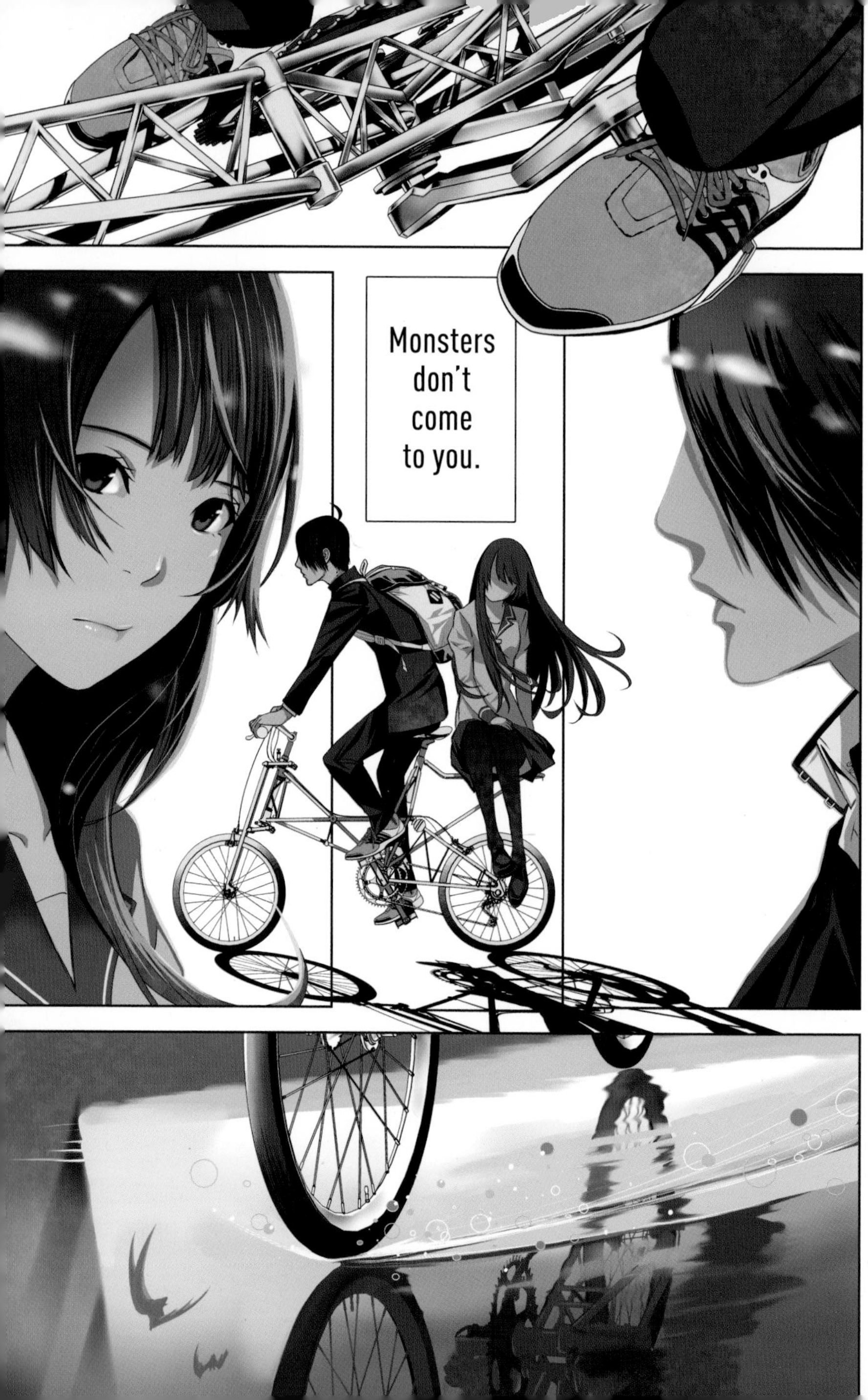
Monsters don't come to you.

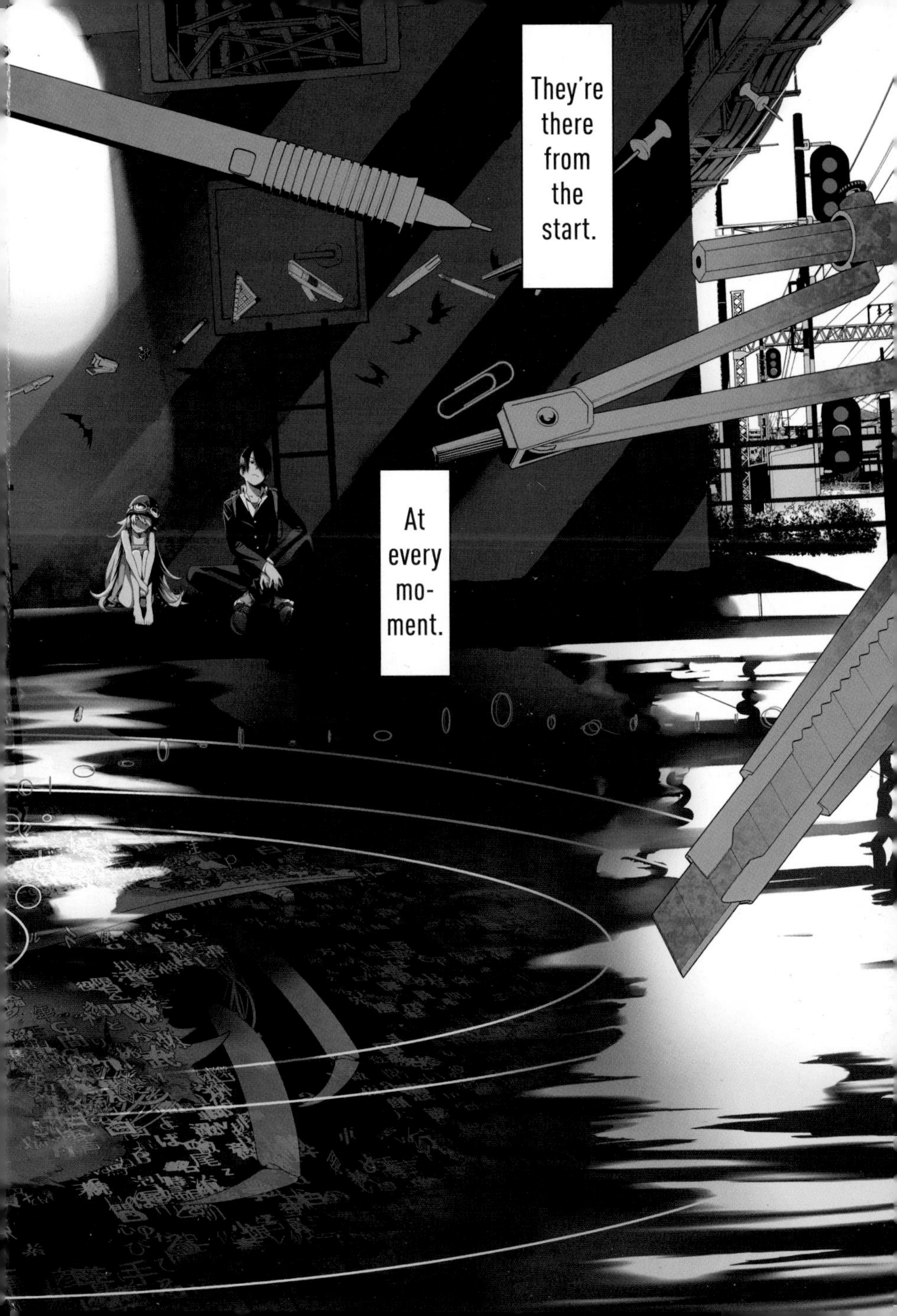
They're there from the start.
At every mo-ment.

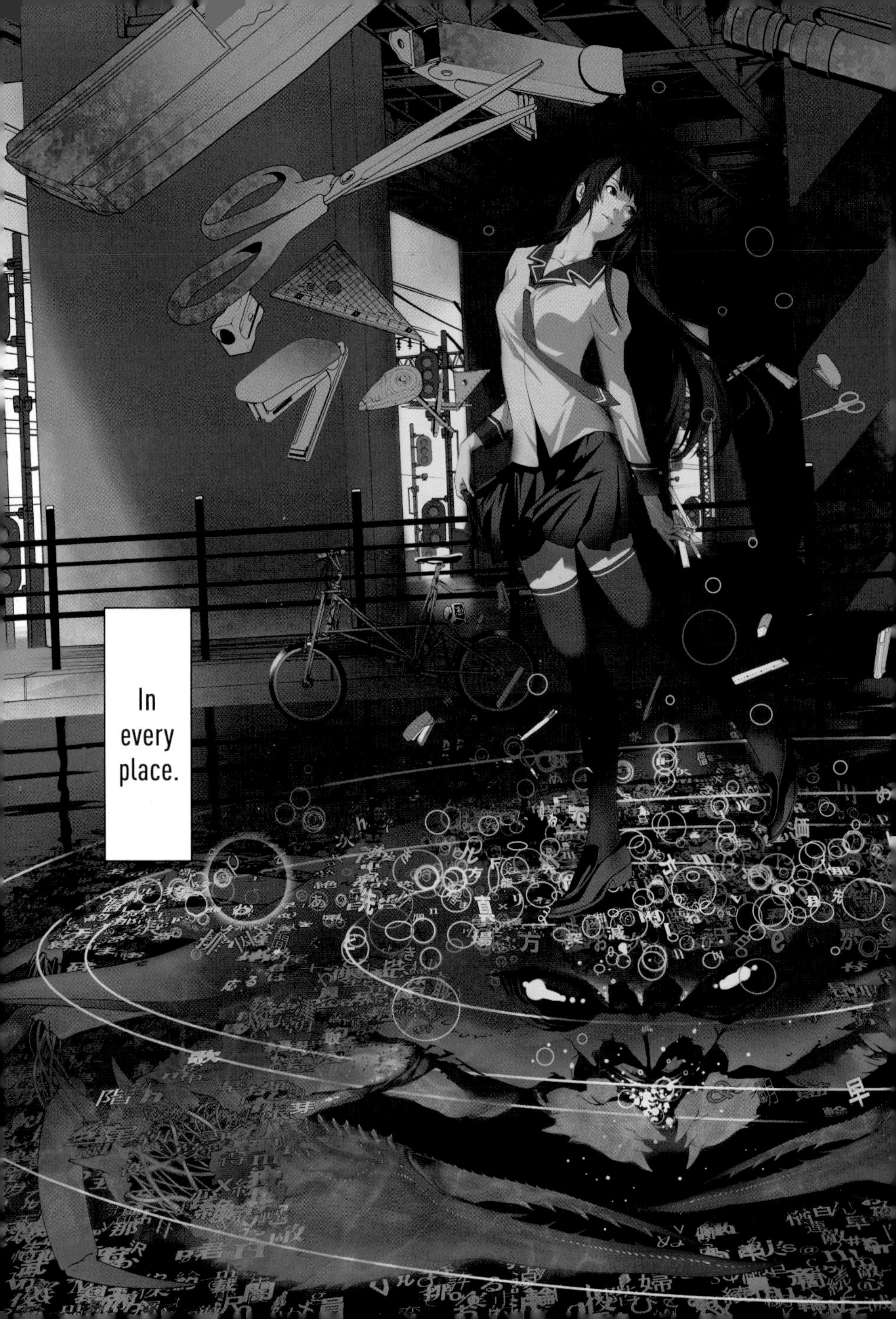
In every place.

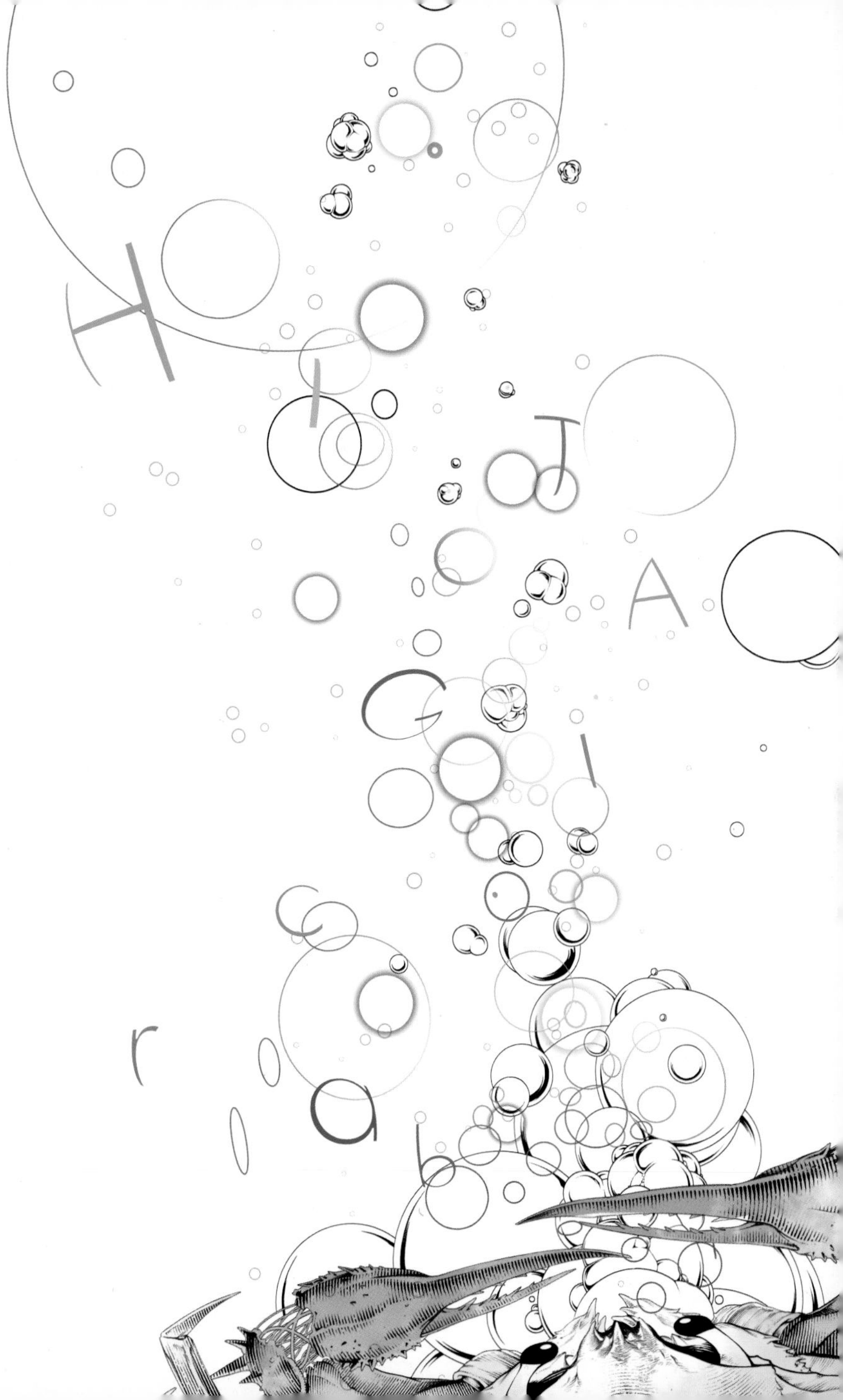

BAKEMONOGATARI

OH!GREAT

Original Story:
NISIOISIN

Original Character
Design: VOFAN

1

Chapter 1 Hitagi Crab

BOOK DESIGN
VEIA

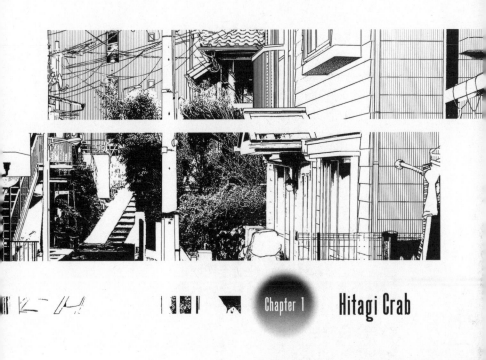

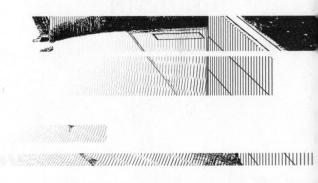

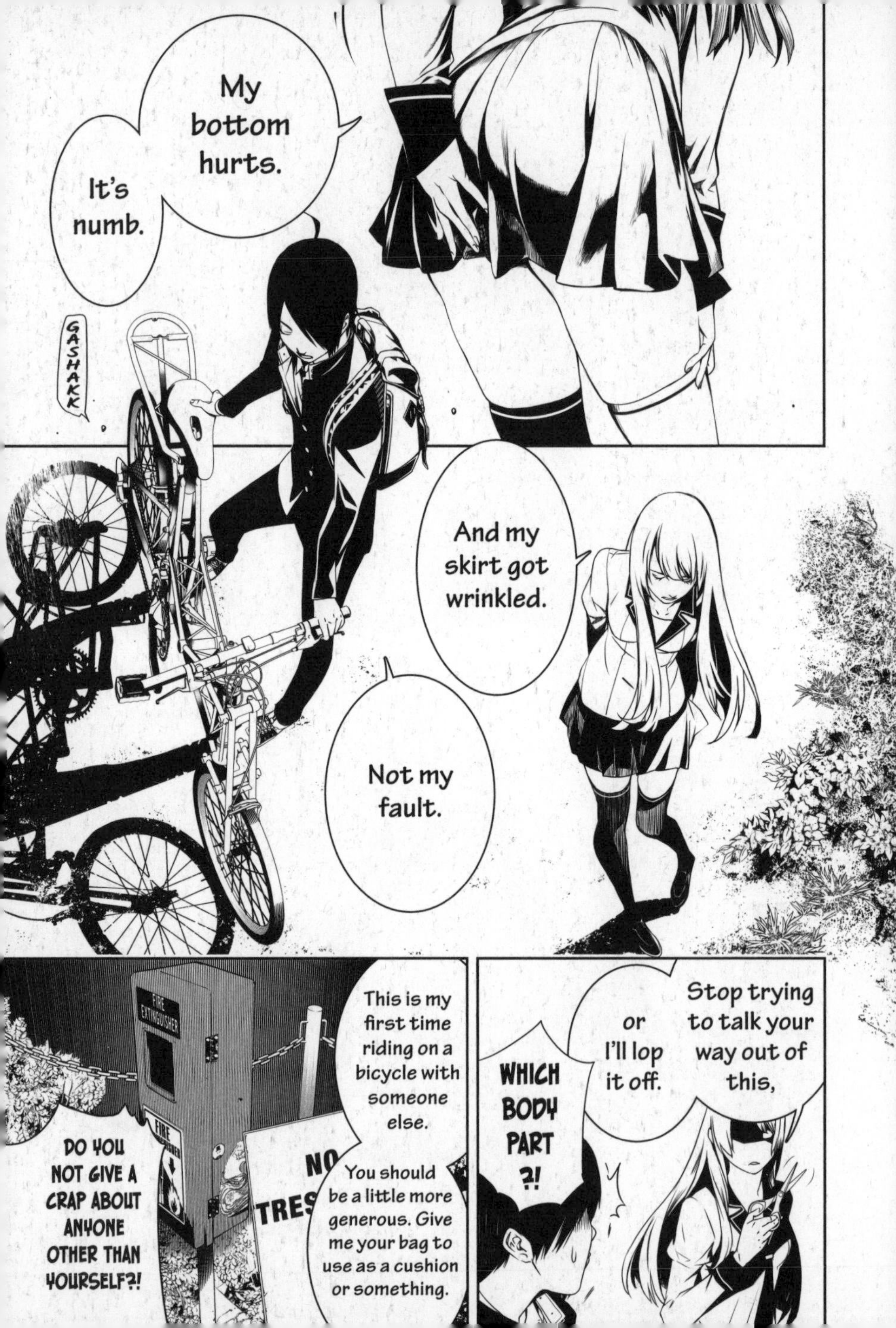

My bottom hurts.
It's numb.
GASHAKK
And my skirt got wrinkled.
Not my fault.
Stop trying to talk your way out of this,
or I'll lop it off.
WHICH BODY PART ?!
This is my first time riding on a bicycle with someone else.
You should be a little more generous. Give me your bag to use as a cushion or something.
DO YOU NOT GIVE A CRAP ABOUT ANYONE OTHER THAN YOURSELF?!
FIRE EXTINGUISHER

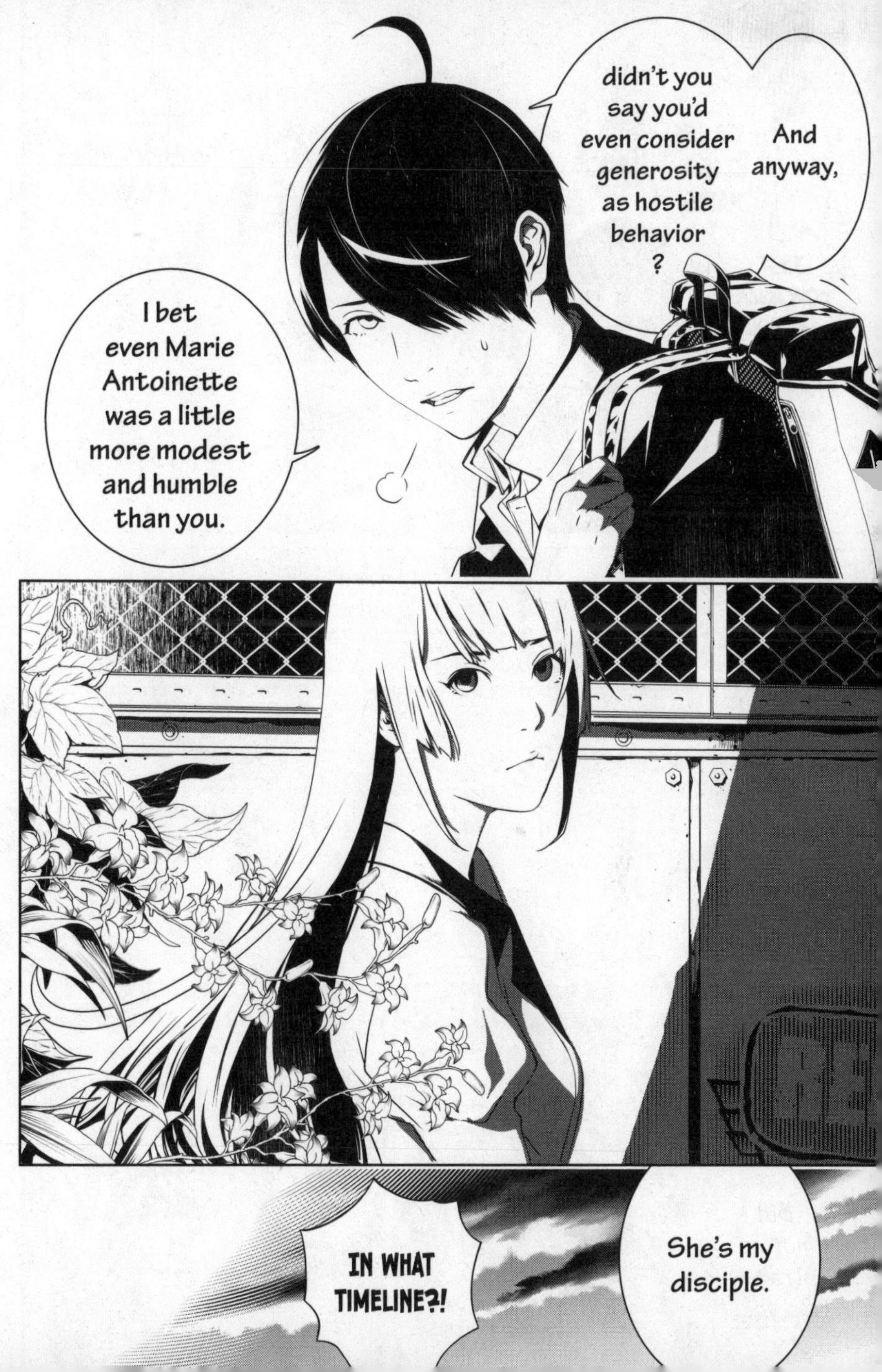
And anyway,
didn't you say you'd even consider generosity as hostile behavior ?
I bet even Marie Antoinette was a little more modest and humble than you.
She's my disciple.
IN WHAT TIMELINE?!

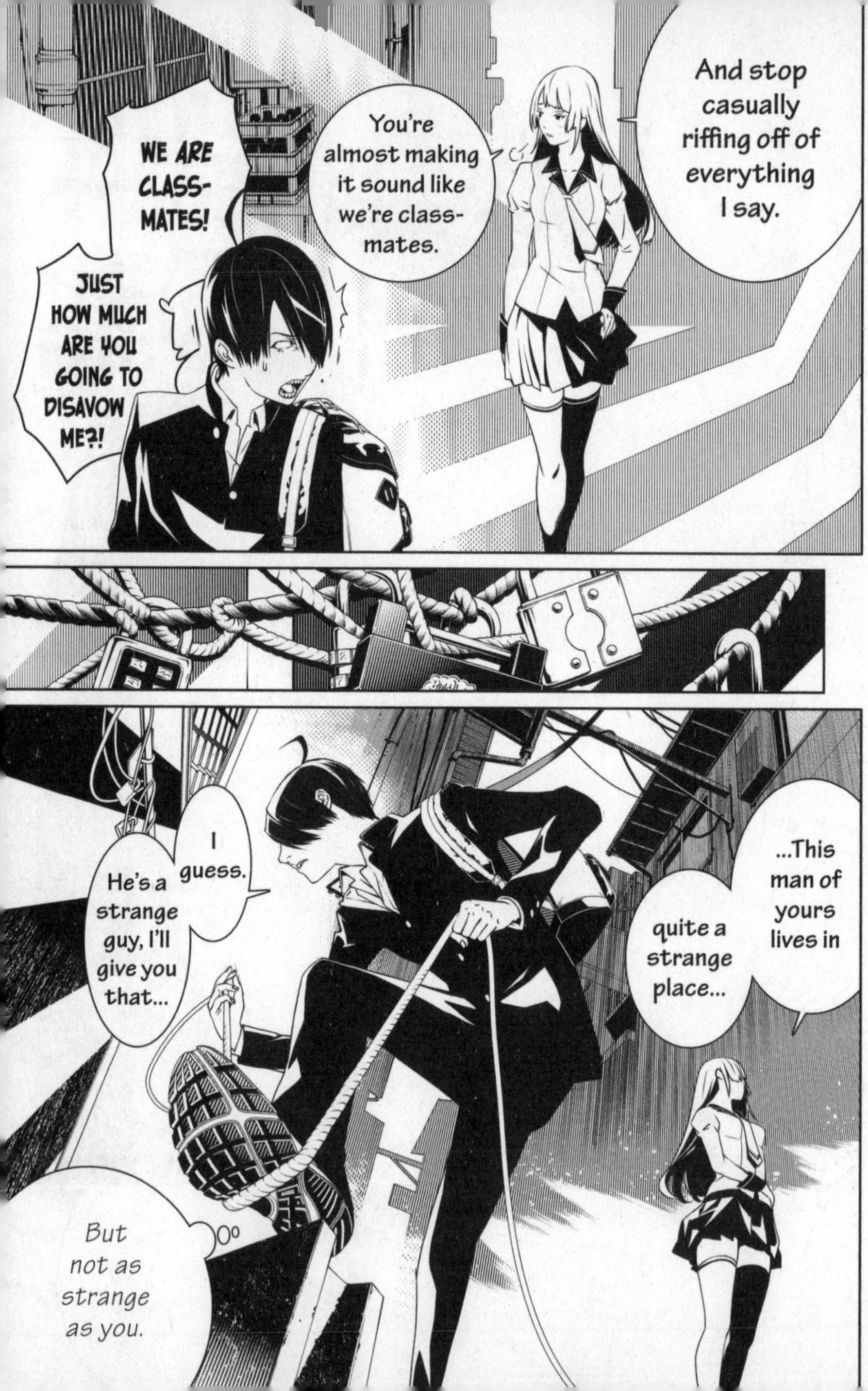
You're almost making it sound like we're classmates.
WE ARE CLASSMATES!
And stop casually riffing off of everything I say.
JUST HOW MUCH ARE YOU GOING TO DISAVOW ME?!
...This man of yours lives in quite a strange place...
He's a strange guy, I'll give you that...
I guess.
But not as strange as you.

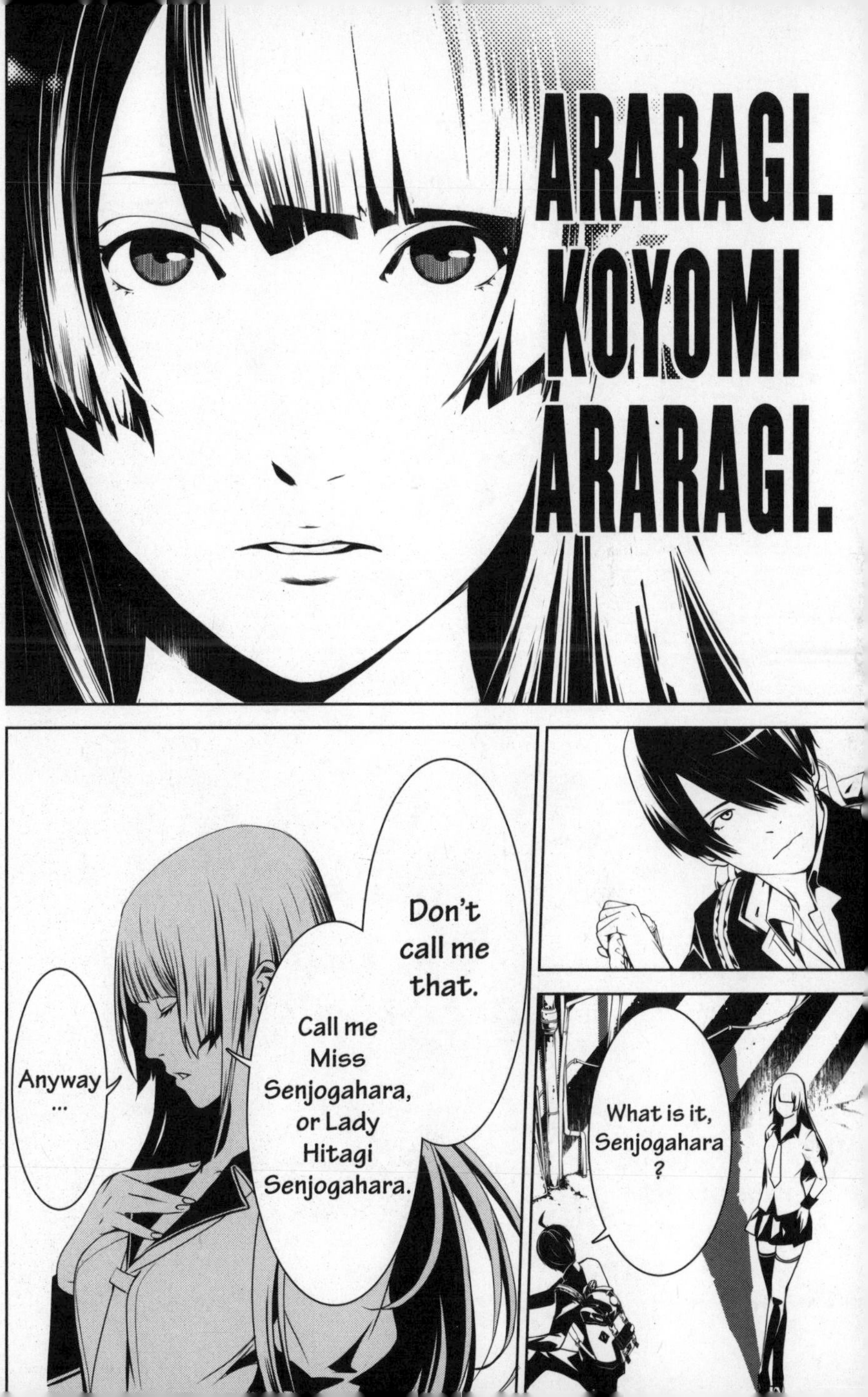

ARARAGI. KOYOMI ARARAGI.
What is it, Senjogahara?
Don't call me that.
Call me Miss Senjogahara, or Lady Hitagi Senjogahara.
Anyway ...

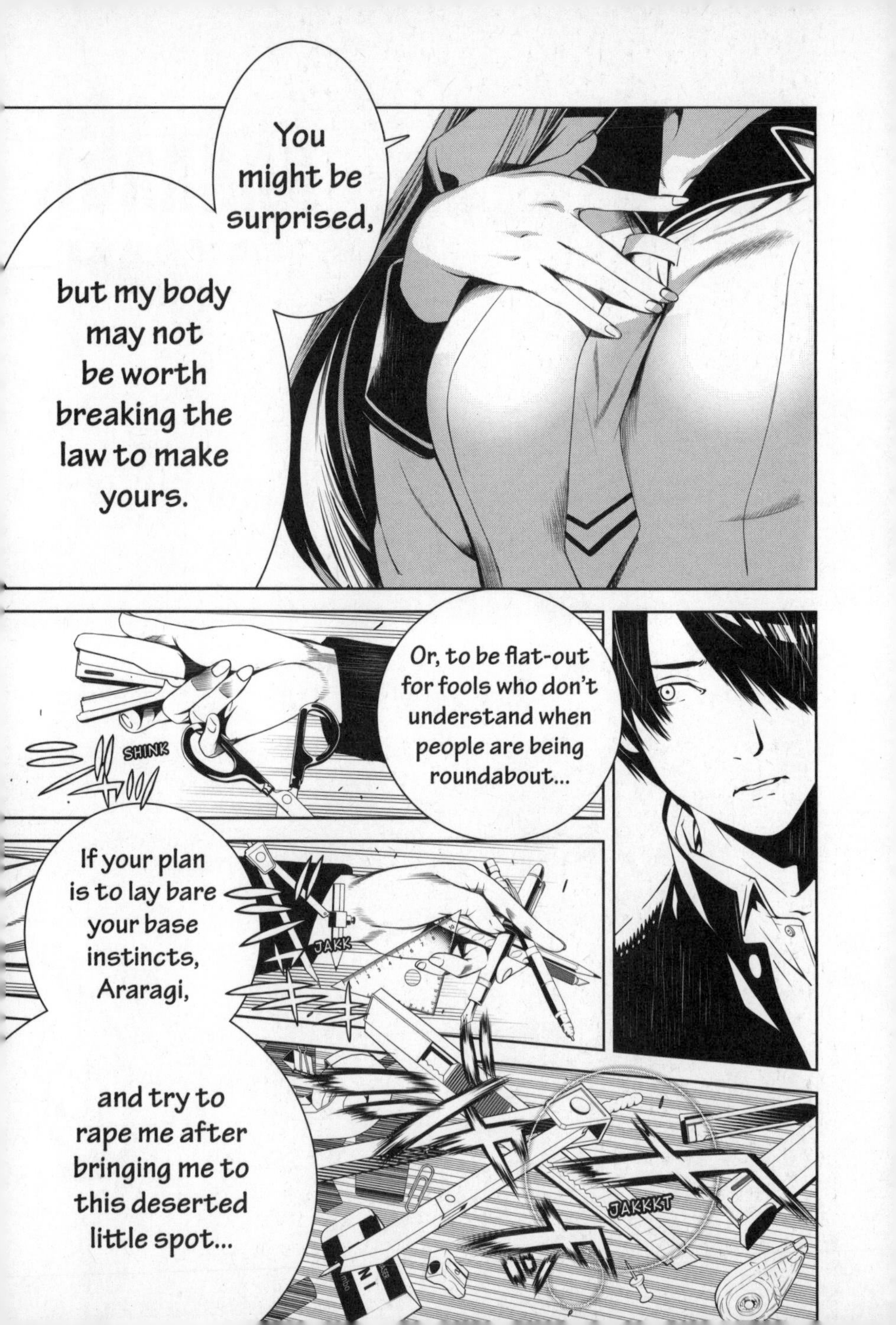

You might be surprised,
but my body may not be worth breaking the law to make yours.
Or, to be flat-out for fools who don't understand when people are being roundabout...
SHINK
If your plan is to lay bare your base instincts, Araragi,
JAKK
and try to rape me after bringing me to this deserted little spot...
JAKKKT

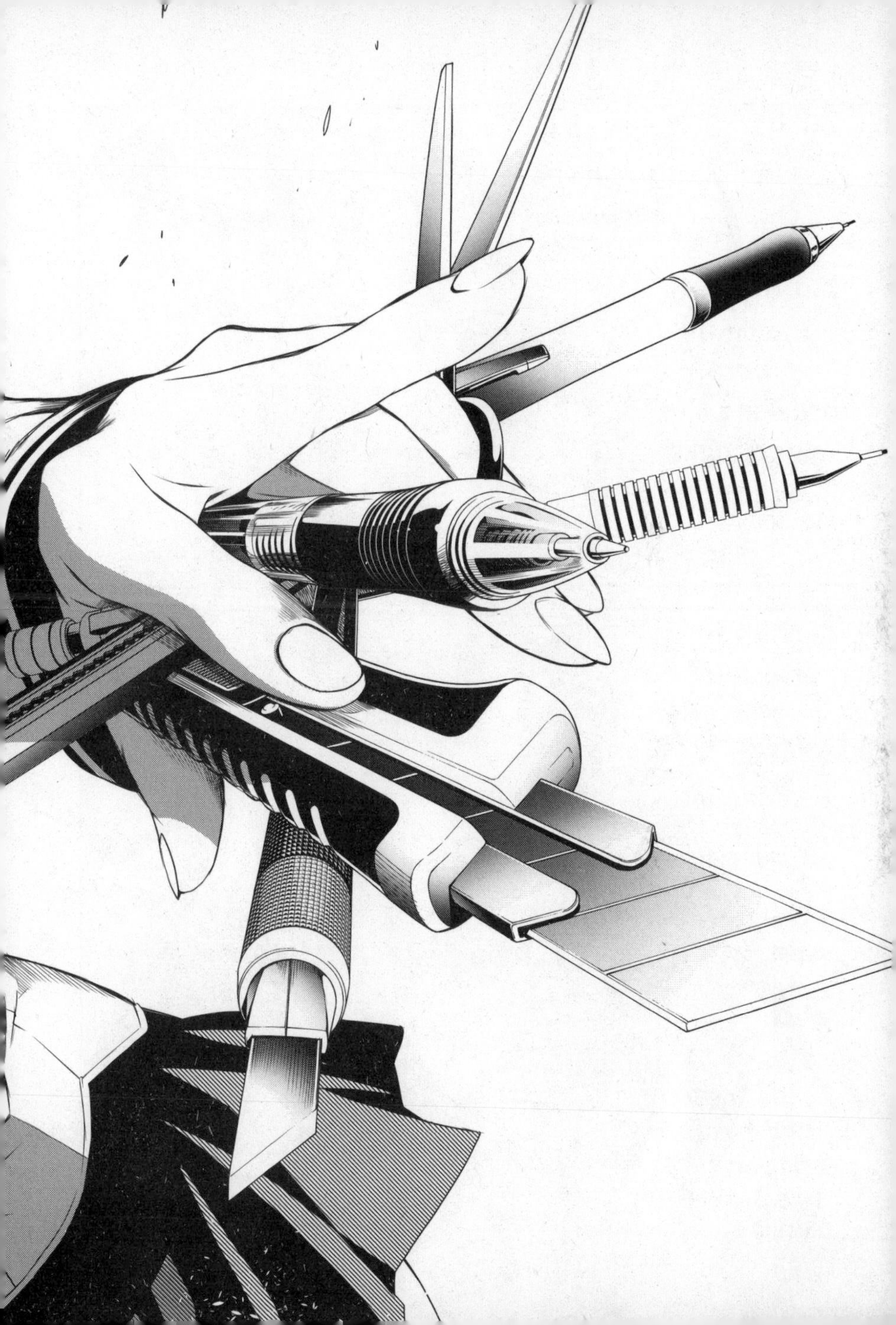

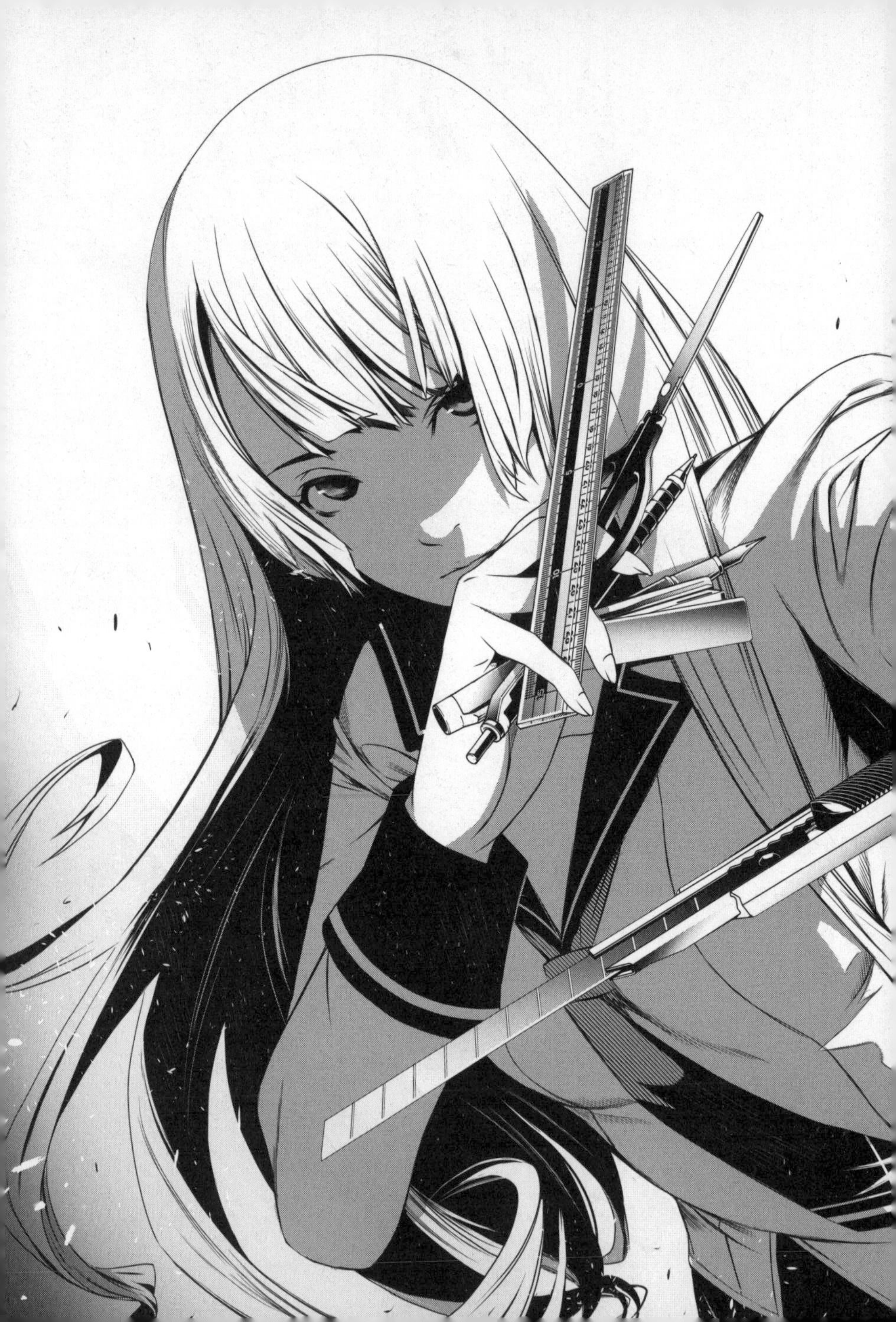

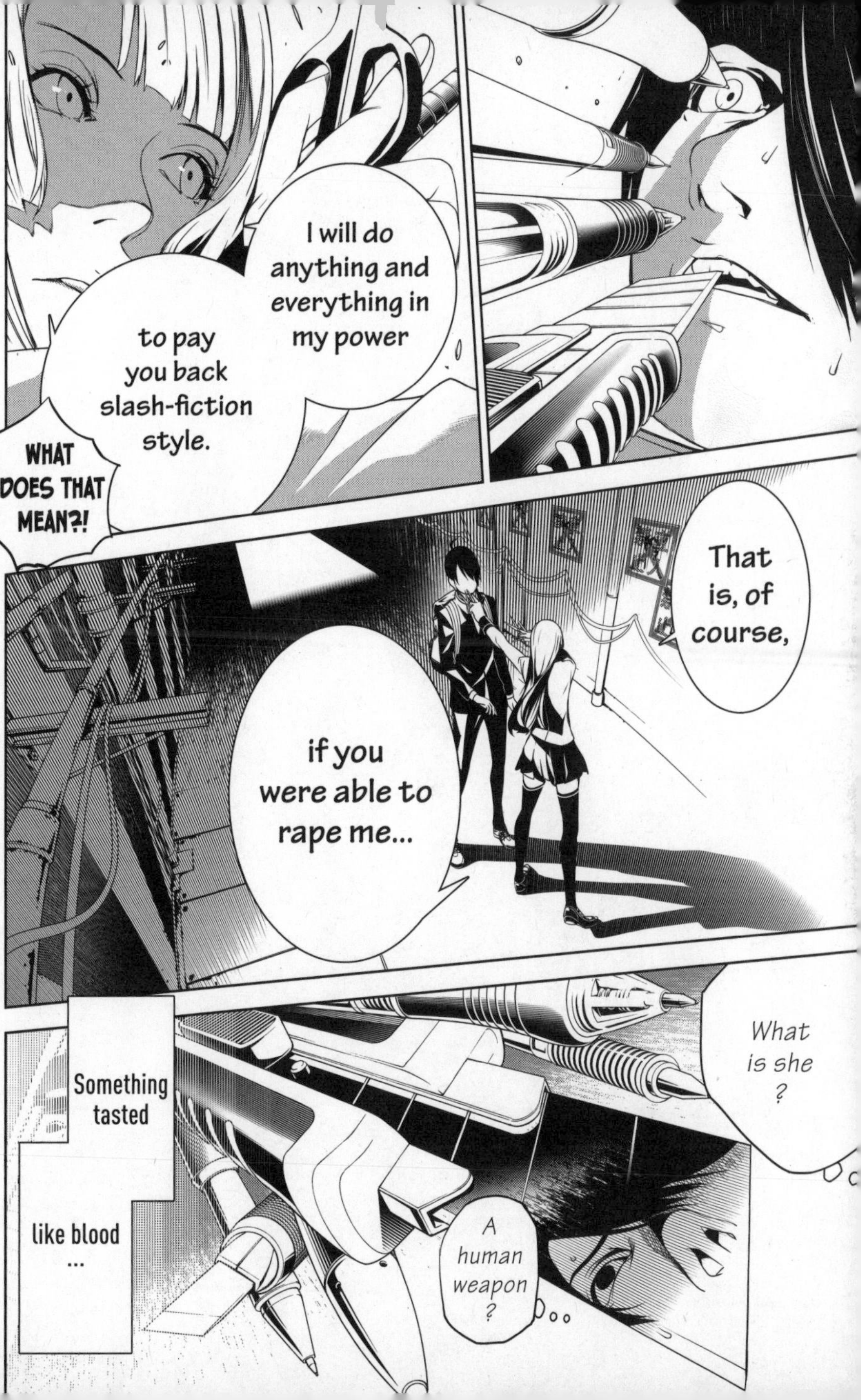
I will do anything and everything in my power
to pay you back slash-fiction style.
WHAT DOES THAT MEAN?!
That is, of course,
if you were able to rape me...
What is she ?
A human weapon ?
Something tasted
like blood ...

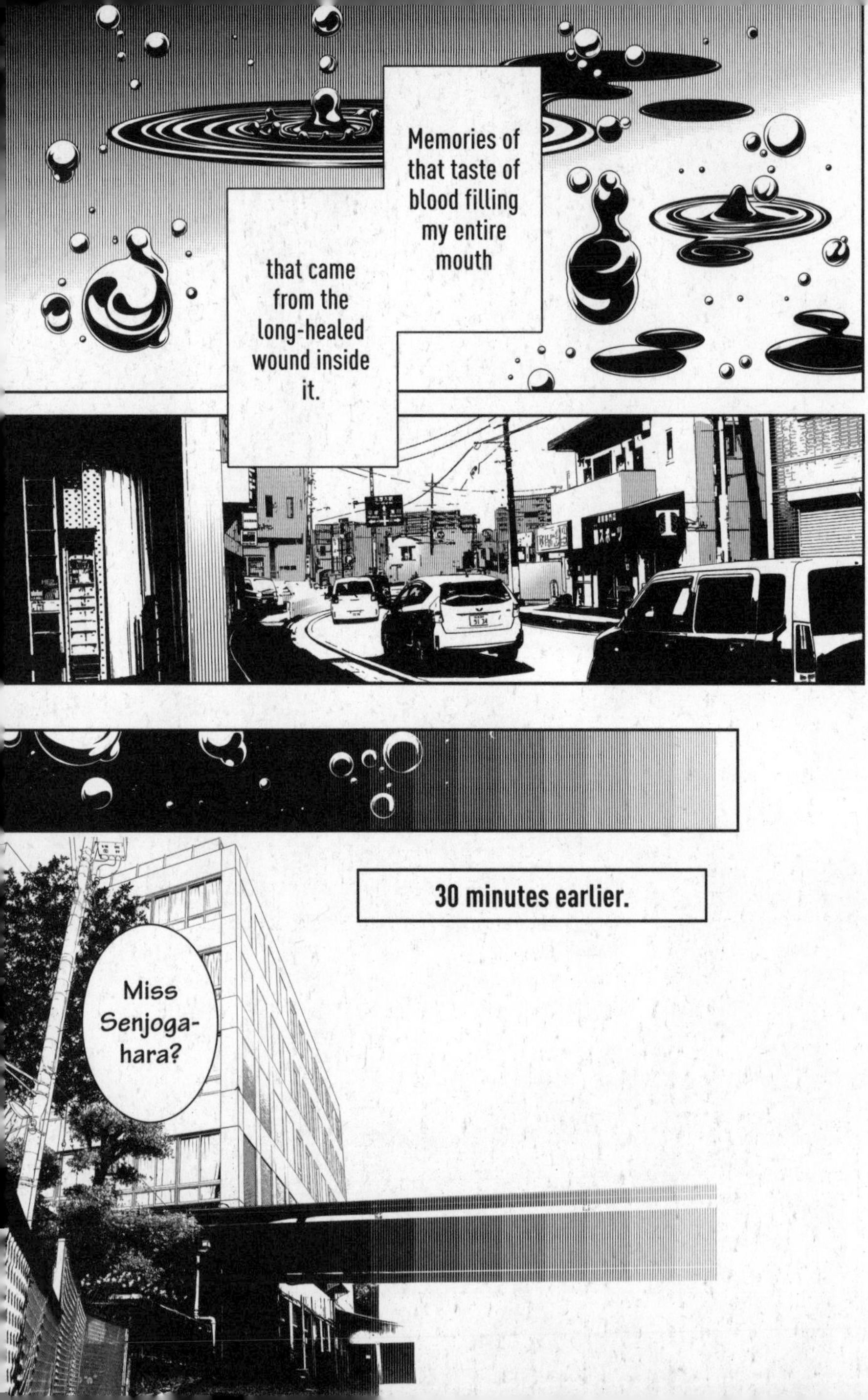
Memories of that taste of blood filling my entire mouth
that came from the long-healed wound inside it.
30 minutes earlier.
Miss Senjoga-hara?

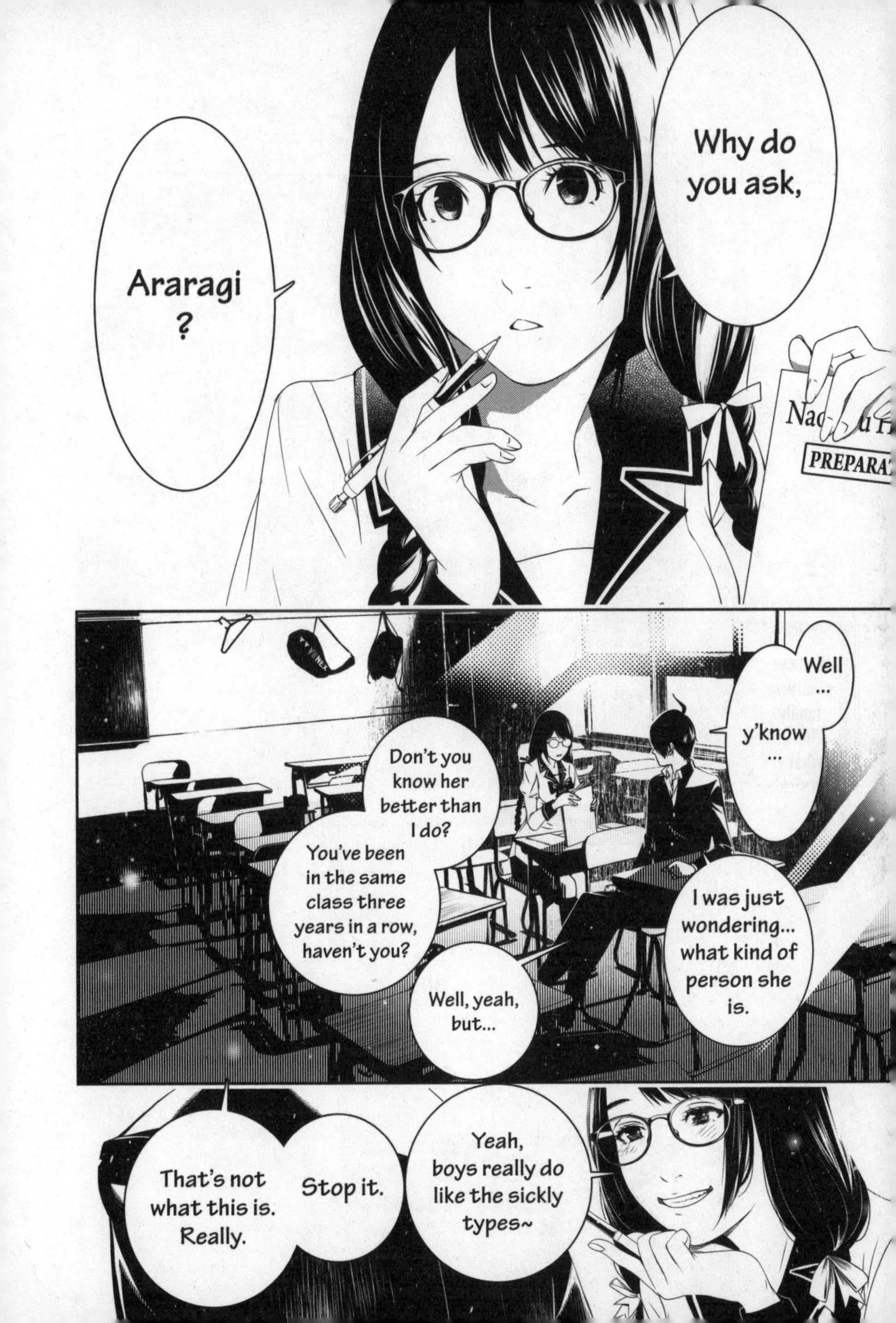
Why do you ask,
Araragi ?
Well ... y'know ...
I was just wondering... what kind of person she is.
Don't you know her better than I do?
You've been in the same class three years in a row, haven't you?
Well, yeah, but...
Yeah, boys really do like the sickly types~
Stop it.
That's not what this is. Really.

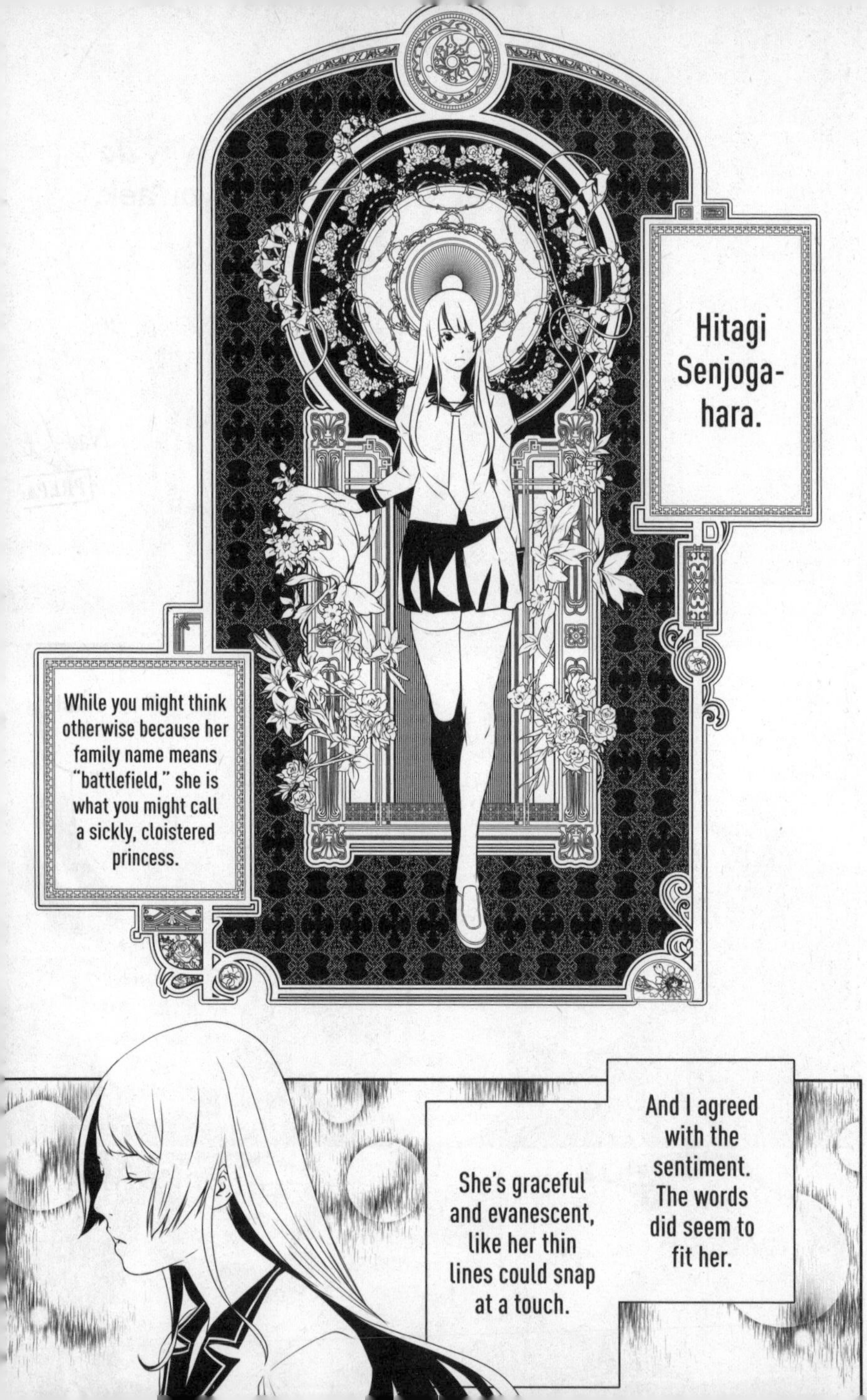
Hitagi Senjoga-hara.
While you might think otherwise because her family name means "battlefield," she is what you might call a sickly, cloistered princess.
And I agreed with the sentiment. The words did seem to fit her.
She's graceful and evanescent, like her thin lines could snap at a touch.

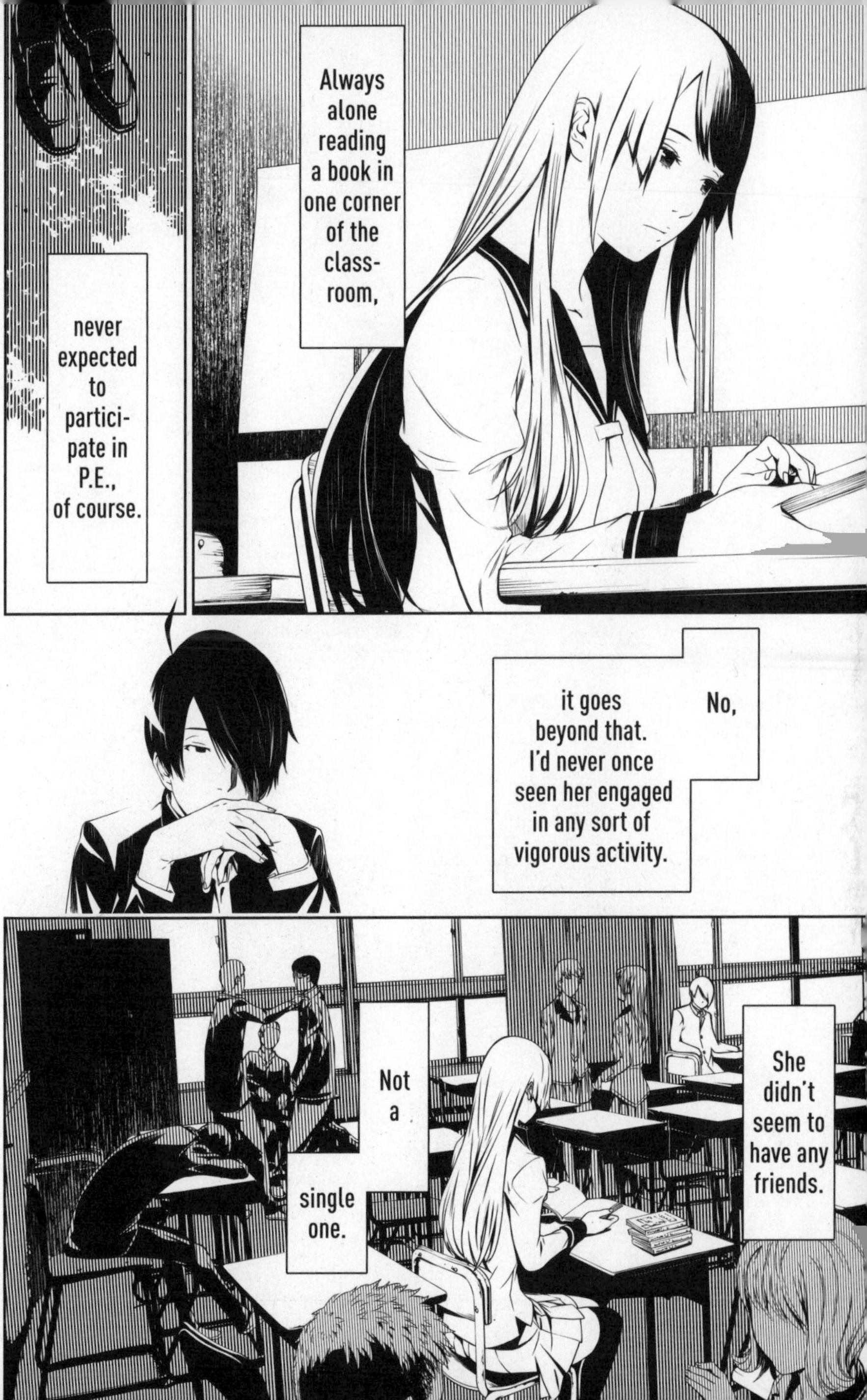
Always alone reading a book in one corner of the class-room,
never expected to partici-pate in P.E., of course.
No,
it goes beyond that. I'd never once seen her engaged in any sort of vigorous activity.
She didn't seem to have any friends.
Not a
single one.

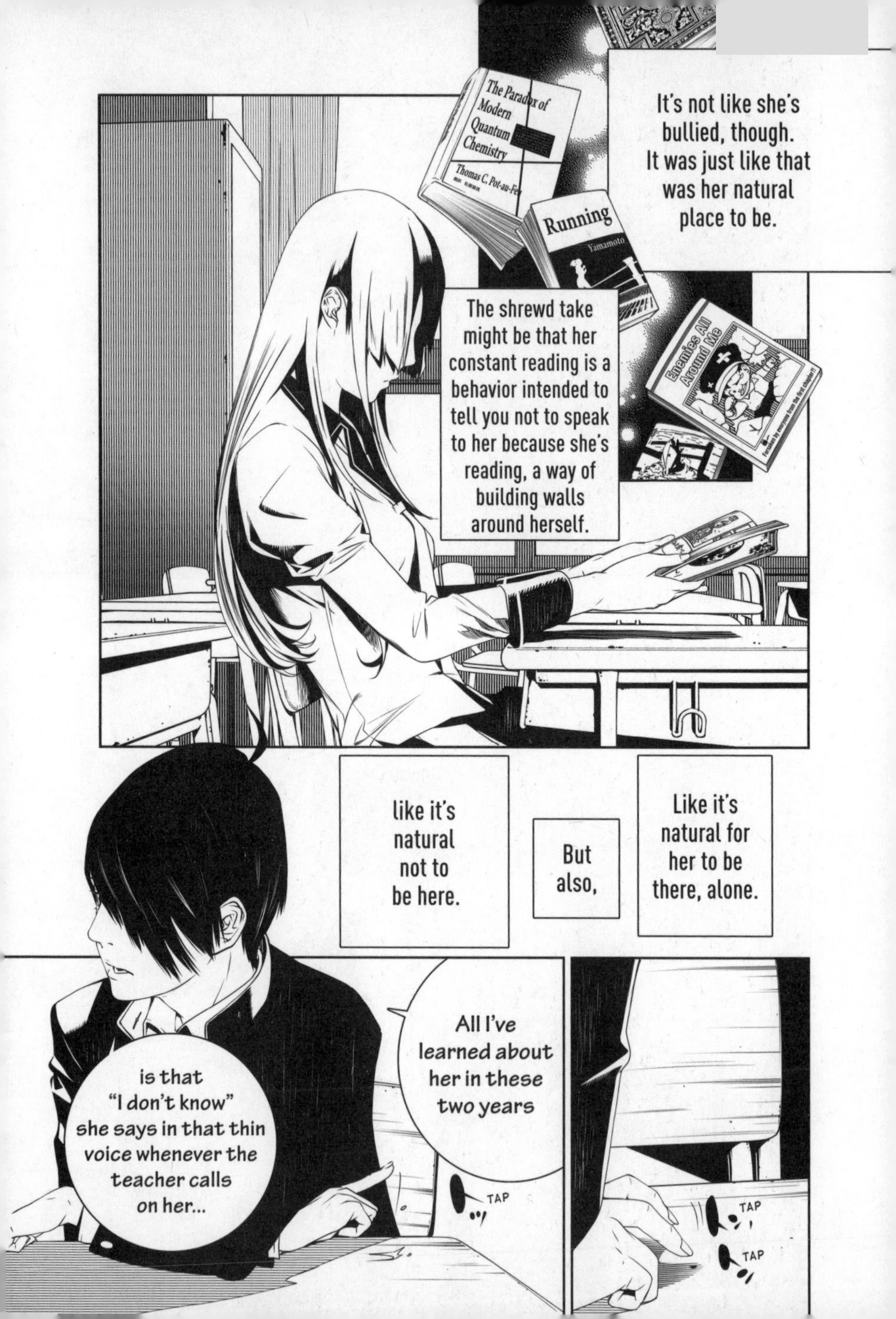
It's not like she's bullied, though. It was just like that was her natural place to be.
The Paradox of Modern Quantum Chemistry
Thomas C. Pot-au-Feu
Running
Yamamoto
Enemies All Around Me
The shrewd take might be that her constant reading is a behavior intended to tell you not to speak to her because she's reading, a way of building walls around herself.
Like it's natural for her to be there, alone.
But also,
like it's natural not to be here.
TAP
TAP
All I've learned about her in these two years
is that "I don't know" she says in that thin voice whenever the teacher calls on her...
TAP

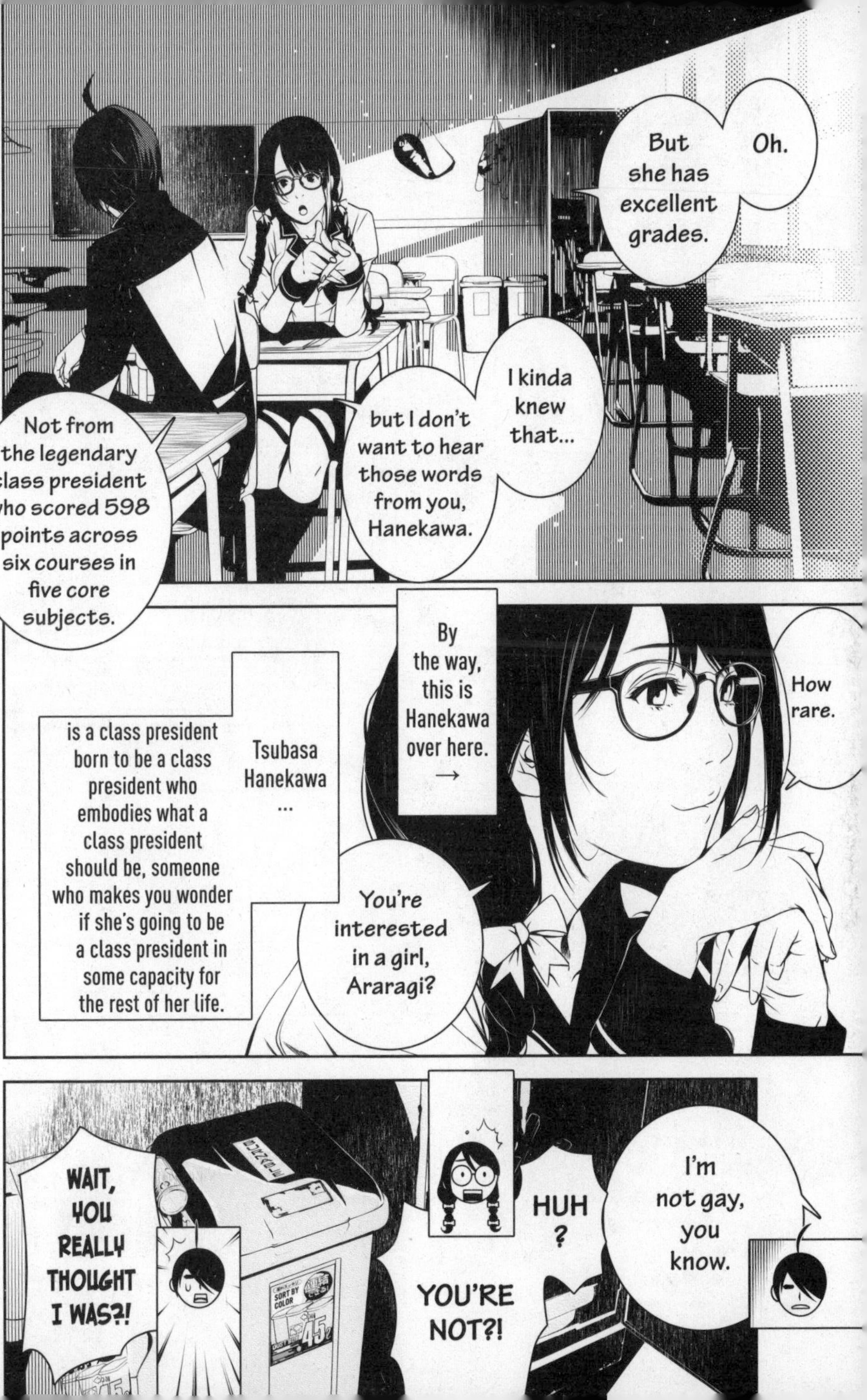
Oh.
But she has excellent grades.
I kinda knew that...
but I don't want to hear those words from you, Hanekawa.
Not from the legendary class president who scored 598 points across six courses in five core subjects.
How rare.
By the way, this is Hanekawa over here. →
Tsubasa Hanekawa ...
is a class president born to be a class president who embodies what a class president should be, someone who makes you wonder if she's going to be a class president in some capacity for the rest of her life.
You're interested in a girl, Araragi?
I'm not gay, you know.
HUH ?
YOU'RE NOT?!
WAIT, YOU REALLY THOUGHT I WAS?!

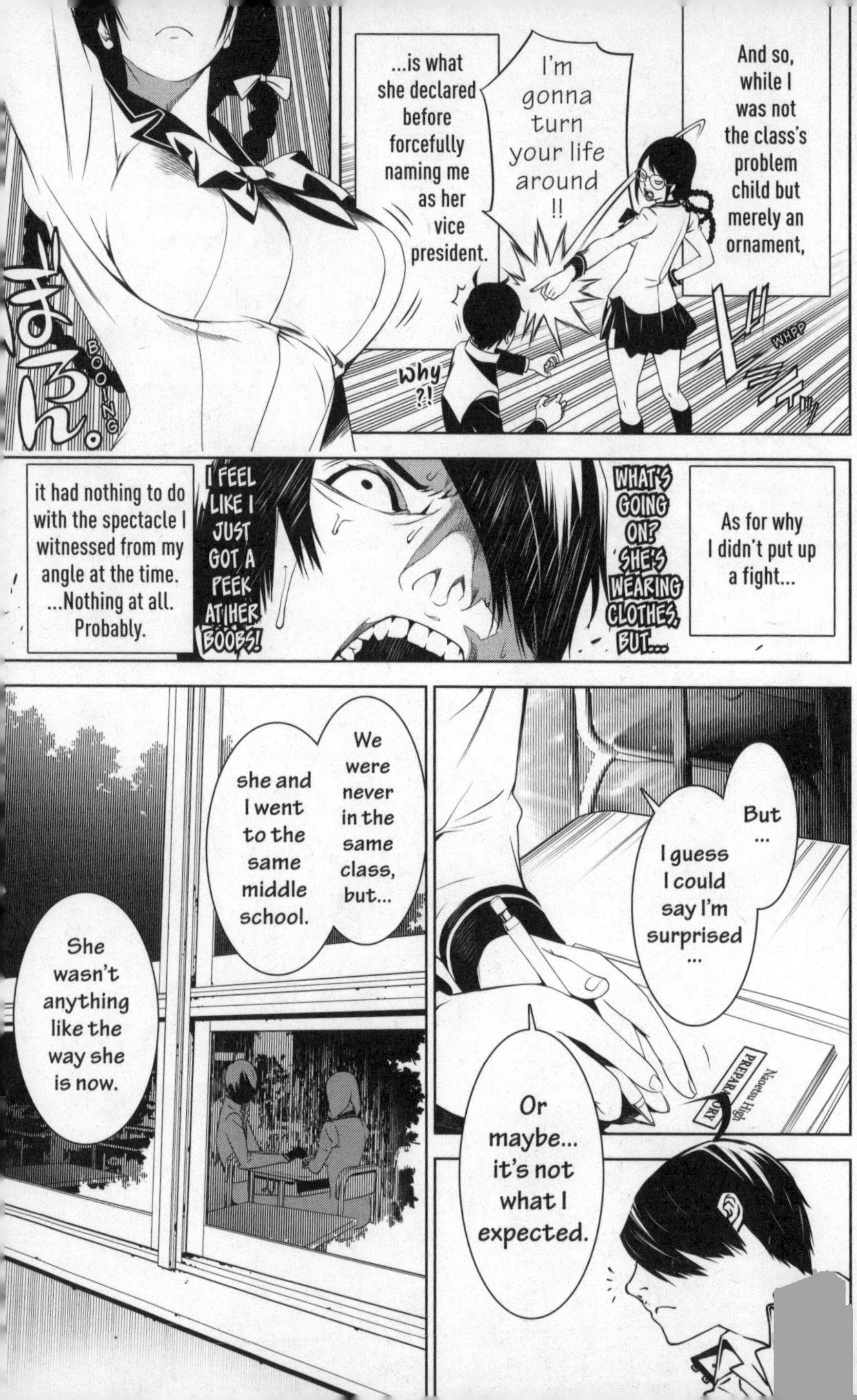
And so, while I was not the class's problem child but merely an ornament,
I'm gonna turn your life around!!
...is what she declared before forcefully naming me as her vice president.
WHPP
why?!
まろん。
BOOING
As for why I didn't put up a fight...
WHAT'S GOING ON? SHE'S WEARING CLOTHES, BUT...
I FEEL LIKE I JUST GOT A PEEK AT HER BOOBS!
it had nothing to do with the spectacle I witnessed from my angle at the time. ...Nothing at all. Probably.
But... I guess I could say I'm surprised...
Naoetsu High
Or maybe... it's not what I expected.
We were never in the same class, but...
she and I went to the same middle school.
She wasn't anything like the way she is now.

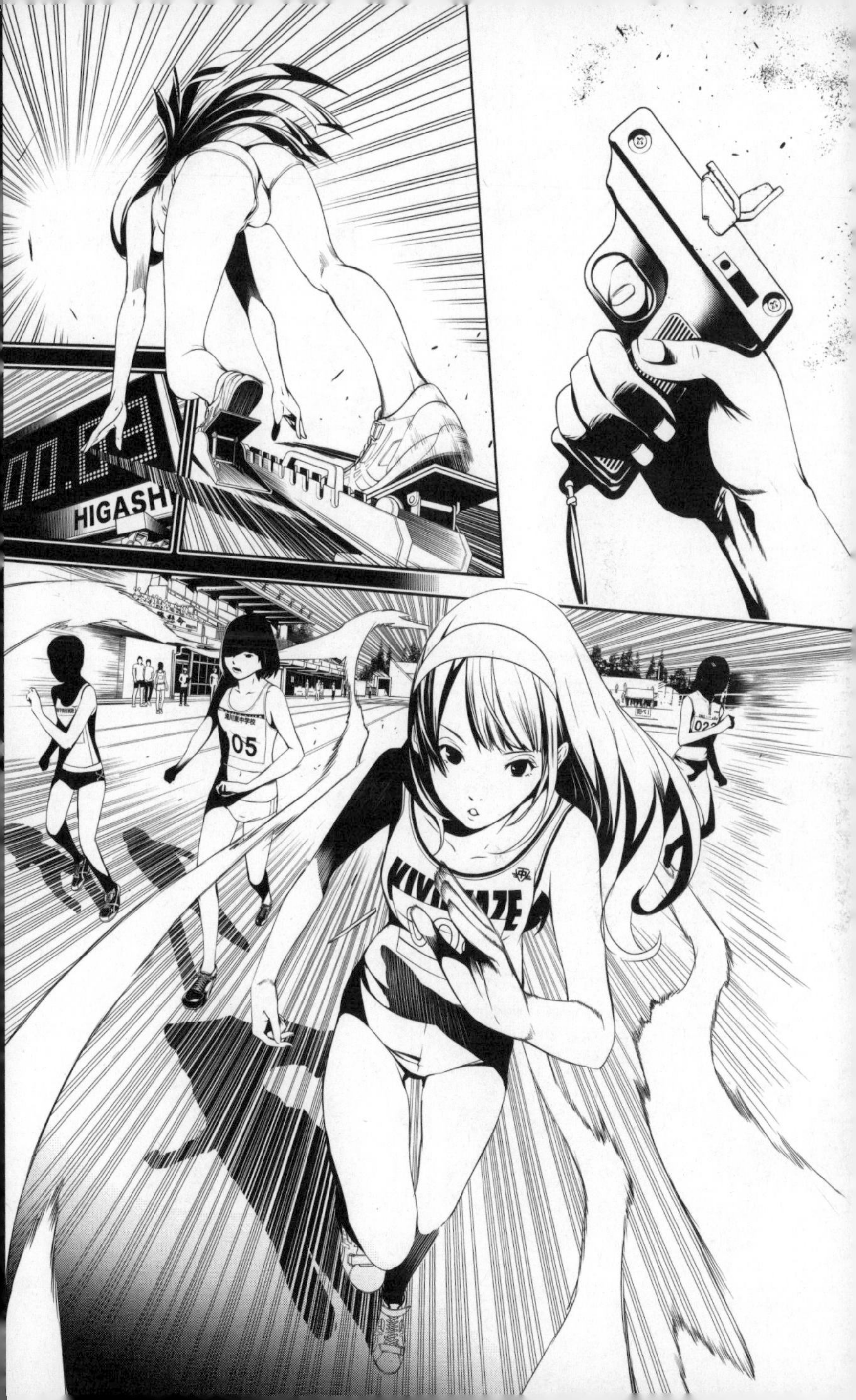
HIGASHI
05

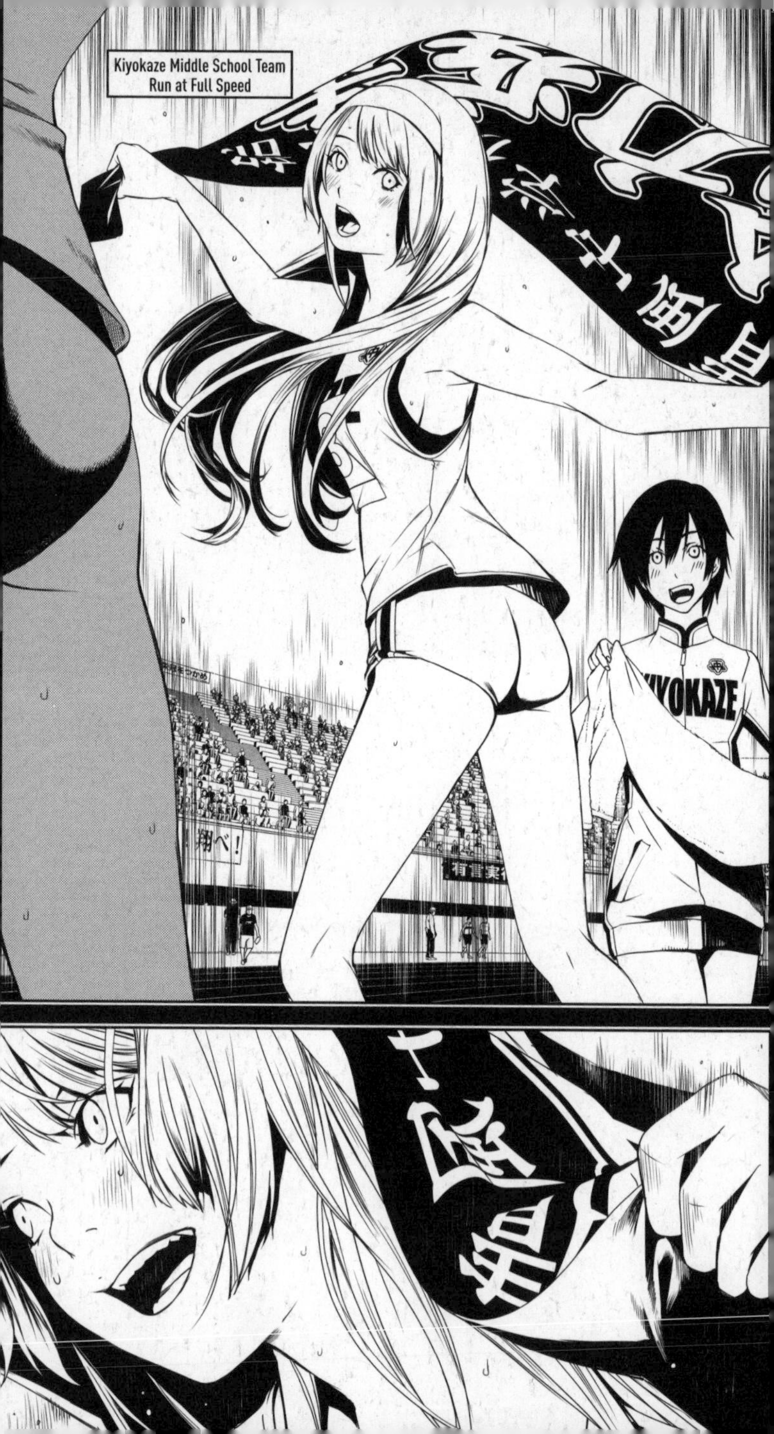
Kiyokaze Middle School Team
Run at Full Speed
KIYOKAZE
翔べ!

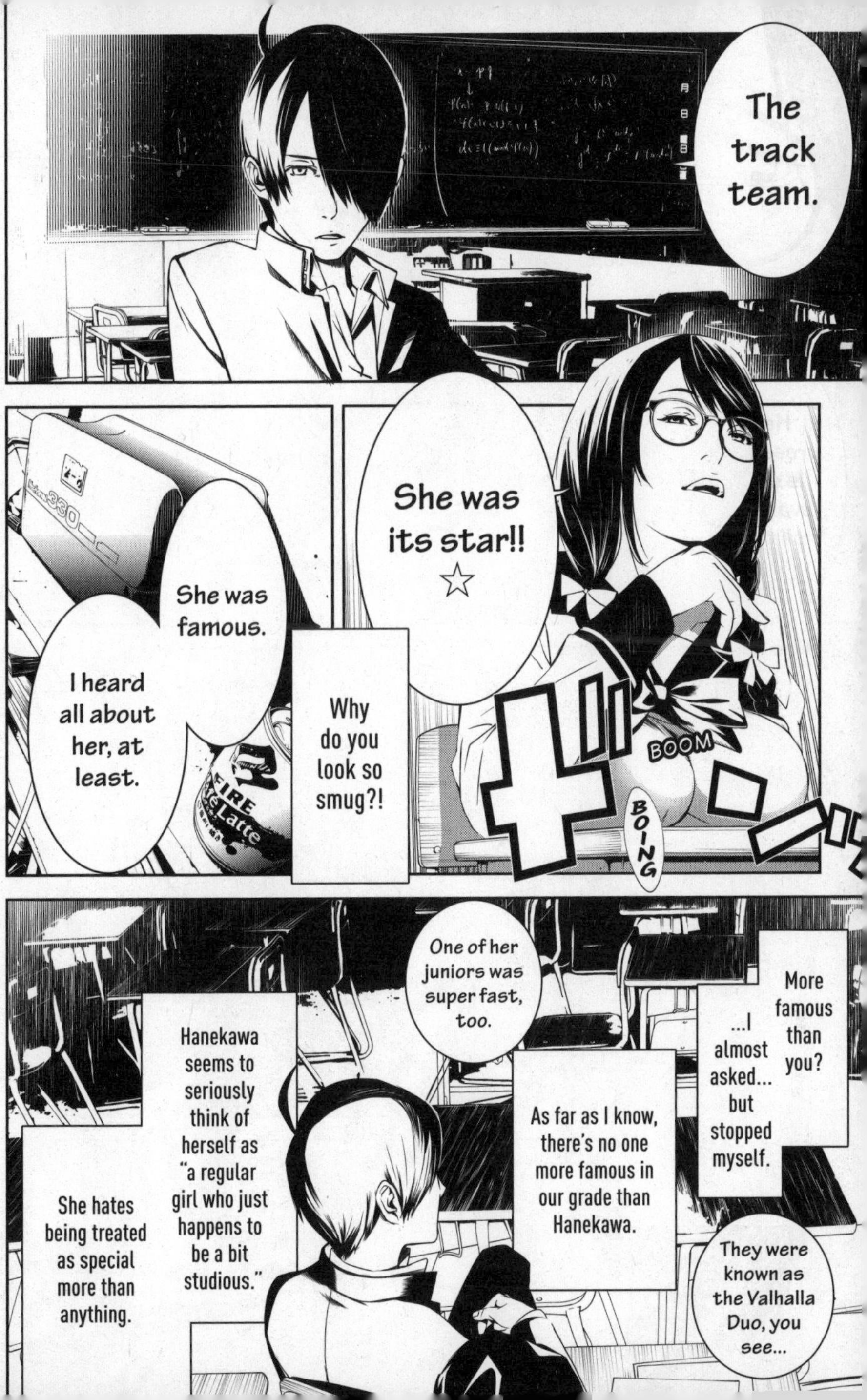
The track team.
She was its star!! ☆
BOOM
BOING
Why do you look so smug?!
She was famous.
I heard all about her, at least.
One of her juniors was super fast, too.
They were known as the Valhalla Duo, you see...
More famous than you?
...I almost asked... but stopped myself.
As far as I know, there's no one more famous in our grade than Hanekawa.
Hanekawa seems to seriously think of herself as "a regular girl who just happens to be a bit studious."
She hates being treated as special more than anything.

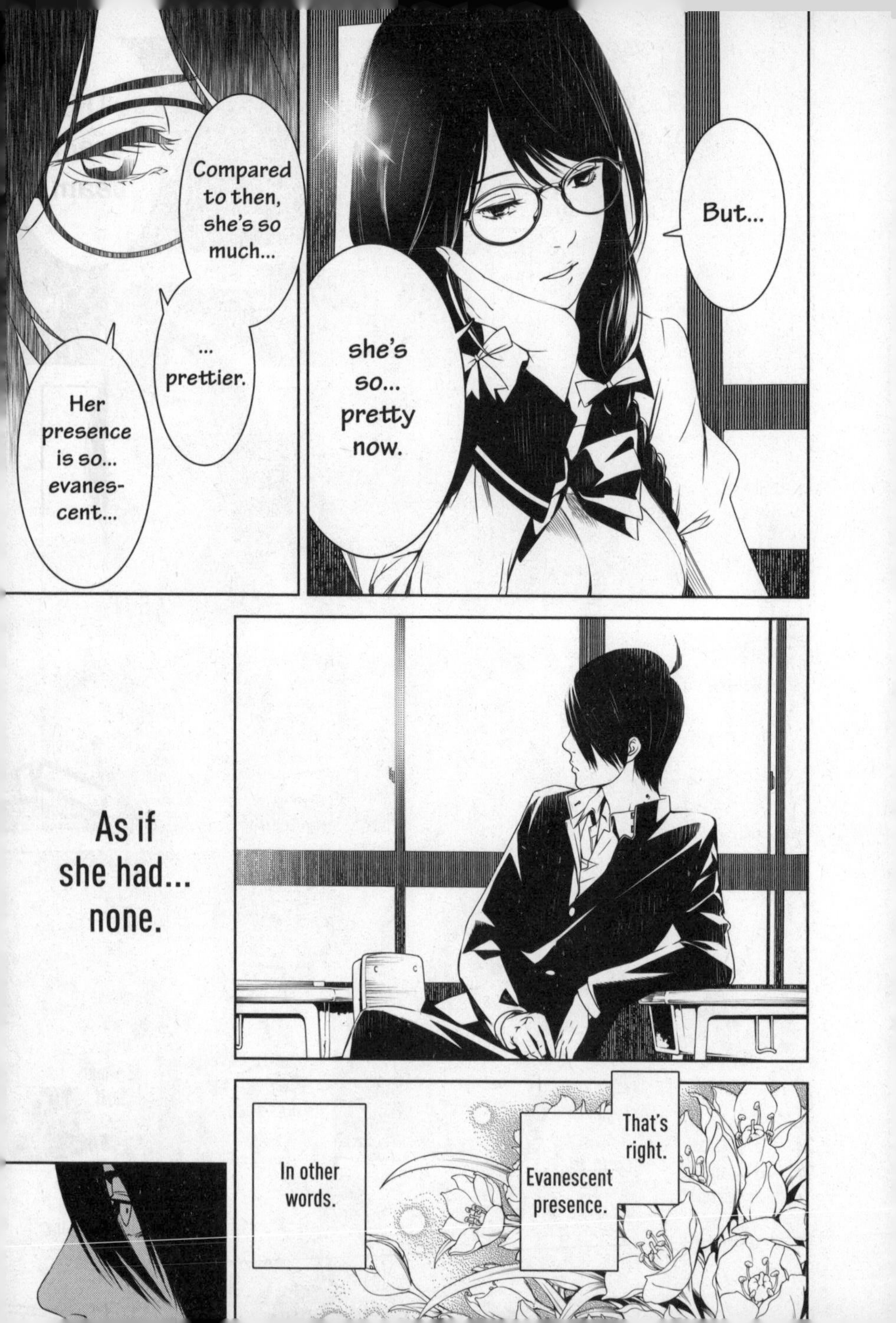
But...
she's so... pretty now.
Compared to then, she's so much...
... prettier.
Her presence is so... evanes-cent...
As if she had... none.
That's right.
Evanescent presence.
In other words.

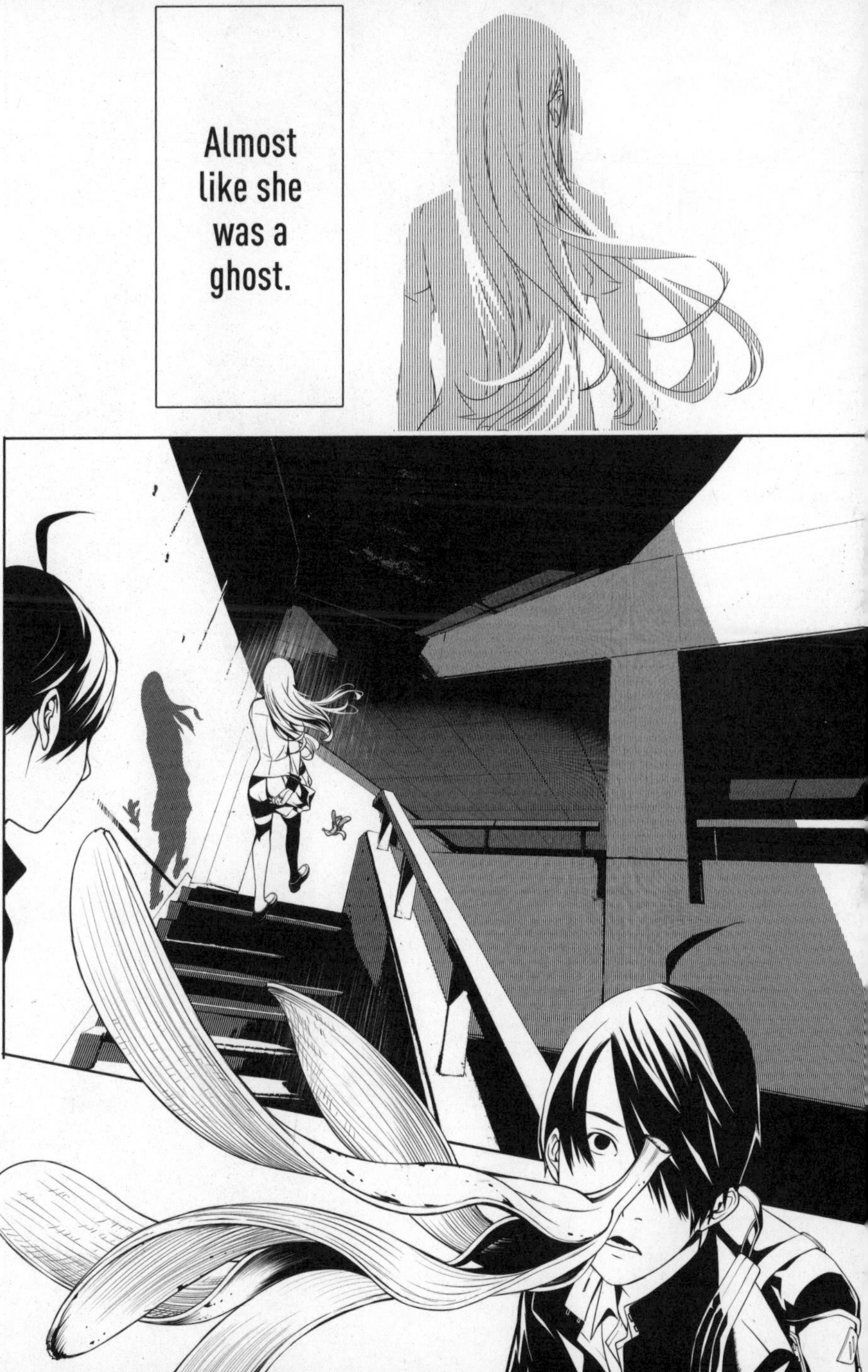
Almost like she was a ghost.

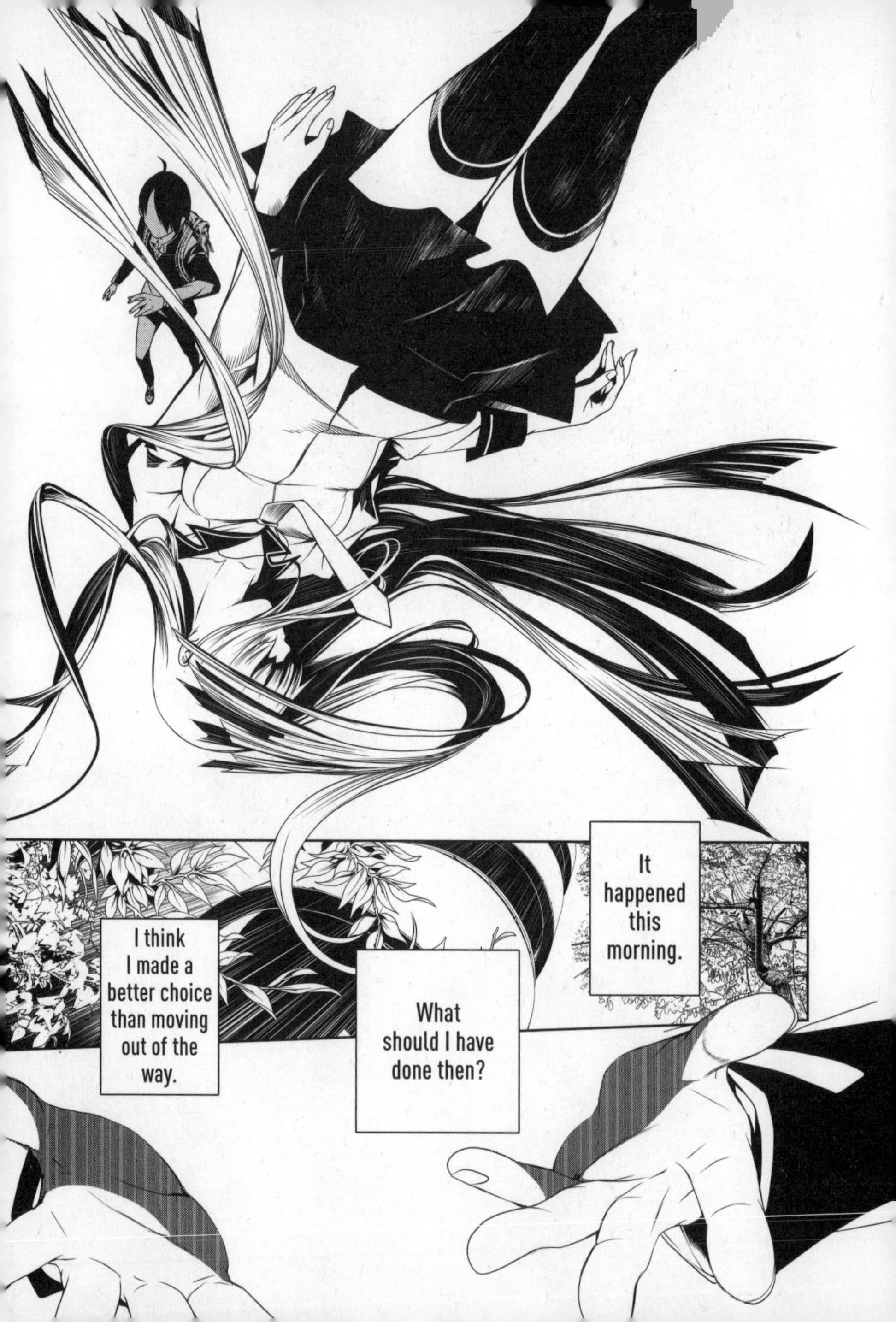
It happened this morning.
What should I have done then?
I think I made a better choice than moving out of the way.

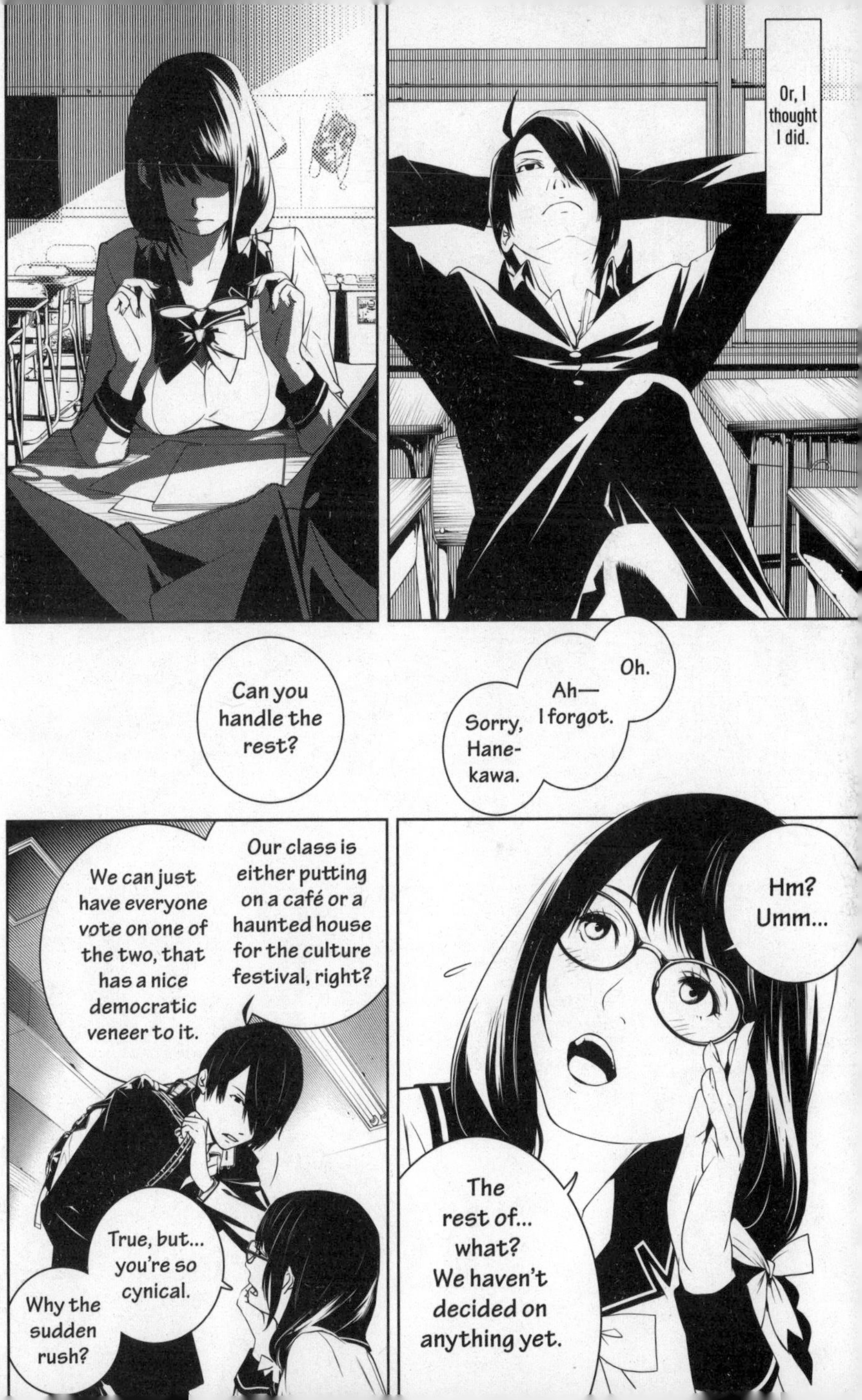
Or, I thought I did.
Oh.
Ah— I forgot.
Sorry, Hane-kawa.
Can you handle the rest?
Hm? Umm...
The rest of... what? We haven't decided on anything yet.
Our class is either putting on a café or a haunted house for the culture festival, right?
We can just have everyone vote on one of the two, that has a nice democratic veneer to it.
True, but... you're so cynical.
Why the sudden rush?

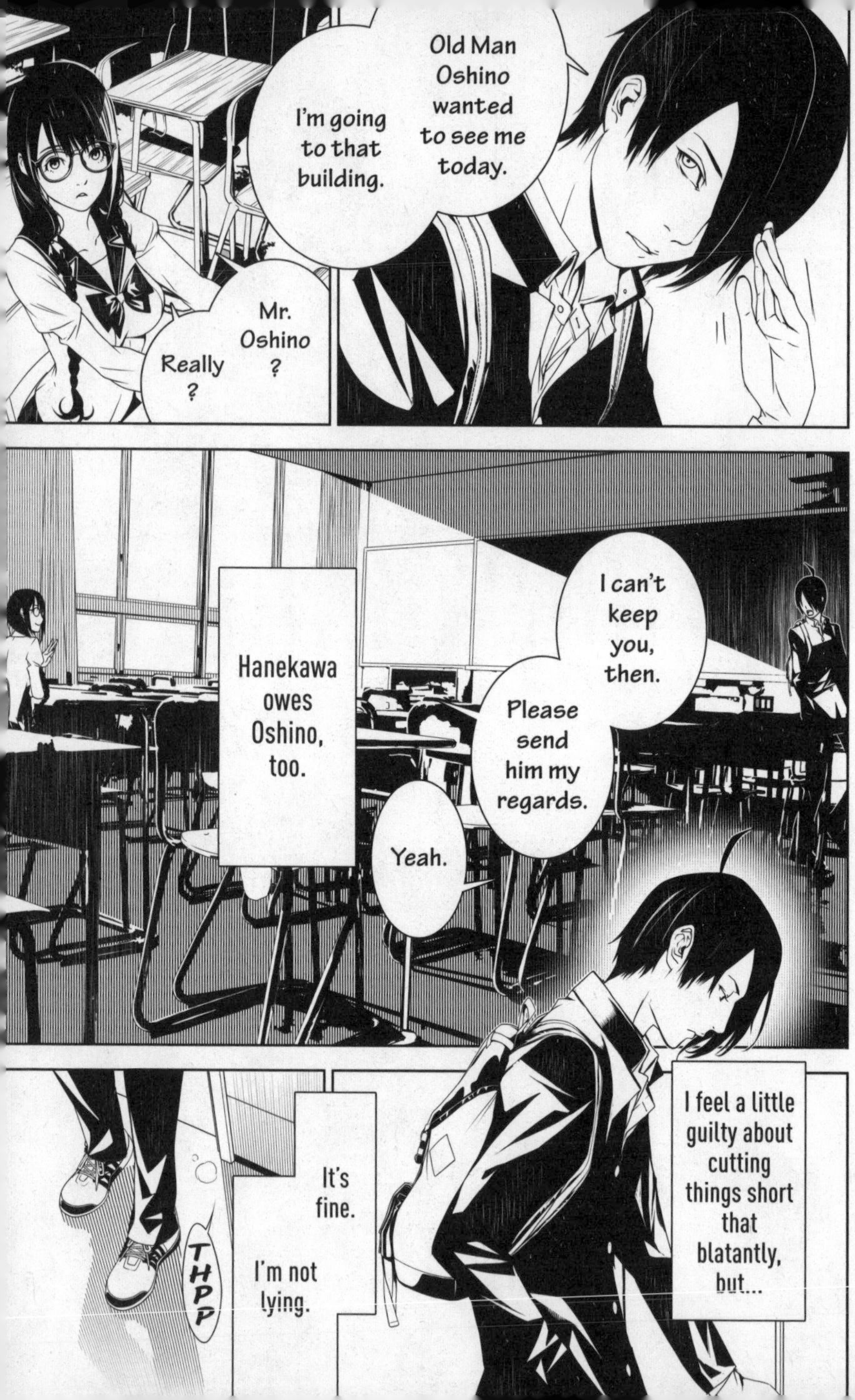
Old Man Oshino wanted to see me today.
I'm going to that building.
Mr. Oshino?
Really?
I can't keep you, then.
Please send him my regards.
Hanekawa owes Oshino, too.
Yeah.
I feel a little guilty about cutting things short that blatantly, but...
It's fine.
I'm not lying.
THPP

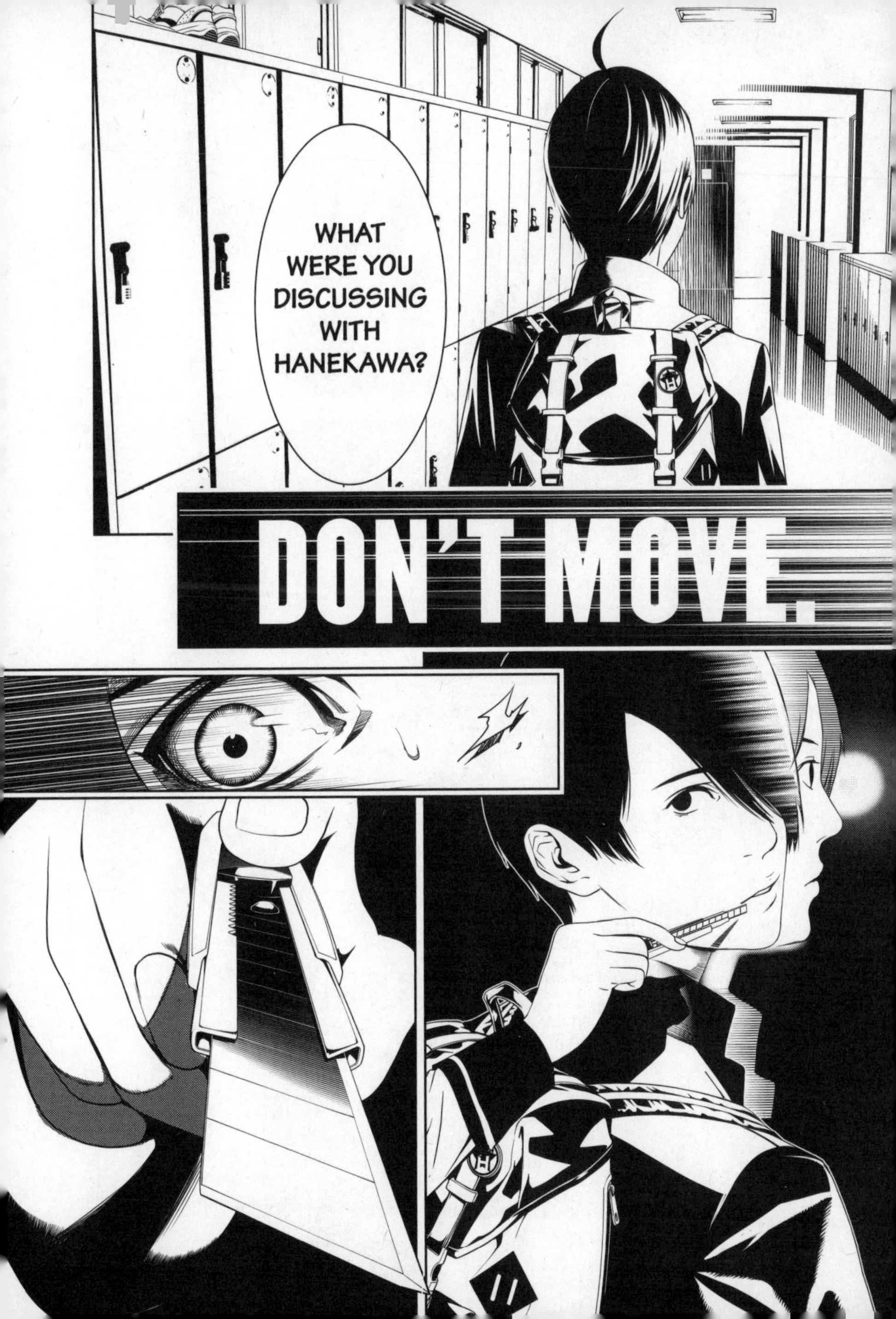
WHAT WERE YOU DISCUSSING WITH HANEKAWA?
DON'T MOVE.

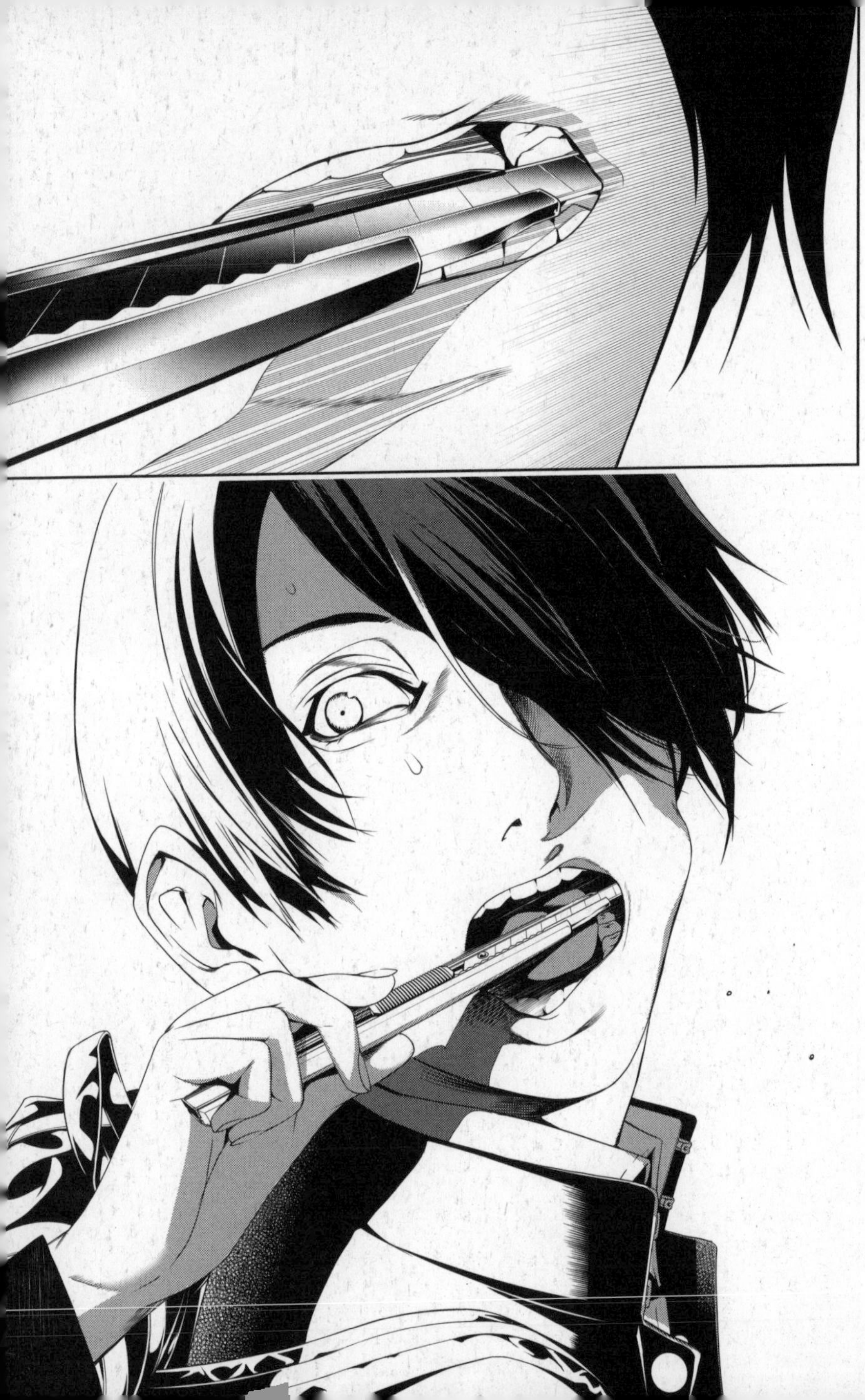

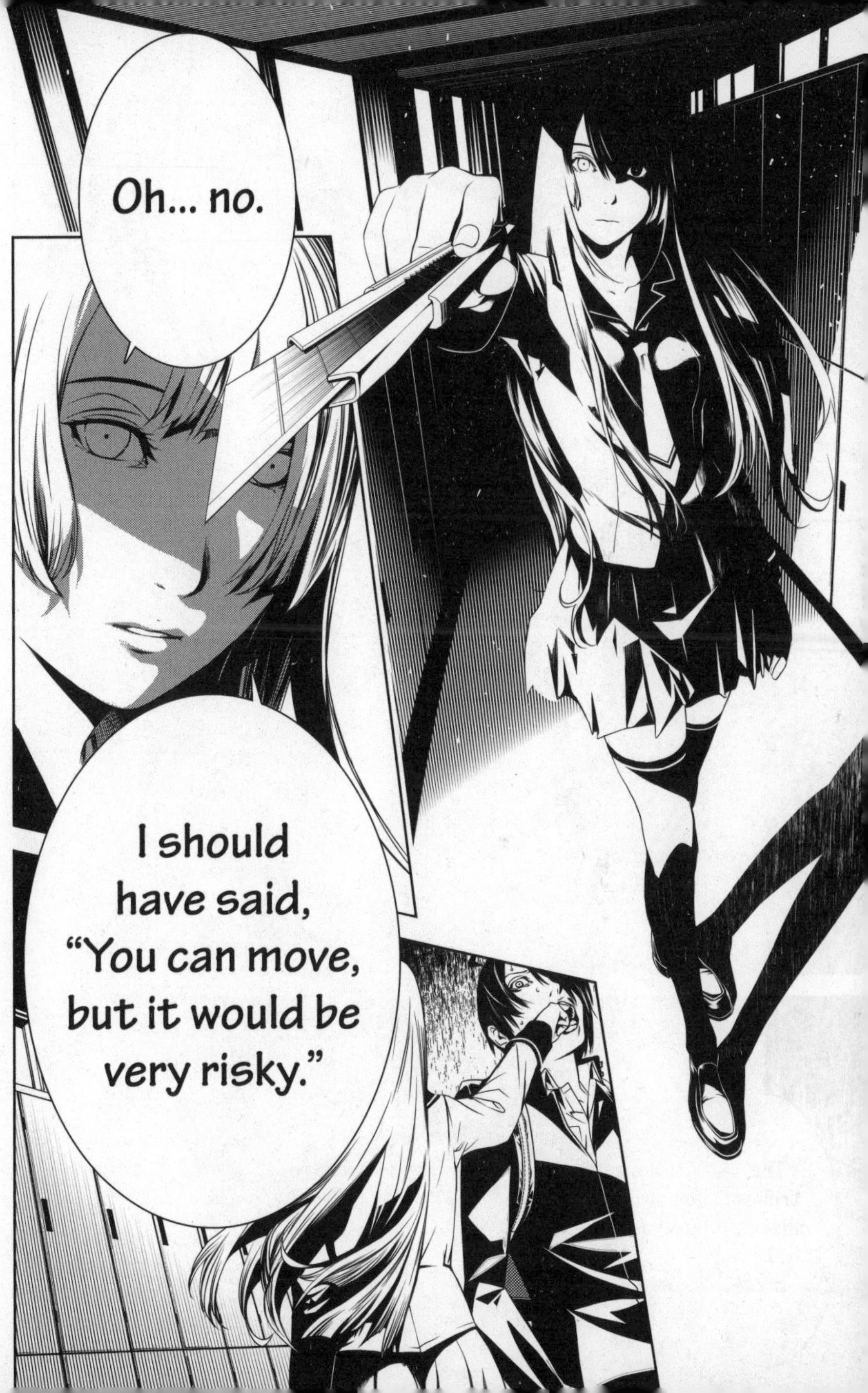
Oh... no.
I should have said, "You can move, but it would be very risky."

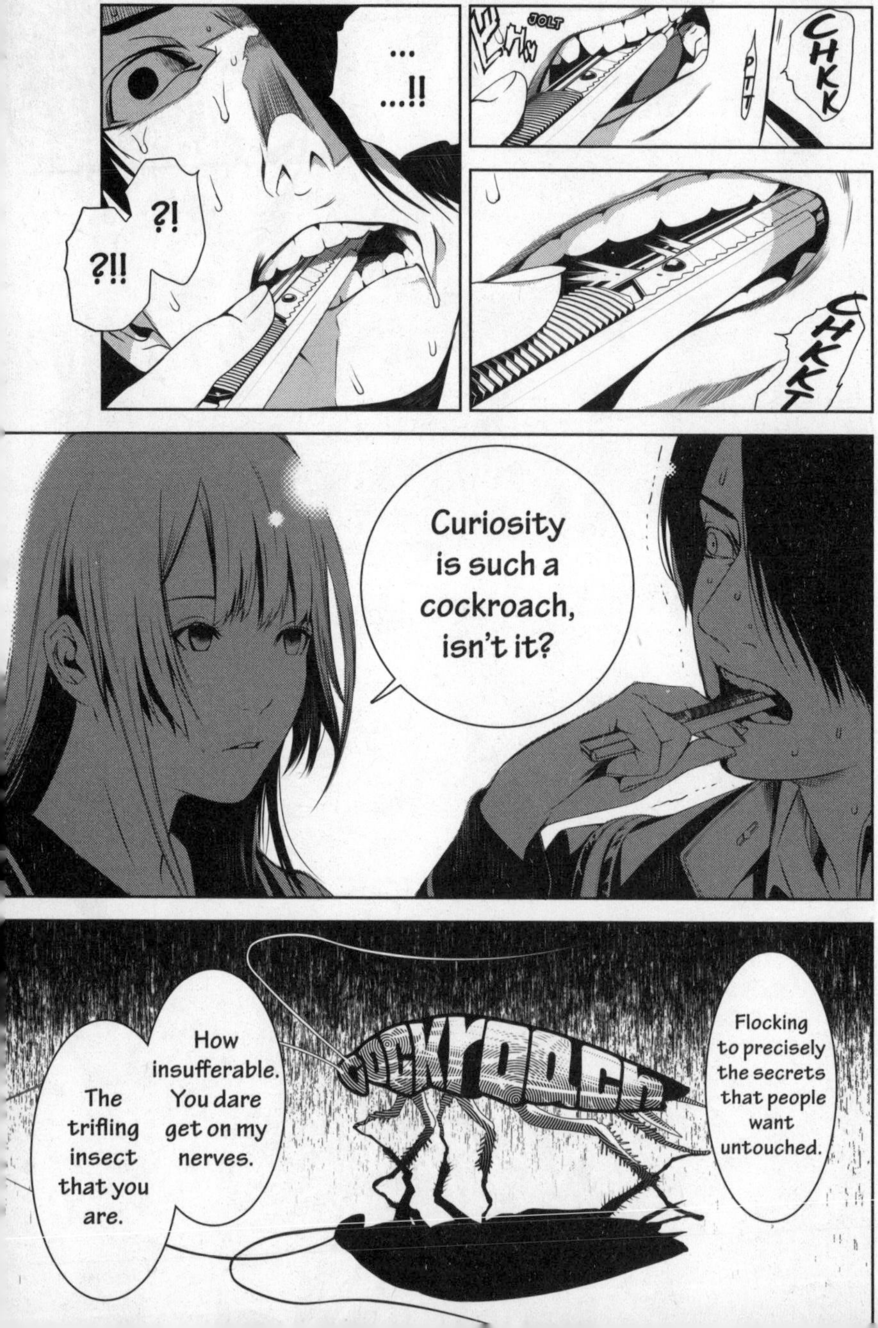
CHKK
PTT
JOLT
CHKKKT
...
...!!
?!
?!!
Curiosity is such a cockroach, isn't it?
Flocking to precisely the secrets that people want untouched.
COCKROACH
How insufferable. You dare get on my nerves.
The trifling insect that you are.

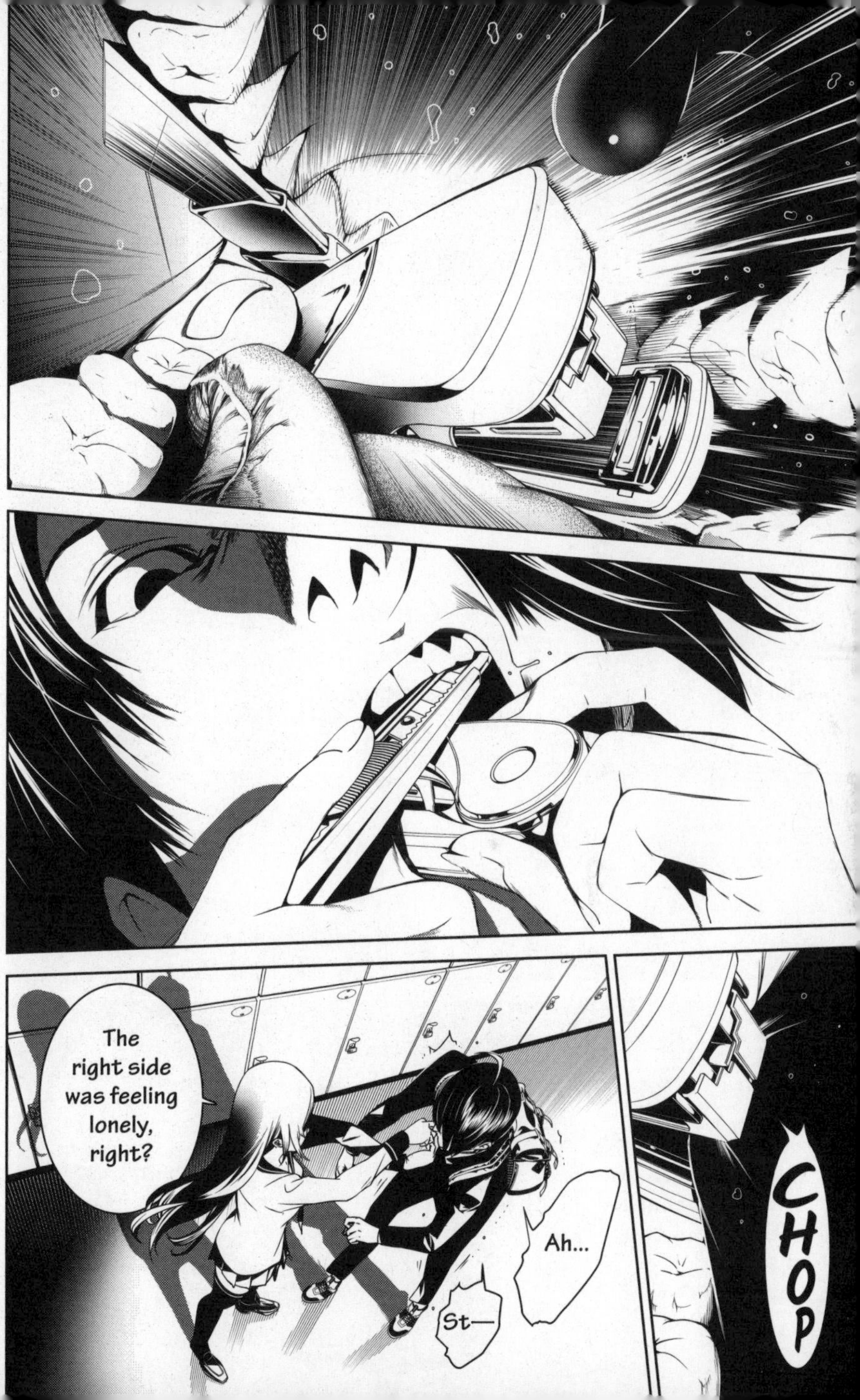
CHOP
The right side was feeling lonely, right?
Ah...
St—

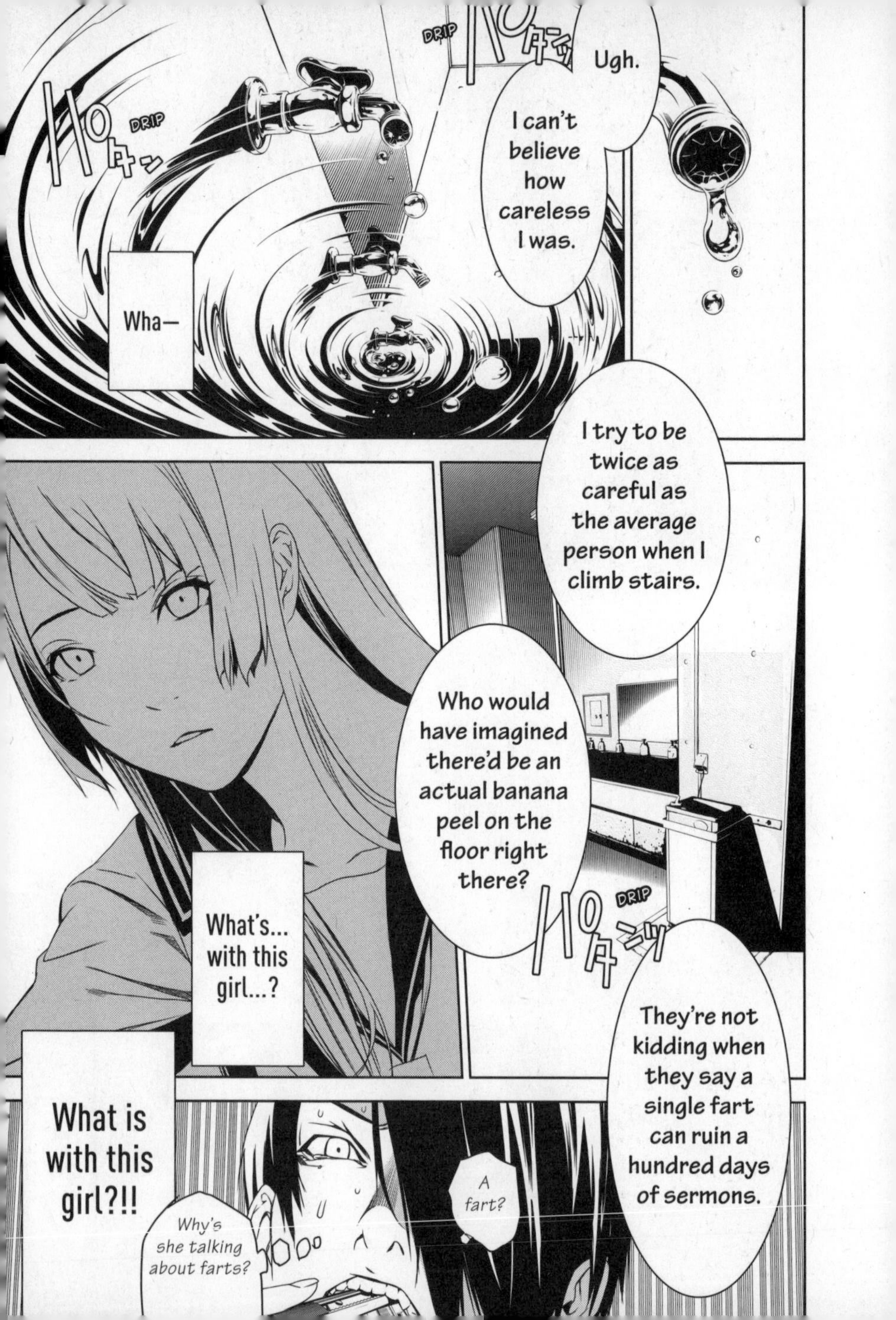
DRIP
Ugh.
I can't believe how careless I was.
DRIP
Wha—
I try to be twice as careful as the average person when I climb stairs.
Who would have imagined there'd be an actual banana peel on the floor right there?
DRIP
What's... with this girl...?
They're not kidding when they say a single fart can ruin a hundred days of sermons.
A fart?
What is with this girl?!!
Why's she talking about farts?

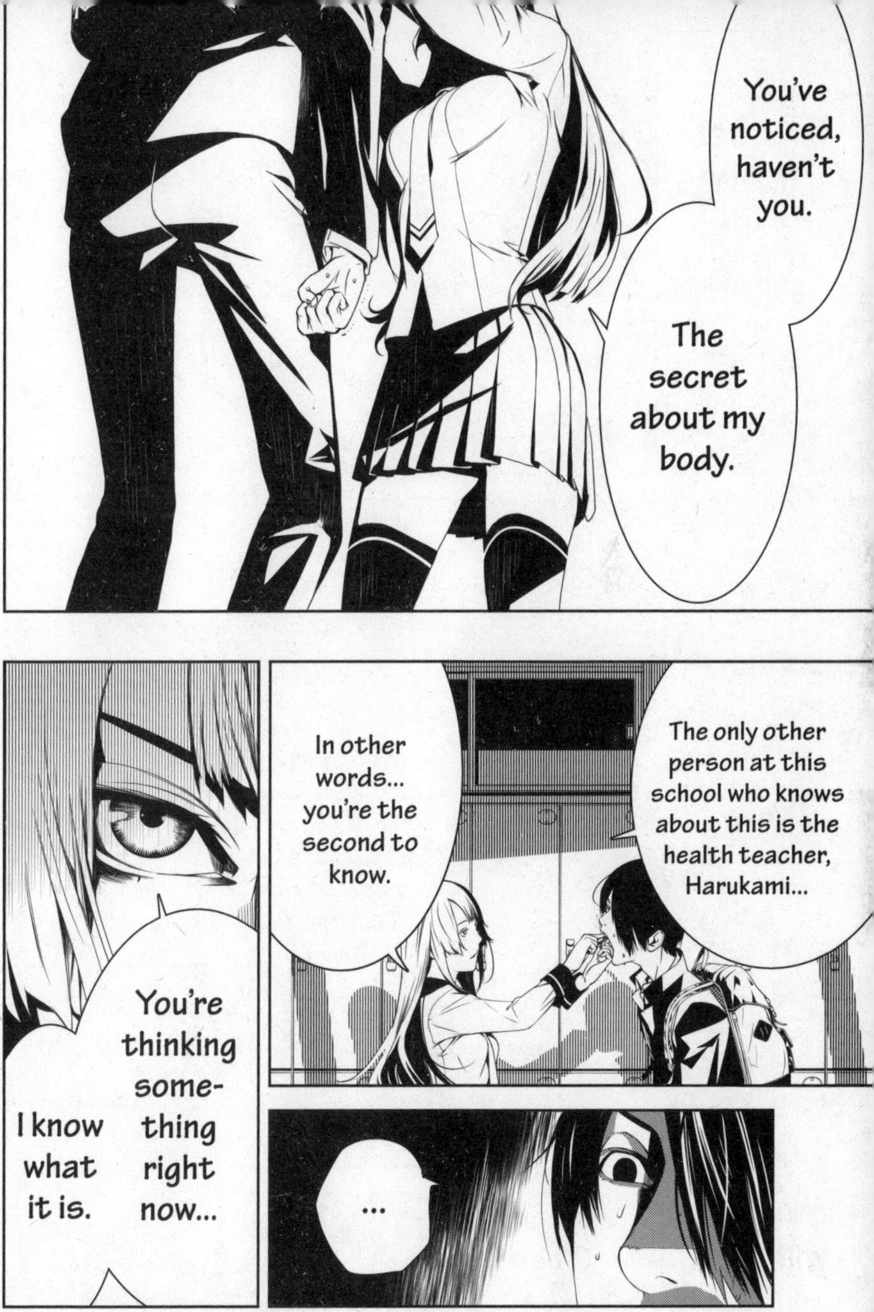
You've noticed, haven't you.
The secret about my body.
The only other person at this school who knows about this is the health teacher, Harukami...
In other words... you're the second to know.
...
You're thinking some-thing right now...
I know what it is.

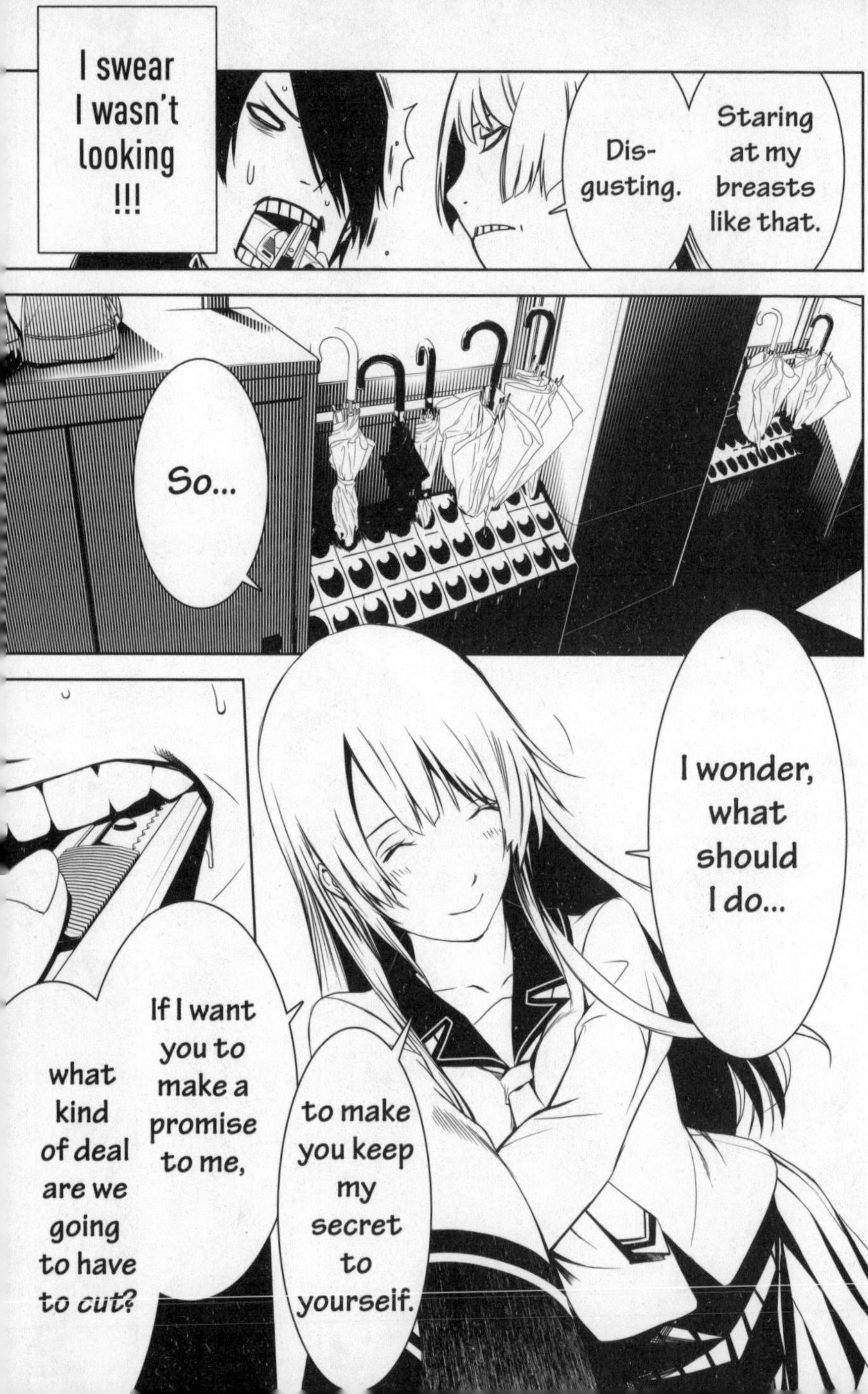
Staring at my breasts like that.
Dis-gusting.
I swear I wasn't looking!!!
So...
I wonder, what should I do...
to make you keep my secret to yourself.
If I want you to make a promise to me,
what kind of deal are we going to have to cut?

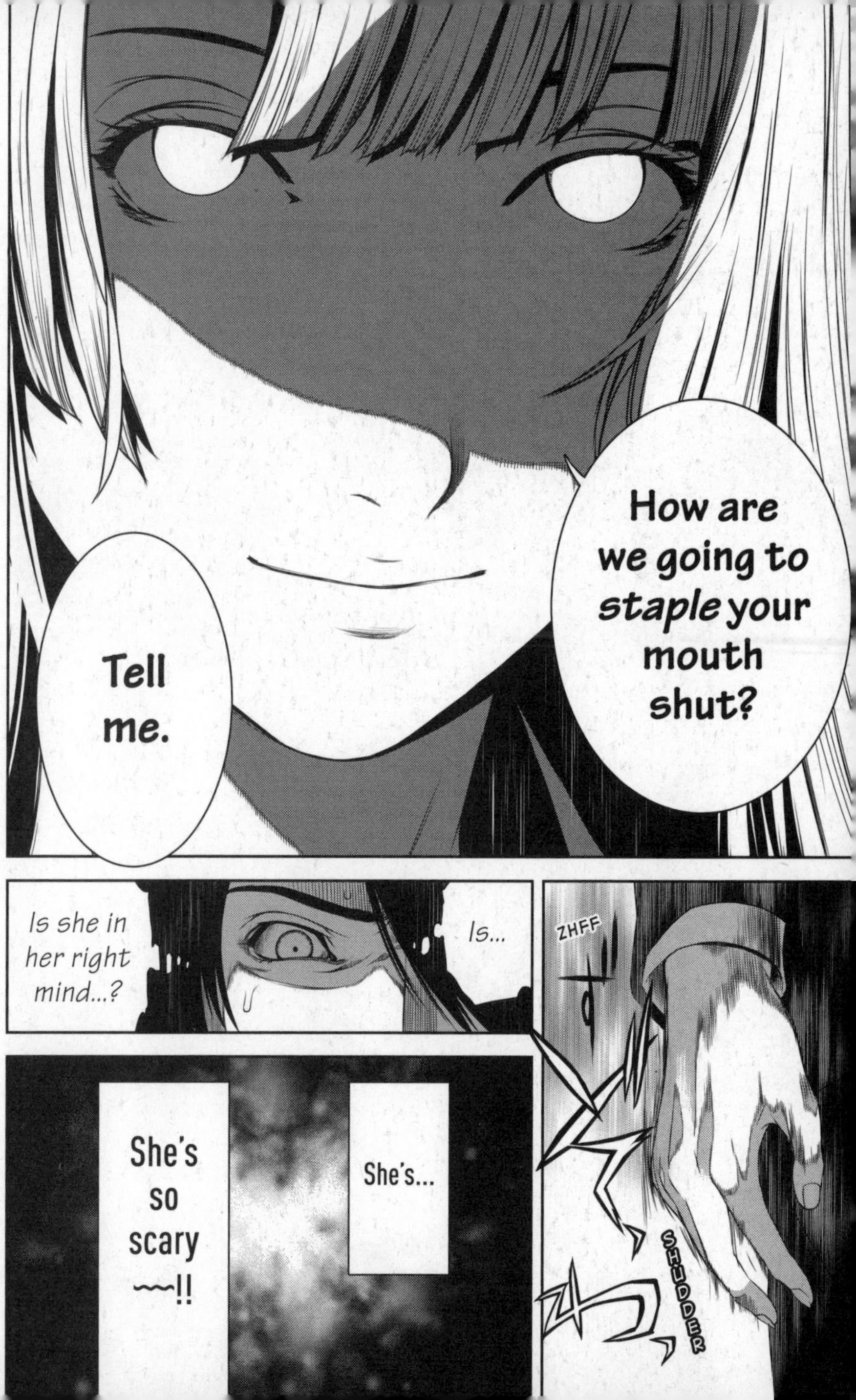
How are we going to *staple* your mouth shut?
Tell me.
ZHFF
SHUDDER
Is...
Is she in her right mind...?
She's...
She's so scary ~~!!

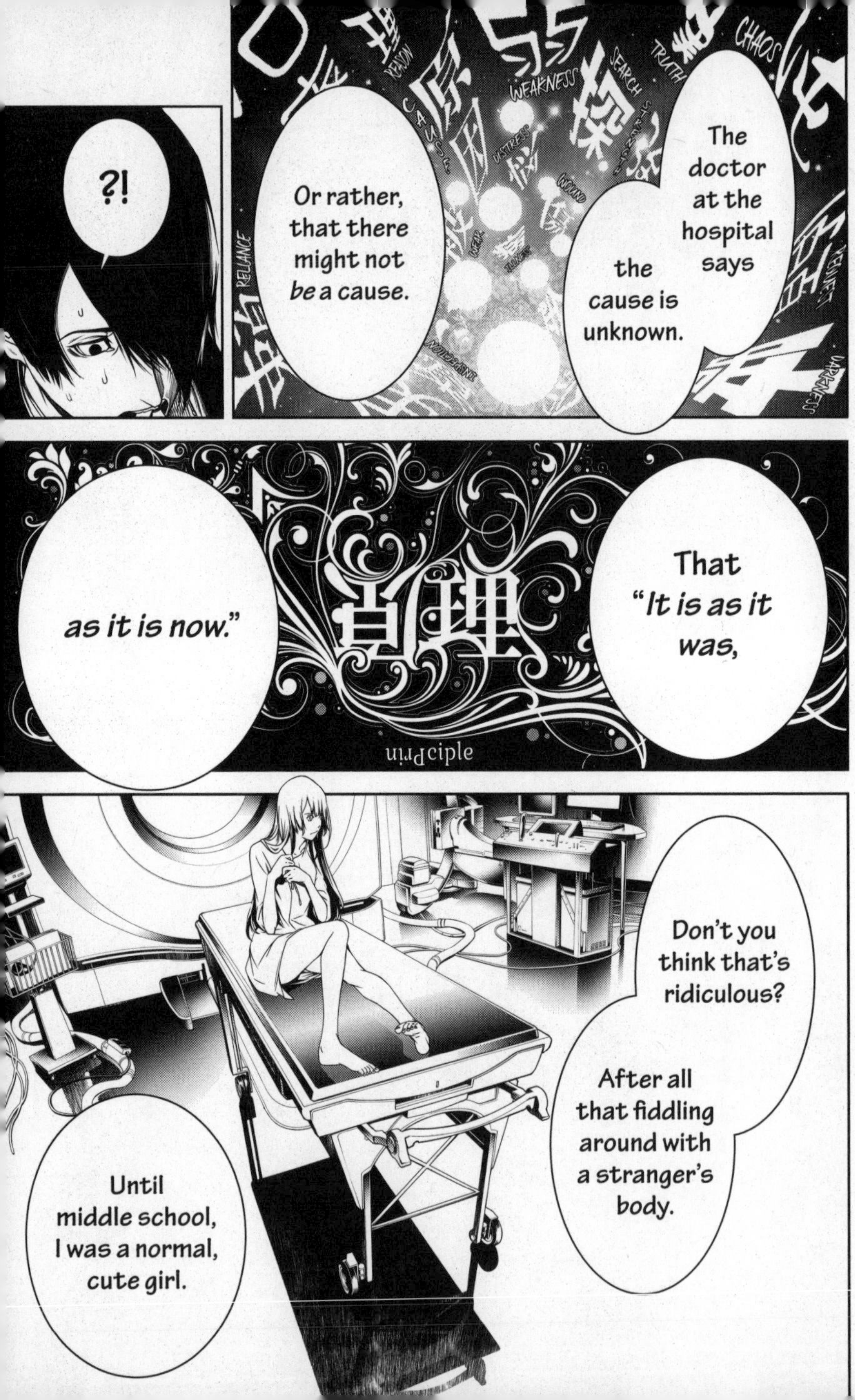
The doctor at the hospital says
the cause is unknown.
Or rather, that there might not *be* a cause.
?!
That "*It is as it was,*
as it is now."
Don't you think that's ridiculous?
After all that fiddling around with a stranger's body.
Until middle school, I was a normal, cute girl.

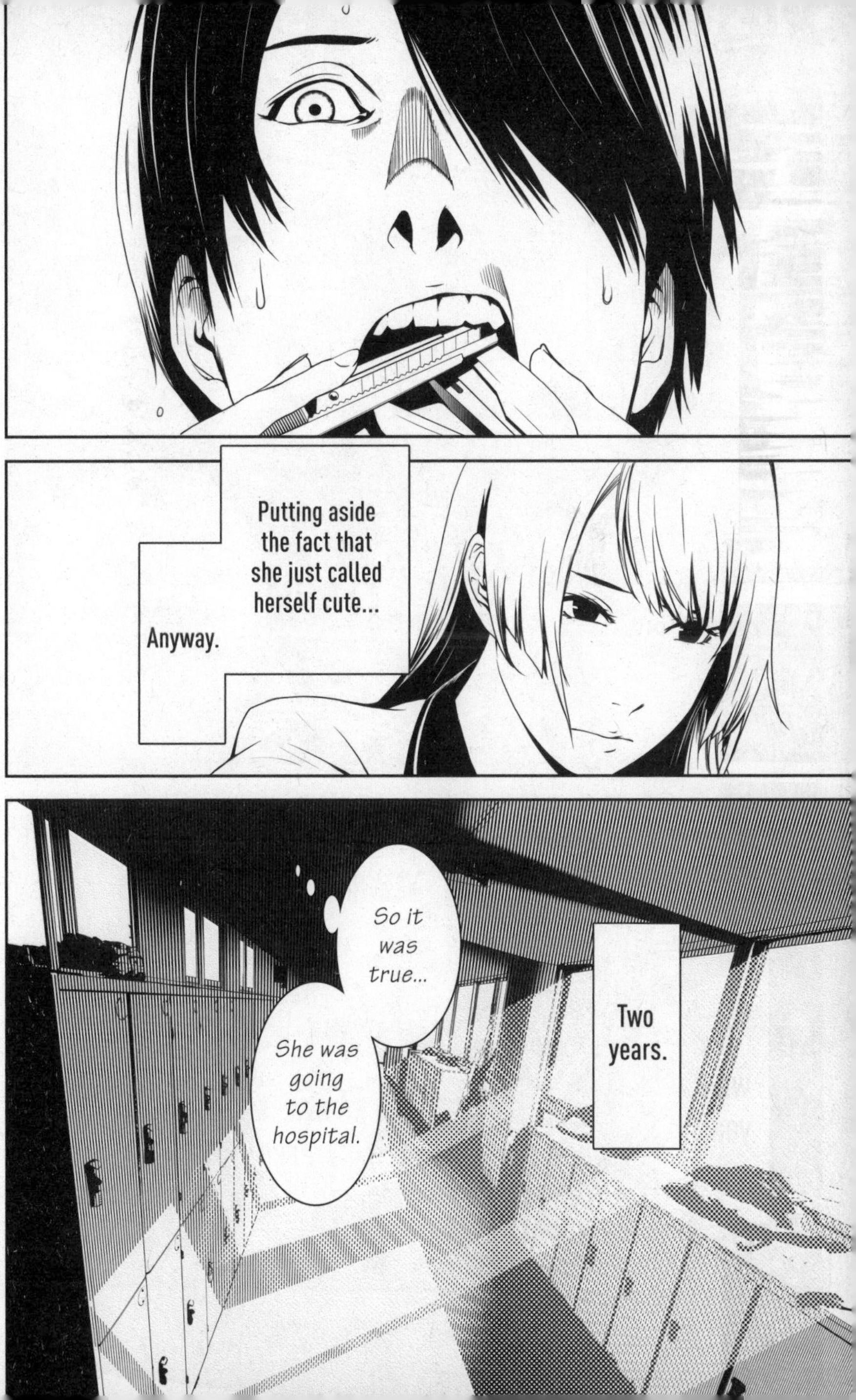
Putting aside the fact that she just called herself cute...
Anyway.
Two years.
So it was true...
She was going to the hospital.

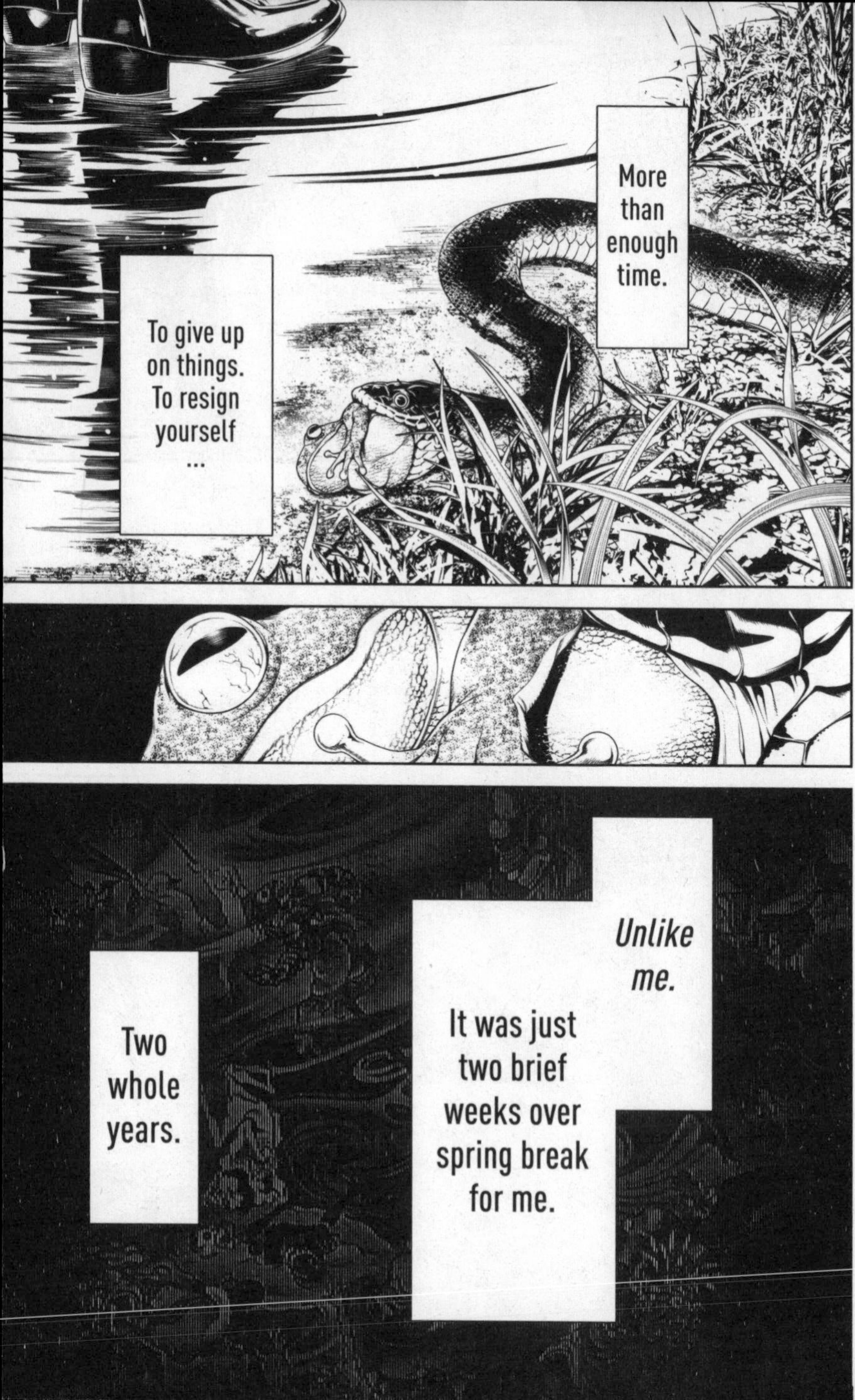
More than enough time.
To give up on things. To resign yourself ...
Unlike me.
It was just two brief weeks over spring break for me.
Two whole years.

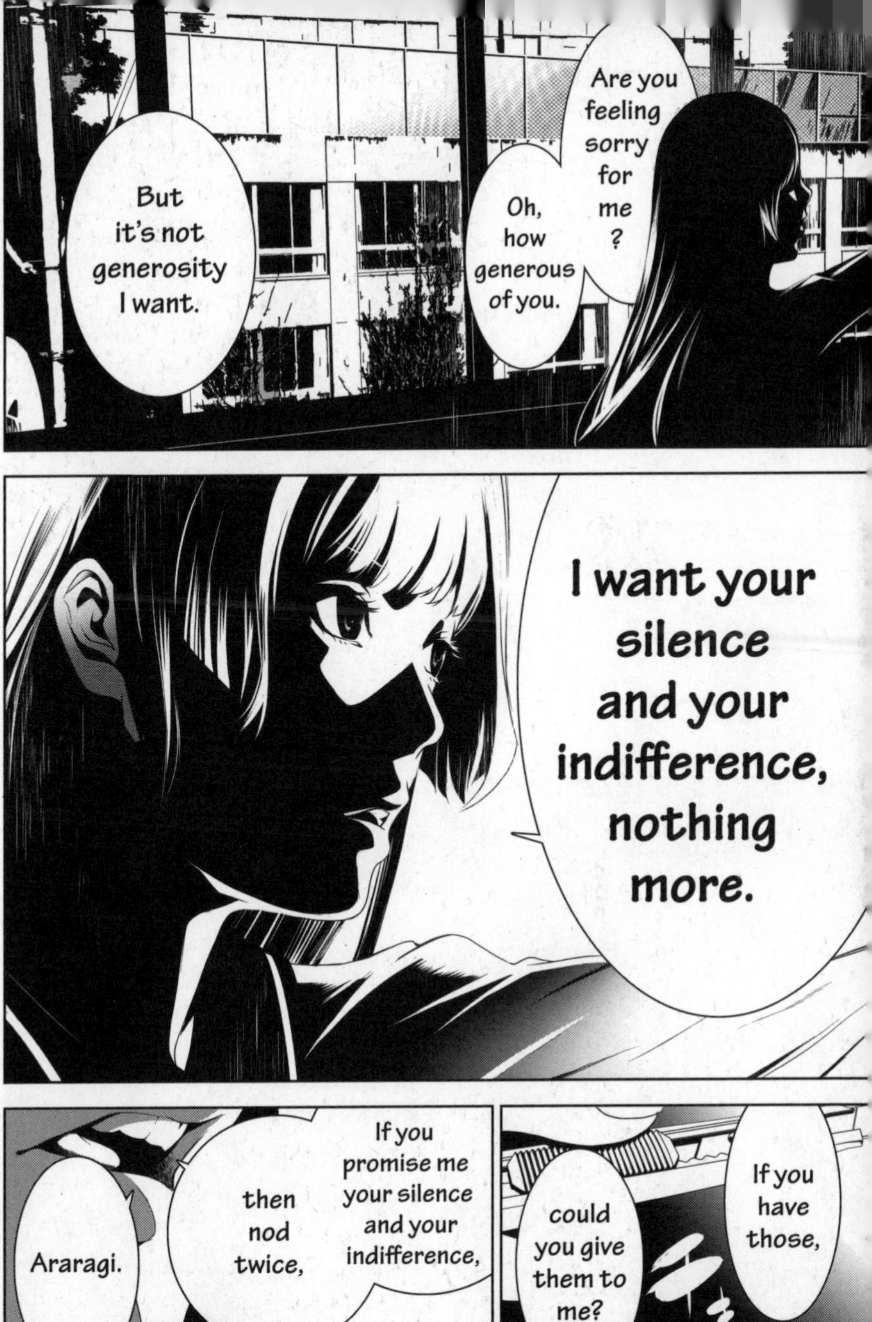
Are you feeling sorry for me?
Oh, how generous of you.
But it's not generosity I want.
I want your silence and your indifference, nothing more.
If you have those,
could you give them to me?
CHKK
If you promise me your silence and your indifference,
then nod twice,
Araragi.

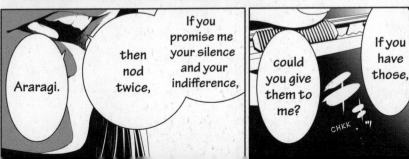

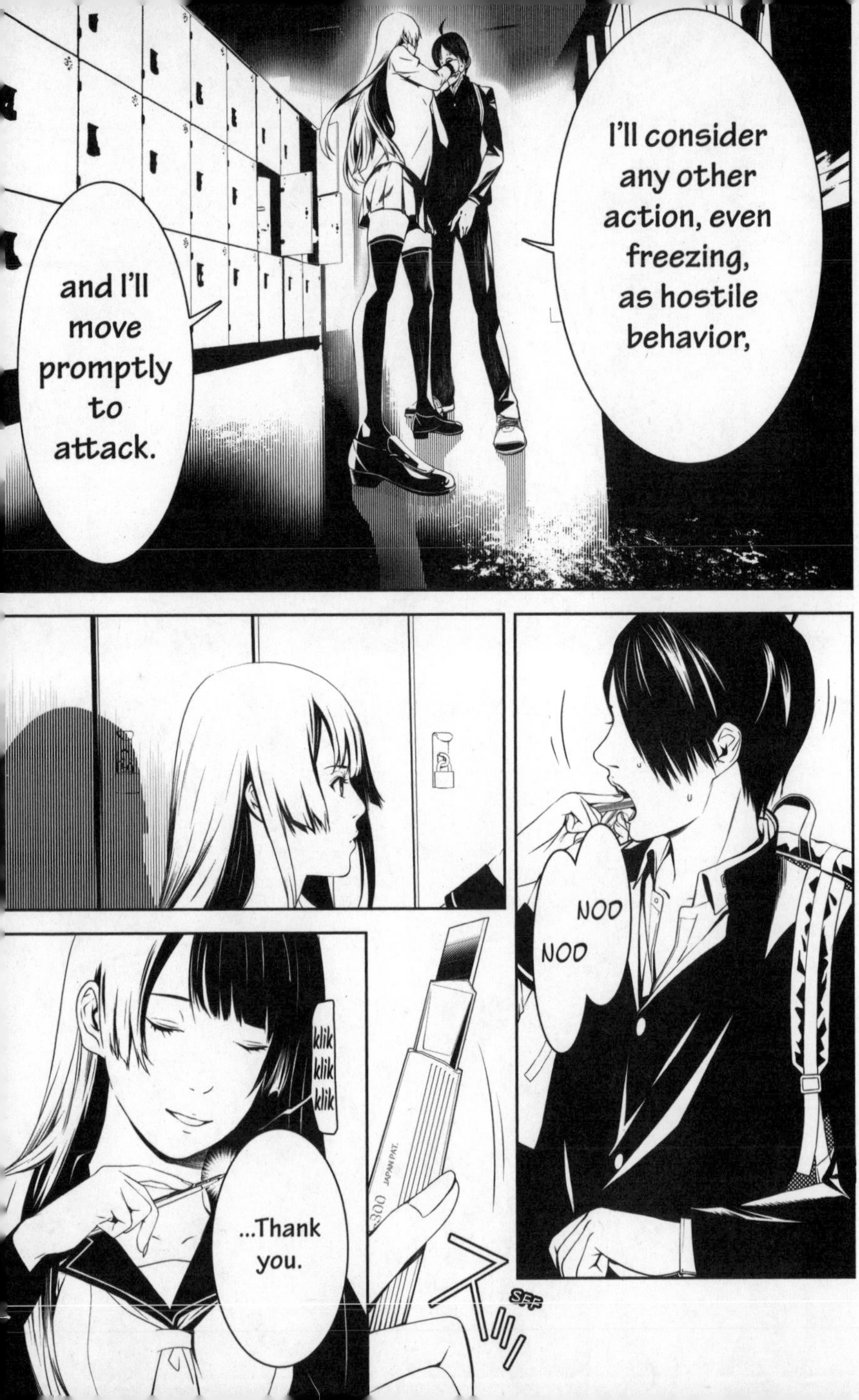
I'll consider any other action, even freezing, as hostile behavior,
and I'll move promptly to attack.
NOD
NOD
klik klik klik
...Thank you.
SFF

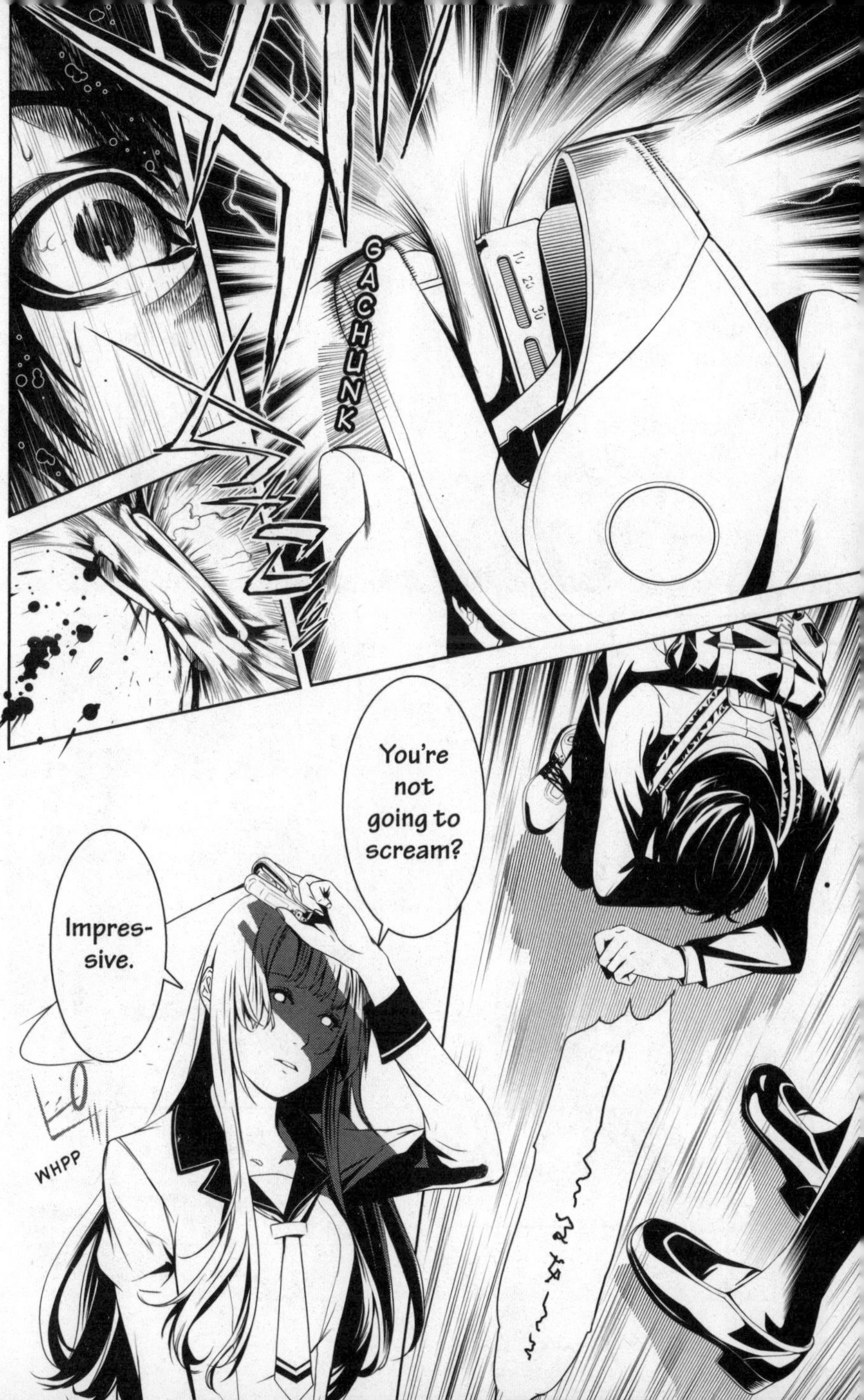
GACHUNK
You're not going to scream?
Impres-
sive.
WHPP

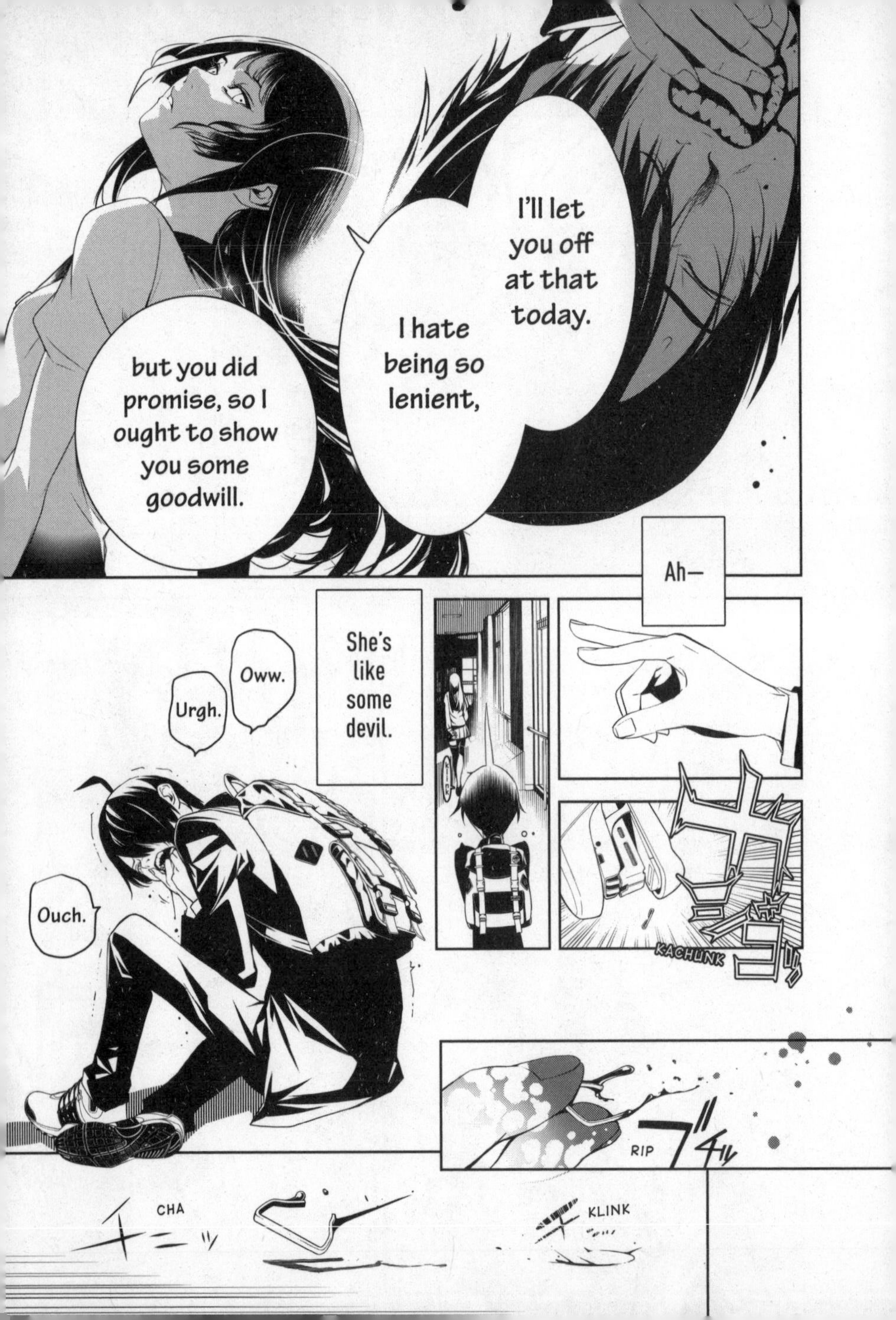
I'll let you off at that today.
I hate being so lenient,
but you did promise, so I ought to show you some goodwill.
Ah—
KACHUNK
KLINK
She's like some devil.
Oww.
Urgh.
Ouch.
RIP
KLINK
CHA

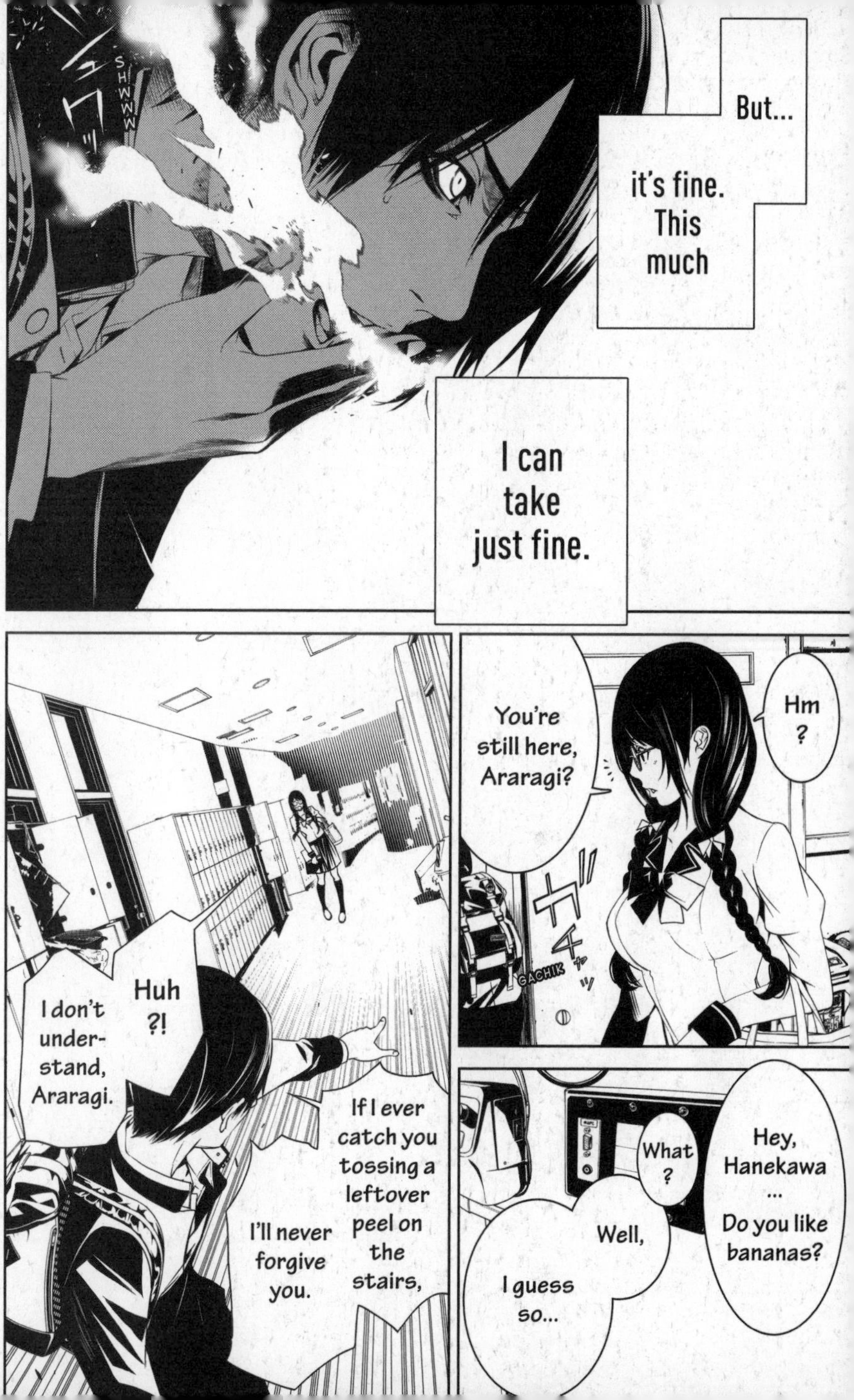
SHWWW
But...
it's fine. This much
I can take just fine.
Hm ?
You're still here, Araragi?
GACHIK
Hey, Hanekawa ... Do you like bananas?
What ?
Well,
I guess so...
If I ever catch you tossing a leftover peel on the stairs,
I'll never forgive you.
Huh ?!
I don't under-stand, Araragi.

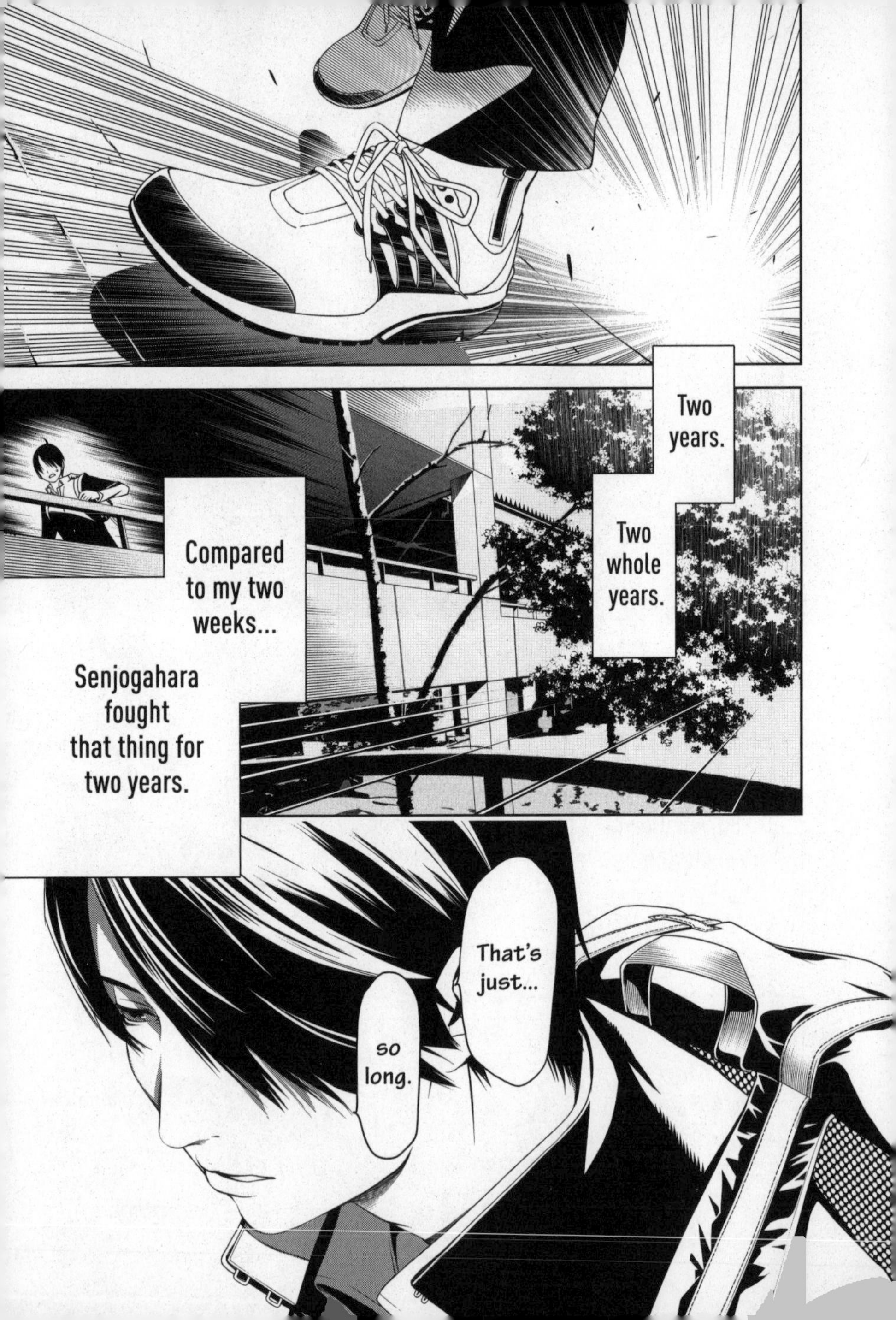
Two years.
Two whole years.
Compared to my two weeks...
Senjogahara fought that thing for two years.
That's just...
so long.

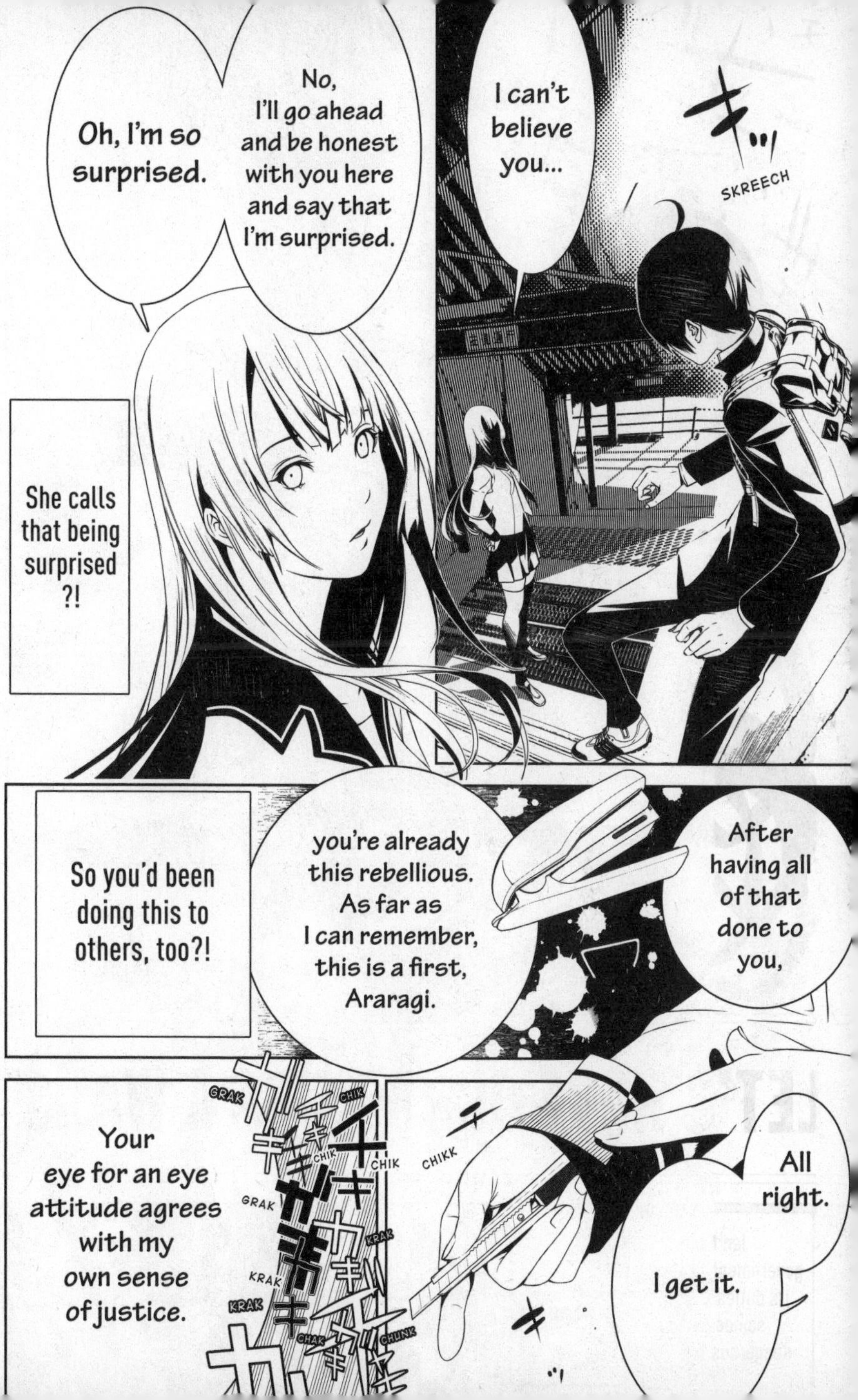
I can't believe you...
SKREECH
No, I'll go ahead and be honest with you here and say that I'm surprised.
Oh, I'm so surprised.
She calls that being surprised?!
After having all of that done to you,
you're already this rebellious. As far as I can remember, this is a first, Araragi.
So you'd been doing this to others, too?!
All right.
I get it.
CHIKK
CHIK
GRAK
CHIK
Your eye for an eye attitude agrees with my own sense of justice.
GRAK
KRAK
KRAK
KRAK
CHAK
CHUNK

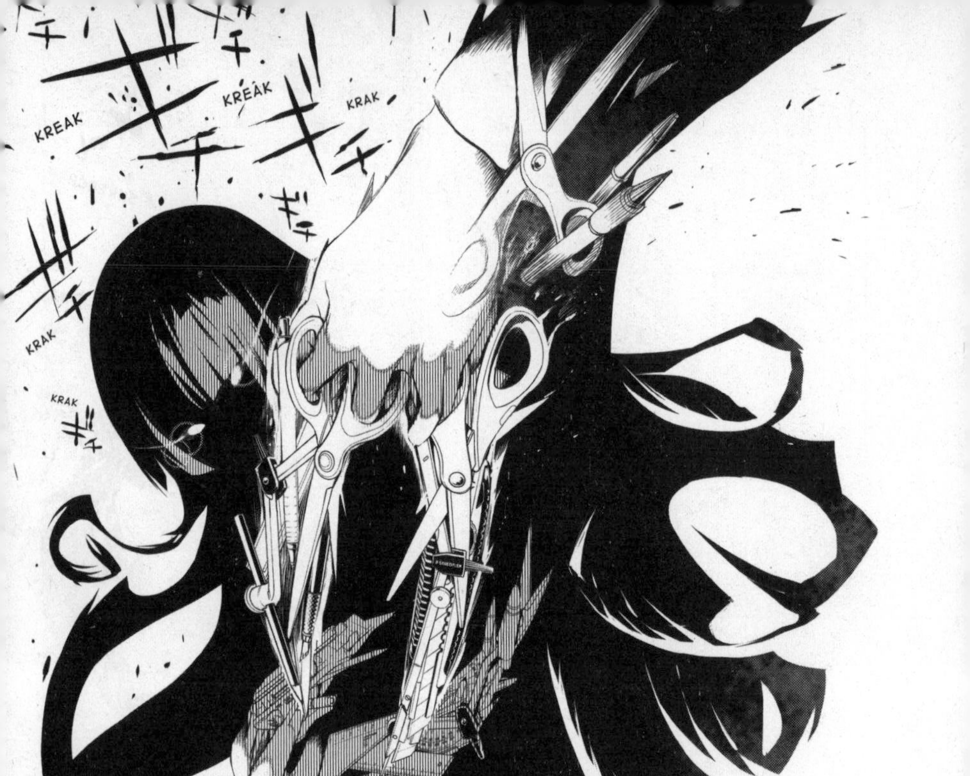
KRAK
KREAK
KREAK
KRAK
KRAK
LET'S HAVE OURSELVES A WAR.

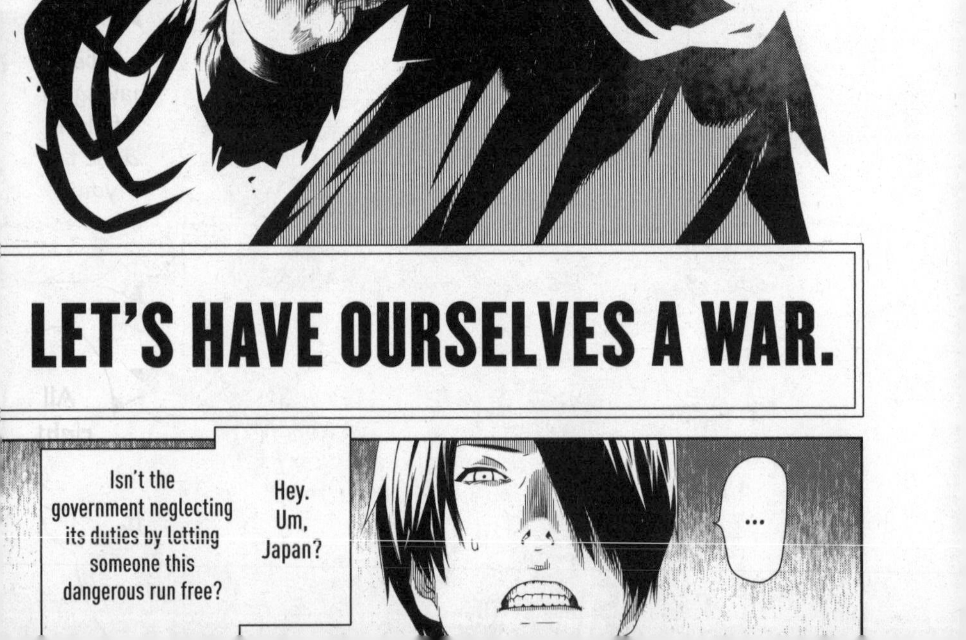
...
Hey. Um, Japan?
Isn't the government neglecting its duties by letting someone this dangerous run free?

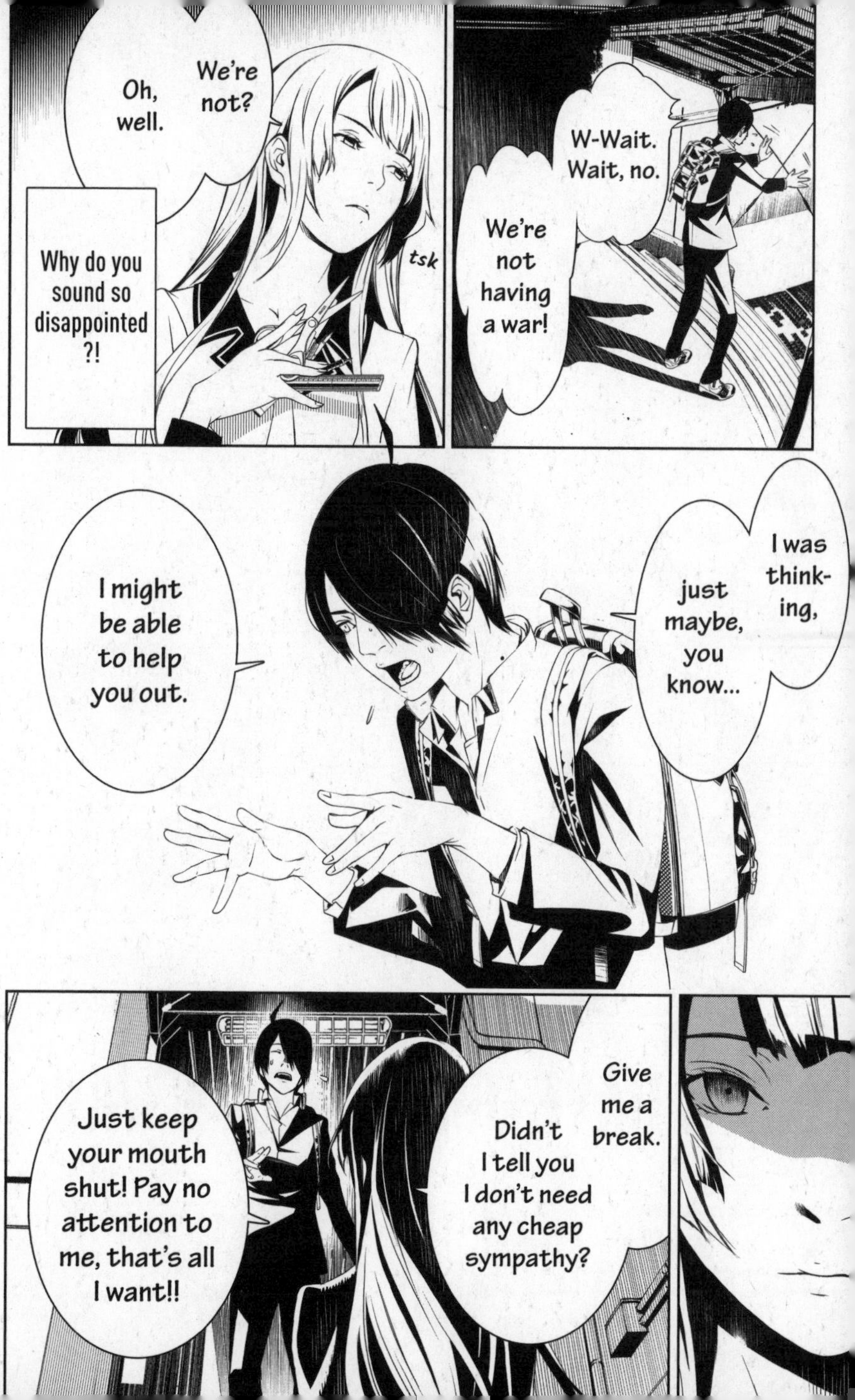
W-Wait. Wait, no.
We're not having a war!
We're not? Oh, well.
tsk
Why do you sound so disappointed ?!
I was thinking, just maybe, you know...
I might be able to help you out.
Give me a break. Didn't I tell you I don't need any cheap sympathy?
Just keep your mouth shut! Pay no attention to me, that's all I want!!

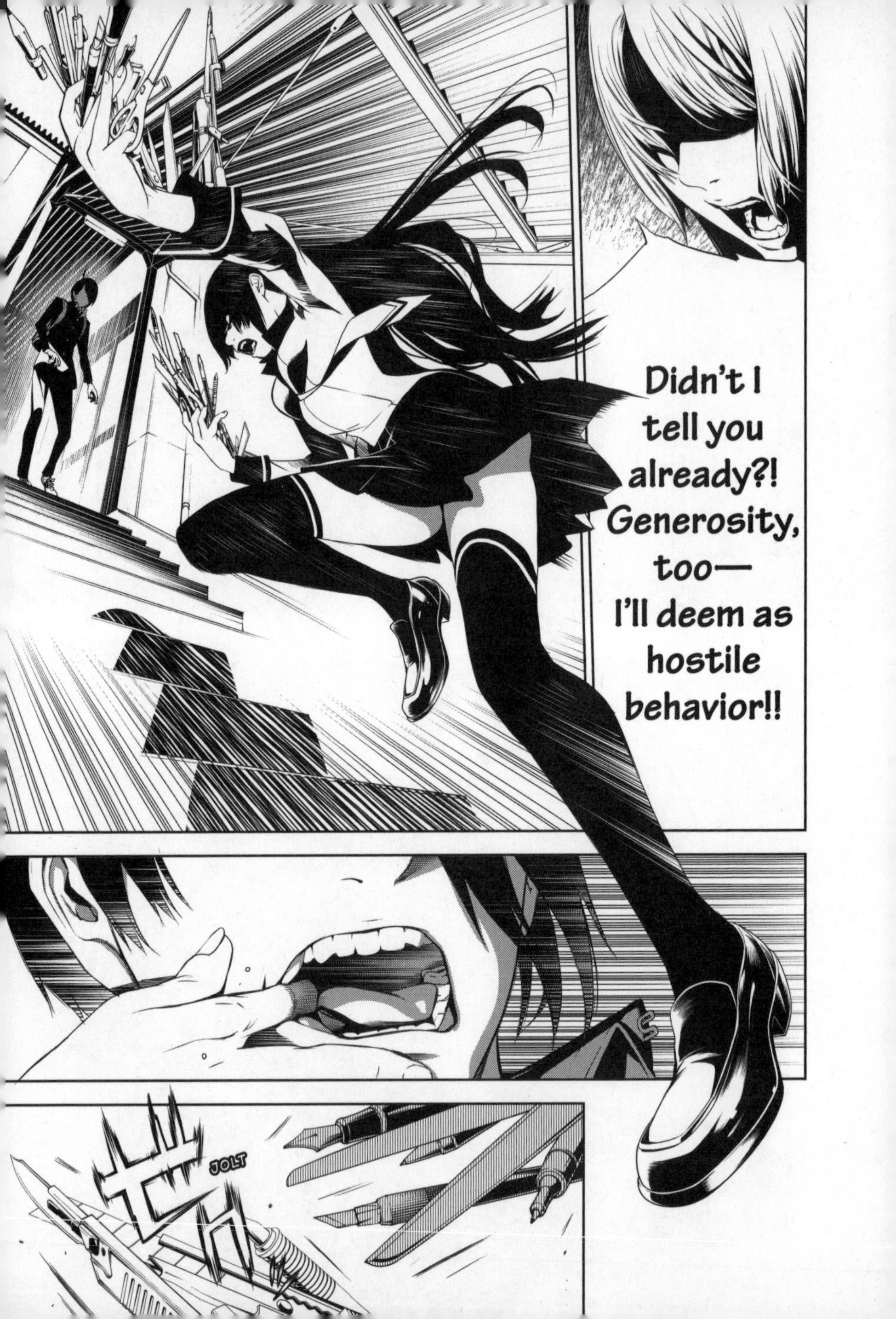
Didn't I tell you already?! Generosity, too— I'll deem as hostile behavior!!
JOLT

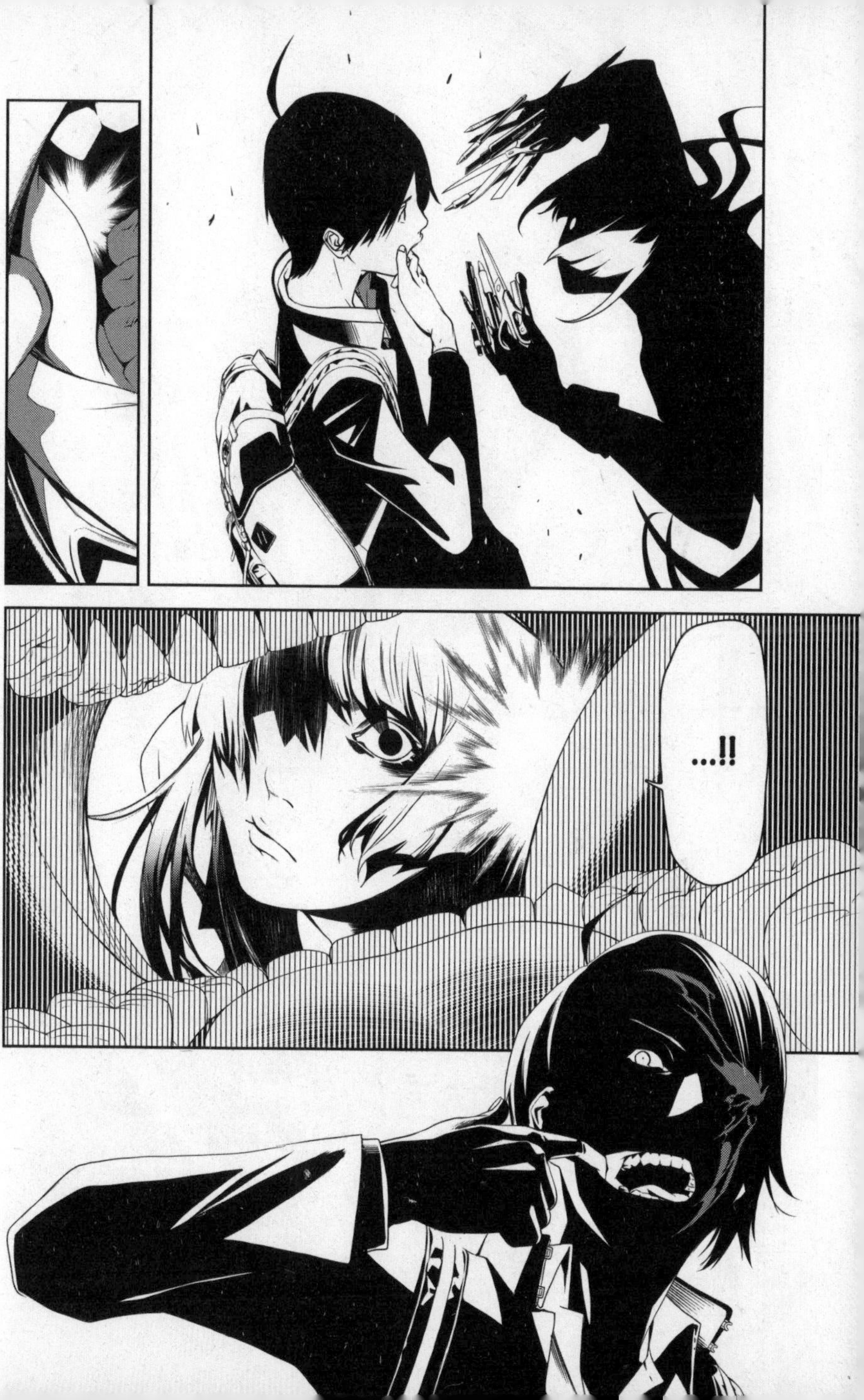
...!!

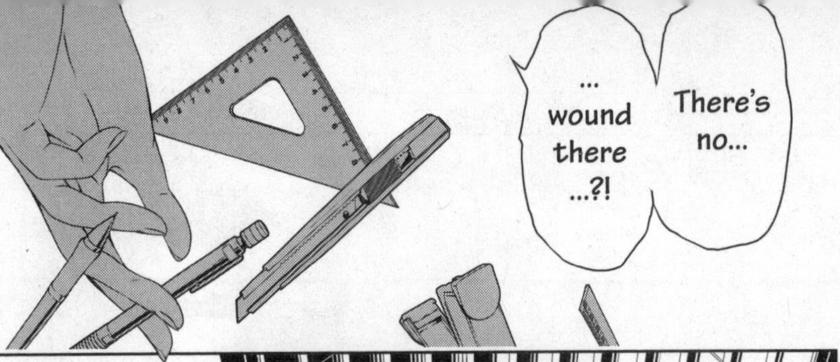
There's no...
...
wound
there
...?!

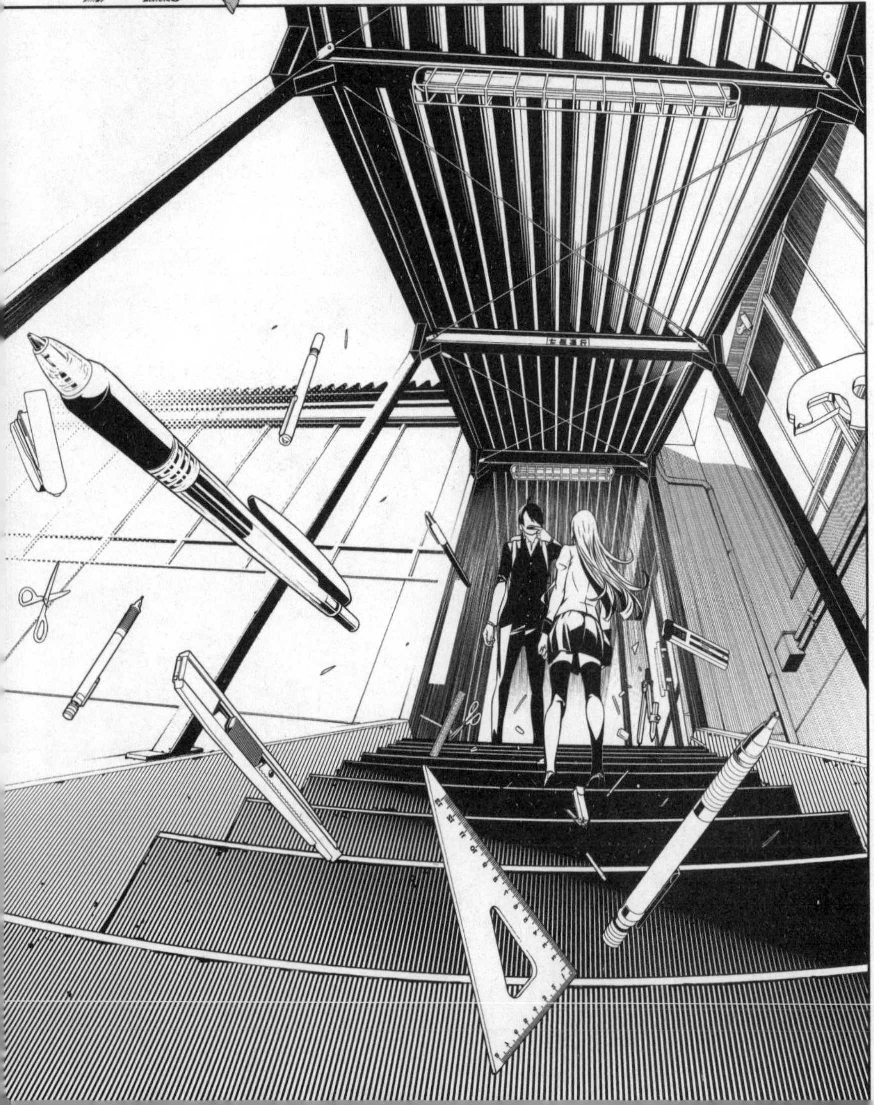

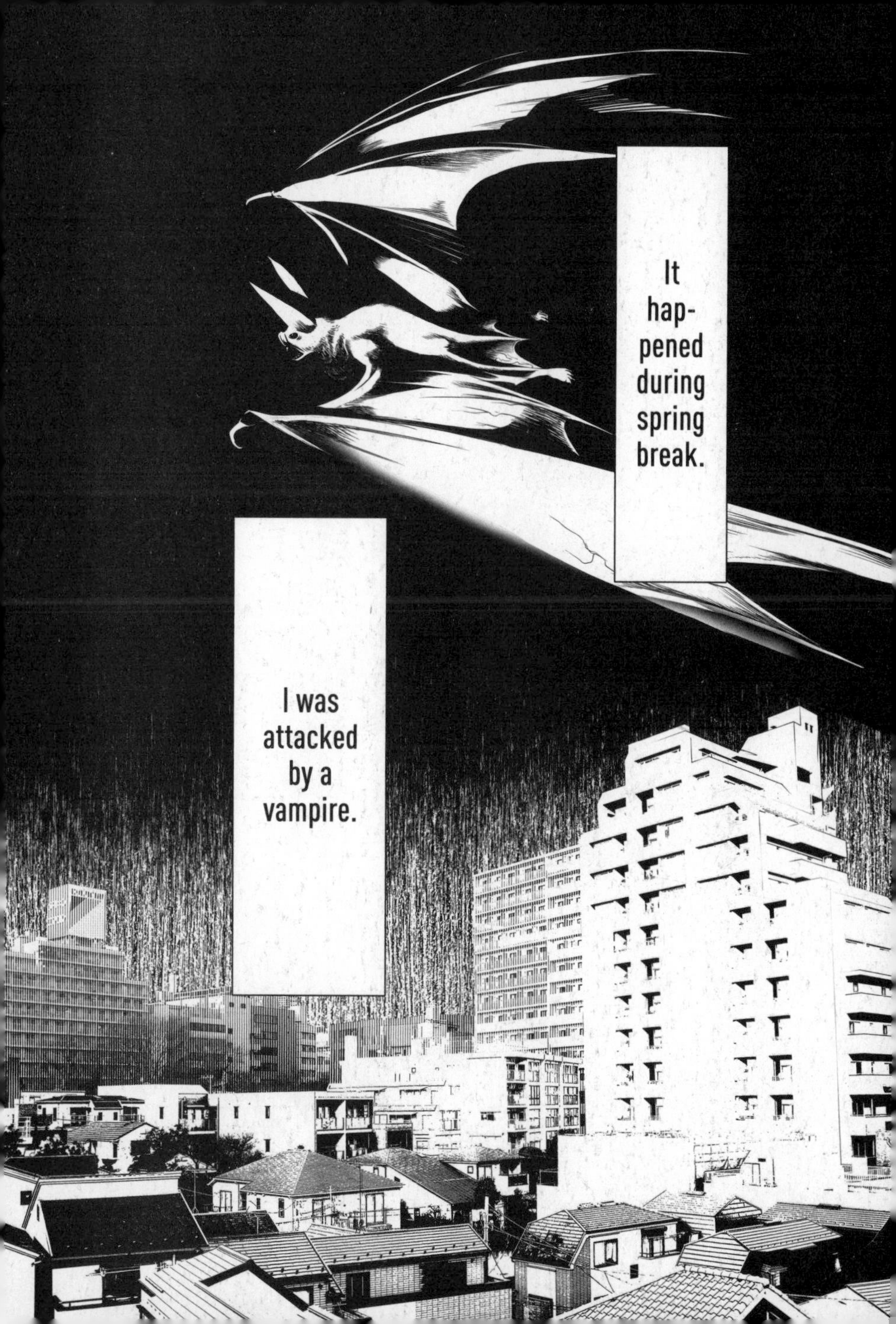
It hap-pened during spring break.
I was attacked by a vampire.

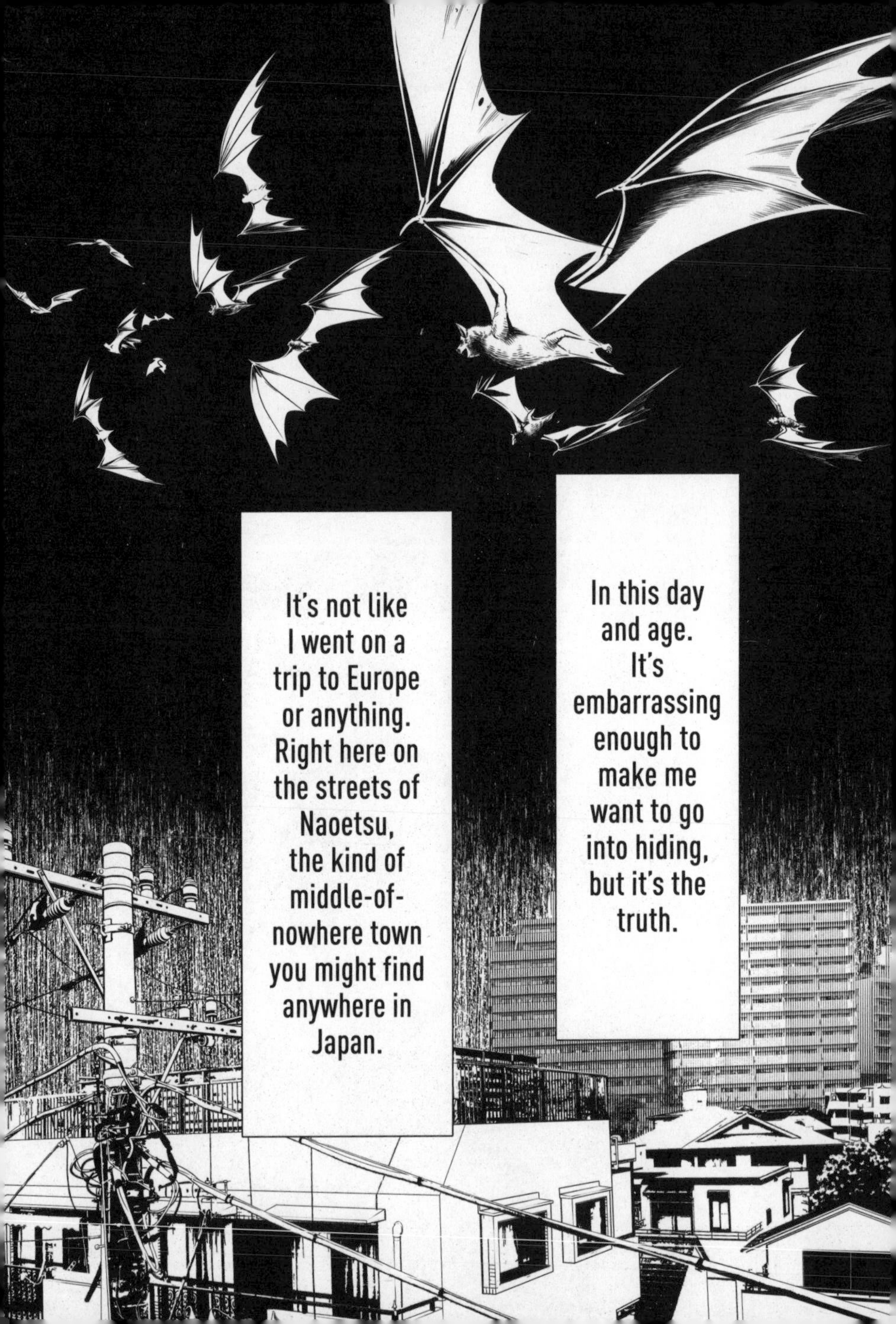
In this day and age. It's embarrassing enough to make me want to go into hiding, but it's the truth.
It's not like I went on a trip to Europe or anything. Right here on the streets of Naoetsu, the kind of middle-of-nowhere town you might find anywhere in Japan.

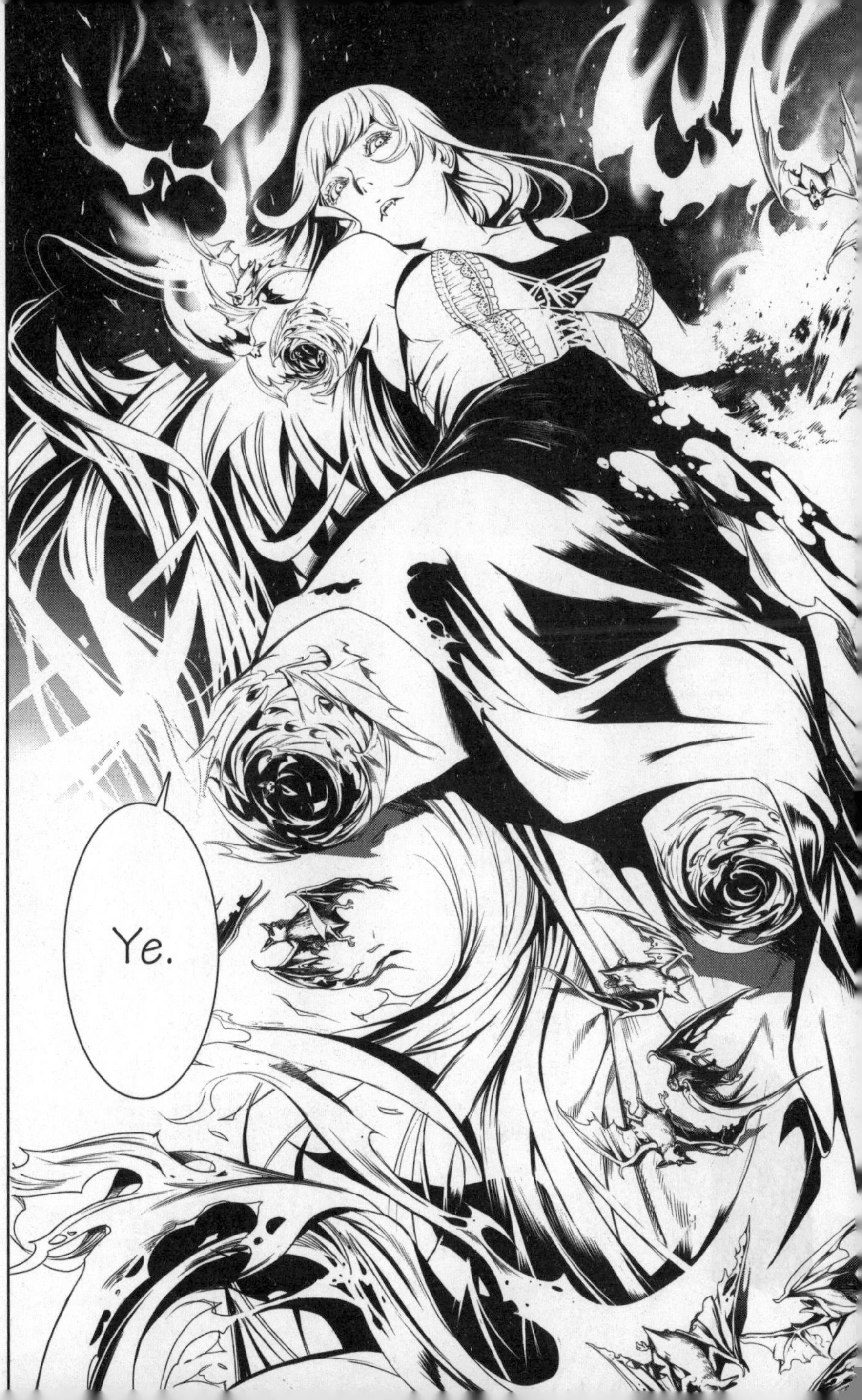
Ye.

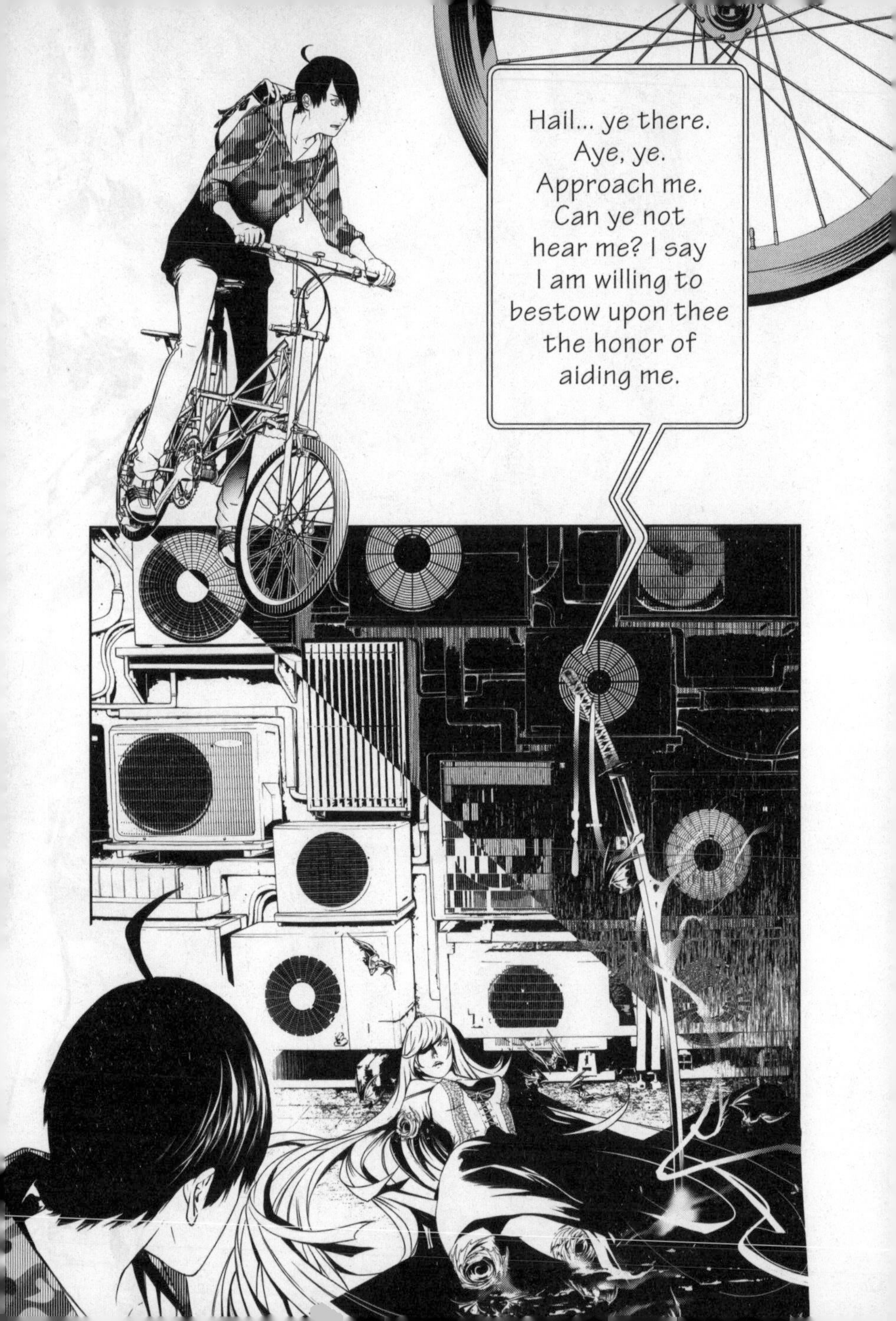
Hail... ye there. Aye, ye. Approach me. Can ye not hear me? I say I am willing to bestow upon thee the honor of aiding me.

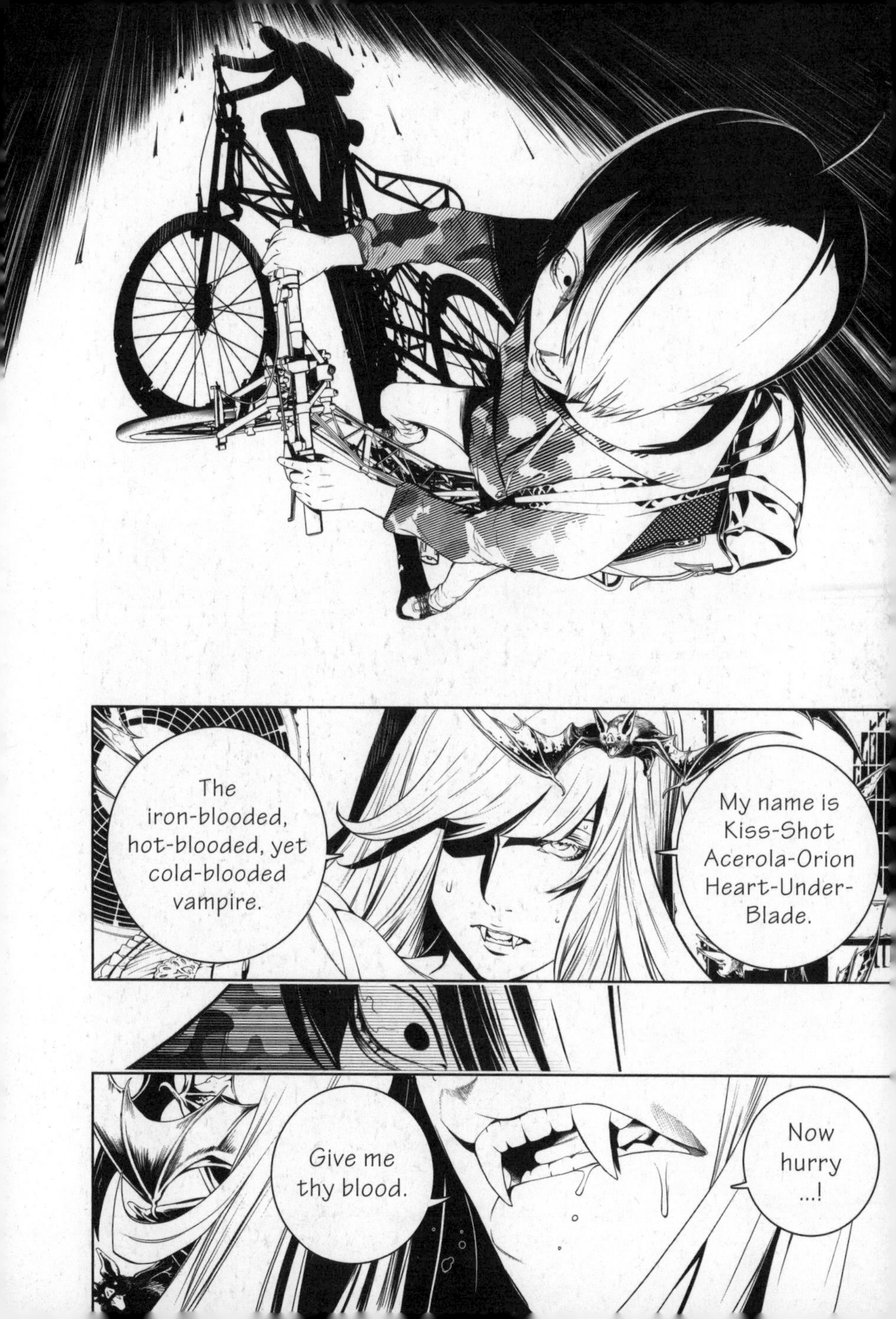
My name is Kiss-Shot Acerola-Orion Heart-Under-Blade.
The iron-blooded, hot-blooded, yet cold-blooded vampire.
Now hurry ...!
Give me thy blood.

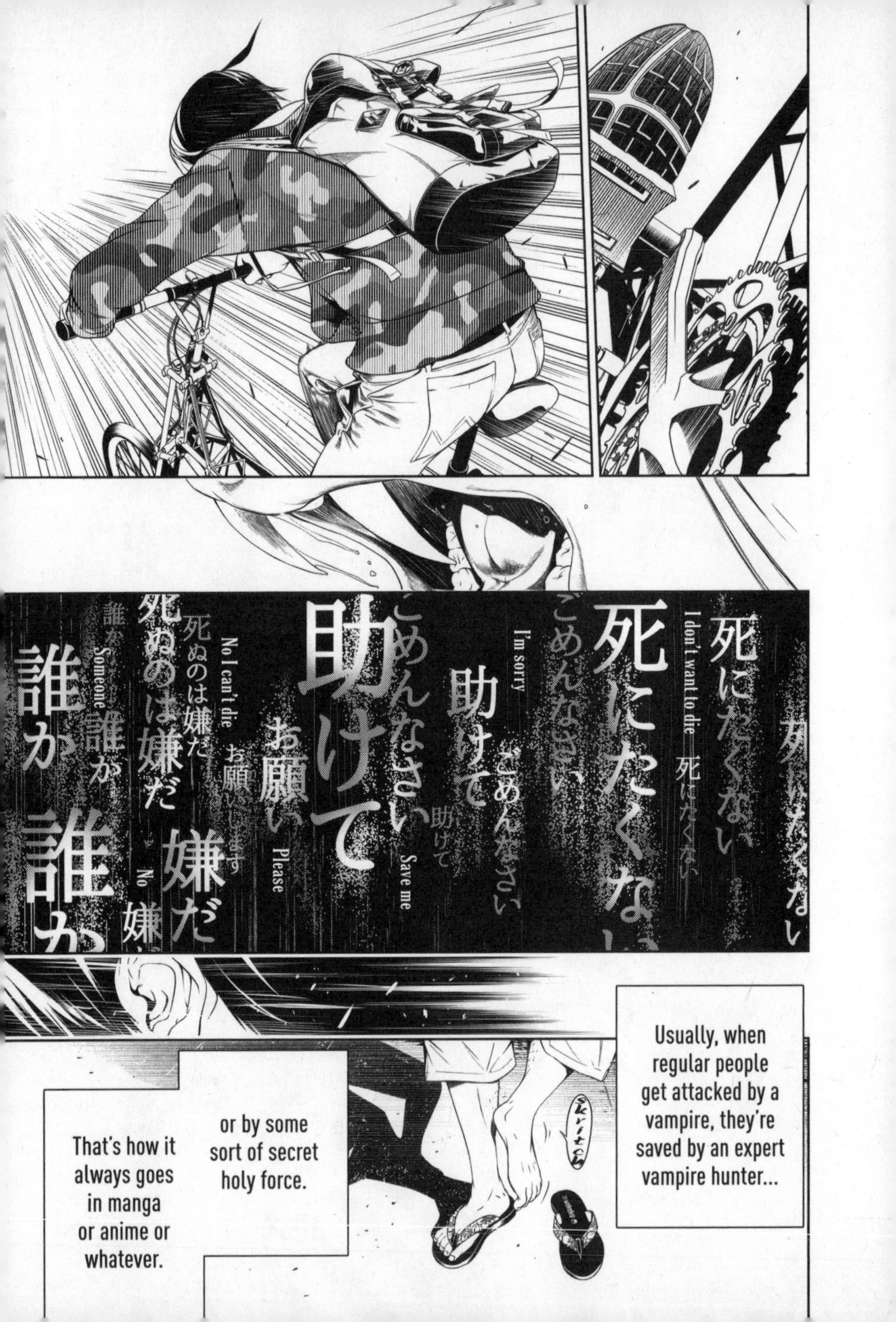
死にたくない
死にたくない
I don't want to die
死にたくない
ごめんなさい
I'm sorry
ごめんなさい
助けて
助けて
Save me
ごめんなさい
助けて
お願い
Please
お願いします
No I can't die
死ぬのは嫌だ
嫌だ
No
嫌
死ぬのは嫌だ
Someone
誰か
誰か
Usually, when regular people get attacked by a vampire, they're saved by an expert vampire hunter...
or by some sort of secret holy force.
That's how it always goes in manga or anime or whatever.

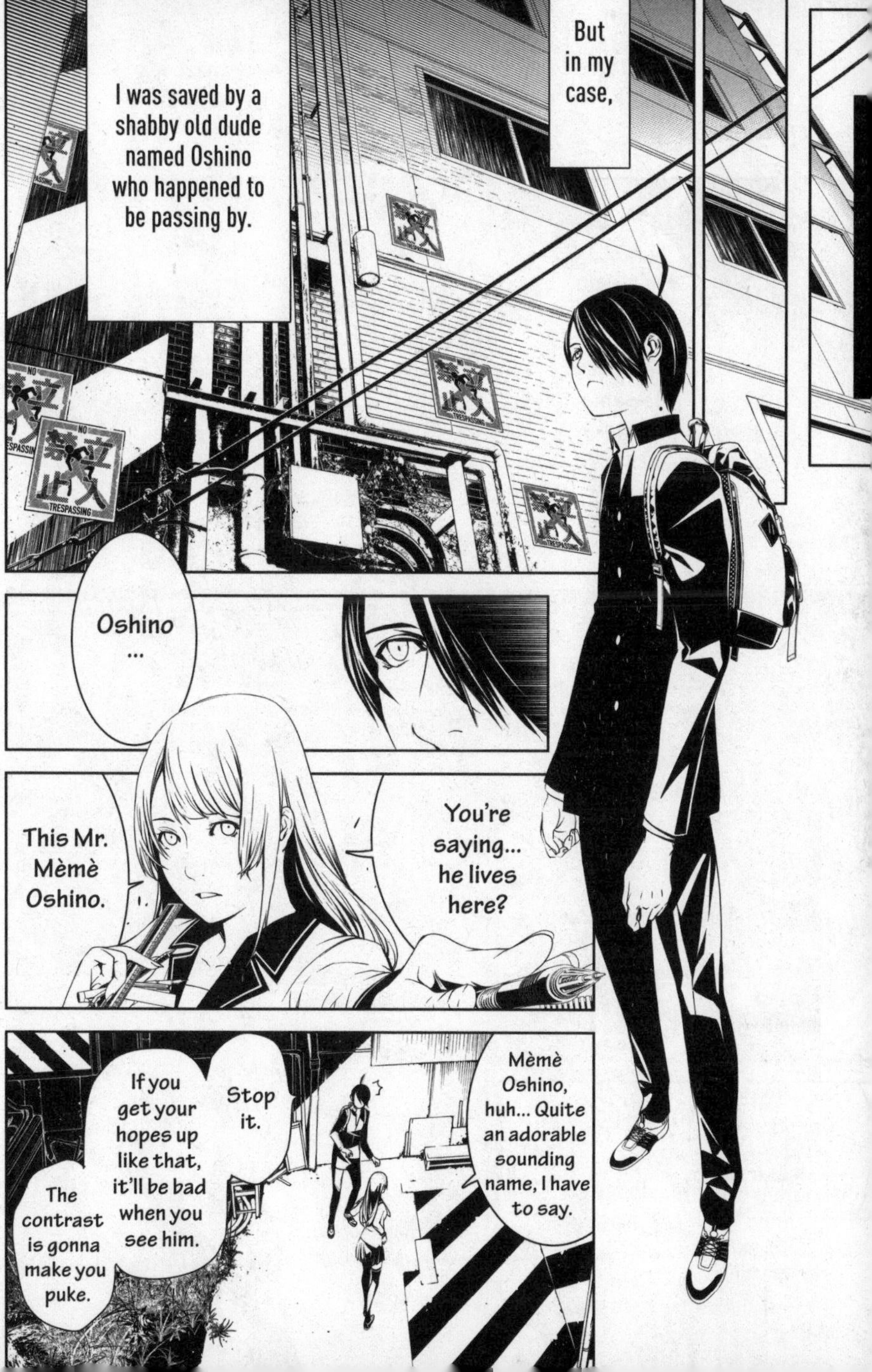
But in my case,
I was saved by a shabby old dude named Oshino who happened to be passing by.
Oshino ...
You're saying... he lives here?
This Mr. Mèmè Oshino.
Mèmè Oshino, huh... Quite an adorable sounding name, I have to say.
Stop it.
If you get your hopes up like that, it'll be bad when you see him.
The contrast is gonna make you puke.

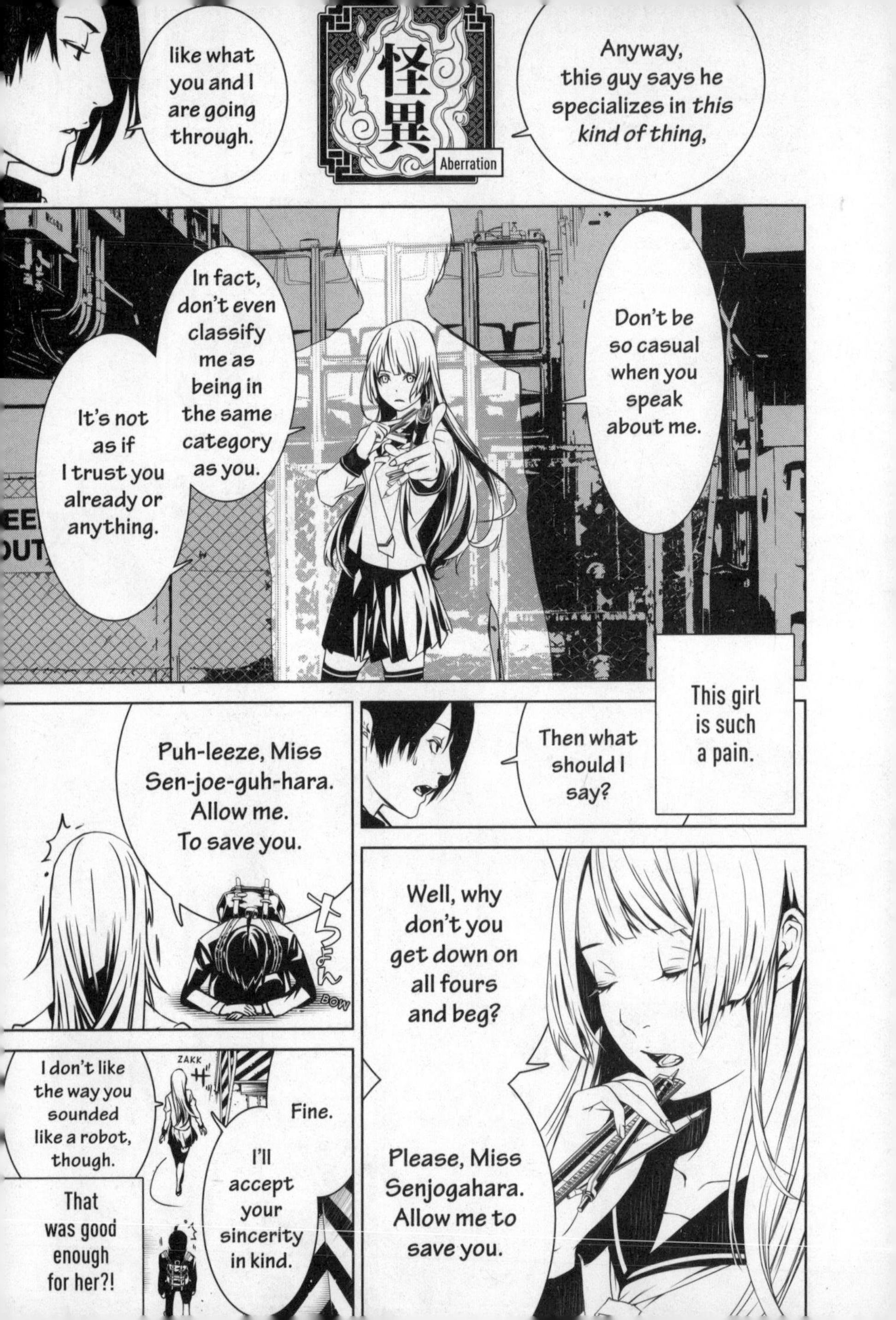

Anyway, this guy says he specializes in *this kind of thing,*
怪異
Aberration
like what you and I are going through.
Don't be so casual when you speak about me.
In fact, don't even classify me as being in the same category as you.
It's not as if I trust you already or anything.
This girl is such a pain.
Then what should I say?
Puh-leeze, Miss Sen-joe-guh-hara. Allow me. To save you.
ちょん
BOW
Well, why don't you get down on all fours and beg?
Please, Miss Senjogahara. Allow me to save you.
ZAKK
Fine.
I'll accept your sincerity in kind.
I don't like the way you sounded like a robot, though.
That was good enough for her?!

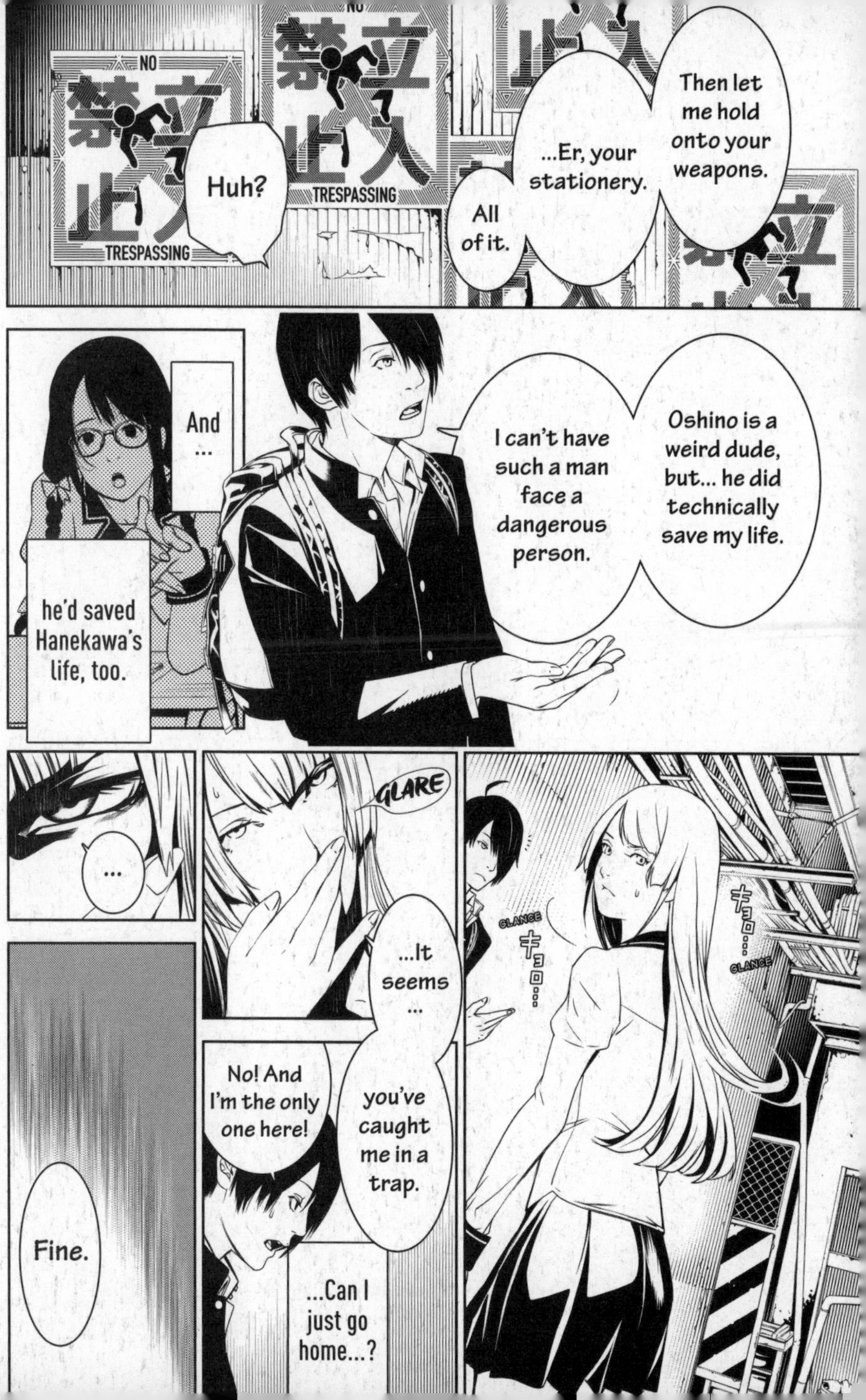

NO
立入禁止
TRESPASSING
Then let me hold onto your weapons.
...Er, your stationery.
All of it.
Huh?
Oshino is a weird dude, but... he did technically save my life.
I can't have such a man face a dangerous person.
And ...
he'd saved Hanekawa's life, too.
キョロ...
GLANCE
キョロ...
GLANCE
GLARE
...
...It seems ...
you've caught me in a trap.
No! And I'm the only one here!
...Can I just go home...?
Fine.

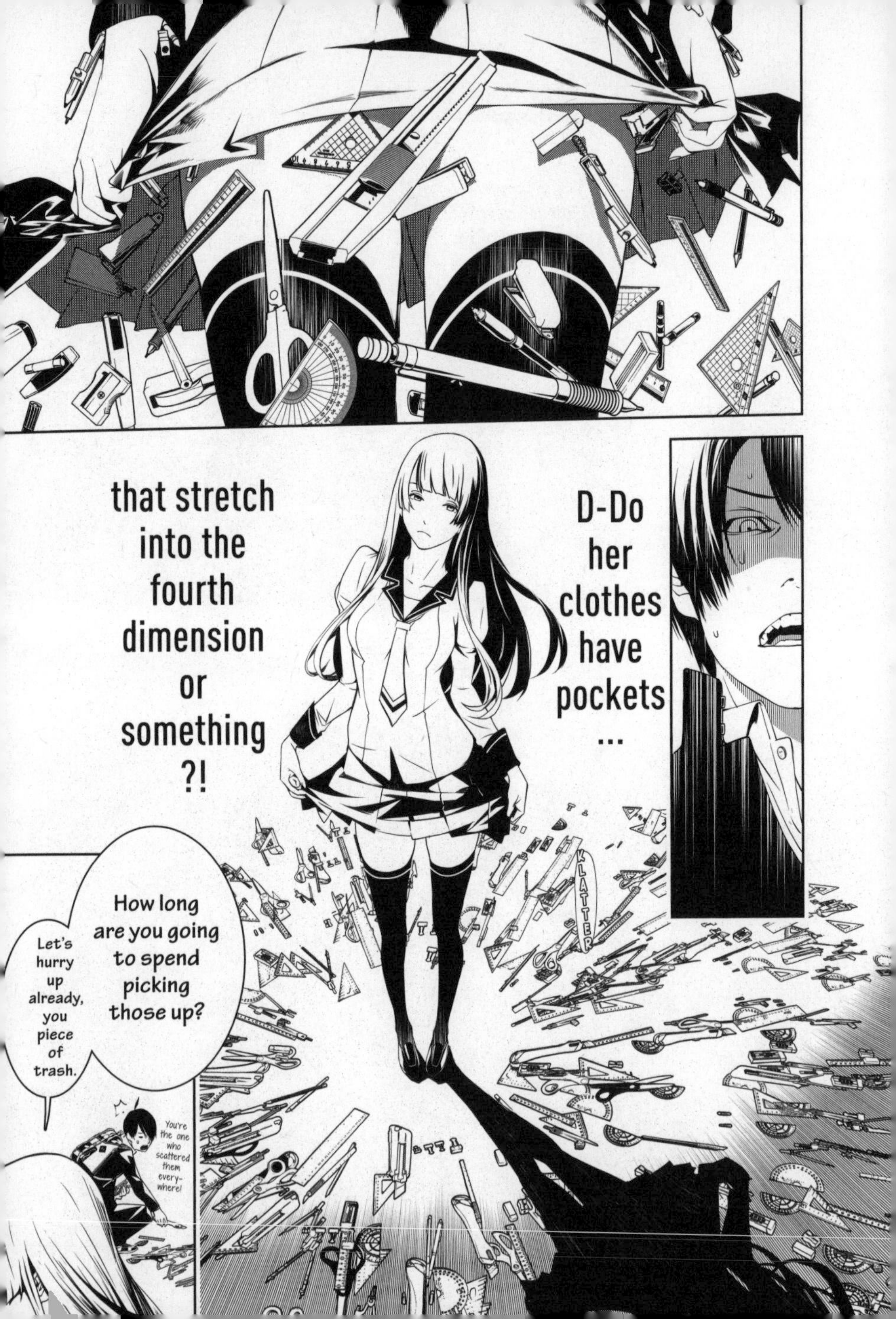
D-Do her clothes have pockets...
that stretch into the fourth dimension or something?!
KLATTER
How long are you going to spend picking those up?
Let's hurry up already, you piece of trash.
You're the one who scattered them everywhere!

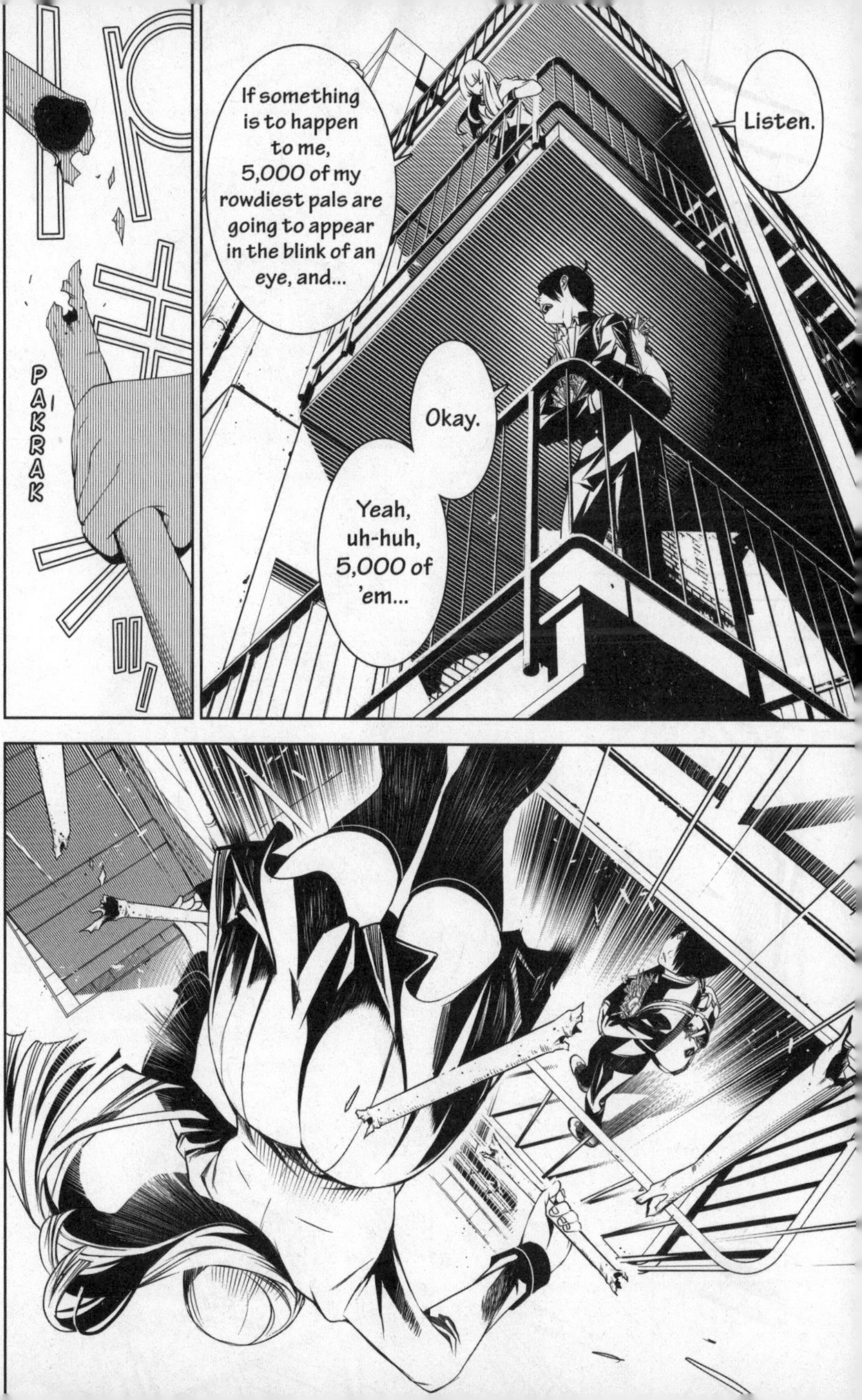
Listen.
If something is to happen to me, 5,000 of my rowdiest pals are going to appear in the blink of an eye, and...
Okay.
Yeah, uh-huh, 5,000 of 'em...
PAKRAK

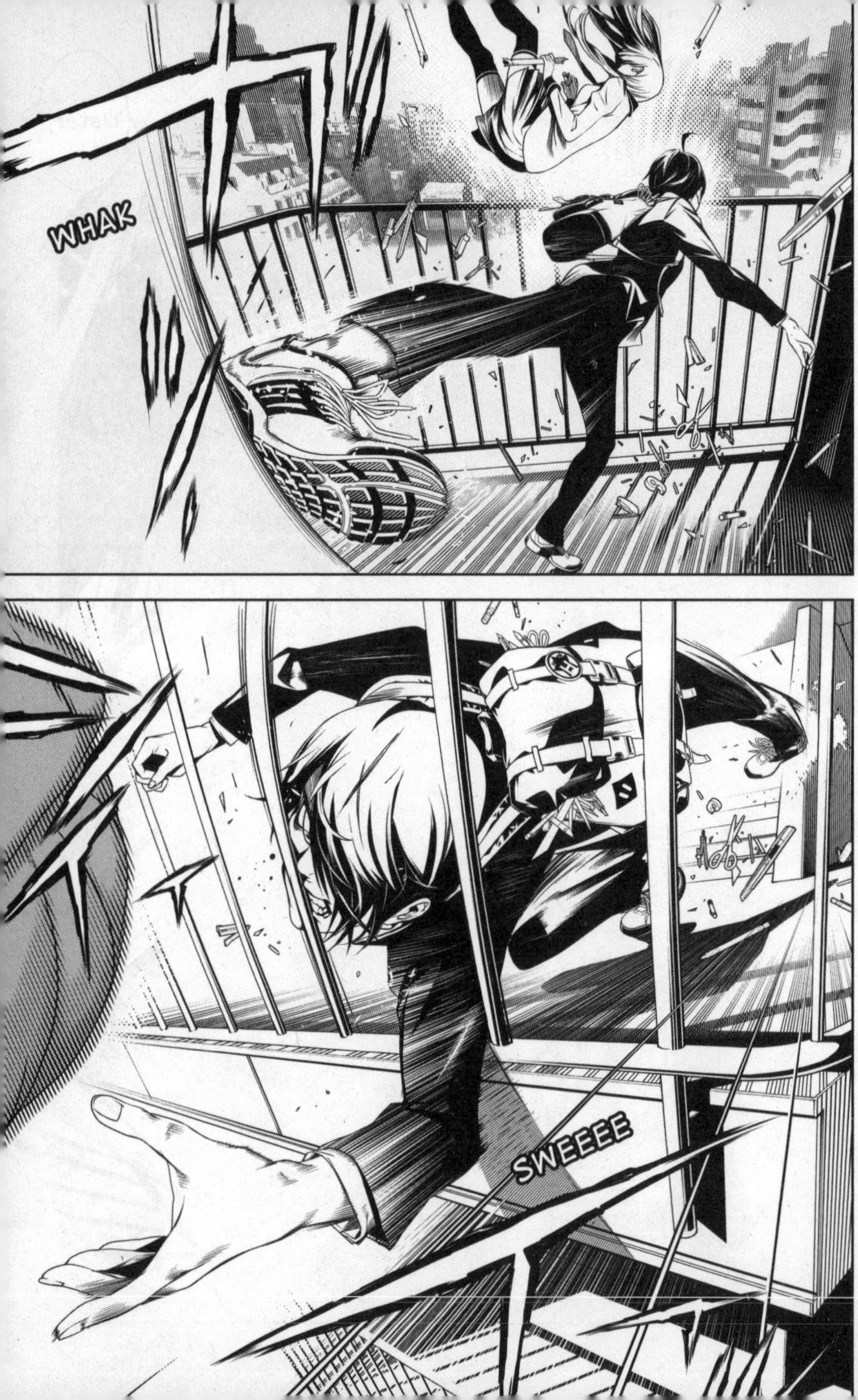
WHAK
SWEEEE

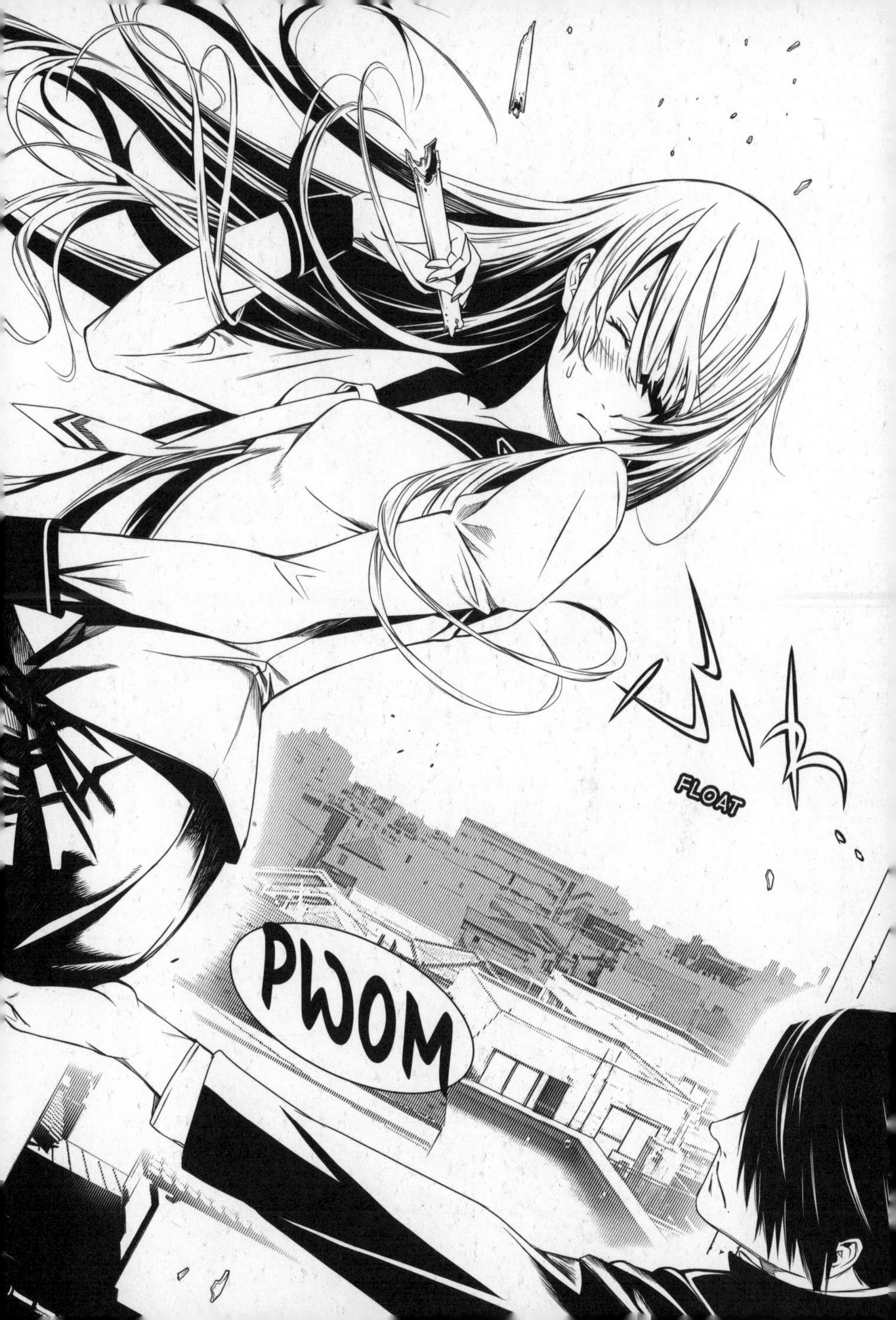
FLOAT
PWOM

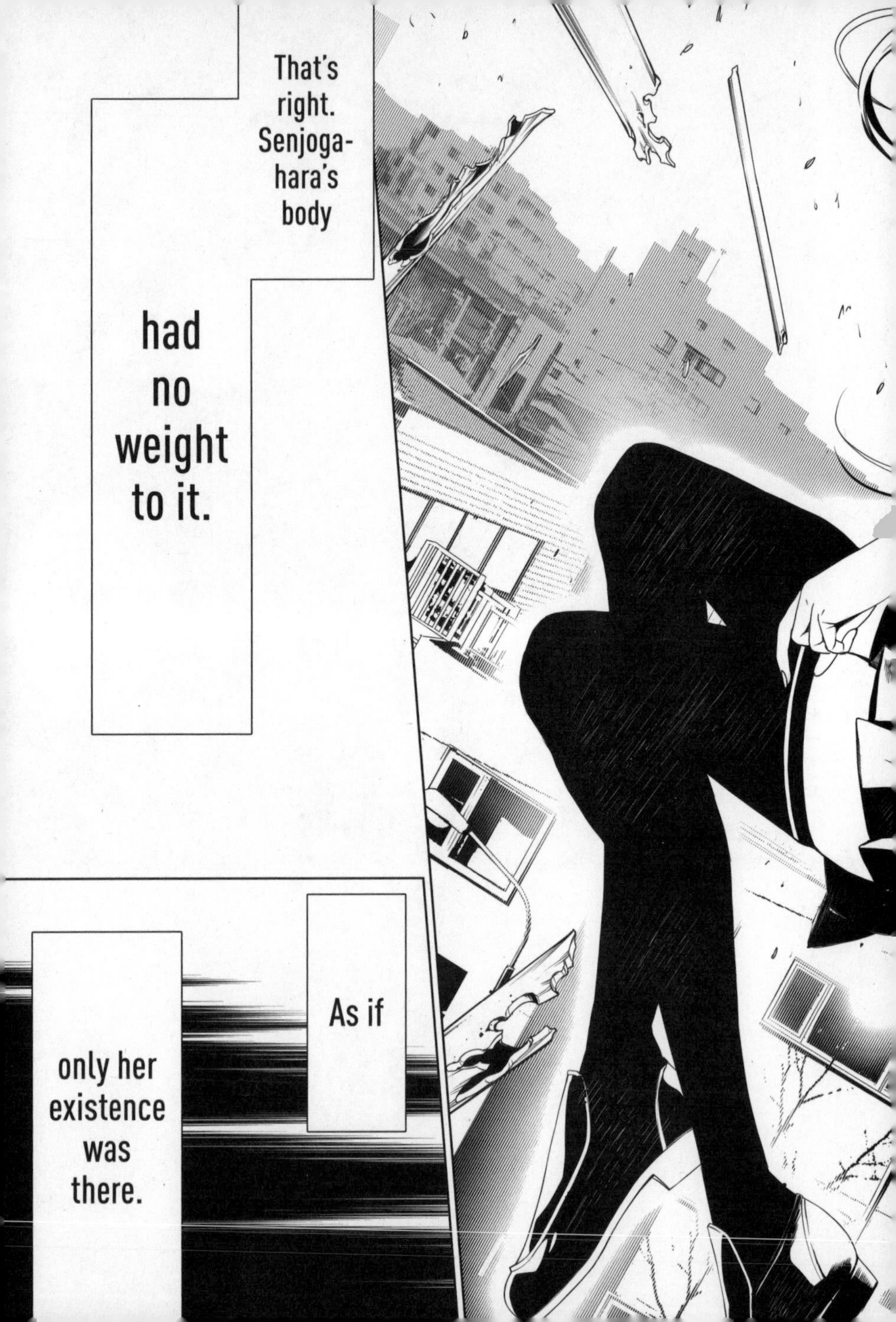
That's right. Senjoga-hara's body
had no weight to it.
As if
only her existence was there.

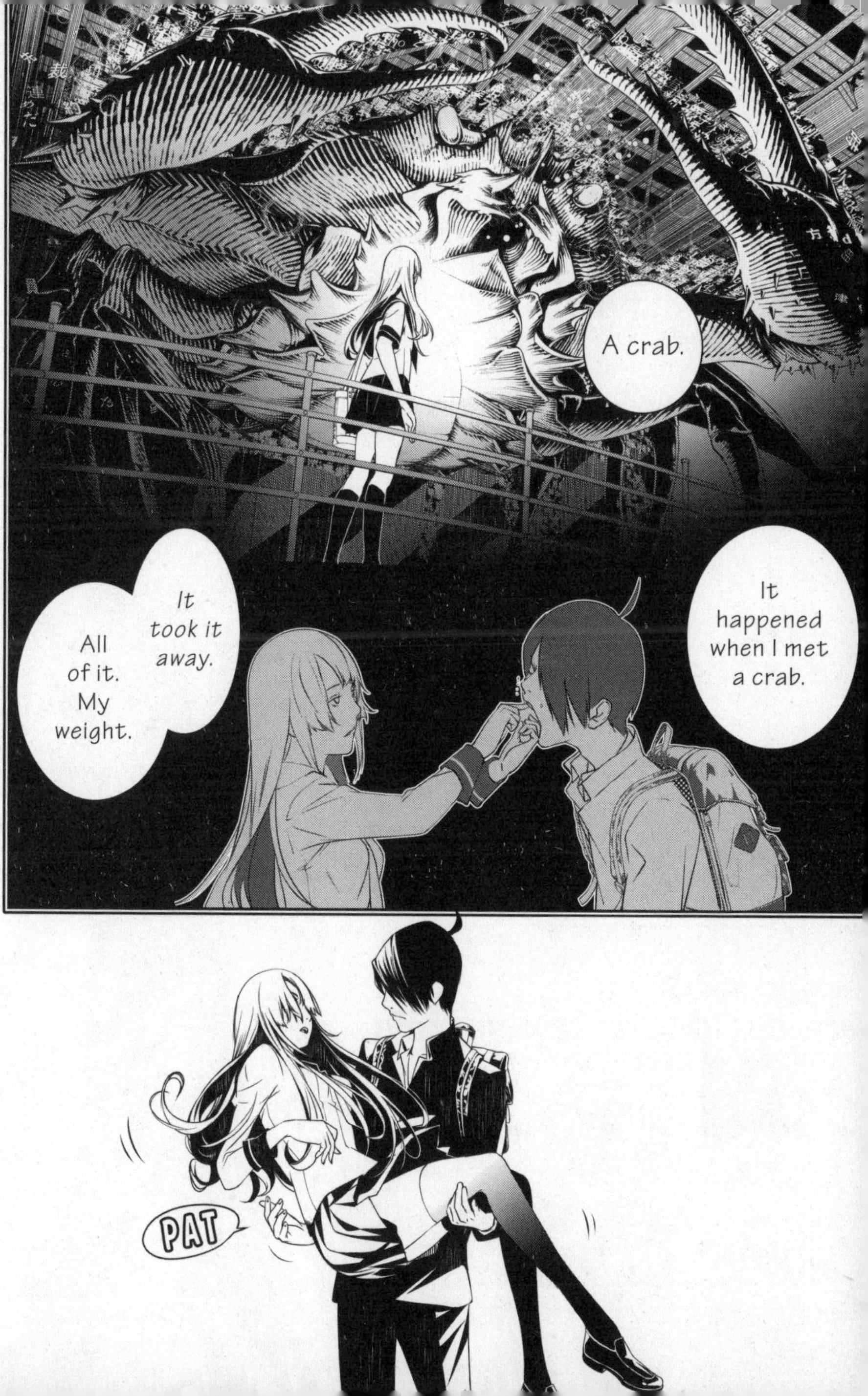
A crab.
It happened when I met a crab.
It took it away.
All of it. My weight.
PAT

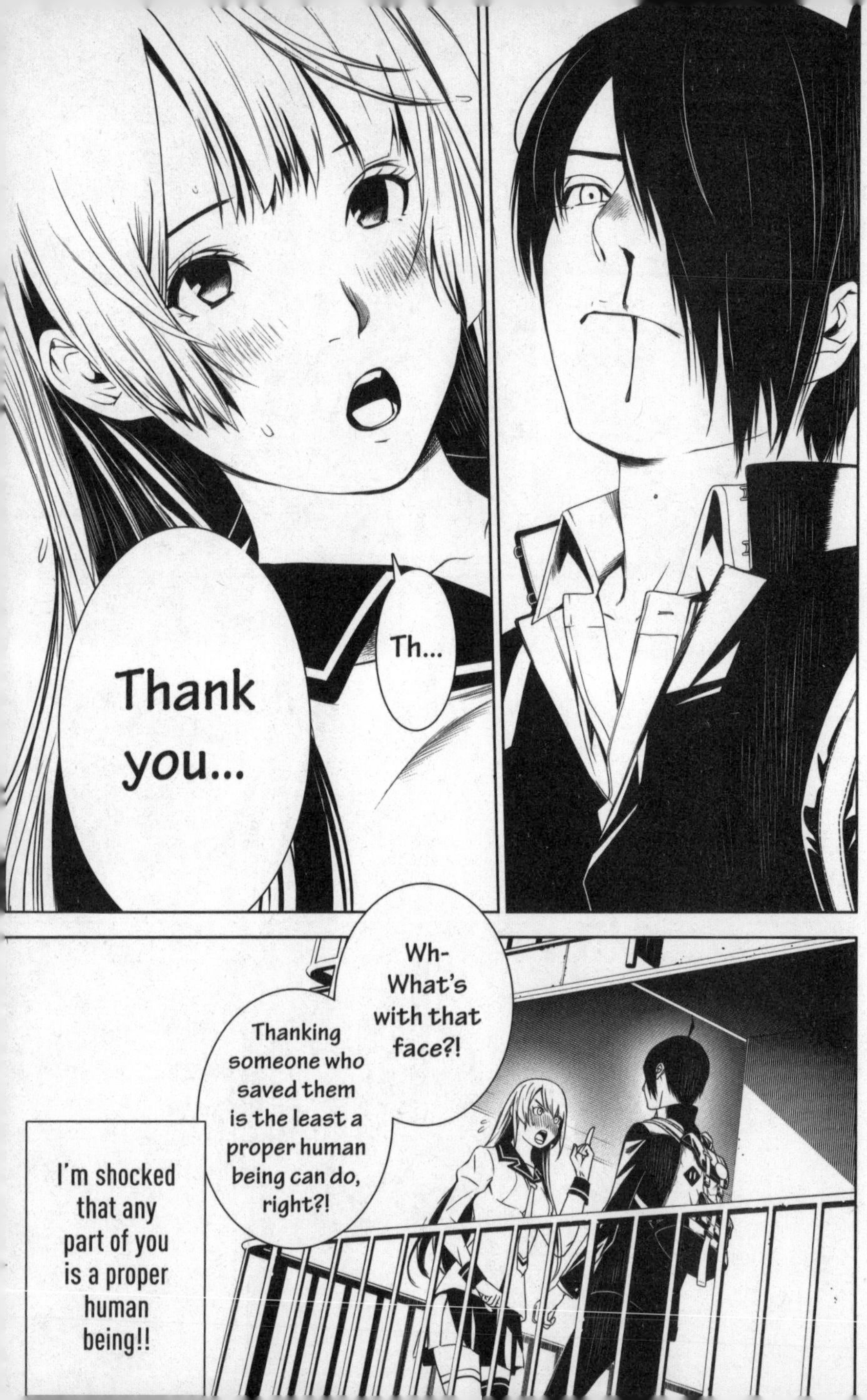
Th...
Thank you...
Wh- What's with that face?!
Thanking someone who saved them is the least a proper human being can do, right?!
I'm shocked that any part of you is a proper human being!!

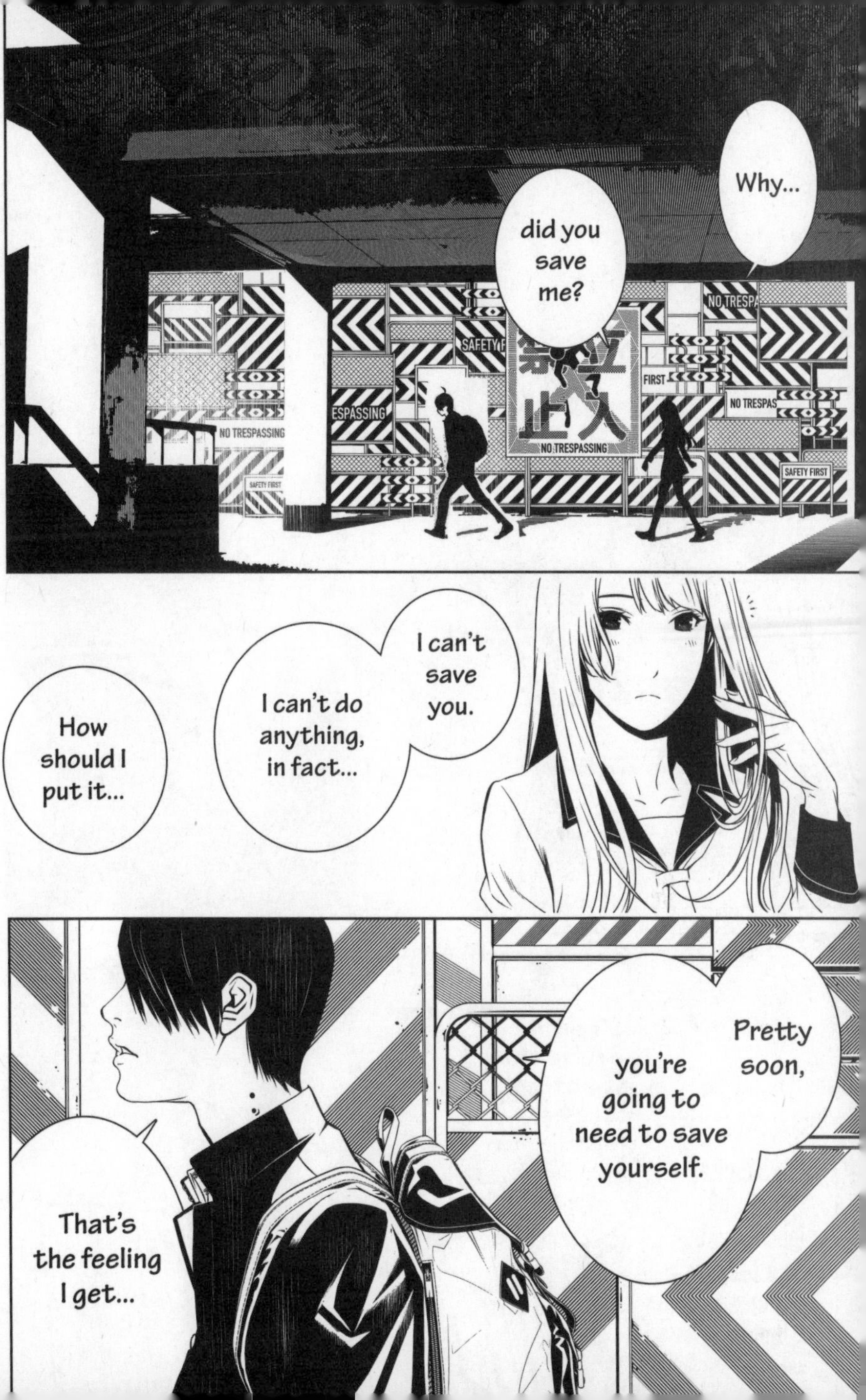
Why...
did you save me?
NO TRESPASSING
SAFETY FIRST
I can't save you.
I can't do anything, in fact...
How should I put it...
Pretty soon, you're going to need to save yourself.
That's the feeling I get...

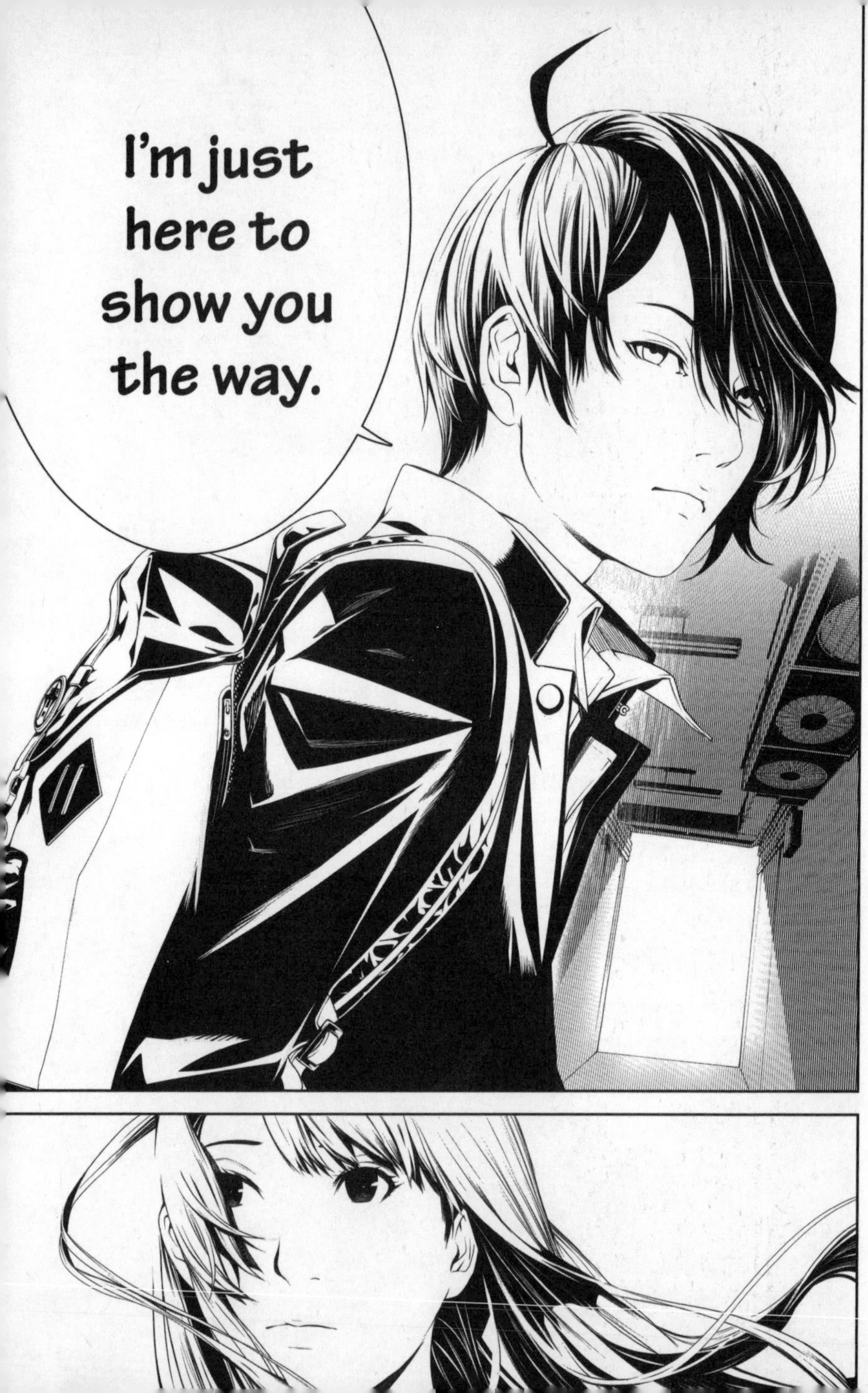
I'm just here to show you the way.

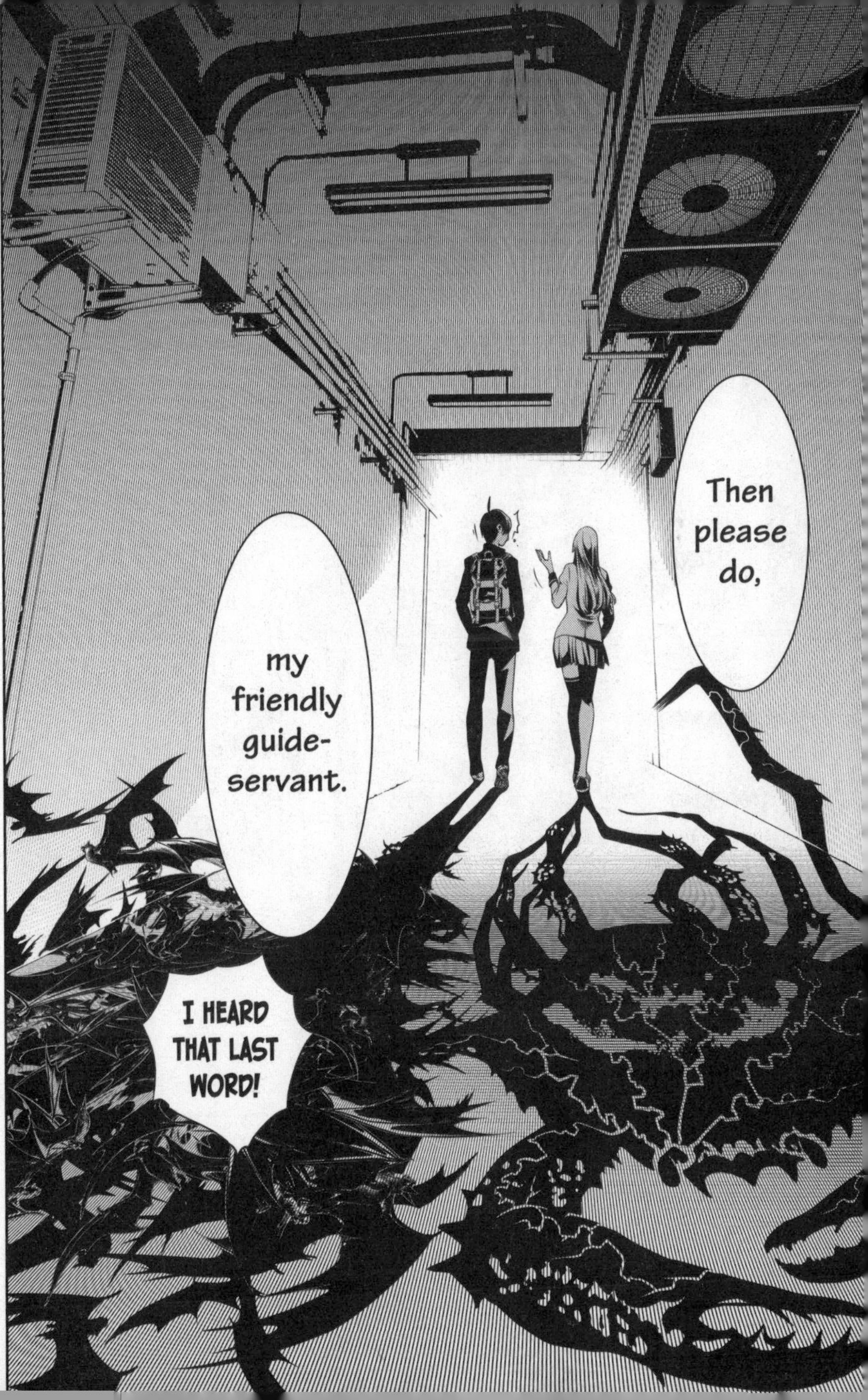
Then please do,
my friendly guide-servant.
I HEARD THAT LAST WORD!

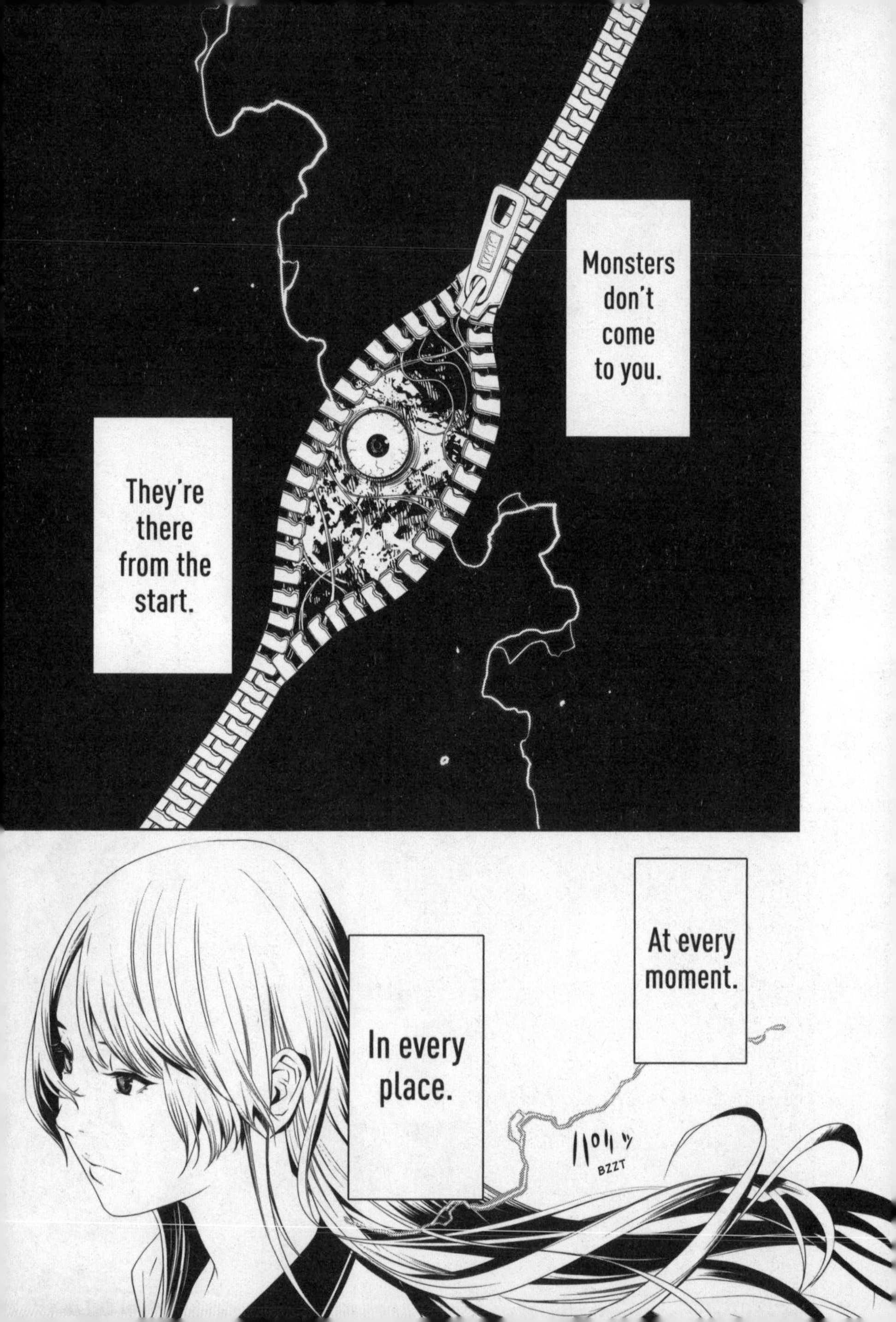
Monsters don't come to you.
They're there from the start.
At every moment.
In every place.
BZZT

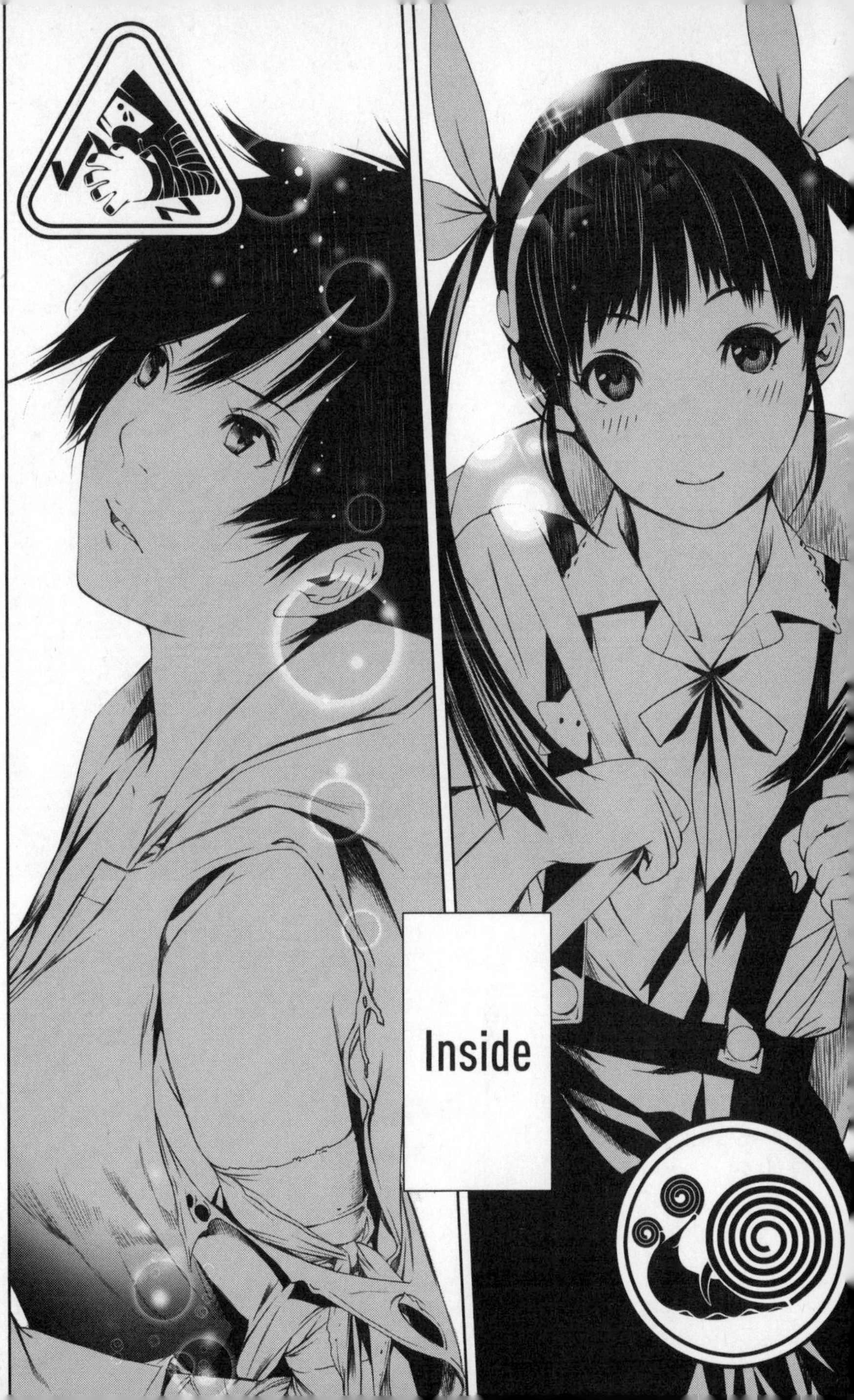
Inside

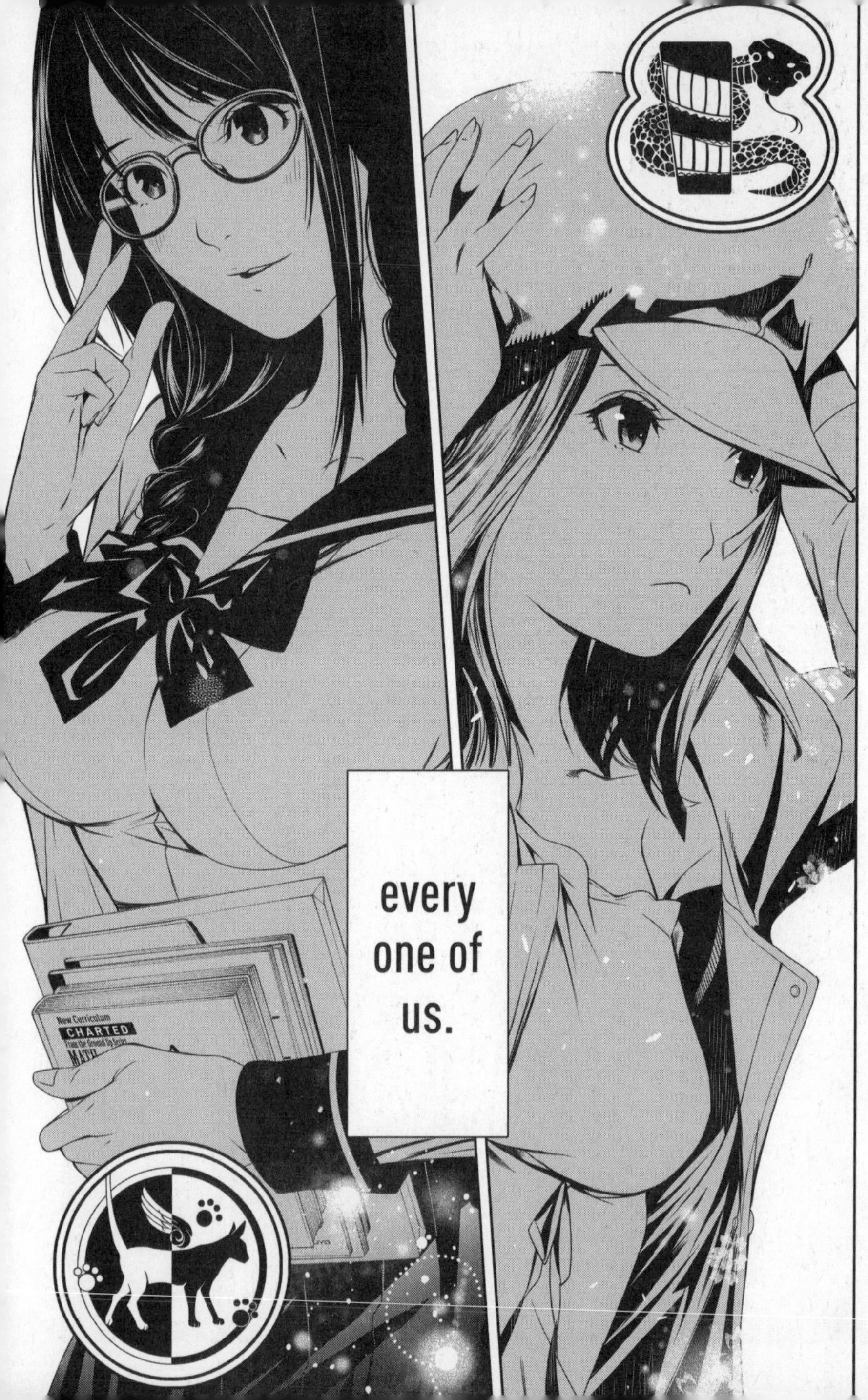
every one of us.
New Curriculum
CHARTED

BAKEMONOGATARI

0 1: Hitagi Crab

化 *bake*

物 *mono*

I
HITAGIcrab

語 *gatari*

bake 化

物 *mono*

HITAGIcrab
1

語 *gatari*

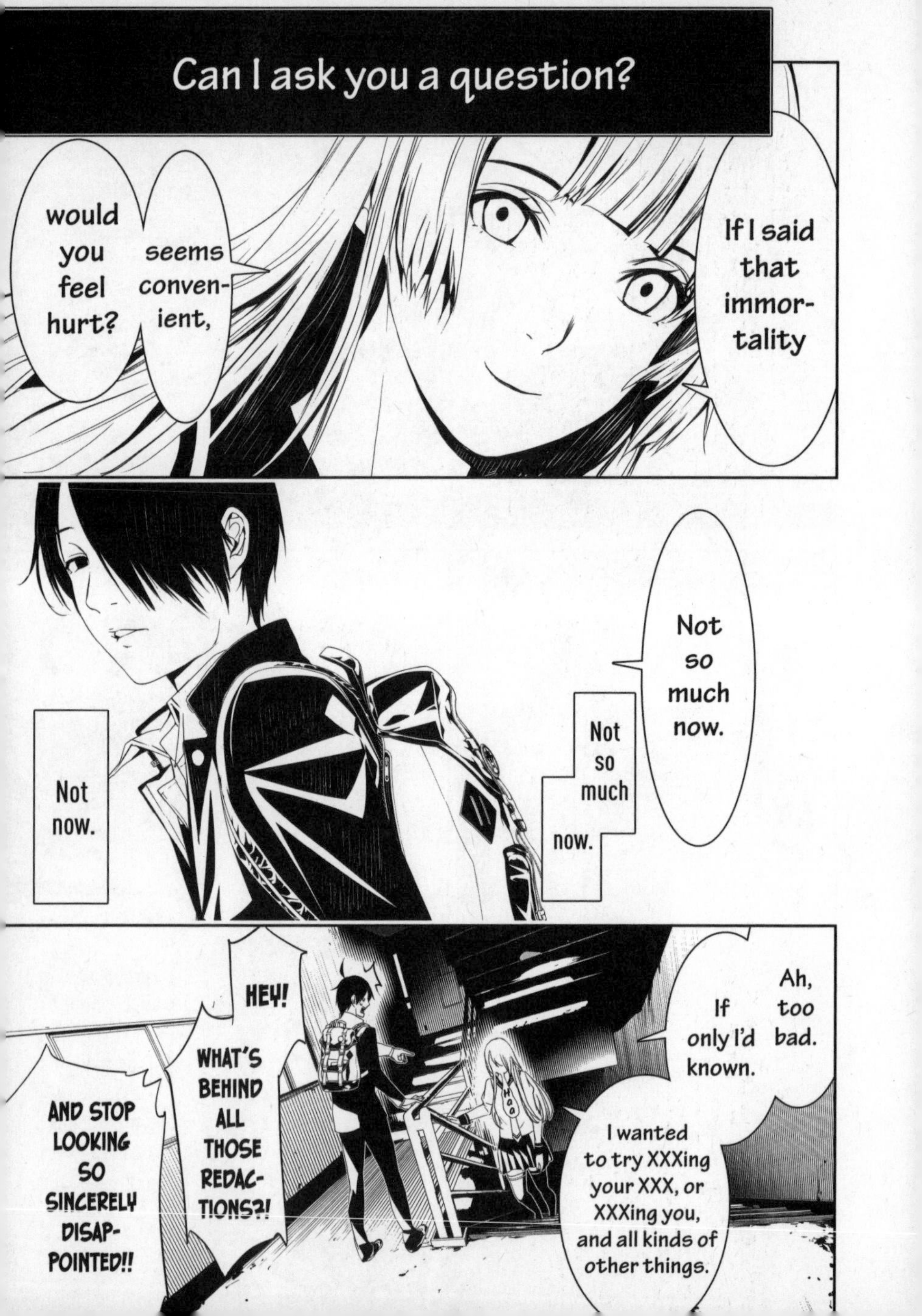
Can I ask you a question?
If I said that immortality
seems convenient,
would you feel hurt?
Not so much now.
Not so much now.
Not now.
Ah, too bad.
If only I'd known.
I wanted to try XXXing your XXX, or XXXing you, and all kinds of other things.
HEY!
WHAT'S BEHIND ALL THOSE REDACTIONS?!
AND STOP LOOKING SO SINCERELY DISAPPOINTED!!

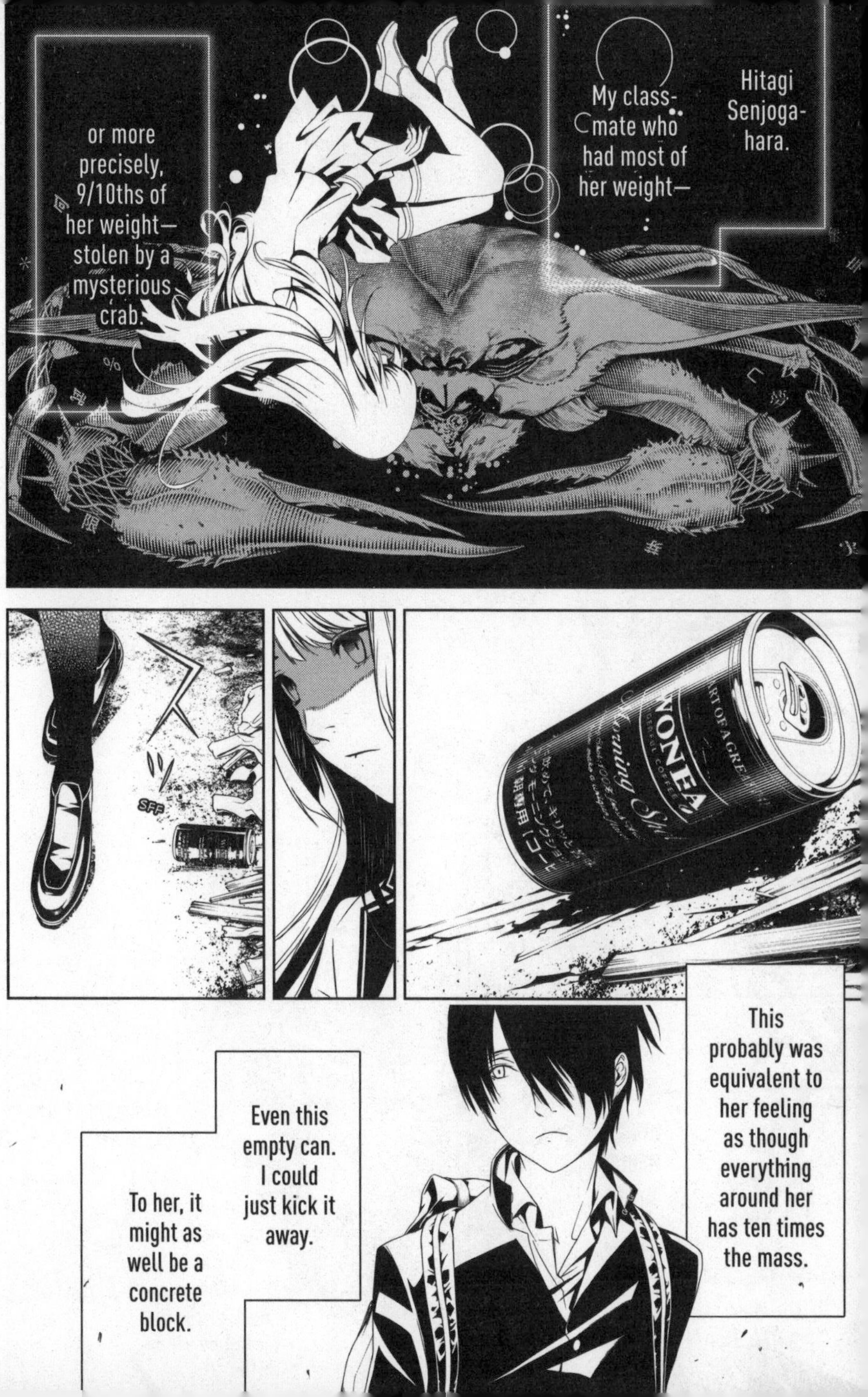
Hitagi Senjogahara.
My classmate who had most of her weight—
or more precisely, 9/10ths of her weight—stolen by a mysterious crab.
SFF
This probably was equivalent to her feeling as though everything around her has ten times the mass.
Even this empty can. I could just kick it away.
To her, it might as well be a concrete block.

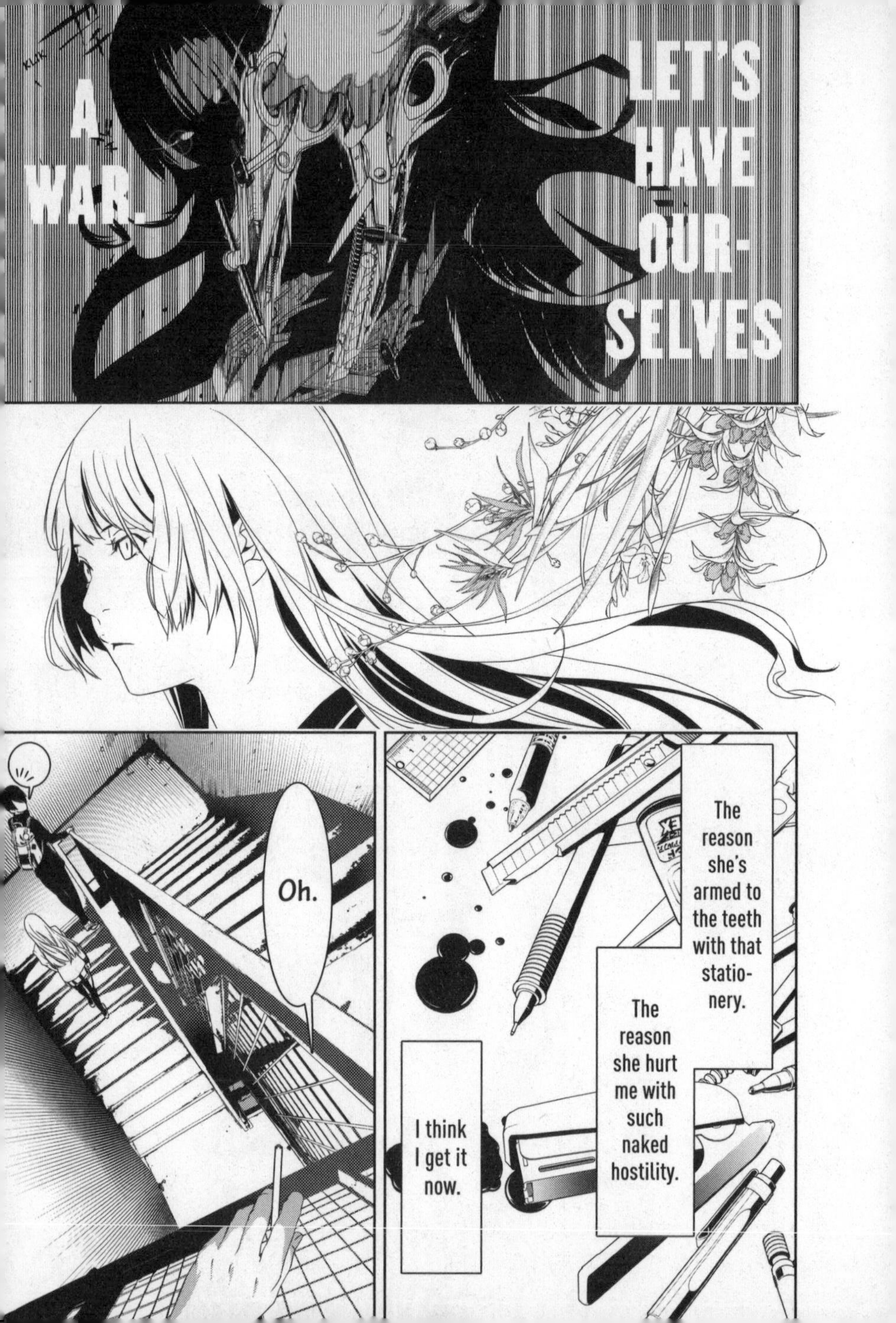
LET'S HAVE OUR-SELVES
A WAR.
The reason she's armed to the teeth with that statio-nery.
The reason she hurt me with such naked hostility.
I think I get it now.
Oh.

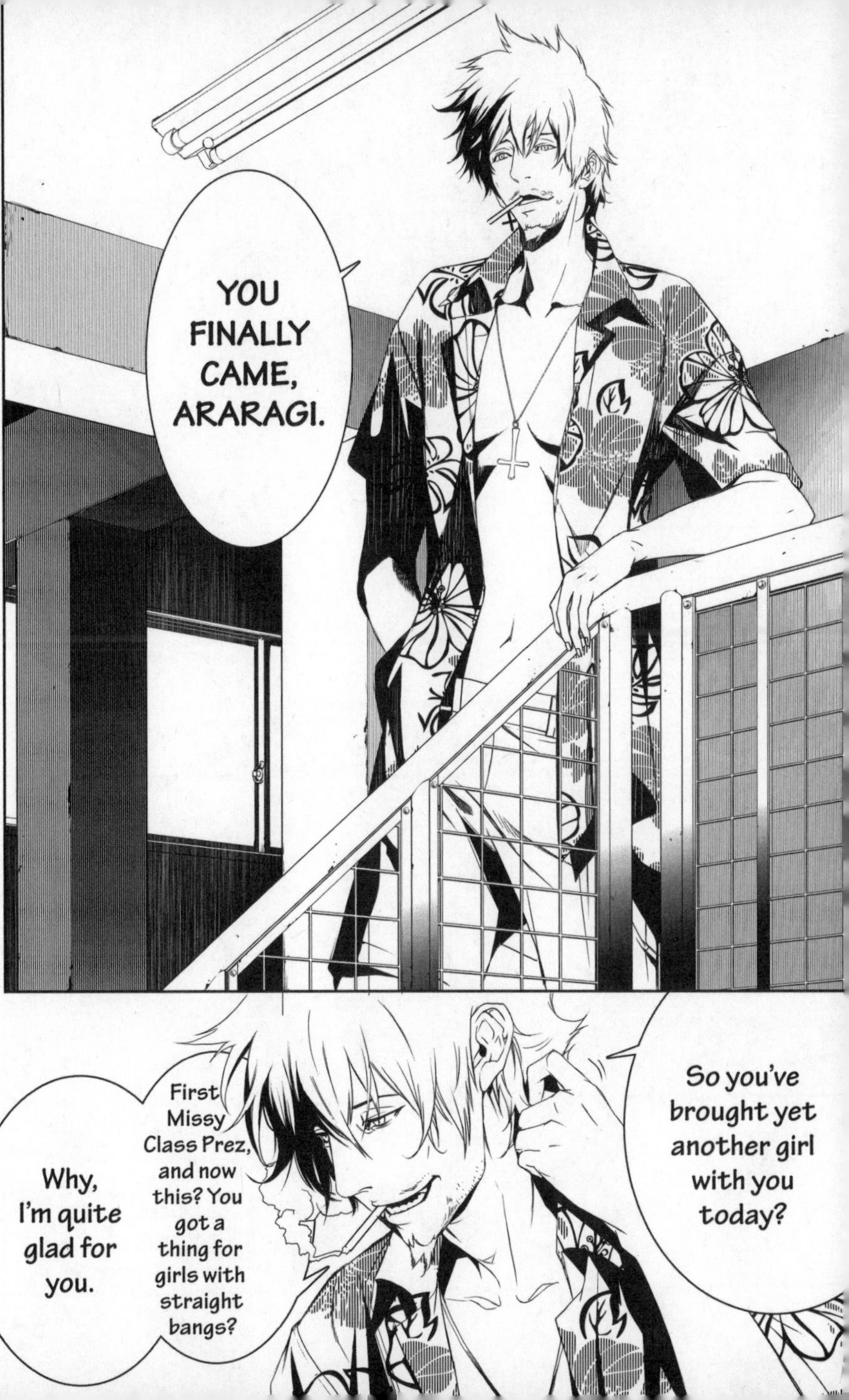
YOU FINALLY CAME, ARARAGI.
So you've brought yet another girl with you today?
First Missy Class Prez, and now this? You got a thing for girls with straight bangs?
Why, I'm quite glad for you.

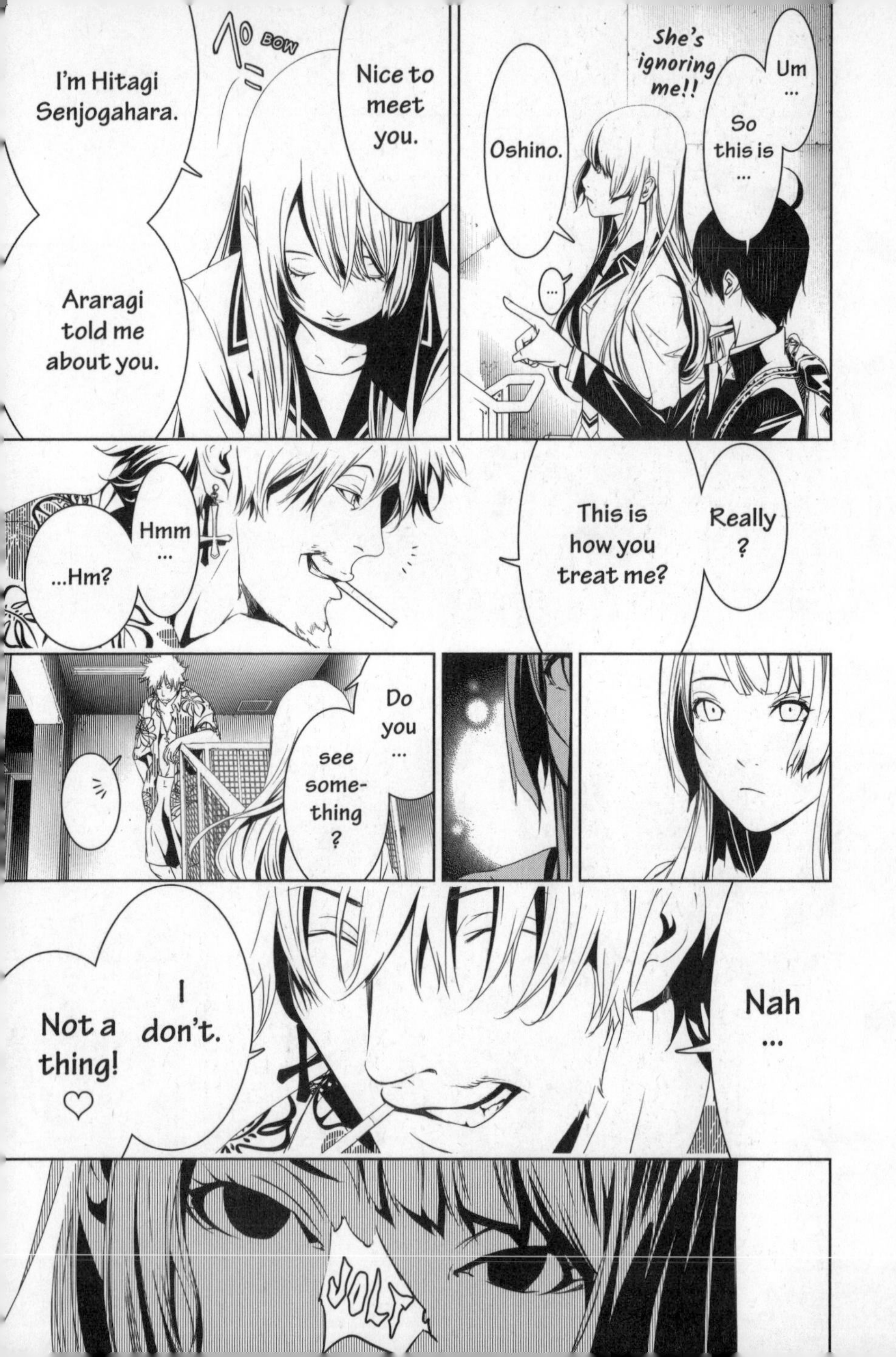
Um ...
She's ignoring me!!
So this is ...
Oshino.
...
Nice to meet you.
BOW
I'm Hitagi Senjogahara.
Araragi told me about you.
Really?
This is how you treat me?
Hmm ...
...Hm?
Do you ...
see something?
Nah ...
I don't.
Not a thing! ♡
JOLT

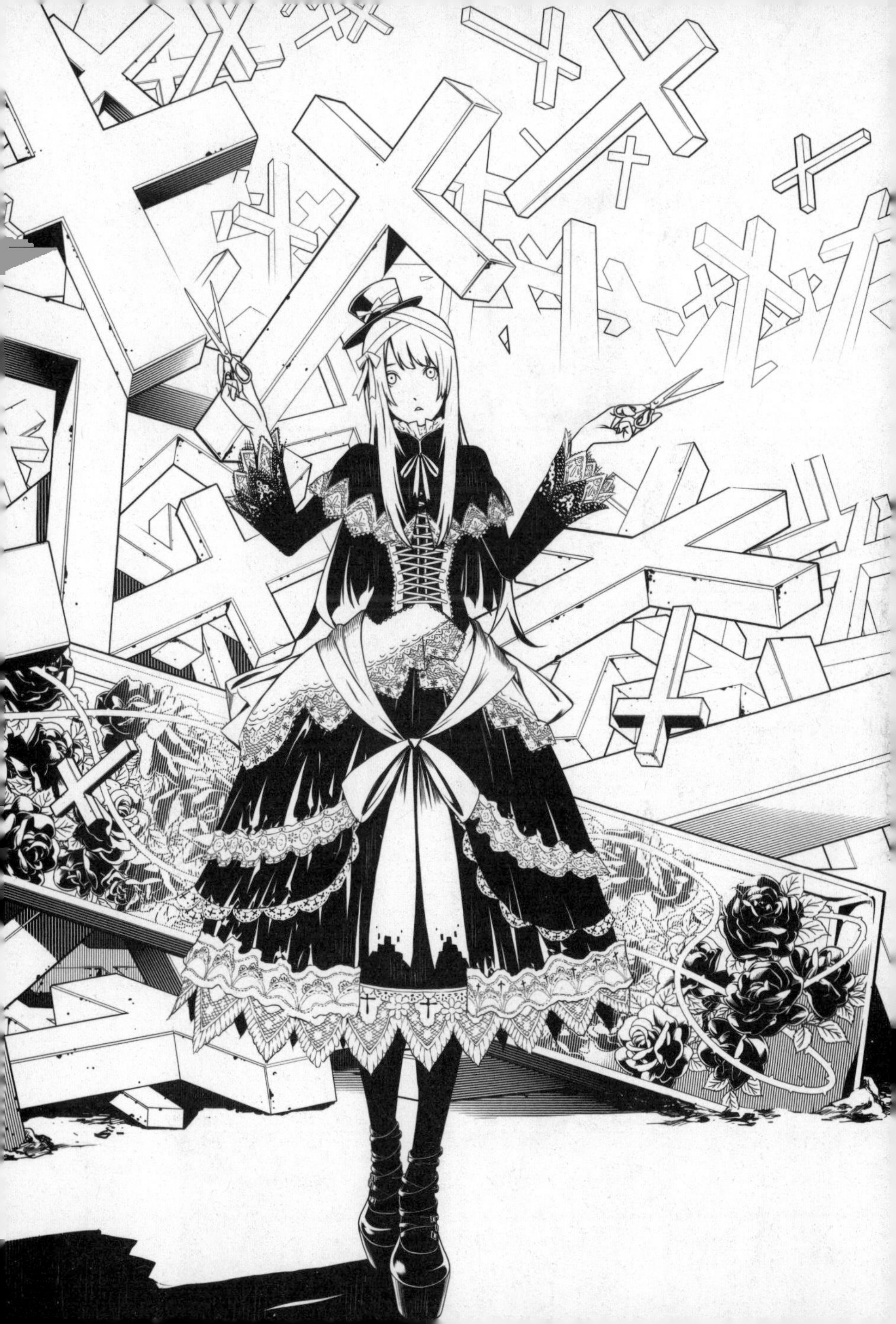

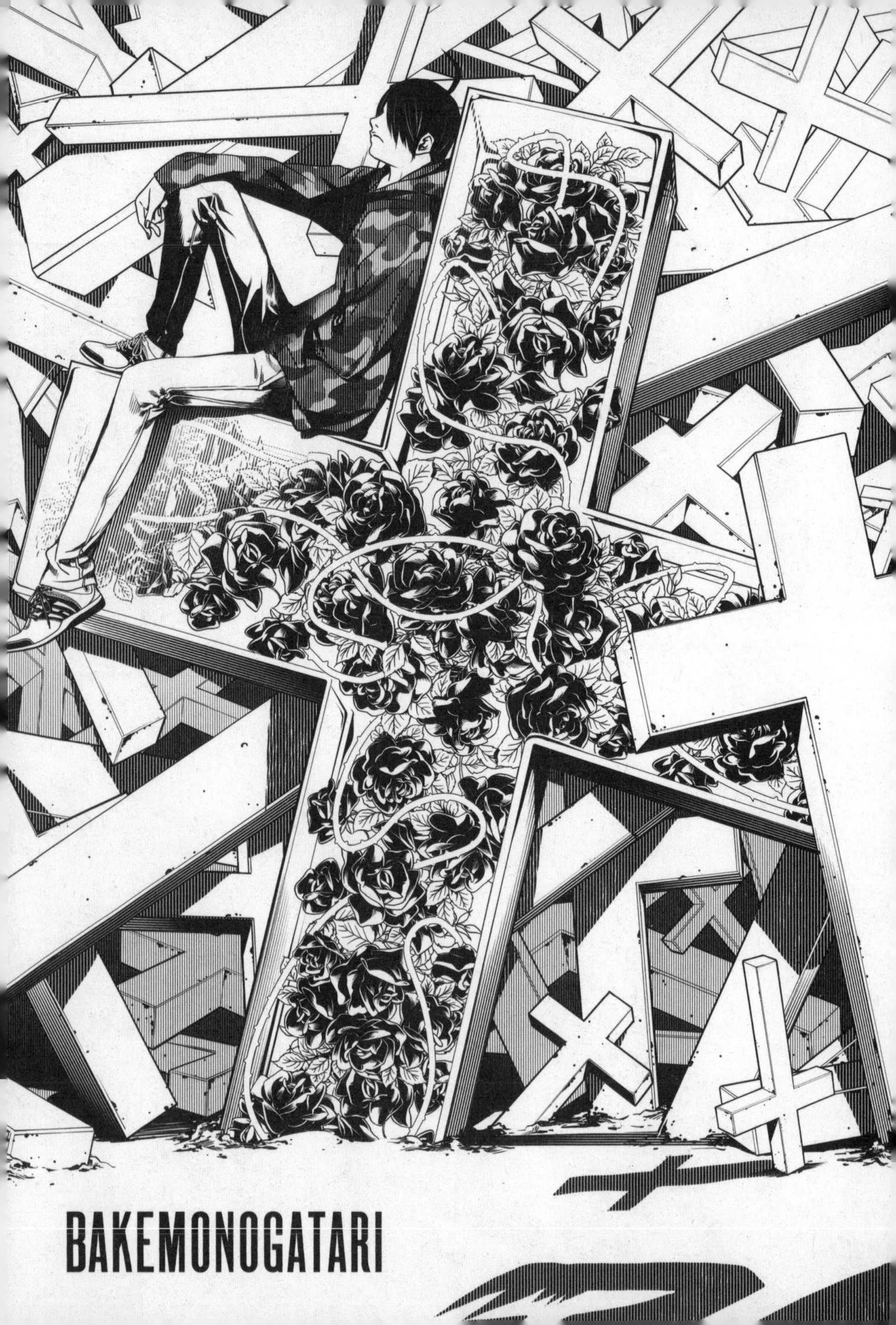
BAKEMONOGATARI

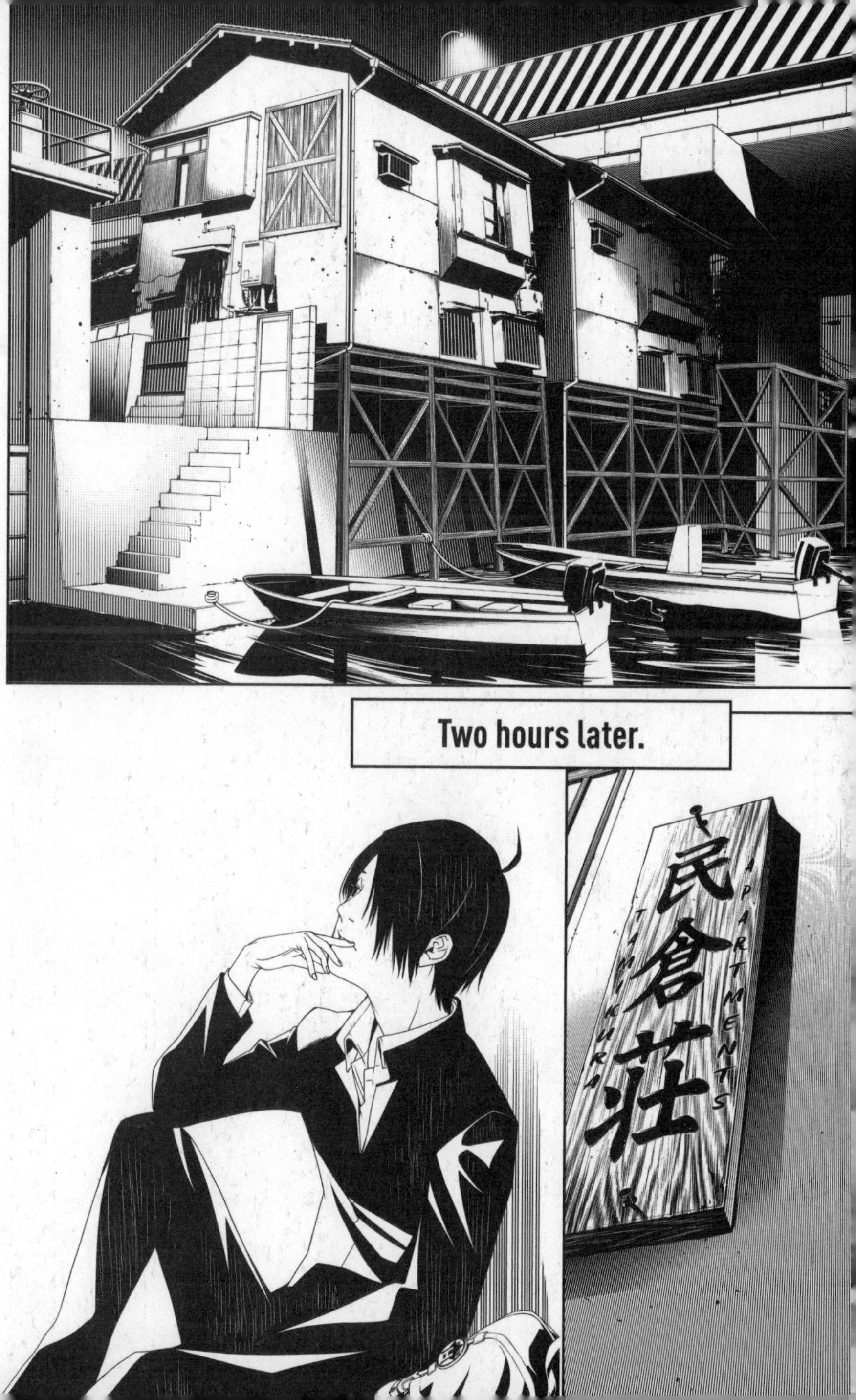
Two hours later.
民倉荘
TAMIKURA APARTMENTS

This room is empty...

ZHAAAAA

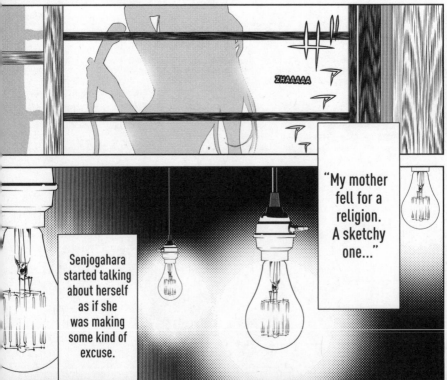

"My mother fell for a religion. A sketchy one..."

Senjogahara started talking about herself as if she was making some kind of excuse.

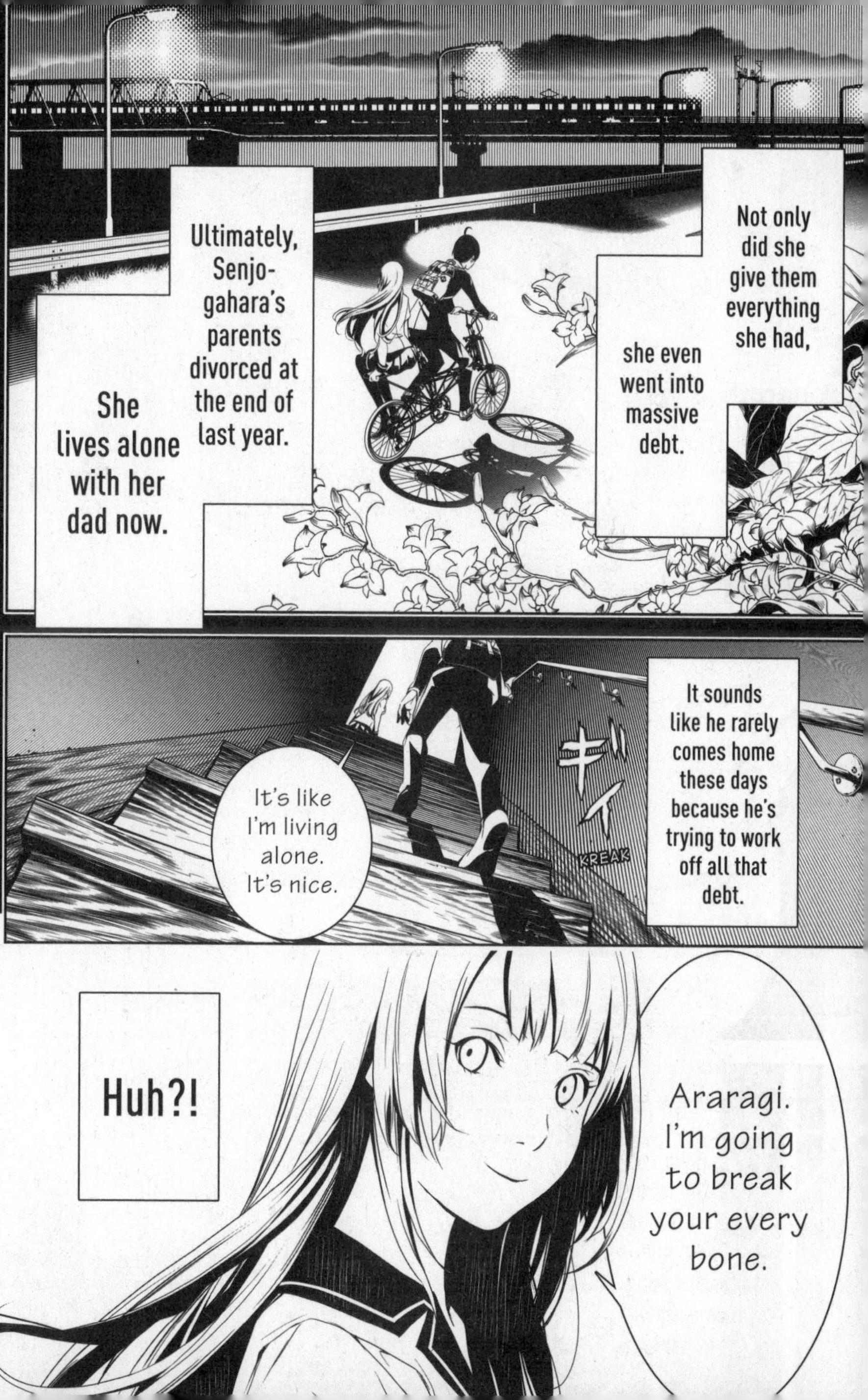
Not only did she give them everything she had,
she even went into massive debt.
Ultimately, Senjo-gahara's parents divorced at the end of last year.
She lives alone with her dad now.
It sounds like he rarely comes home these days because he's trying to work off all that debt.
KREAK
It's like I'm living alone. It's nice.
Araragi. I'm going to break your every bone.
Huh?!

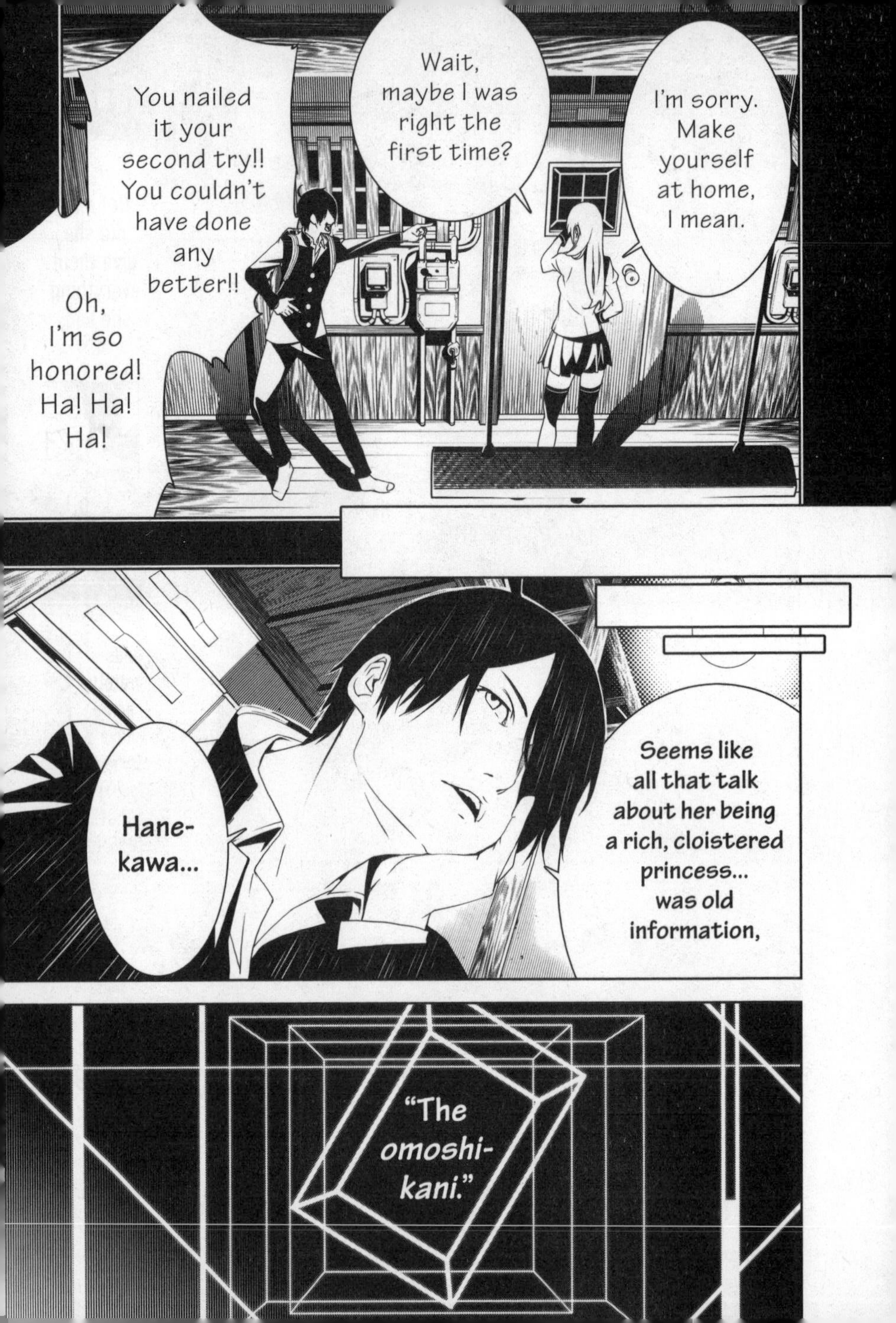
I'm sorry. Make yourself at home, I mean.
Wait, maybe I was right the first time?
You nailed it your second try!! You couldn't have done any better!!
Oh, I'm so honored! Ha! Ha! Ha!
Seems like all that talk about her being a rich, cloistered princess... was old information,
Hane-kawa...
"The omoshi-kani."

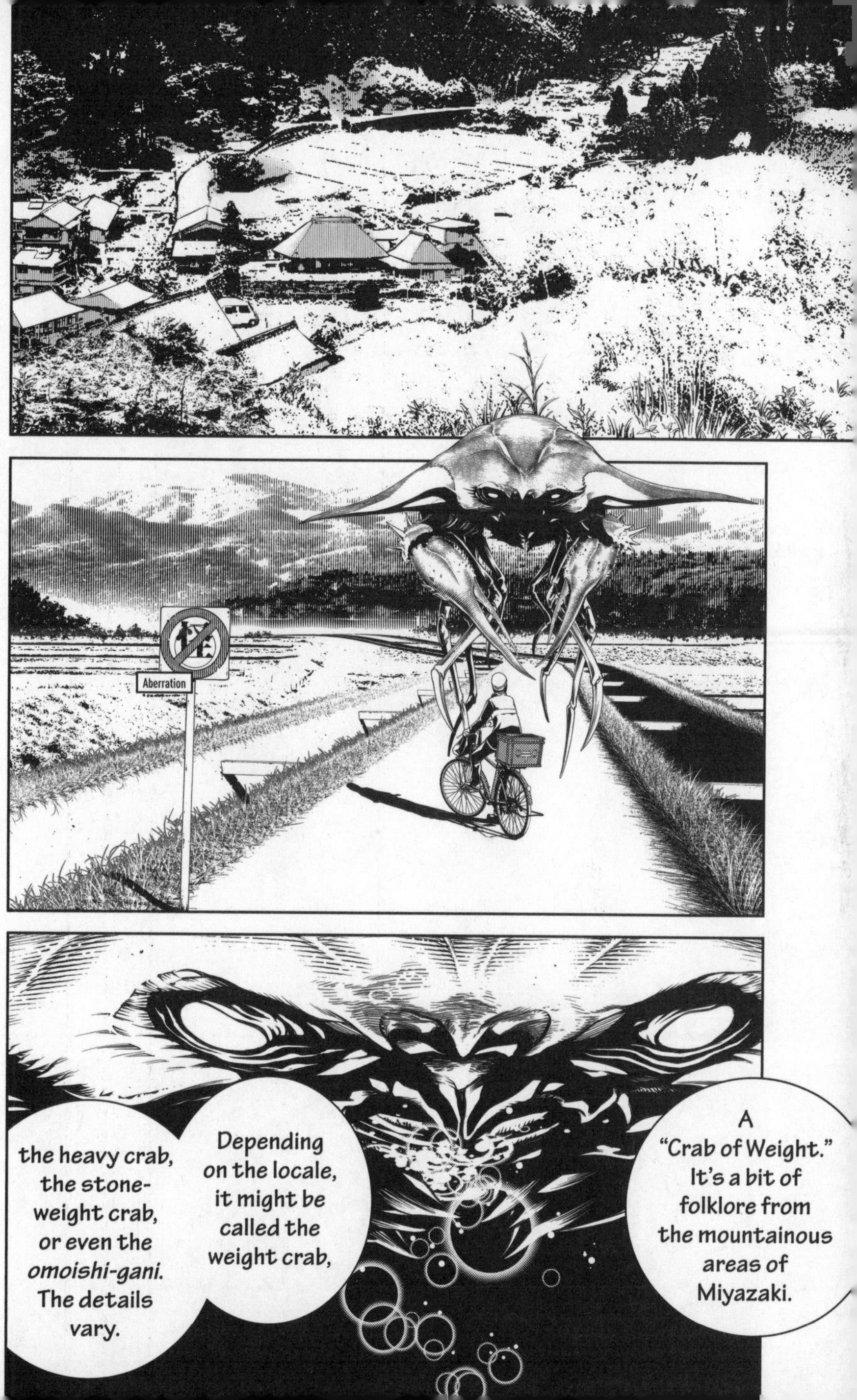
Aberration
A "Crab of Weight." It's a bit of folklore from the mountainous areas of Miyazaki.
Depending on the locale, it might be called the weight crab,
the heavy crab, the stone-weight crab, or even the *omoishi-gani*. The details vary.

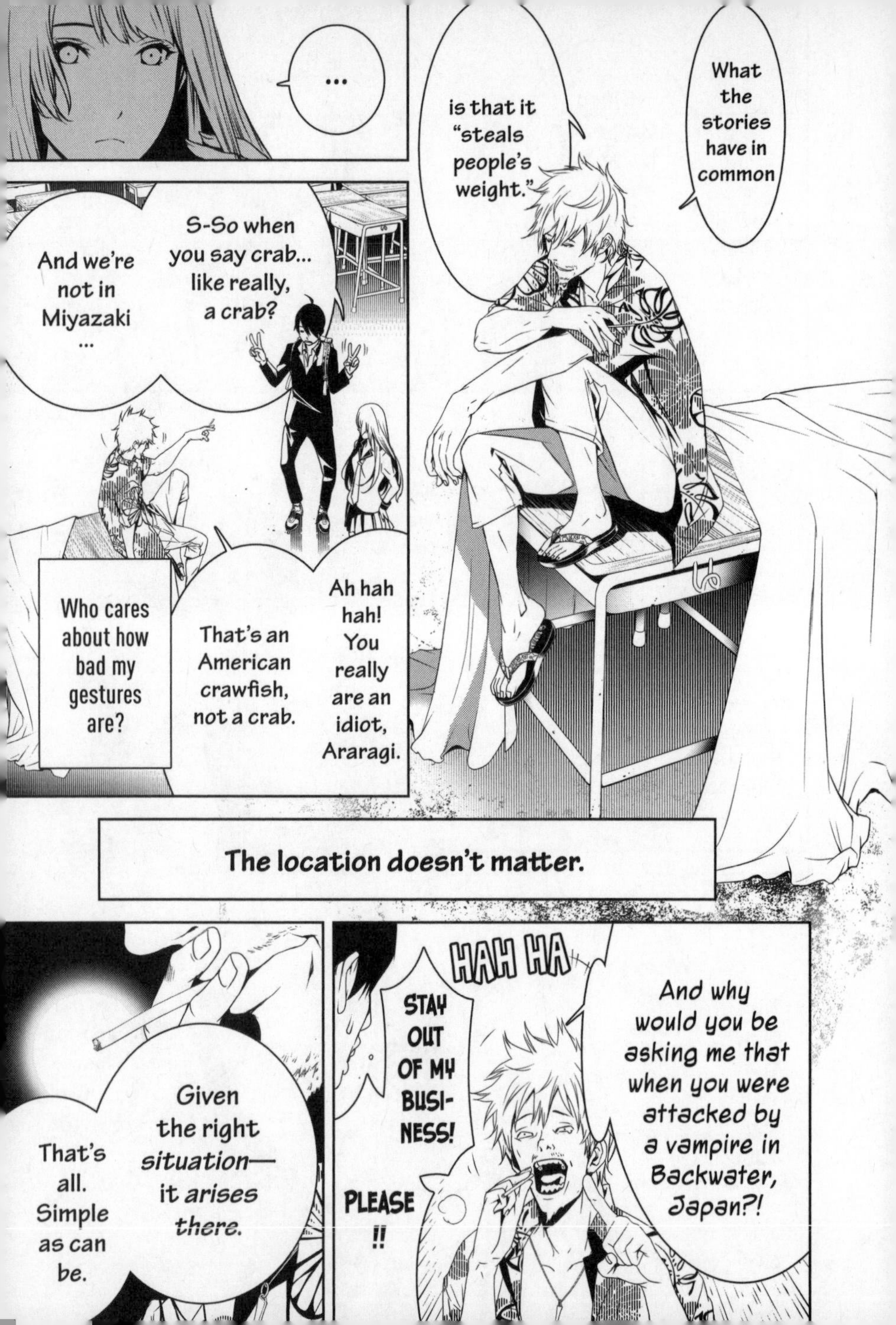
What the stories have in common
is that it "steals people's weight."
...
S-So when you say crab... like really, a crab?
And we're not in Miyazaki ...
Ah hah hah! You really are an idiot, Araragi.
That's an American crawfish, not a crab.
Who cares about how bad my gestures are?
The location doesn't matter.
And why would you be asking me that when you were attacked by a vampire in Backwater, Japan?!
HAH HA
STAY OUT OF MY BUSI-NESS!
PLEASE !!
Given the right situation— it arises there.
That's all. Simple as can be.

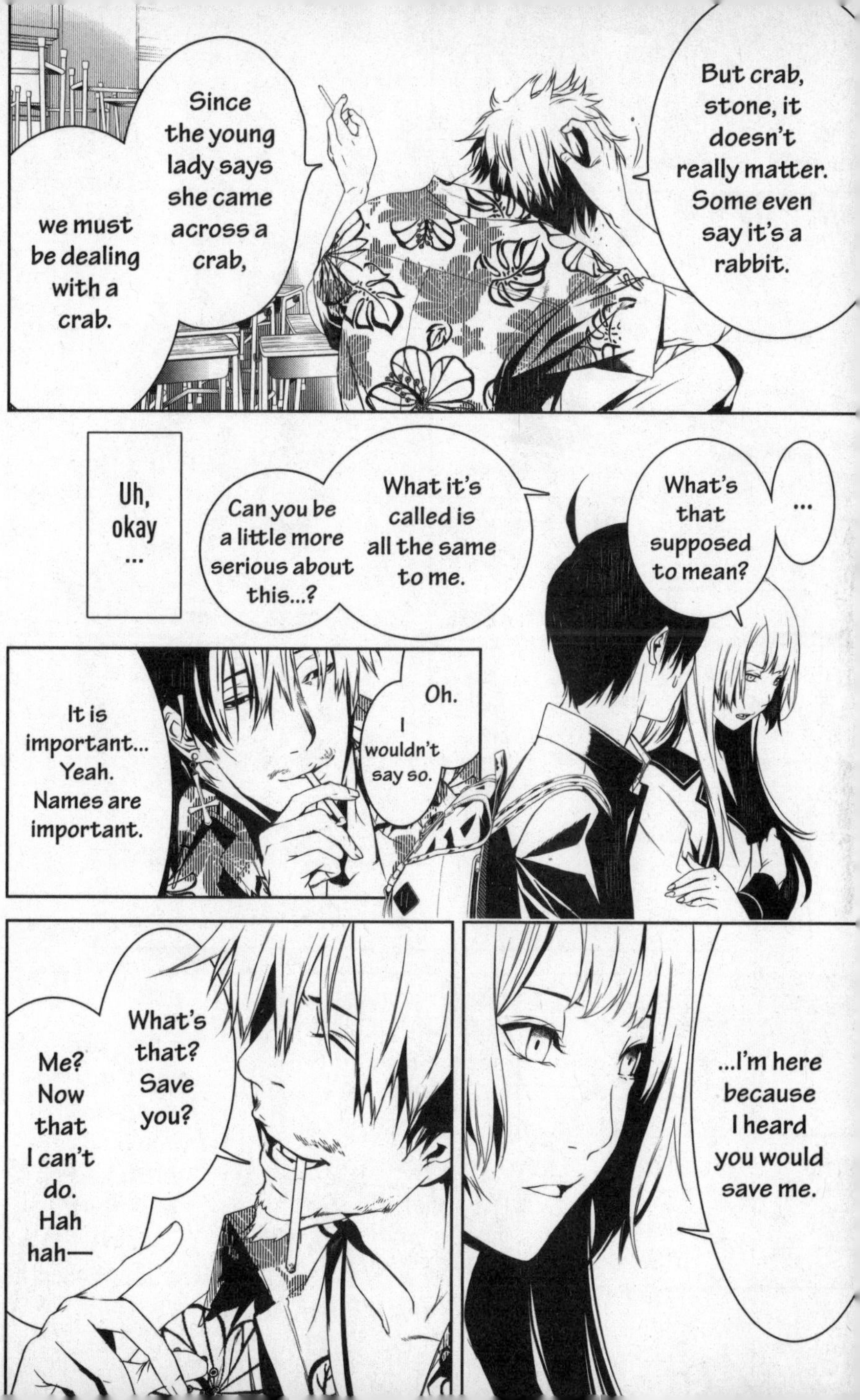
But crab, stone, it doesn't really matter. Some even say it's a rabbit.
Since the young lady says she came across a crab,
we must be dealing with a crab.
...
What's that supposed to mean?
What it's called is all the same to me.
Can you be a little more serious about this...?
Uh, okay ...
Oh. I wouldn't say so.
It is important... Yeah. Names are important.
...I'm here because I heard you would save me.
What's that? Save you?
Me? Now that I can't do. Hah hah—

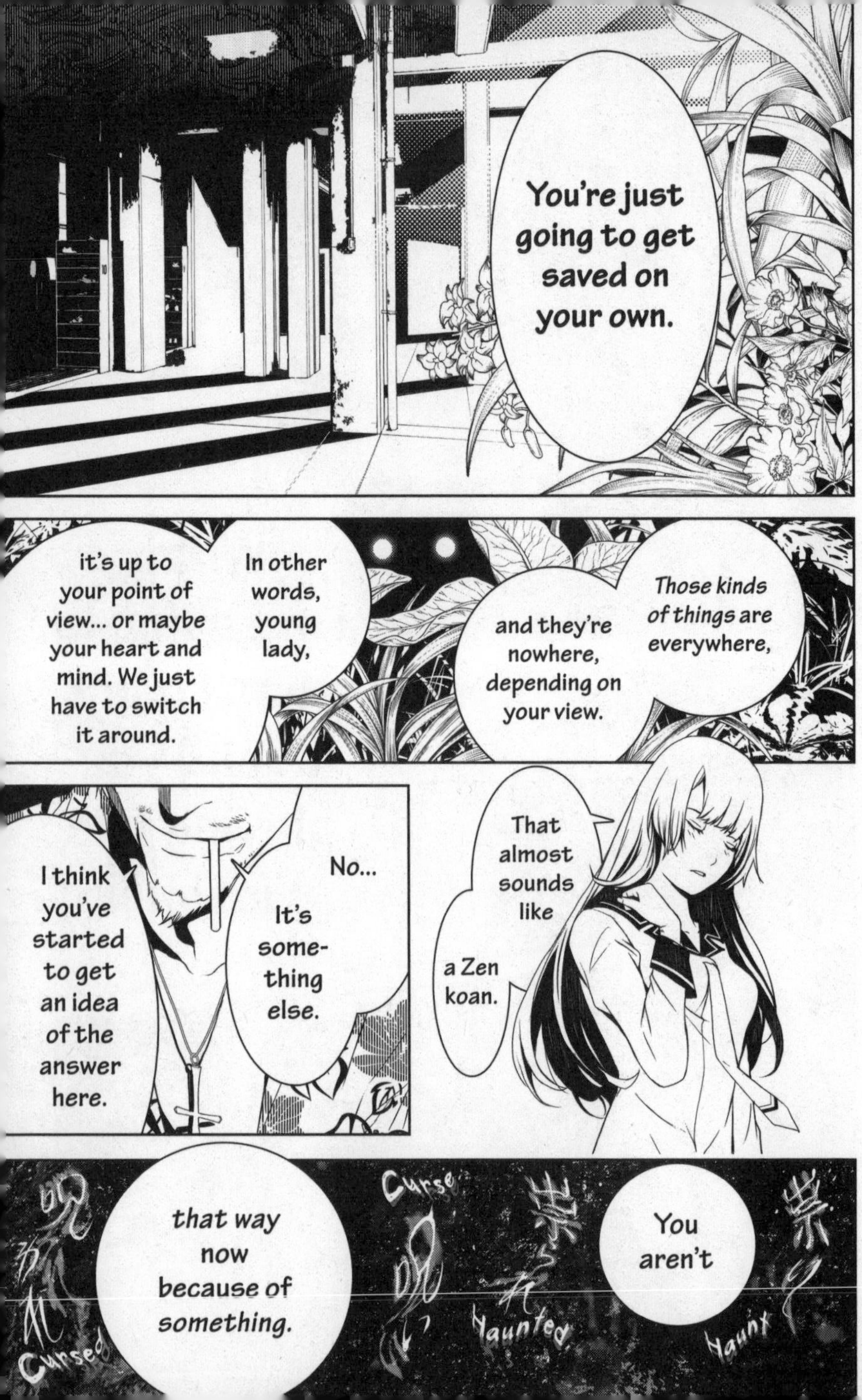
You're just going to get saved on your own.
Those kinds of things are everywhere,
and they're nowhere, depending on your view.
In other words, young lady,
it's up to your point of view... or maybe your heart and mind. We just have to switch it around.
That almost sounds like
a Zen koan.
No...
It's something else.
I think you've started to get an idea of the answer here.
Haunt
You aren't
Haunted
Curse
that way now because of something.
Cursed

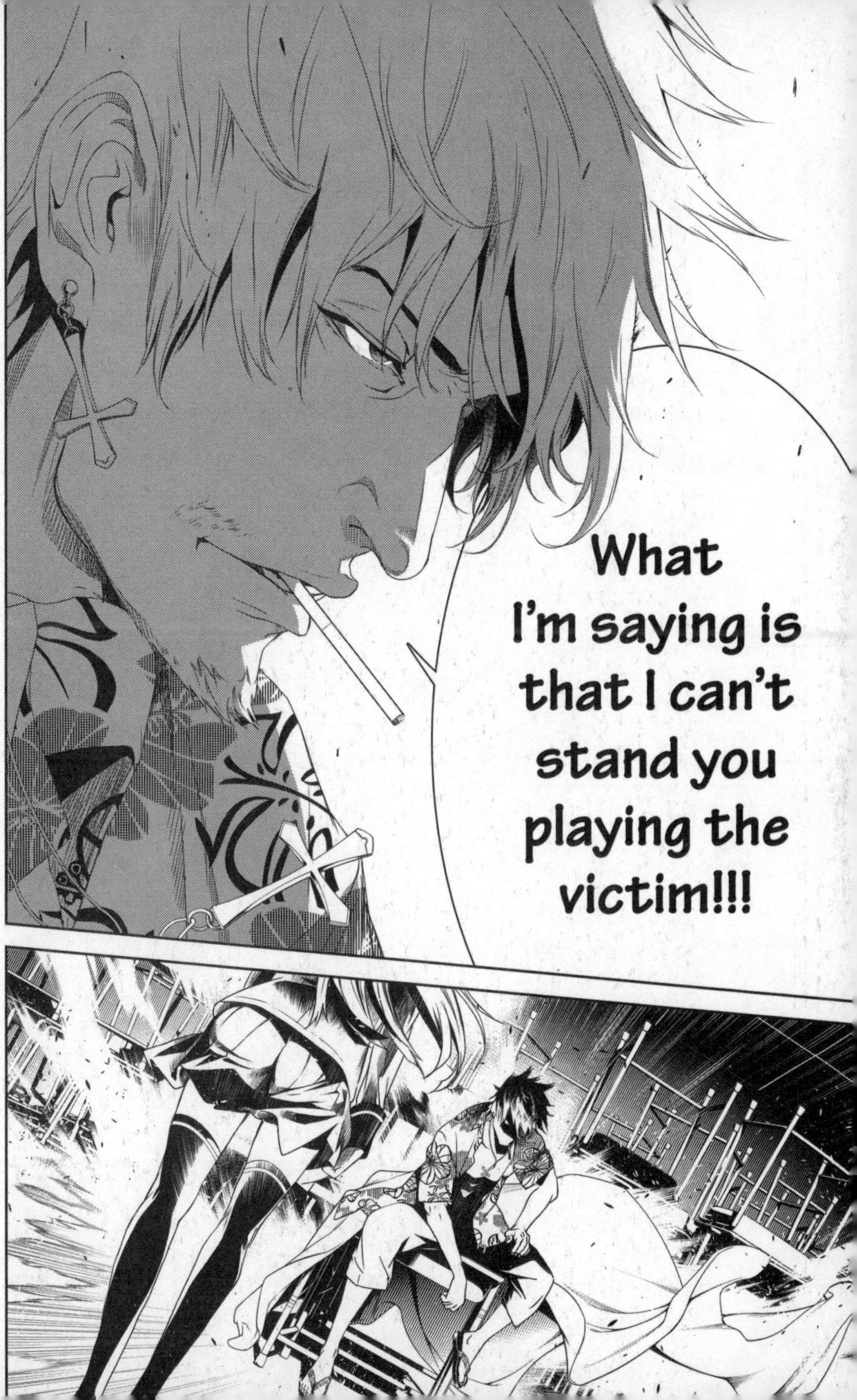
What I'm saying is that I can't stand you playing the victim!!!

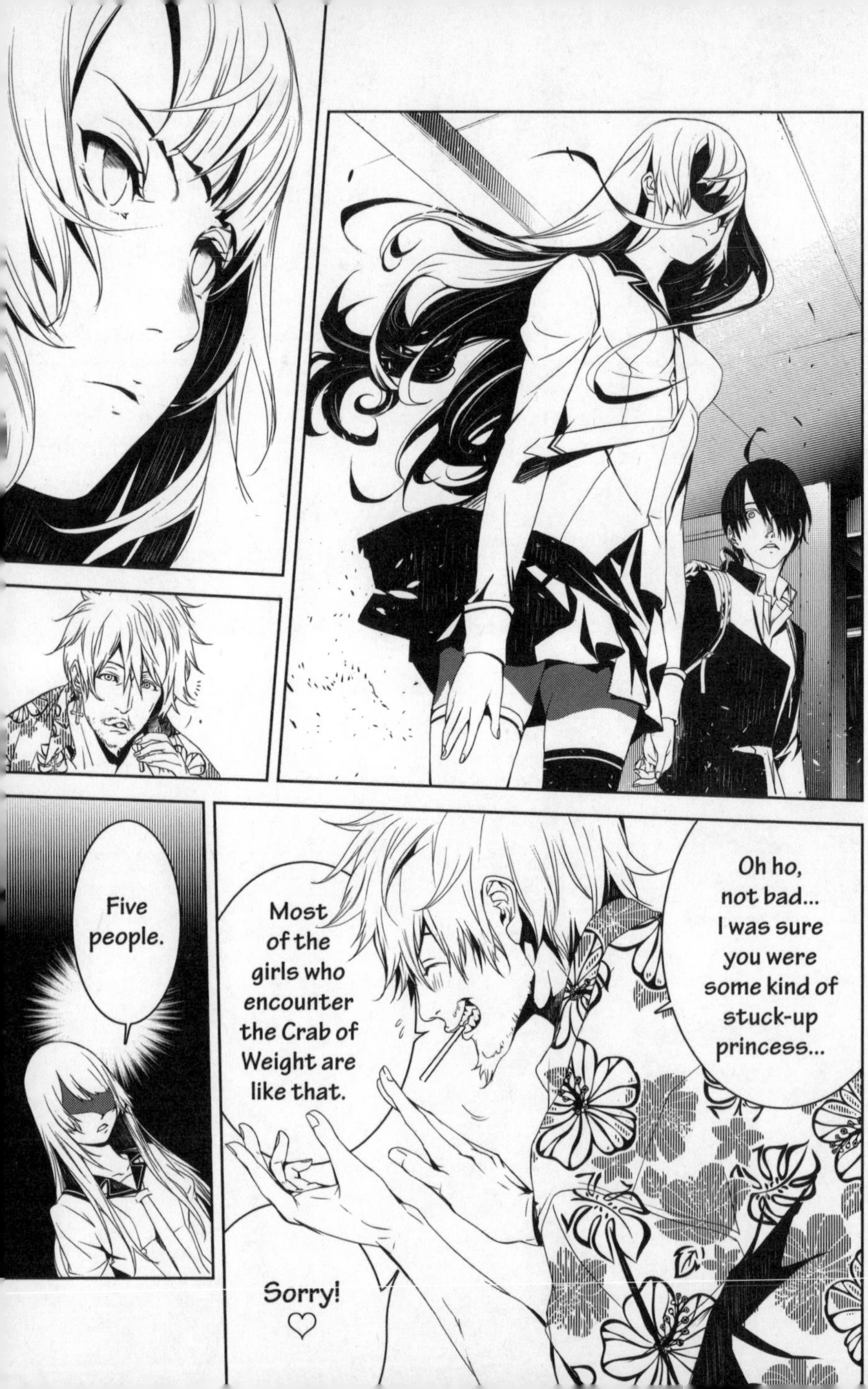
Oh ho, not bad... I was sure you were some kind of stuck-up princess...
Most of the girls who encounter the Crab of Weight are like that.
Sorry! ♡
Five people.

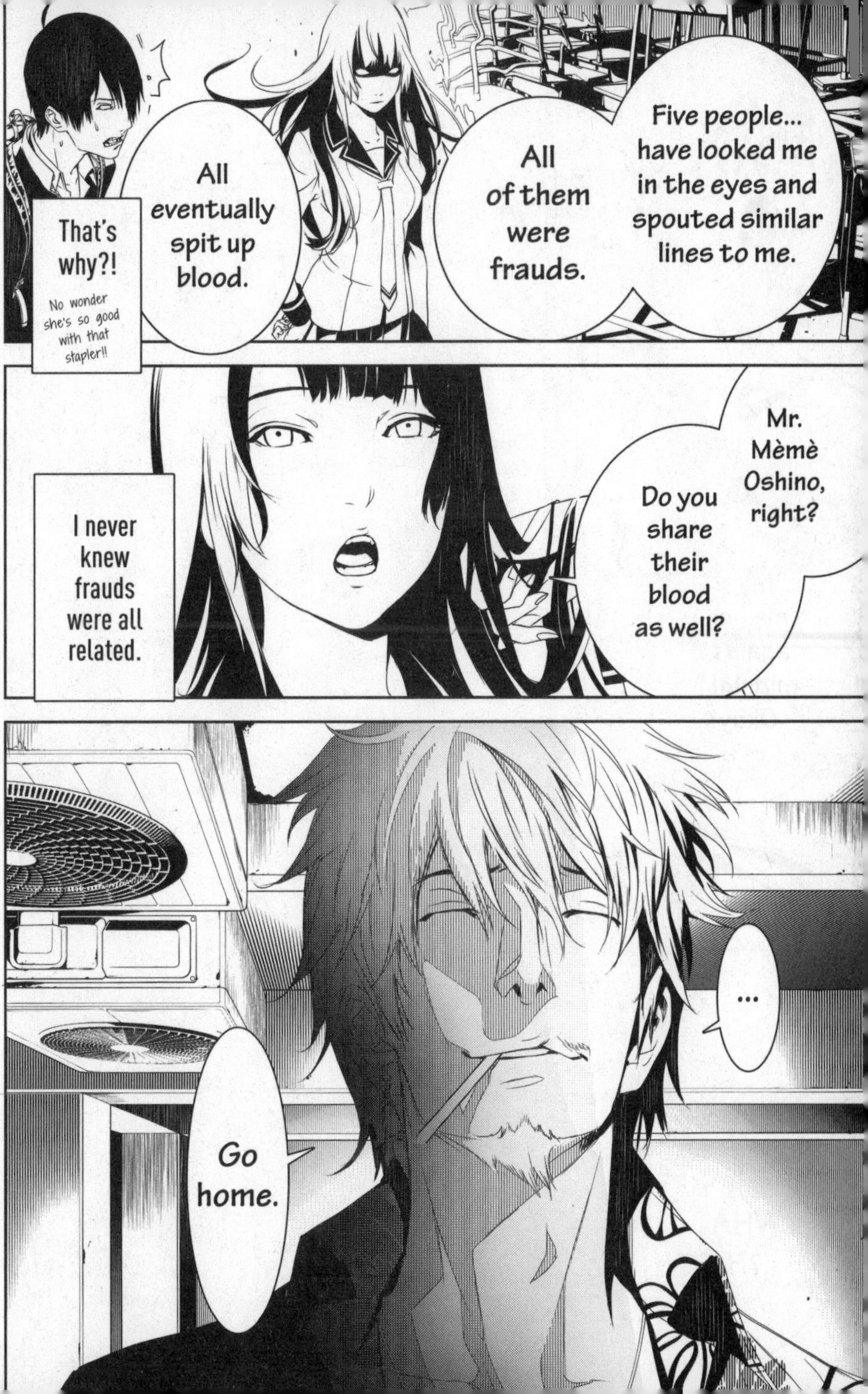
Five people... have looked me in the eyes and spouted similar lines to me.
All of them were frauds.
All eventually spit up blood.
That's why?!
No wonder she's so good with that stapler!!
Mr. Mèmè Oshino, right?
Do you share their blood as well?
I never knew frauds were all related.
...
Go home.

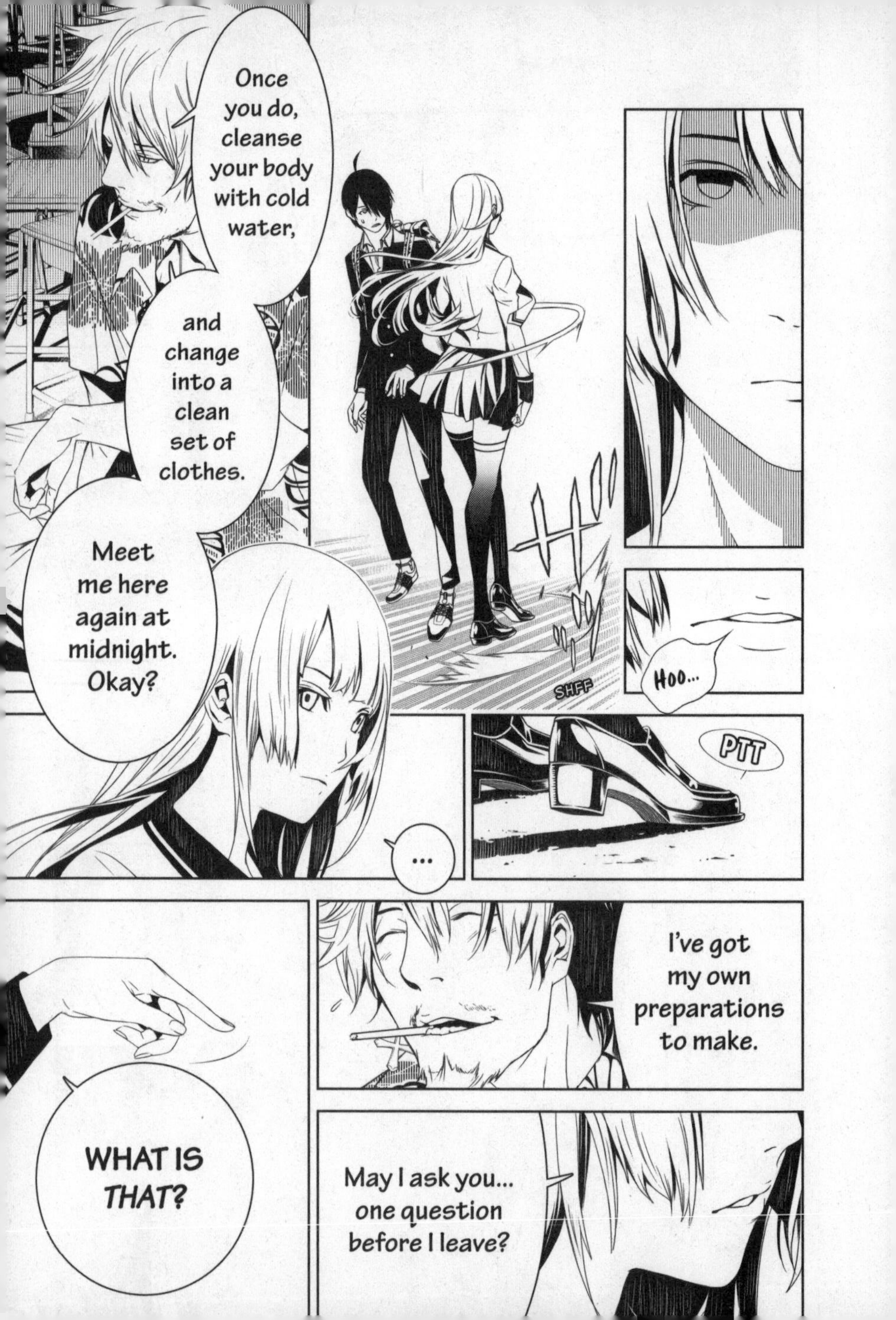
Hoo...
SHFF
Once you do, cleanse your body with cold water,
and change into a clean set of clothes.
Meet me here again at midnight. Okay?
PTT
...
I've got my own preparations to make.
May I ask you... one question before I leave?
WHAT IS *THAT?*

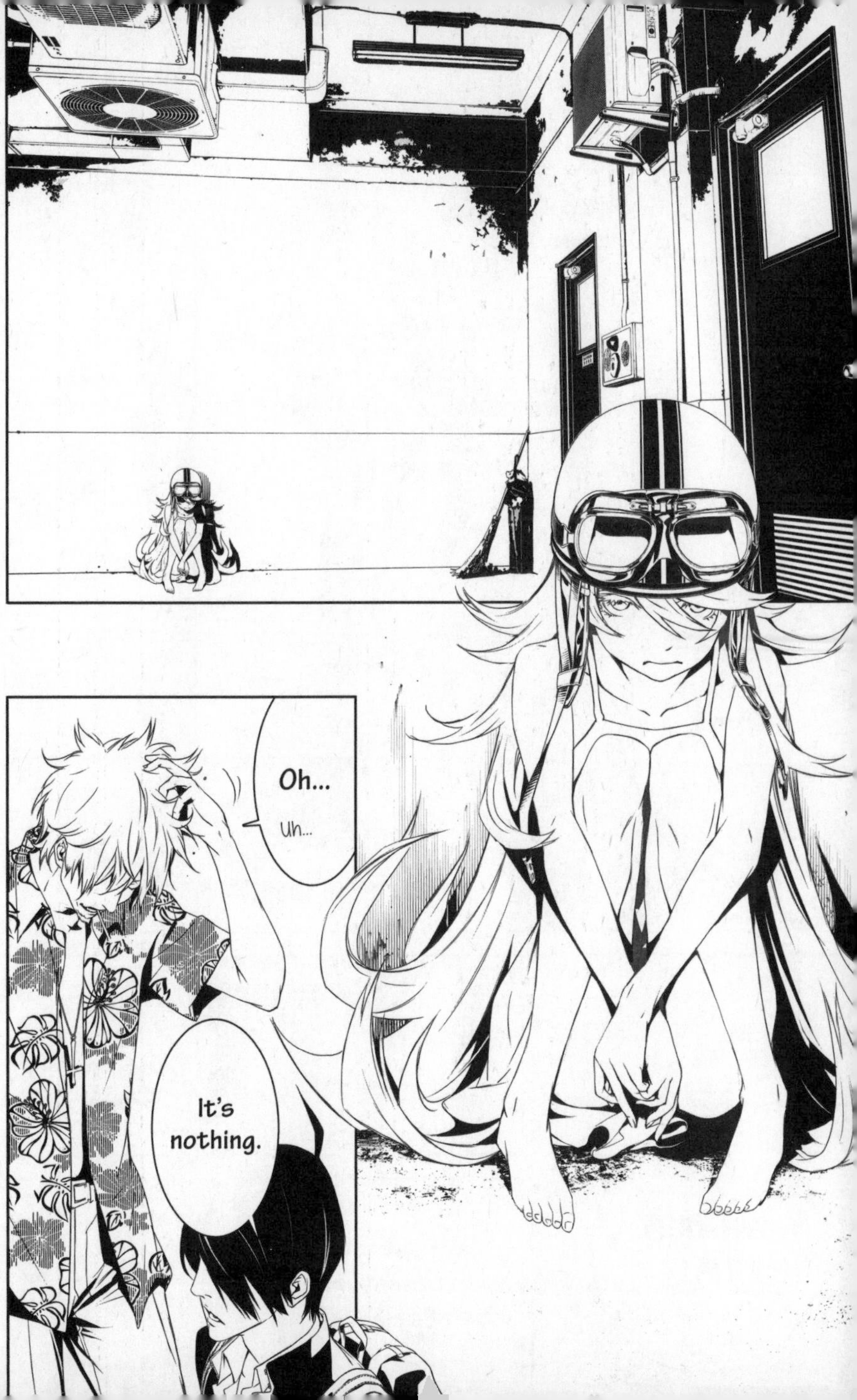
Oh... Uh...
It's nothing.

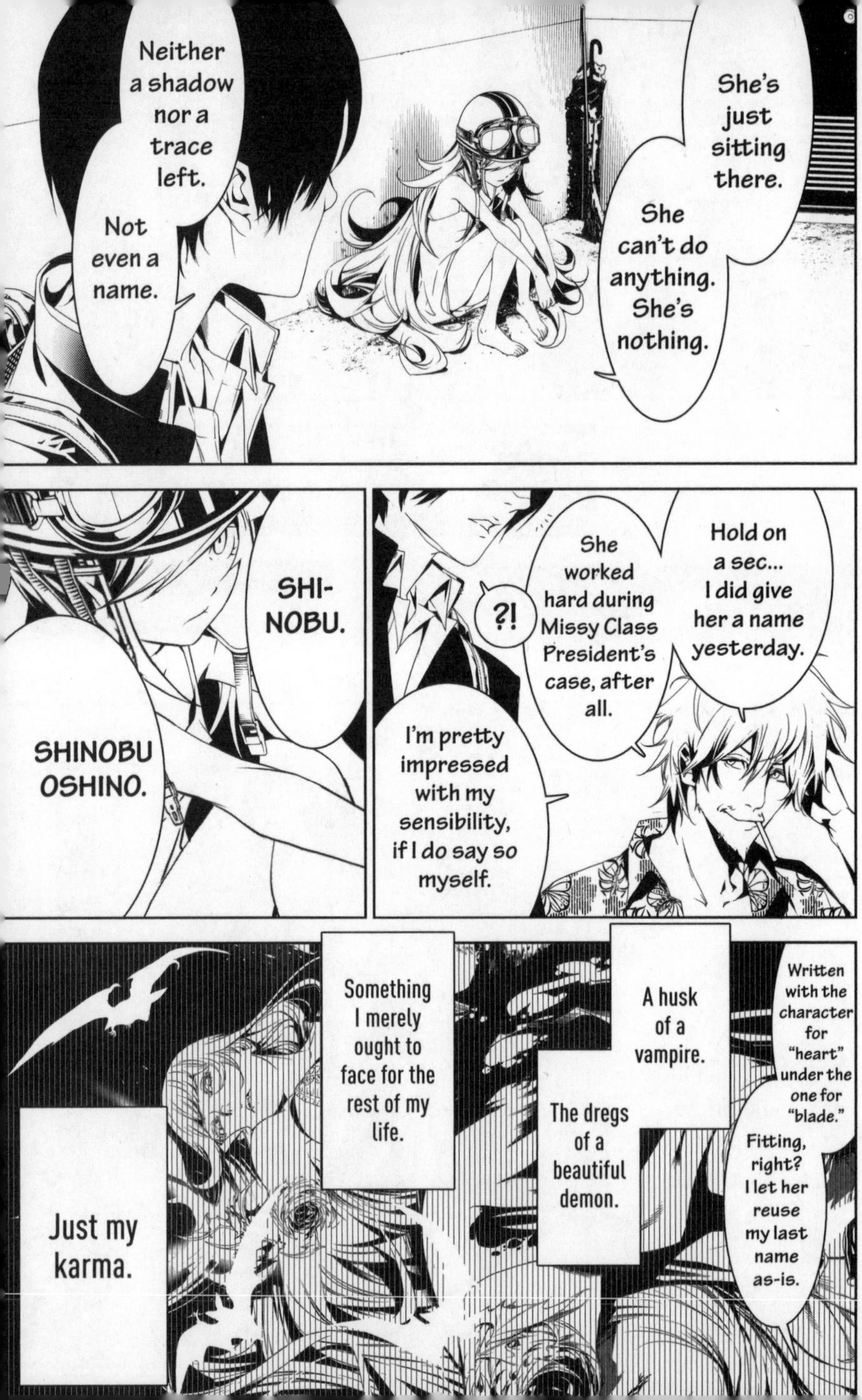
She's just sitting there.
She can't do anything. She's nothing.
Neither a shadow nor a trace left.
Not even a name.
Hold on a sec... I did give her a name yesterday.
She worked hard during Missy Class President's case, after all.
?!
I'm pretty impressed with my sensibility, if I do say so myself.
SHI-NOBU.
SHINOBU OSHINO.
Written with the character for "heart" under the one for "blade."
Fitting, right? I let her reuse my last name as-is.
A husk of a vampire.
The dregs of a beautiful demon.
Something I merely ought to face for the rest of my life.
Just my karma.

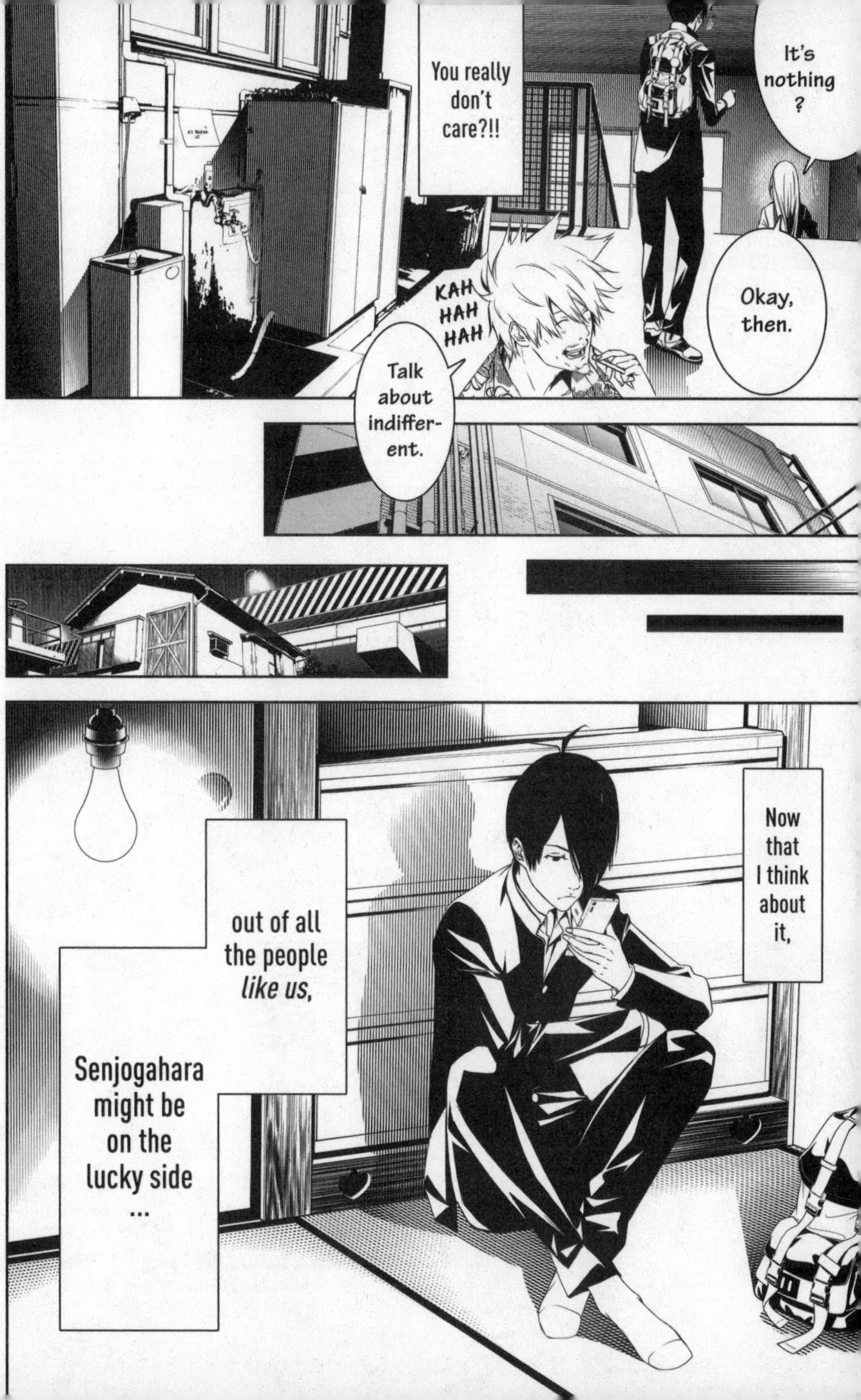
It's nothing?
Okay, then.
You really don't care?!!
KAH HAH HAH
Talk about indiffer-ent.
Now that I think about it,
out of all the people *like us*,
Senjogahara might be on the lucky side ...

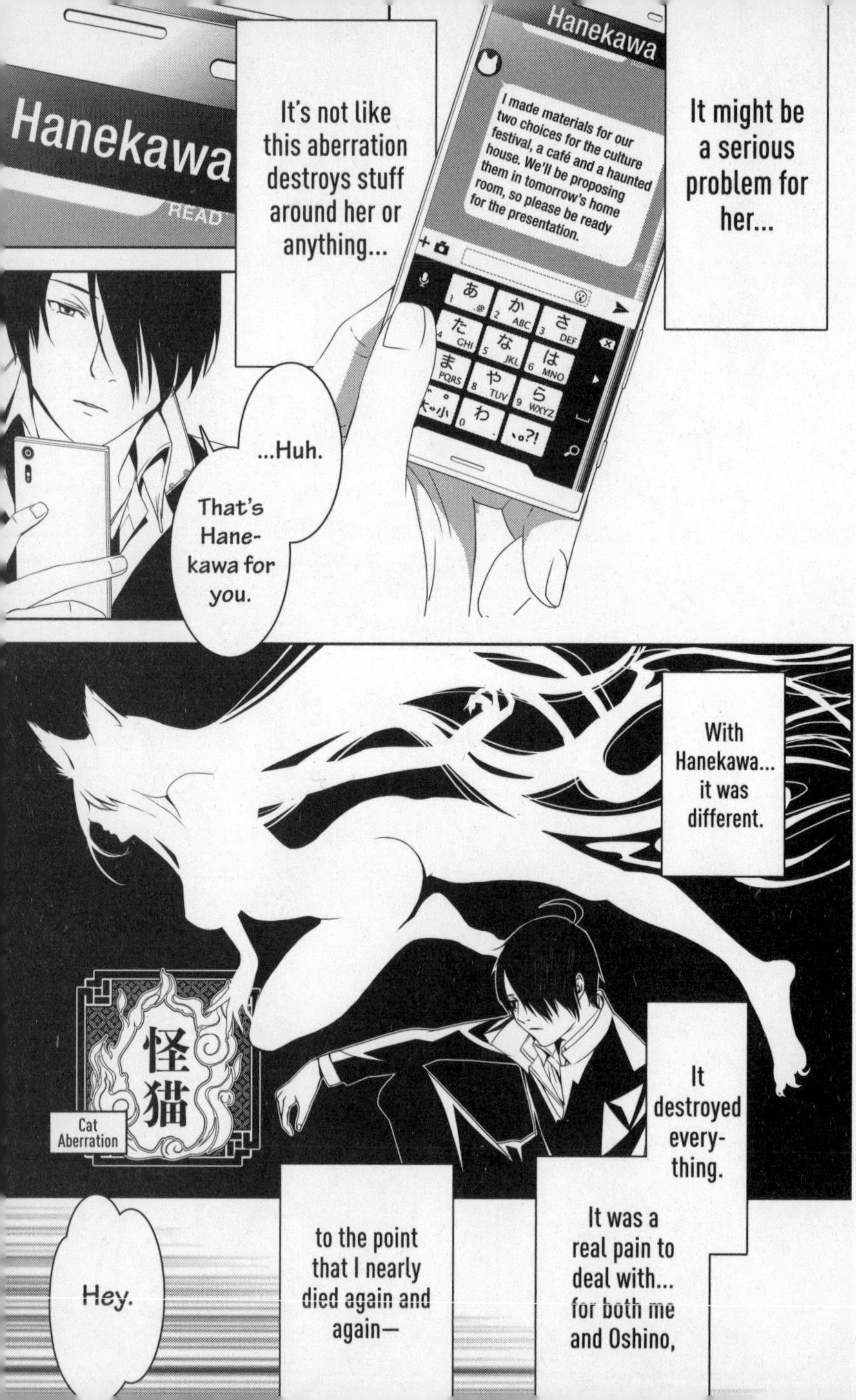

It might be a serious problem for her...
It's not like this aberration destroys stuff around her or anything...
Hanekawa
I made materials for our two choices for the culture festival, a café and a haunted house. We'll be proposing them in tomorrow's home room, so please be ready for the presentation.
Hanekawa
READ
...Huh.
That's Hanekawa for you.
With Hanekawa... it was different.
It destroyed everything.
怪猫
Cat Aberration
It was a real pain to deal with... for both me and Oshino,
to the point that I nearly died again and again—
Hey.

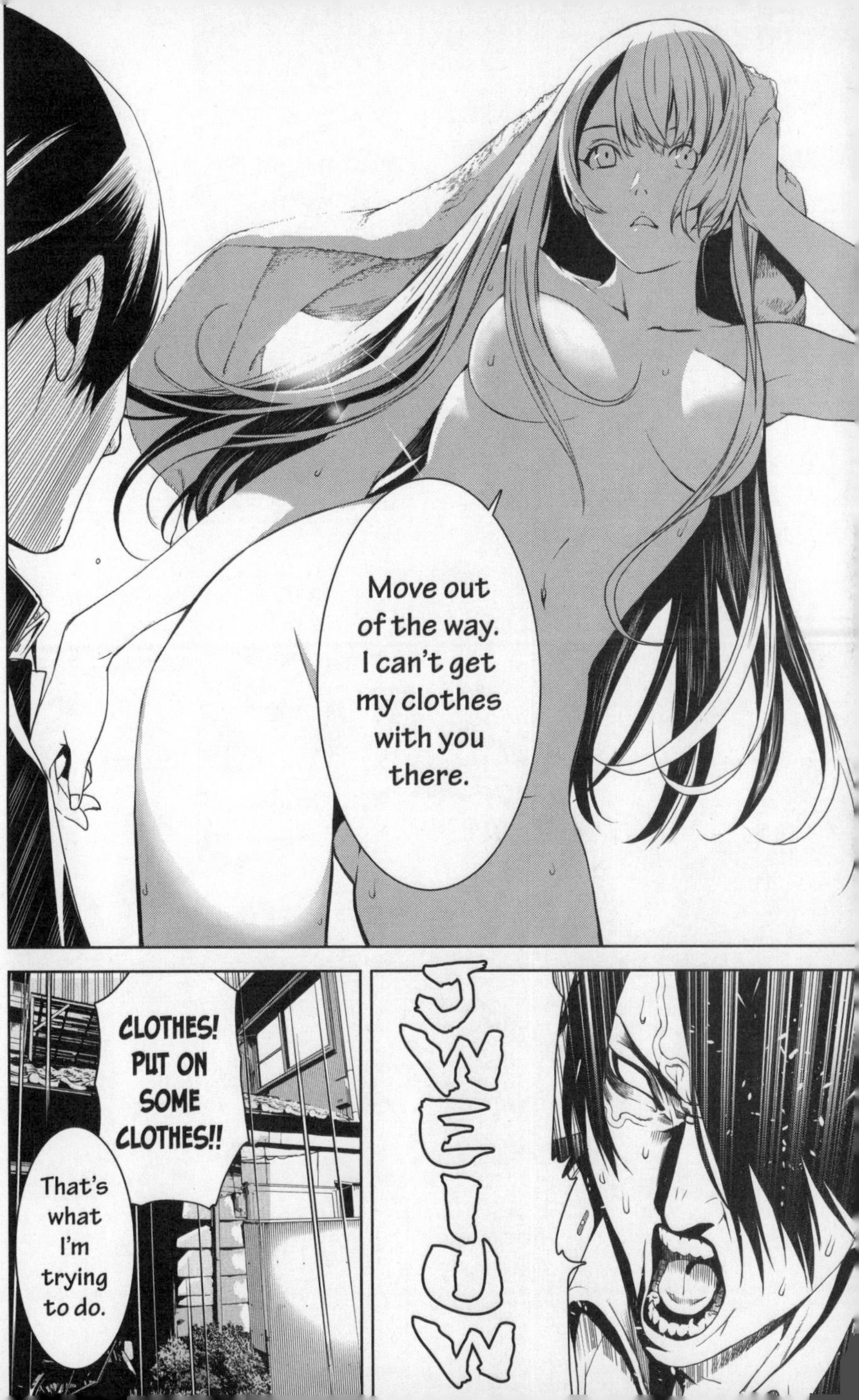
Move out of the way. I can't get my clothes with you there.
JWEUW
CLOTHES! PUT ON SOME CLOTHES!!
That's what I'm trying to do.

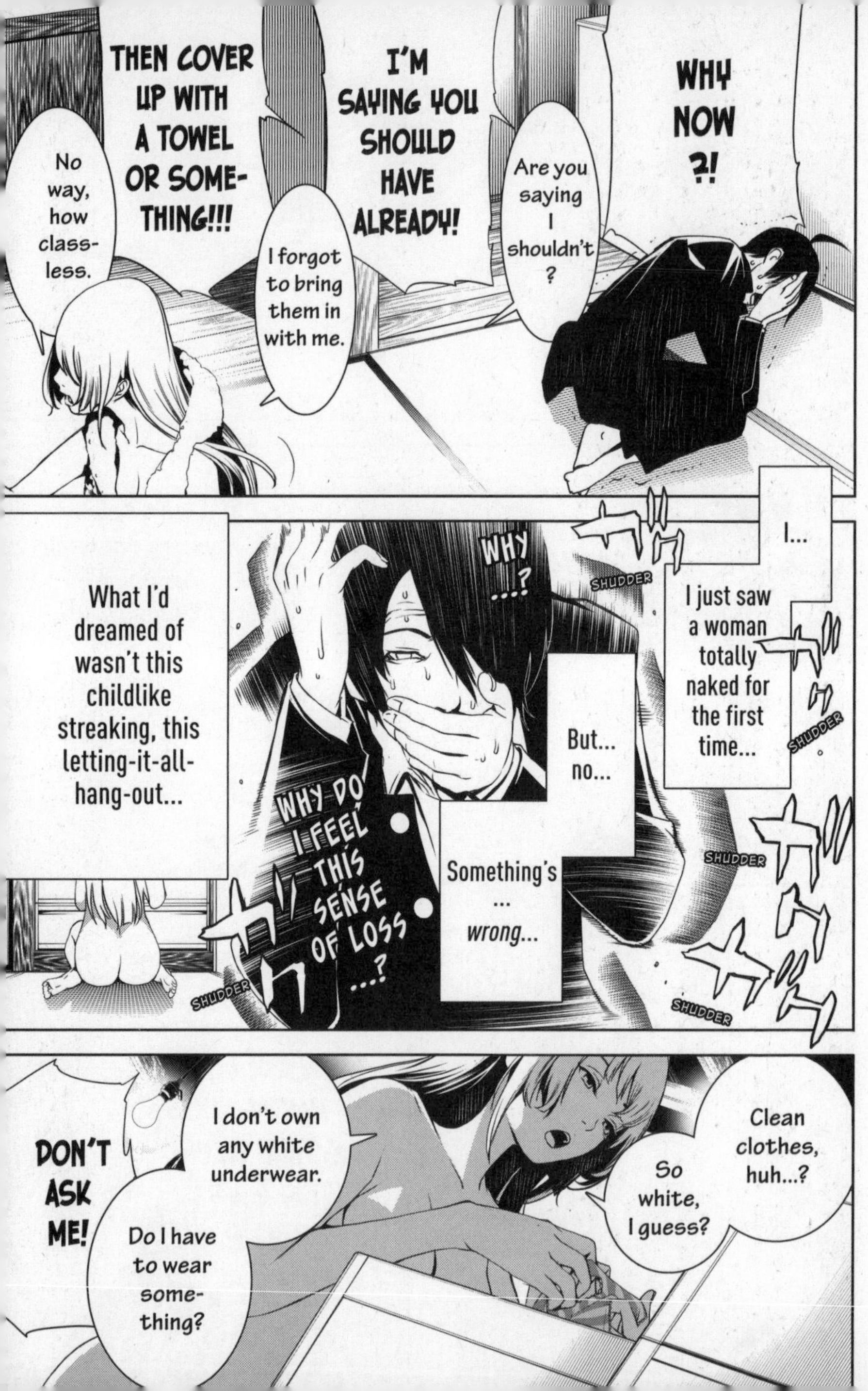
WHY NOW ?!
Are you saying I shouldn't ?
I'M SAYING YOU SHOULD HAVE ALREADY!
I forgot to bring them in with me.
THEN COVER UP WITH A TOWEL OR SOME-THING!!!
No way, how class-less.
I...
I just saw a woman totally naked for the first time...
SHUDDER
SHUDDER
SHUDDER
But... no...
Something's ... *wrong*...
WHY ...?
WHY DO I FEEL THIS SENSE OF LOSS ...?
SHUDDER
SHUDDER
What I'd dreamed of wasn't this childlike streaking, this letting-it-all-hang-out...
Clean clothes, huh...?
So white, I guess?
I don't own any white underwear.
DON'T ASK ME!
Do I have to wear something?

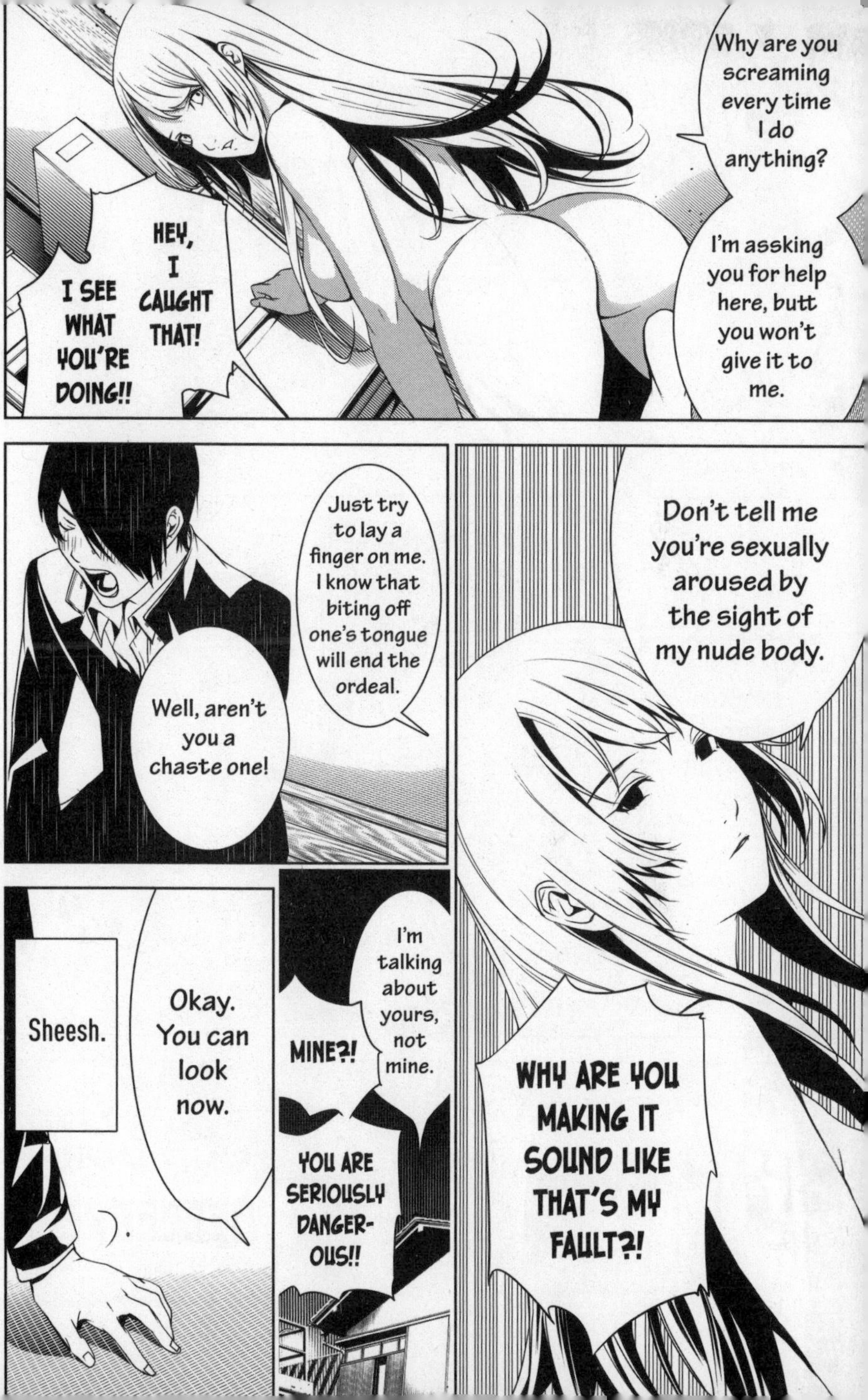
Why are you screaming every time I do anything?
I'm assking you for help here, butt you won't give it to me.
HEY, I CAUGHT THAT!
I SEE WHAT YOU'RE DOING!!
Don't tell me you're sexually aroused by the sight of my nude body.
WHY ARE YOU MAKING IT SOUND LIKE THAT'S MY FAULT?!
Just try to lay a finger on me. I know that biting off one's tongue will end the ordeal.
Well, aren't you a chaste one!
I'm talking about yours, not mine.
MINE?!
YOU ARE SERIOUSLY DANGER-OUS!!
Okay. You can look now.
Sheesh.

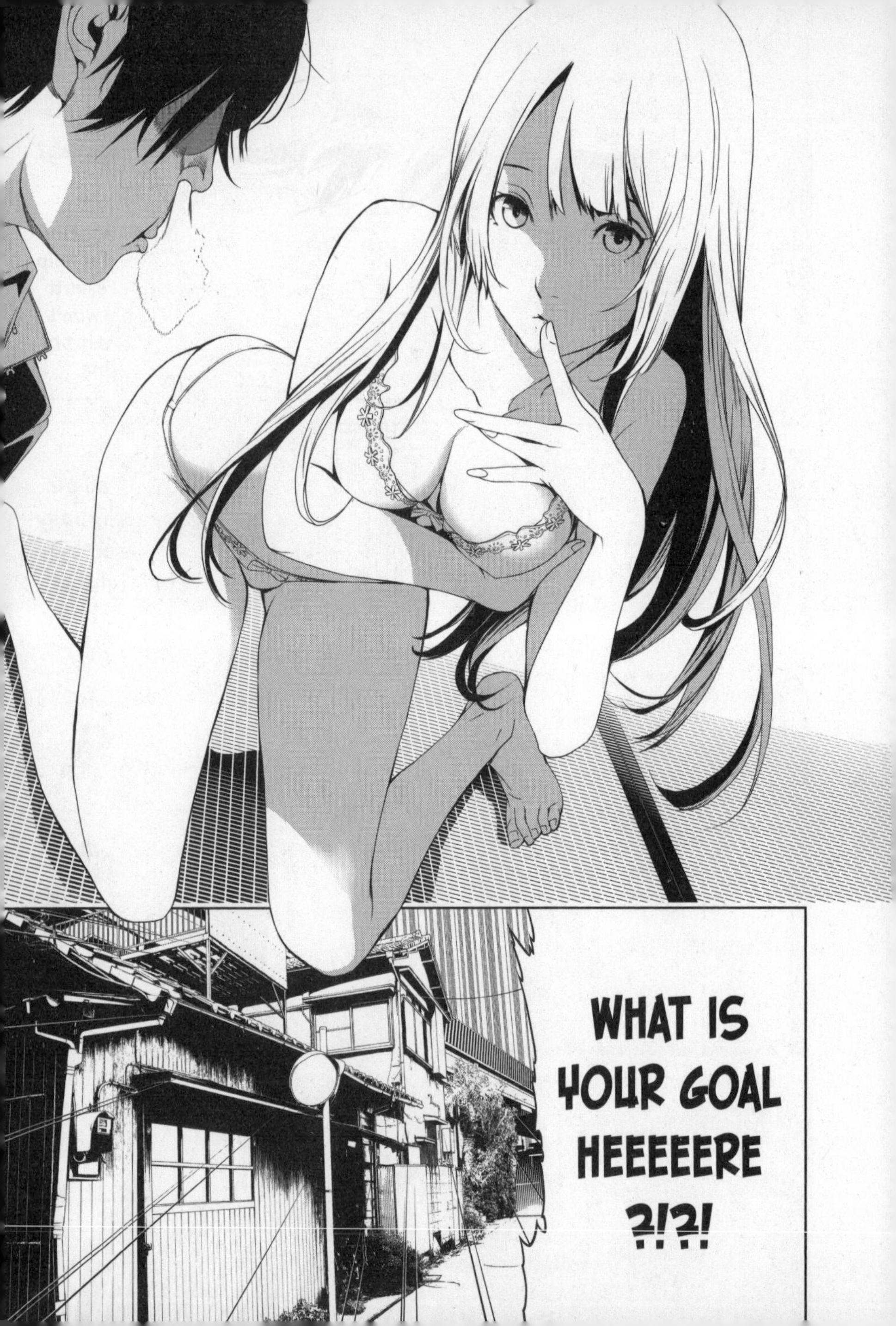
WHAT IS YOUR GOAL HEEEEERE ?!?!

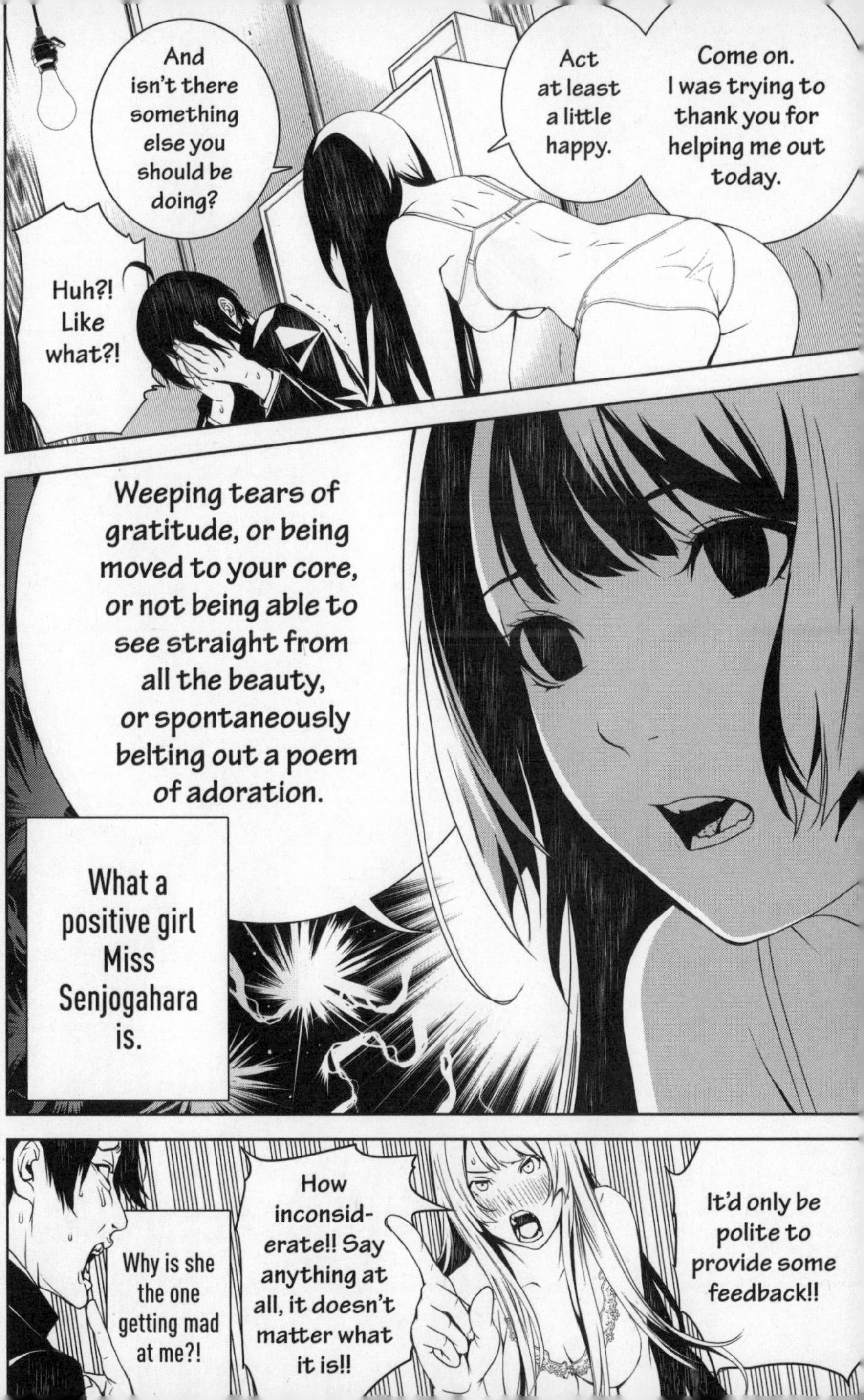
Come on. I was trying to thank you for helping me out today.
Act at least a little happy.
And isn't there something else you should be doing?
Huh?! Like what?!
Weeping tears of gratitude, or being moved to your core, or not being able to see straight from all the beauty, or spontaneously belting out a poem of adoration.
What a positive girl Miss Senjogahara is.
It'd only be polite to provide some feedback!!
How inconsid-erate!! Say anything at all, it doesn't matter what it is!!
Why is she the one getting mad at me?!

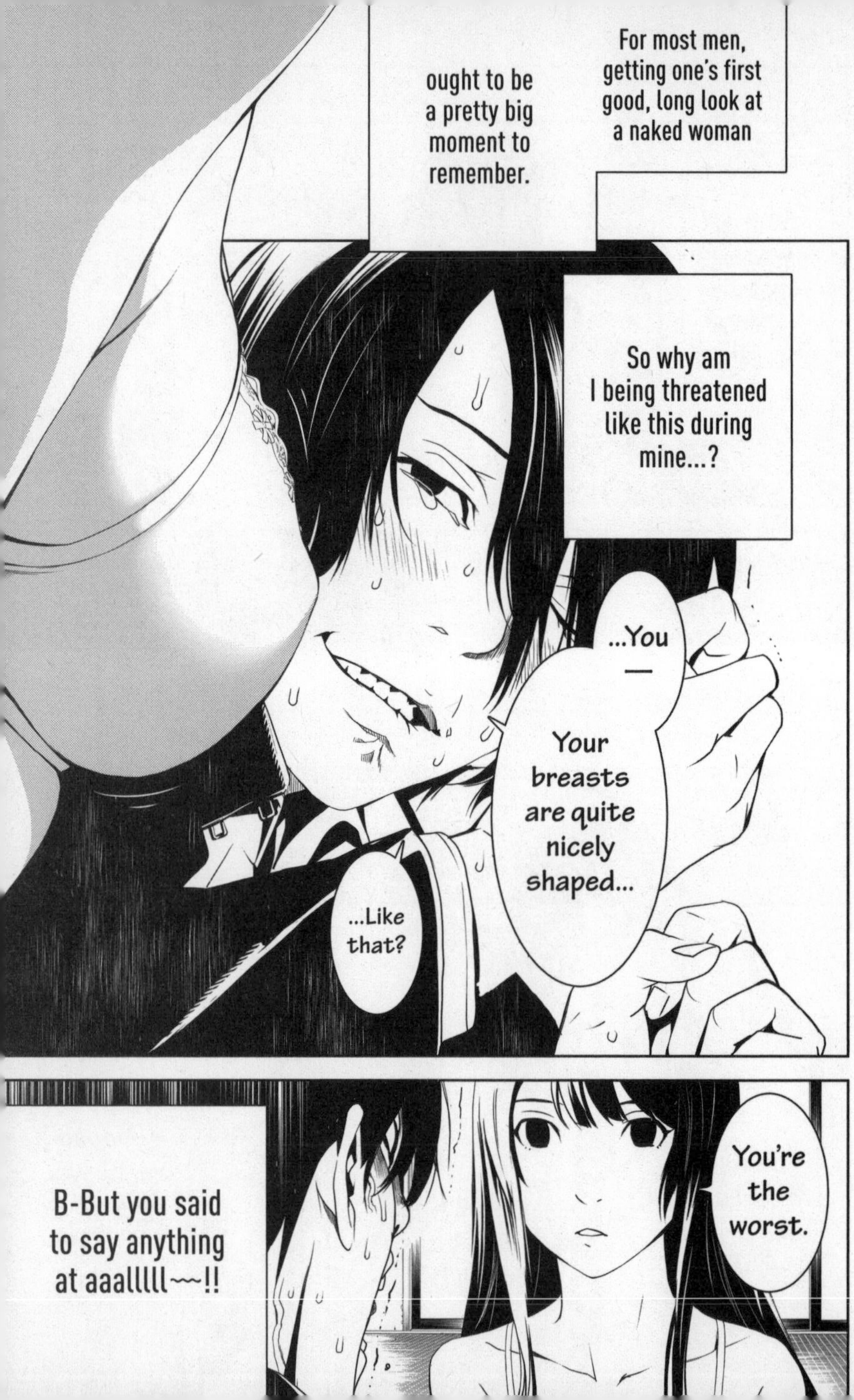
For most men, getting one's first good, long look at a naked woman
ought to be a pretty big moment to remember.
So why am I being threatened like this during mine...?
...You —
Your breasts are quite nicely shaped...
...Like that?
You're the worst.
B-But you said to say anything at aaallllll~~!!

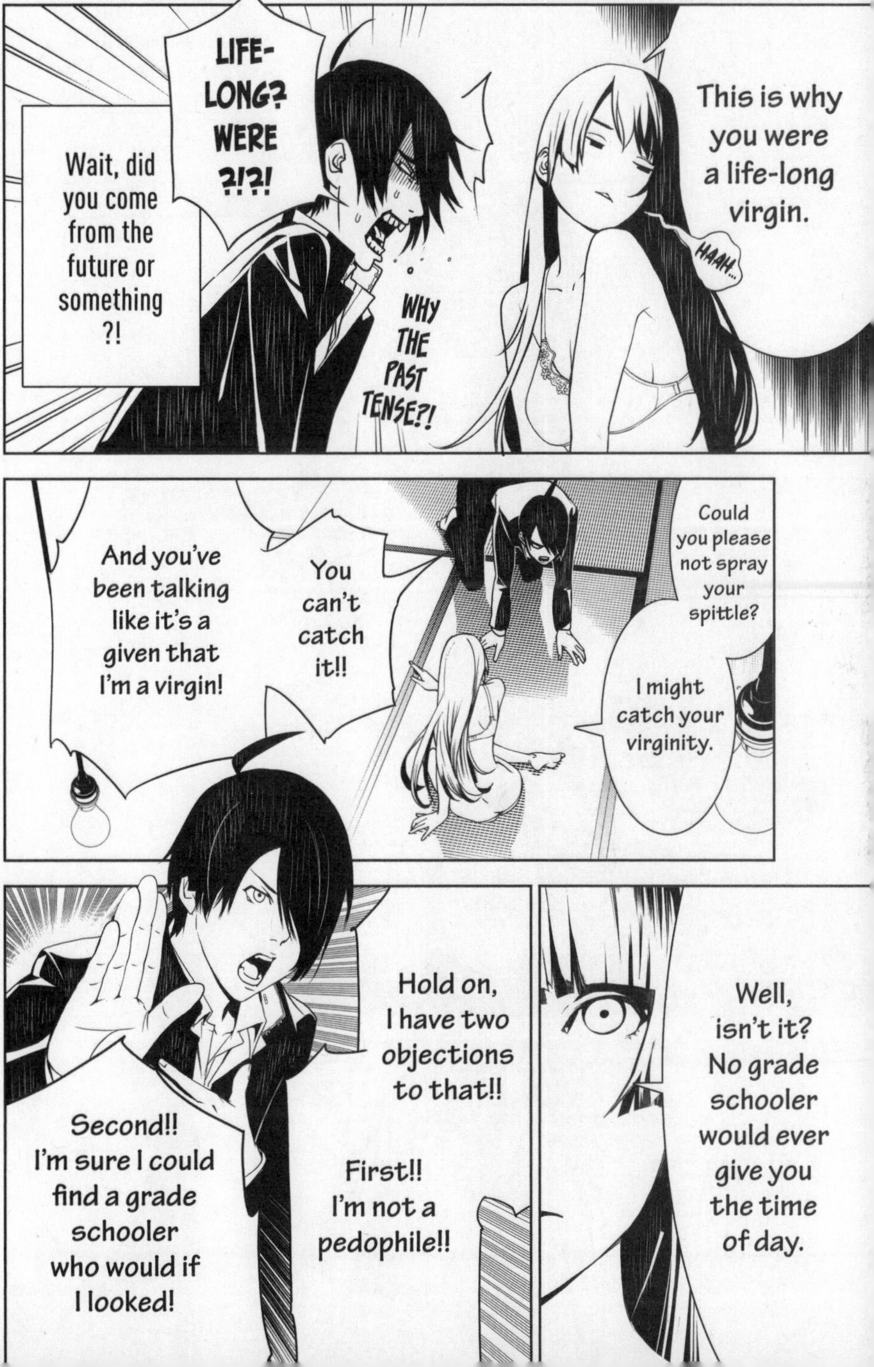
This is why you were a life-long virgin.
HAAH...
LIFE-LONG? WERE ?!?!
WHY THE PAST TENSE?!
Wait, did you come from the future or something ?!
Could you please not spray your spittle?
I might catch your virginity.
You can't catch it!!
And you've been talking like it's a given that I'm a virgin!
Well, isn't it? No grade schooler would ever give you the time of day.
Hold on, I have two objections to that!!
First!! I'm not a pedophile!!
Second!! I'm sure I could find a grade schooler who would if I looked!

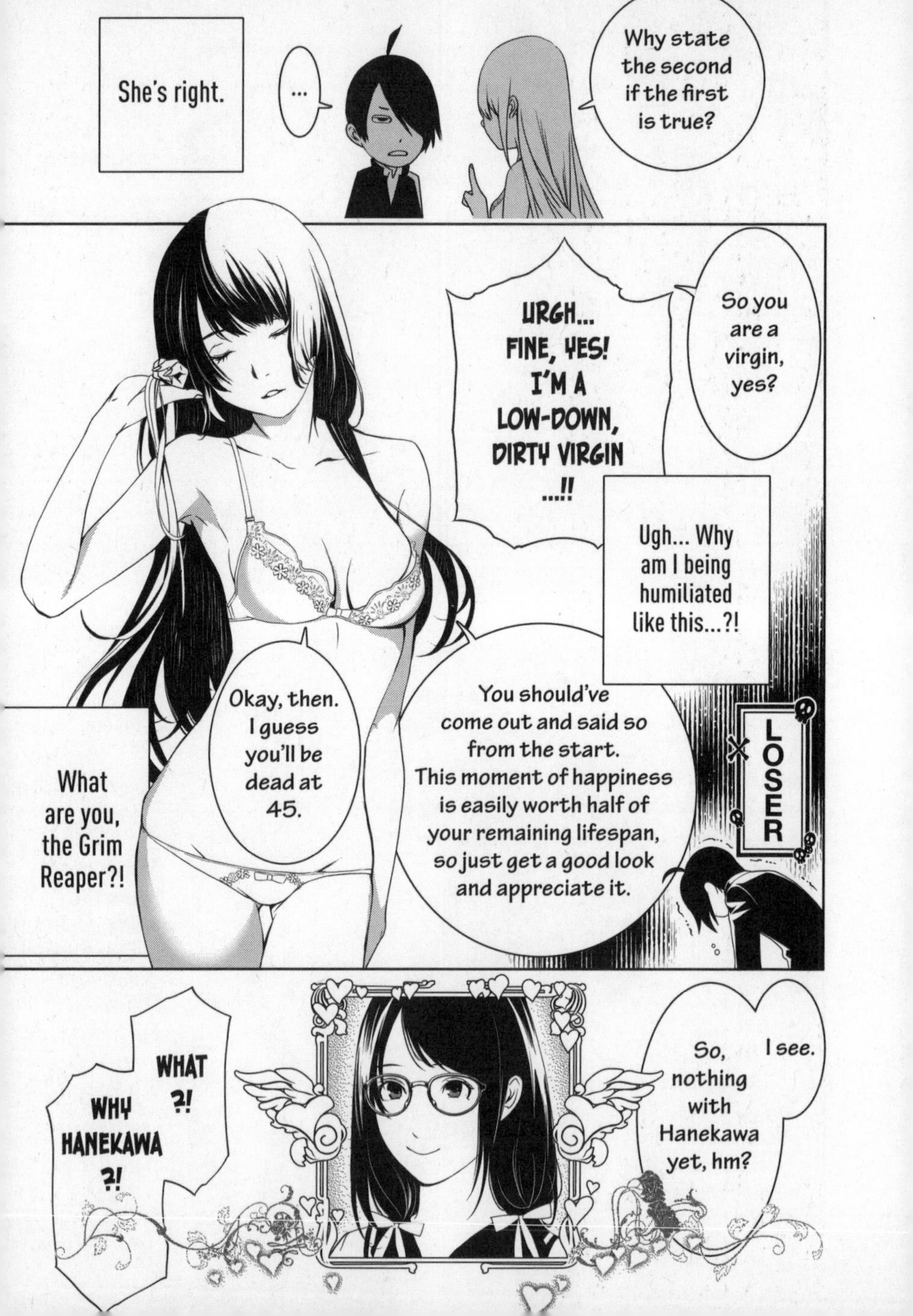
Why state the second if the first is true?
...
She's right.
So you are a virgin, yes?
URGH... FINE, YES! I'M A LOW-DOWN, DIRTY VIRGIN ...!!
Ugh... Why am I being humiliated like this...?!
LOSER
You should've come out and said so from the start. This moment of happiness is easily worth half of your remaining lifespan, so just get a good look and appreciate it.
Okay, then. I guess you'll be dead at 45.
What are you, the Grim Reaper?!
I see.
So, nothing with Hanekawa yet, hm?
WHAT ?!
WHY HANEKAWA ?!

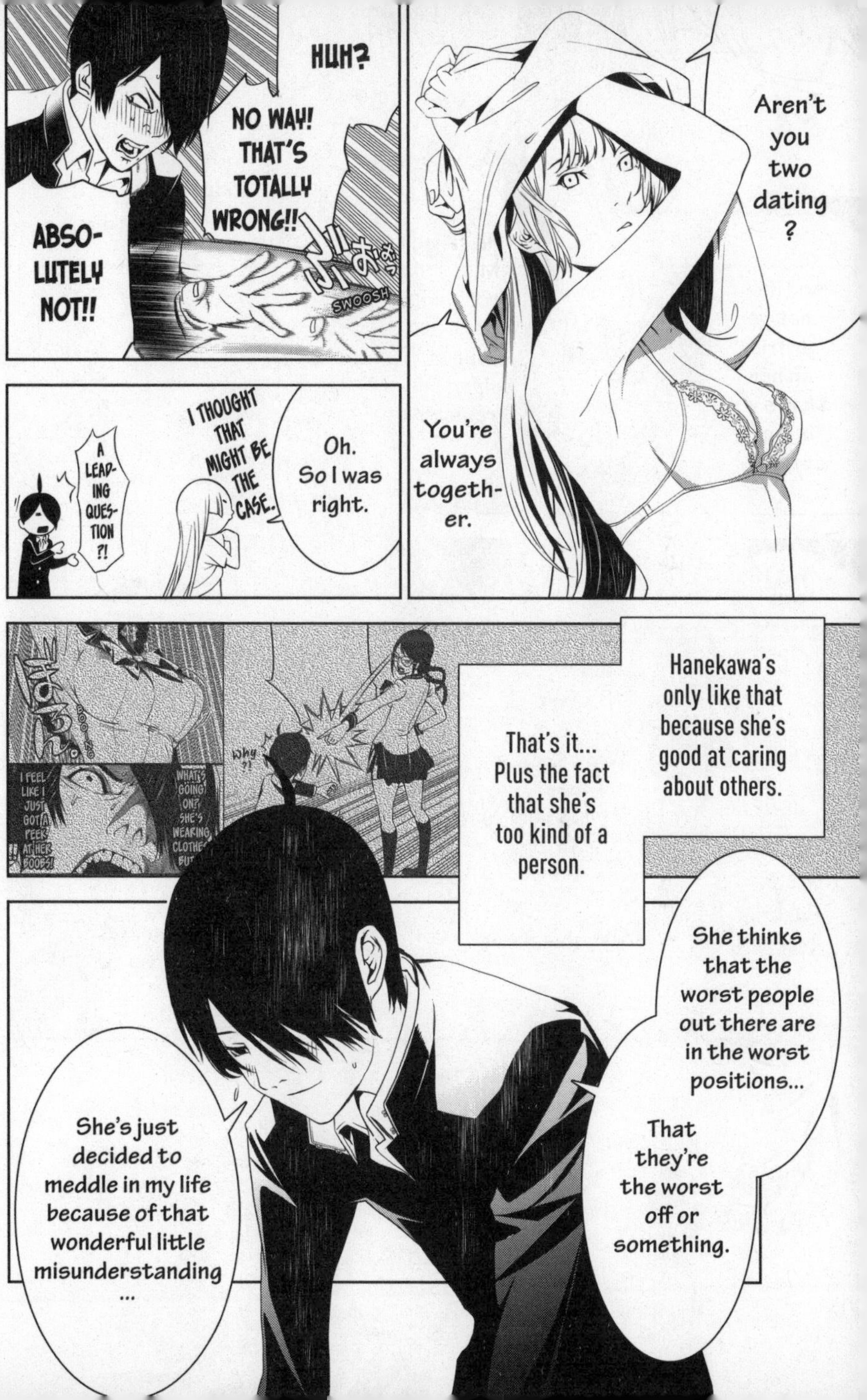
Aren't you two dating?
You're always together.
HUH?
NO WAY! THAT'S TOTALLY WRONG!!
ABSOLUTELY NOT!!
SWOOSH
Oh. So I was right.
I THOUGHT THAT MIGHT BE THE CASE.
A LEADING QUESTION?!
Hanekawa's only like that because she's good at caring about others.
That's it... Plus the fact that she's too kind of a person.
Why?!
BOING
WHAT'S GOING ON? SHE'S WEARING CLOTHES BUT...
I FEEL LIKE I JUST GOT A PEEK AT HER BOOBS!
She thinks that the worst people out there are in the worst positions...
That they're the worst off or something.
She's just decided to meddle in my life because of that wonderful little misunderstanding...

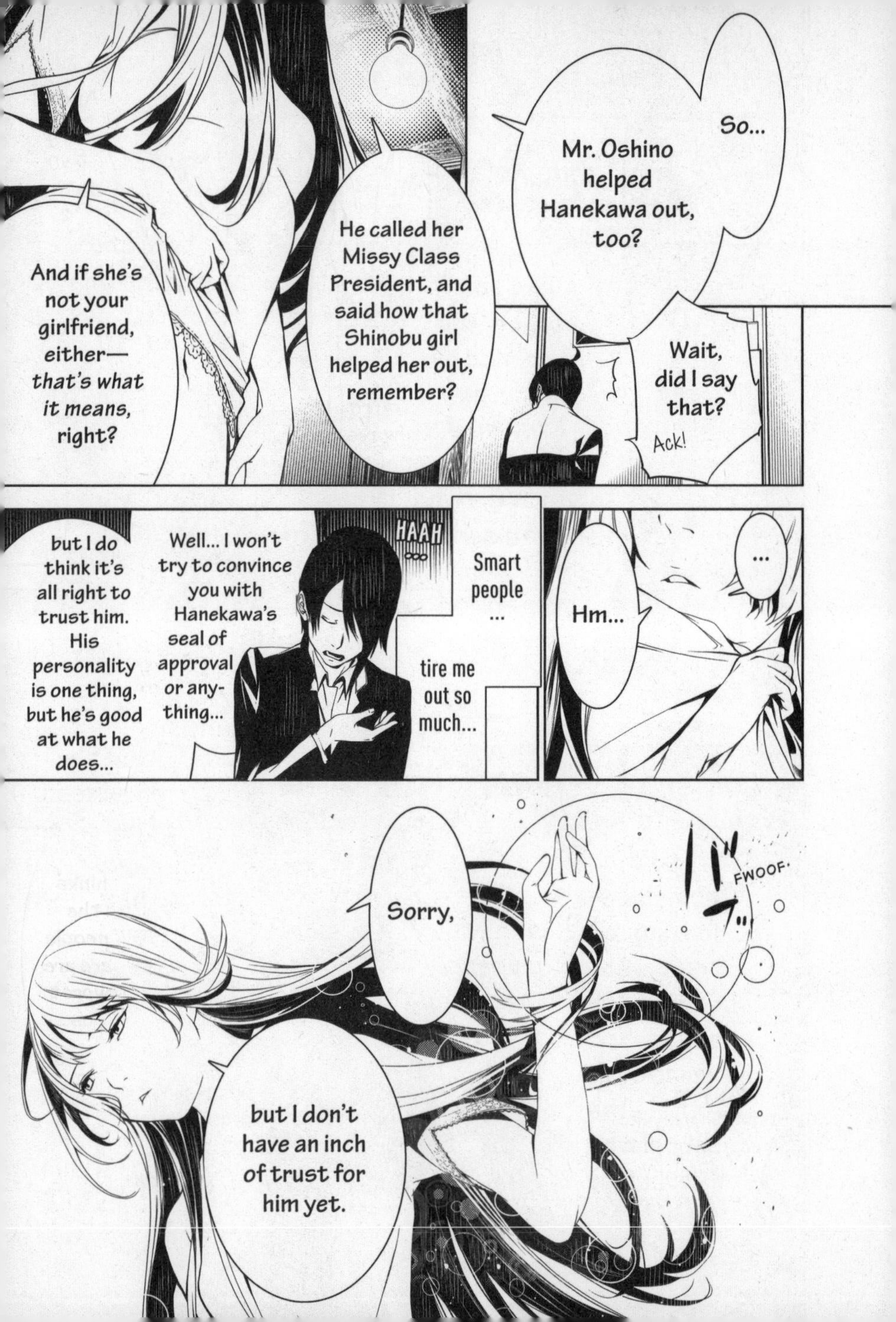

So...
Mr. Oshino helped Hanekawa out, too?
Wait, did I say that?
Ack!
He called her Missy Class President, and said how that Shinobu girl helped her out, remember?
And if she's not your girlfriend, either— *that's what it means,* right?
...
Hm...
HAAH
Smart people ...
tire me out so much...
Well... I won't try to convince you with Hanekawa's seal of approval or any-thing...
but I do think it's all right to trust him. His personality is one thing, but he's good at what he does...
FWOOF
Sorry,
but I don't have an inch of trust for him yet.

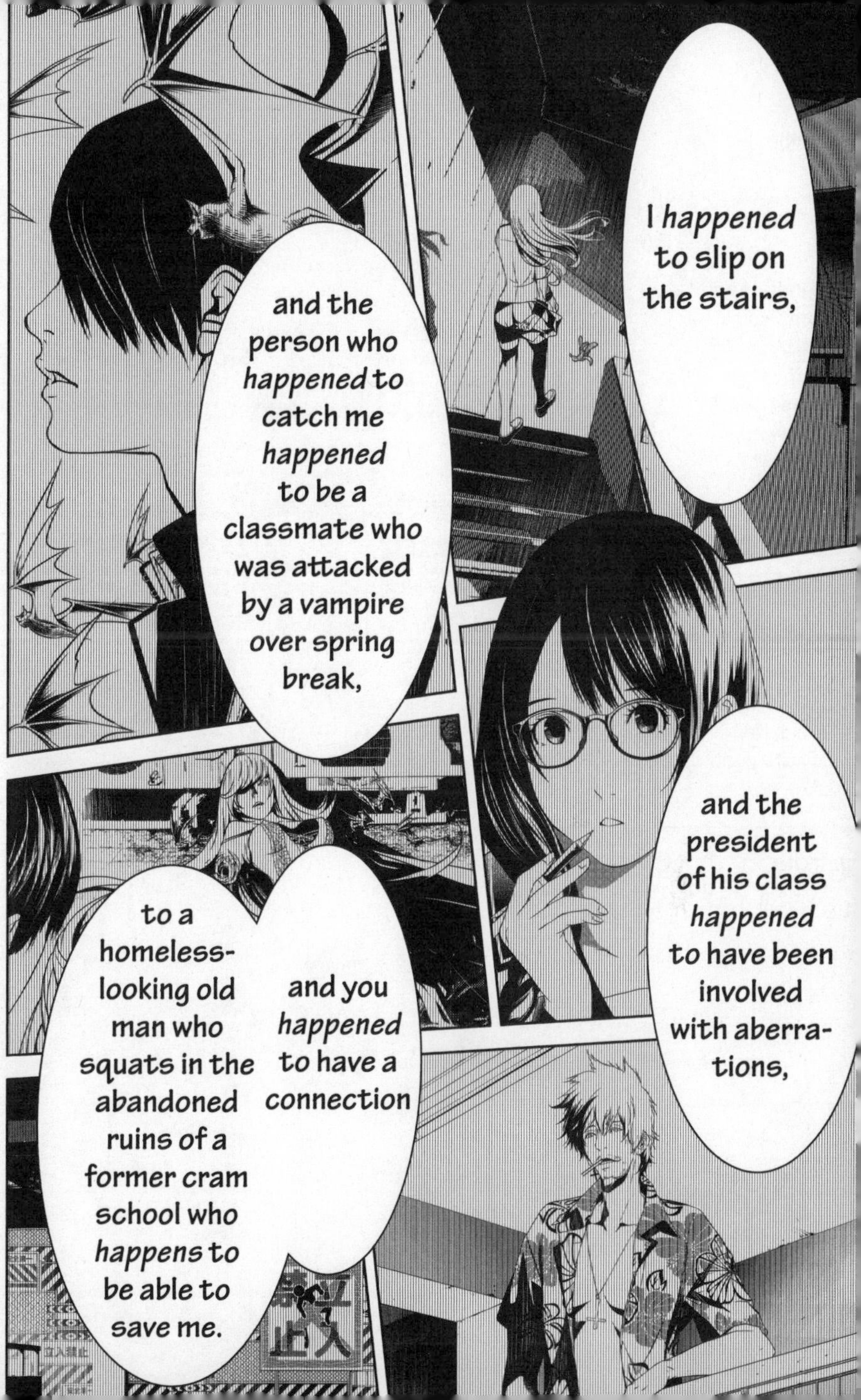
I happened to slip on the stairs,
and the person who happened to catch me happened to be a classmate who was attacked by a vampire over spring break,
and the president of his class happened to have been involved with aberrations,
and you happened to have a connection
to a homeless-looking old man who squats in the abandoned ruins of a former cram school who happens to be able to save me.

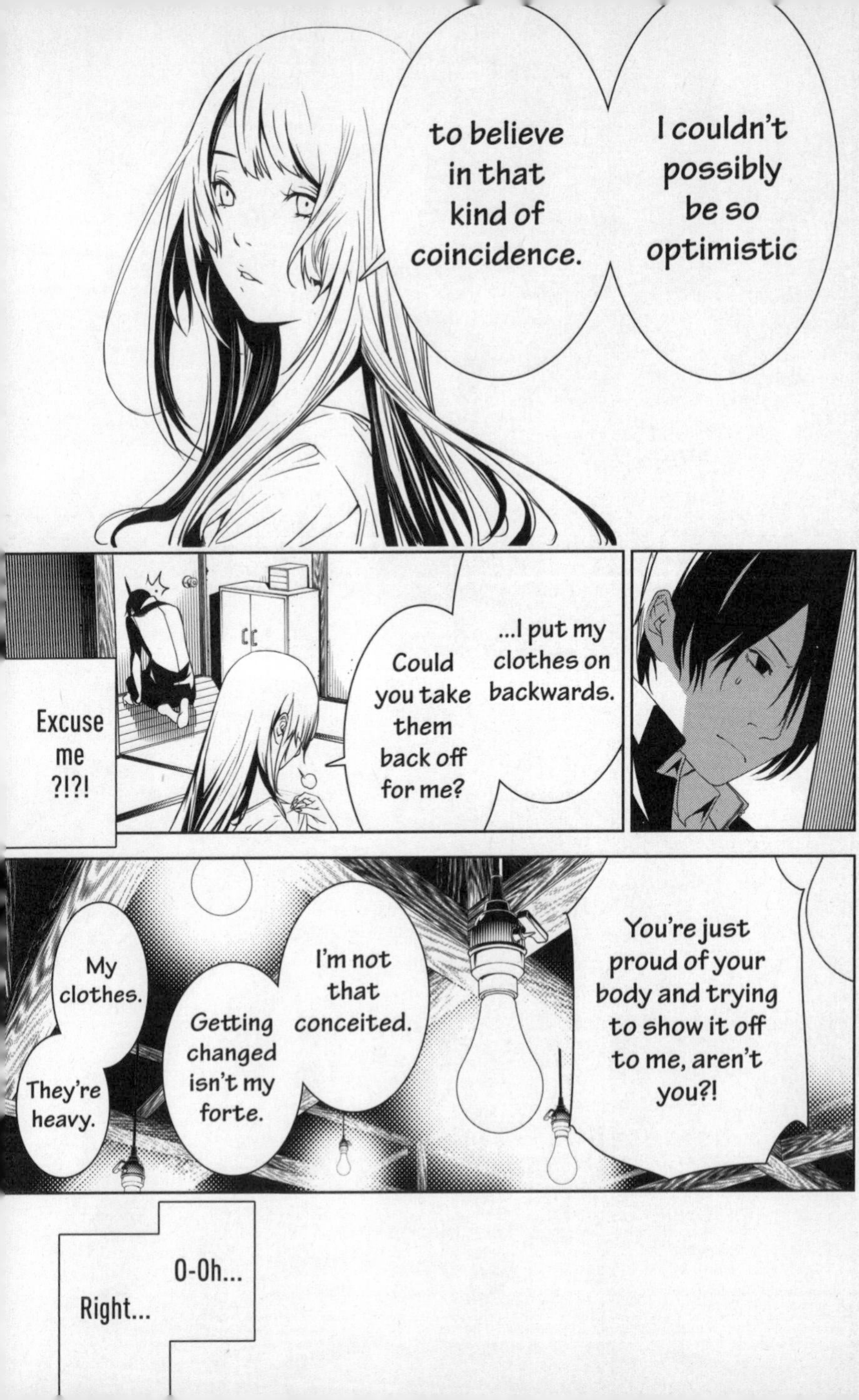

I couldn't possibly be so optimistic
to believe in that kind of coincidence.
...I put my clothes on backwards.
Could you take them back off for me?
Excuse me ?!?!
You're just proud of your body and trying to show it off to me, aren't you?!
I'm not that conceited.
Getting changed isn't my forte.
My clothes.
They're heavy.
O-Oh...
Right...

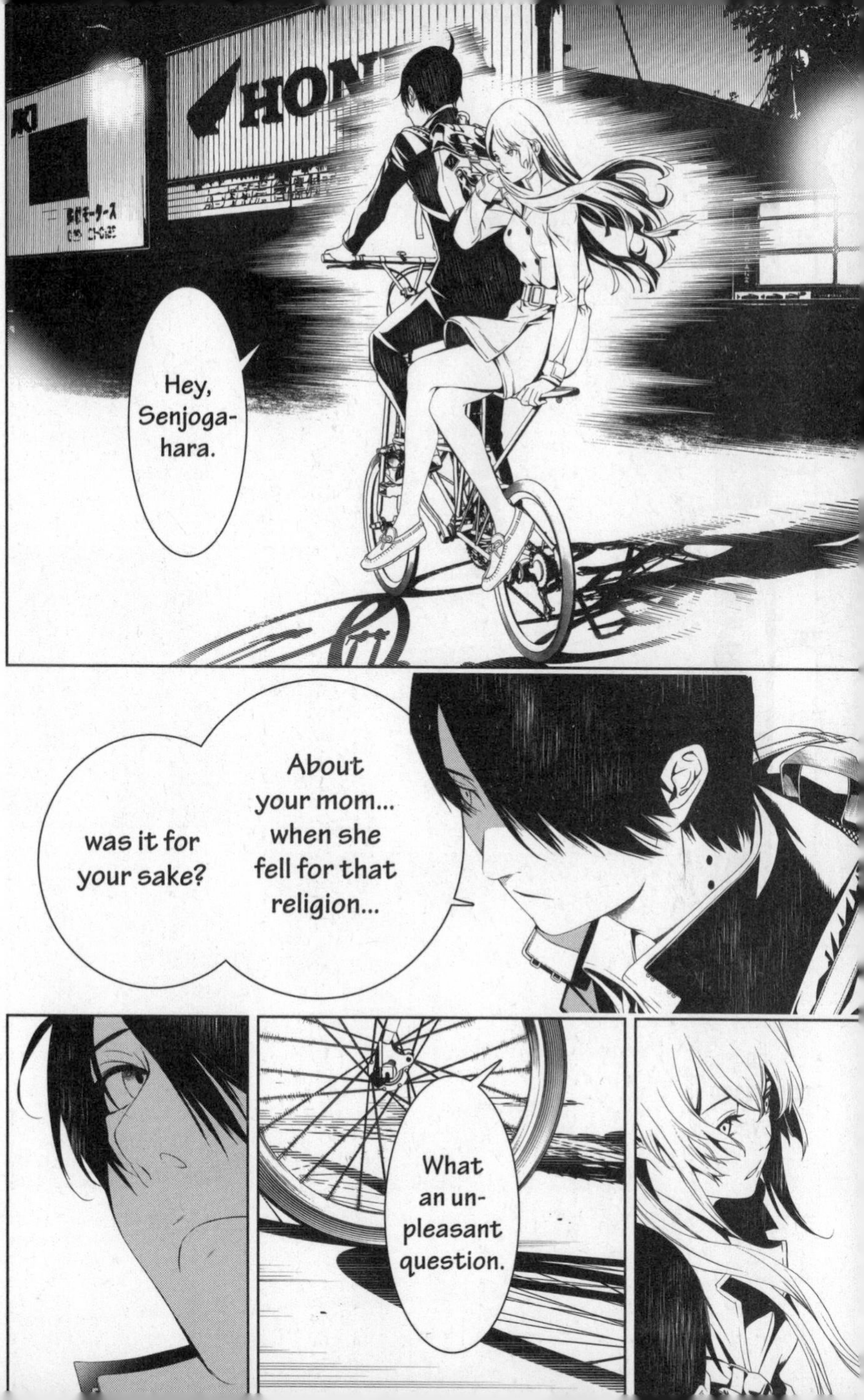
Hey, Senjoga-hara.
About your mom... when she fell for that religion...
was it for your sake?
What an un-pleasant question.

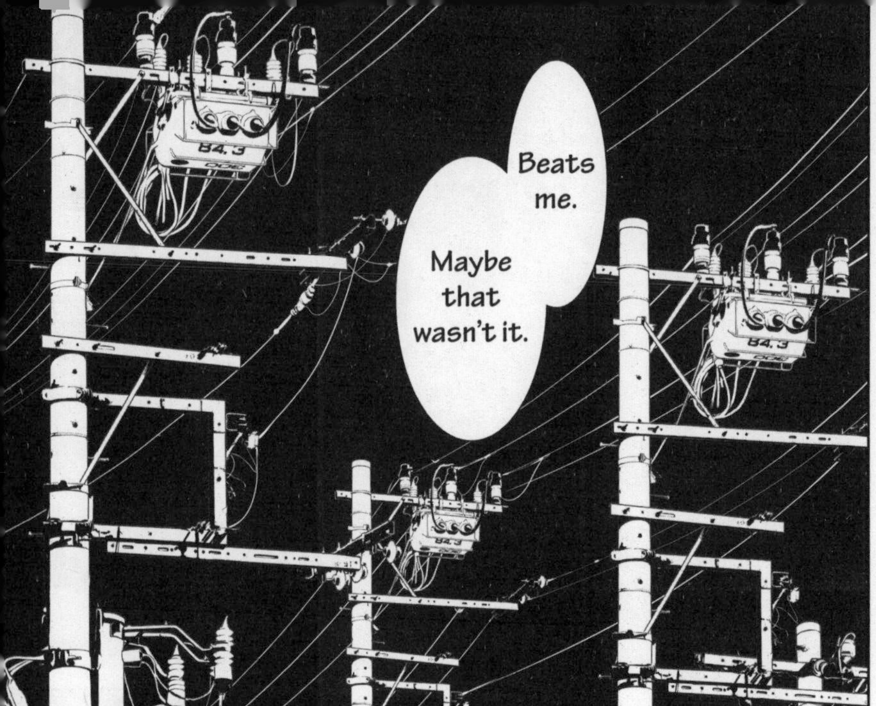
Beats me.
Maybe that wasn't it.

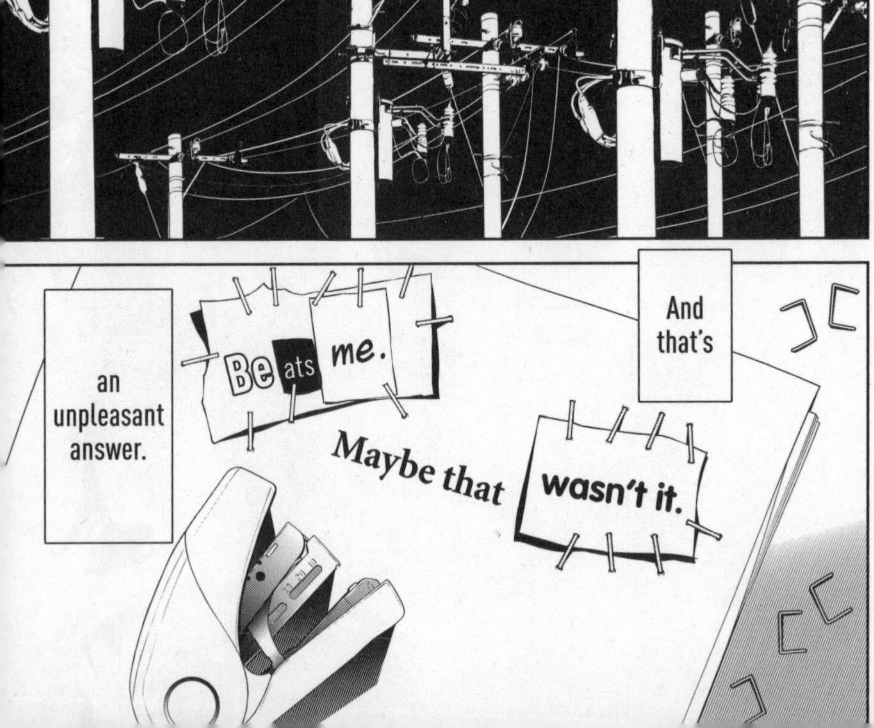
And that's
Beats me.
Maybe that wasn't it.
an unpleasant answer.

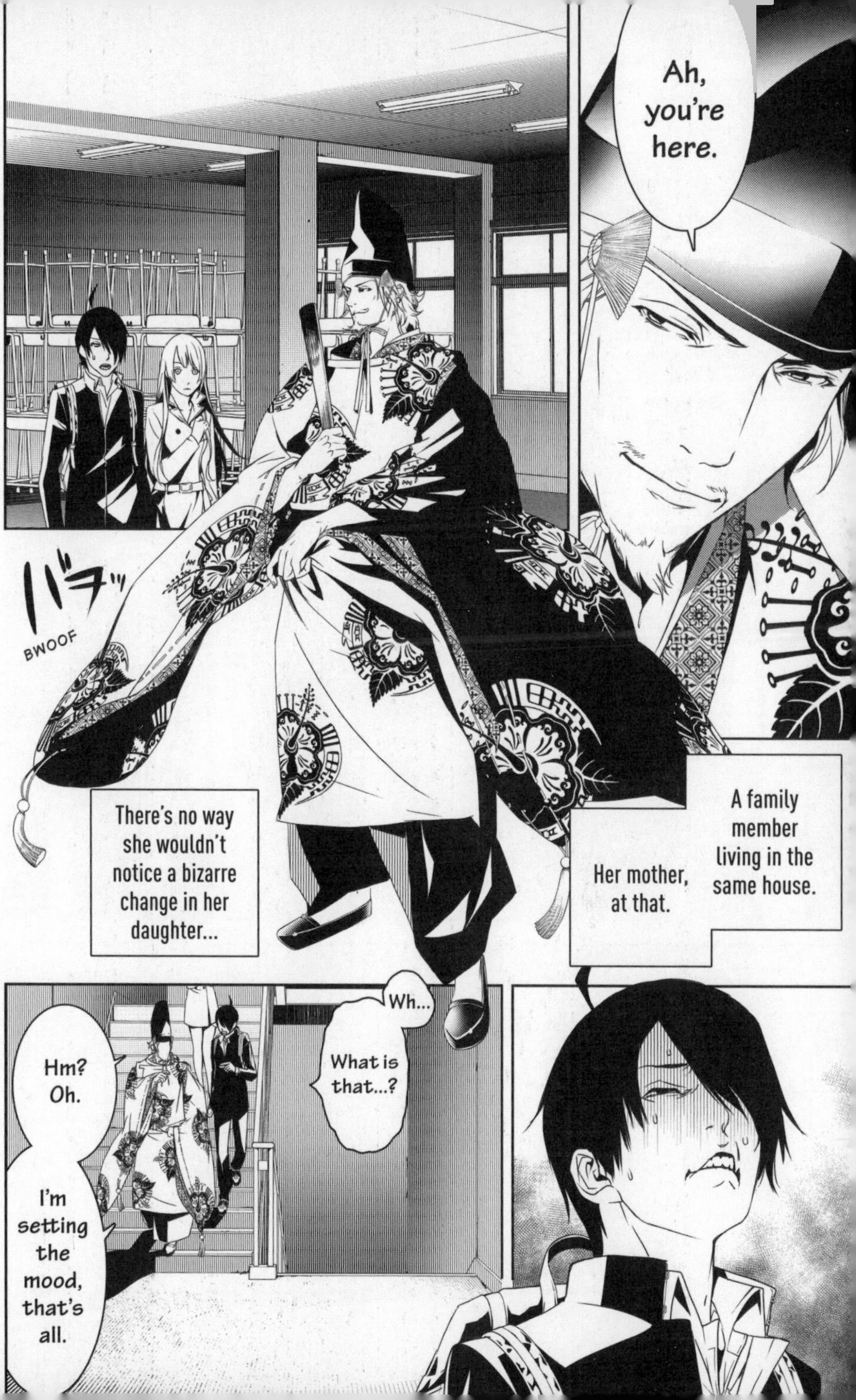

Ah, you're here.
バヲッ
BWOOF
A family member living in the same house.
Her mother, at that.
There's no way she wouldn't notice a bizarre change in her daughter...
Wh...
What is that...?
Hm? Oh.
I'm setting the mood, that's all.

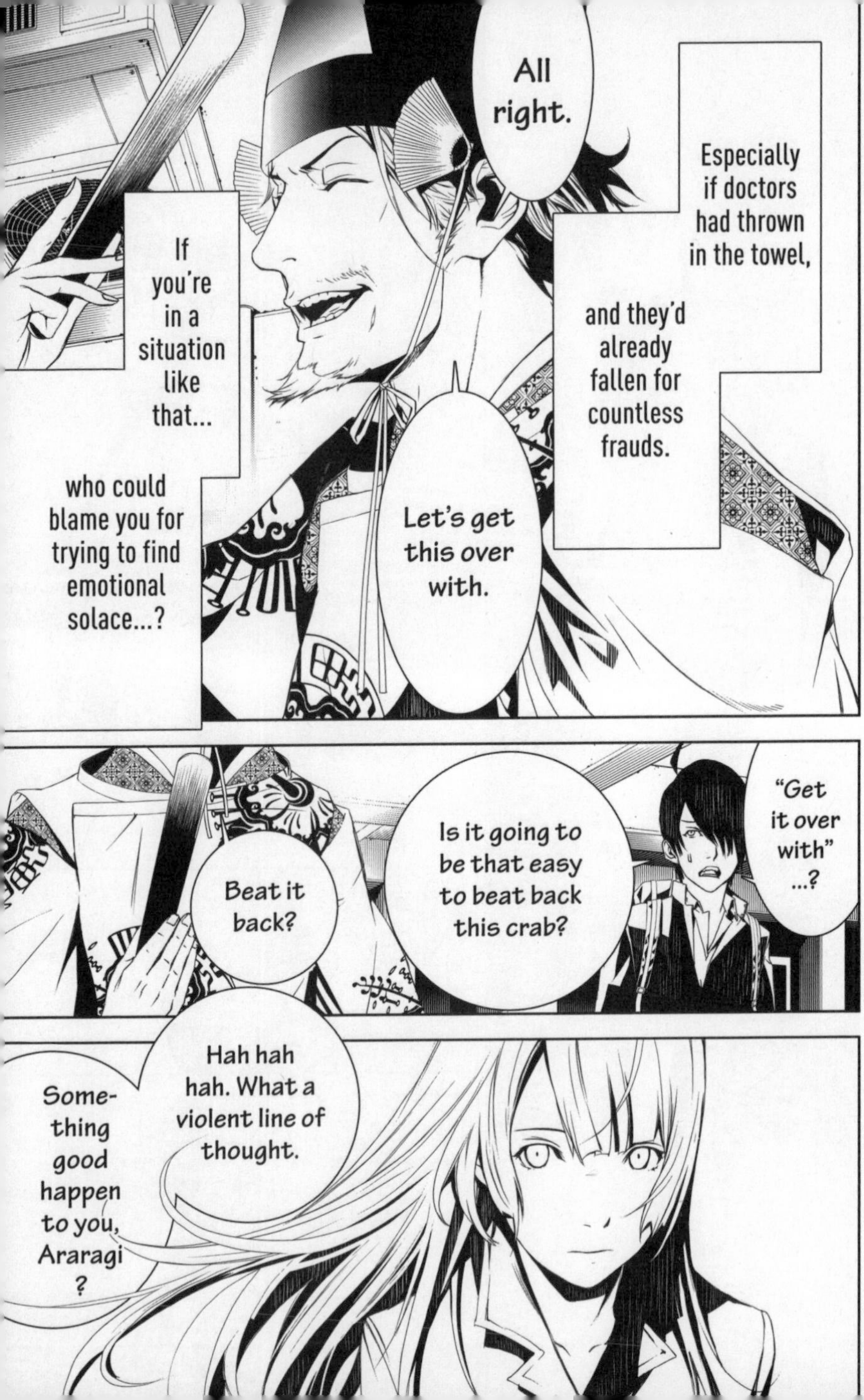
Especially if doctors had thrown in the towel,
and they'd already fallen for countless frauds.
If you're in a situation like that...
who could blame you for trying to find emotional solace...?
All right.
Let's get this over with.
"Get it over with" ...?
Is it going to be that easy to beat back this crab?
Beat it back?
Hah hah hah. What a violent line of thought.
Some-thing good happen to you, Araragi?

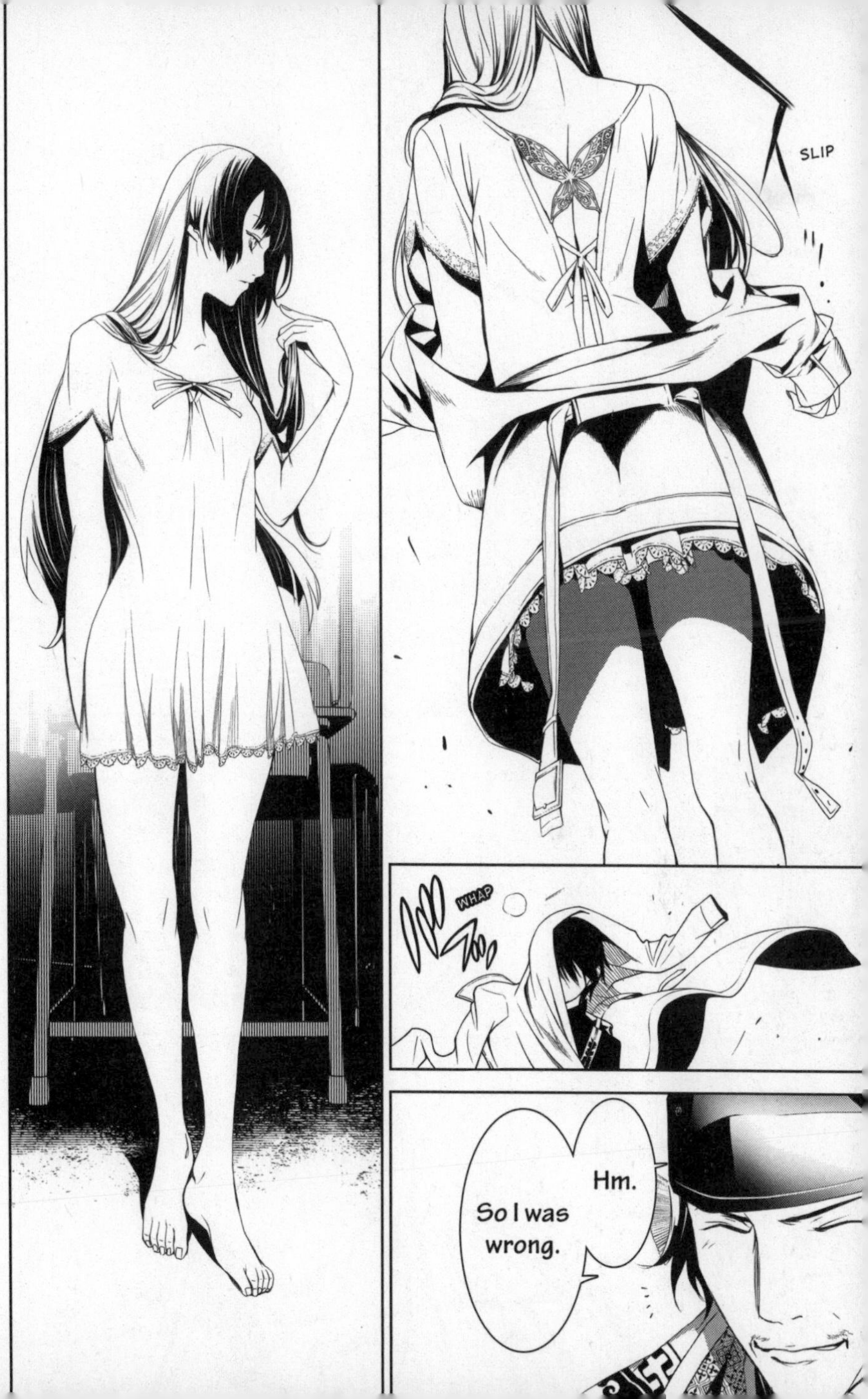
SLIP
WHAP
Hm.
So I was wrong.

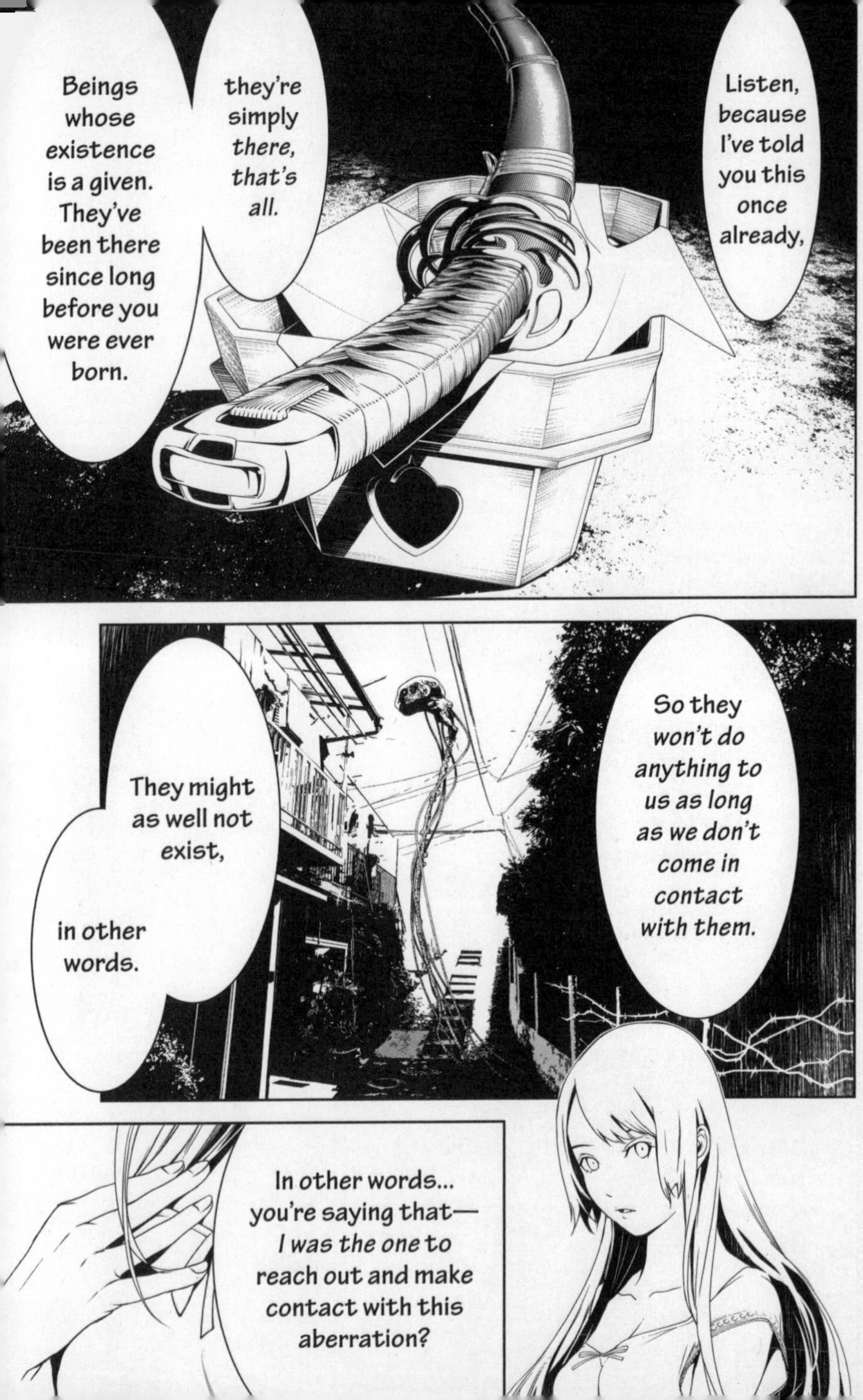
Listen, because I've told you this once already,
they're simply *there, that's all.*
Beings whose existence is a given. They've been there since long before you were ever born.
So they won't do anything to us as long as we don't come in contact with them.
They might as well not exist,
in other words.
In other words... you're saying that— *I was the one to* reach out and make contact with this aberration?

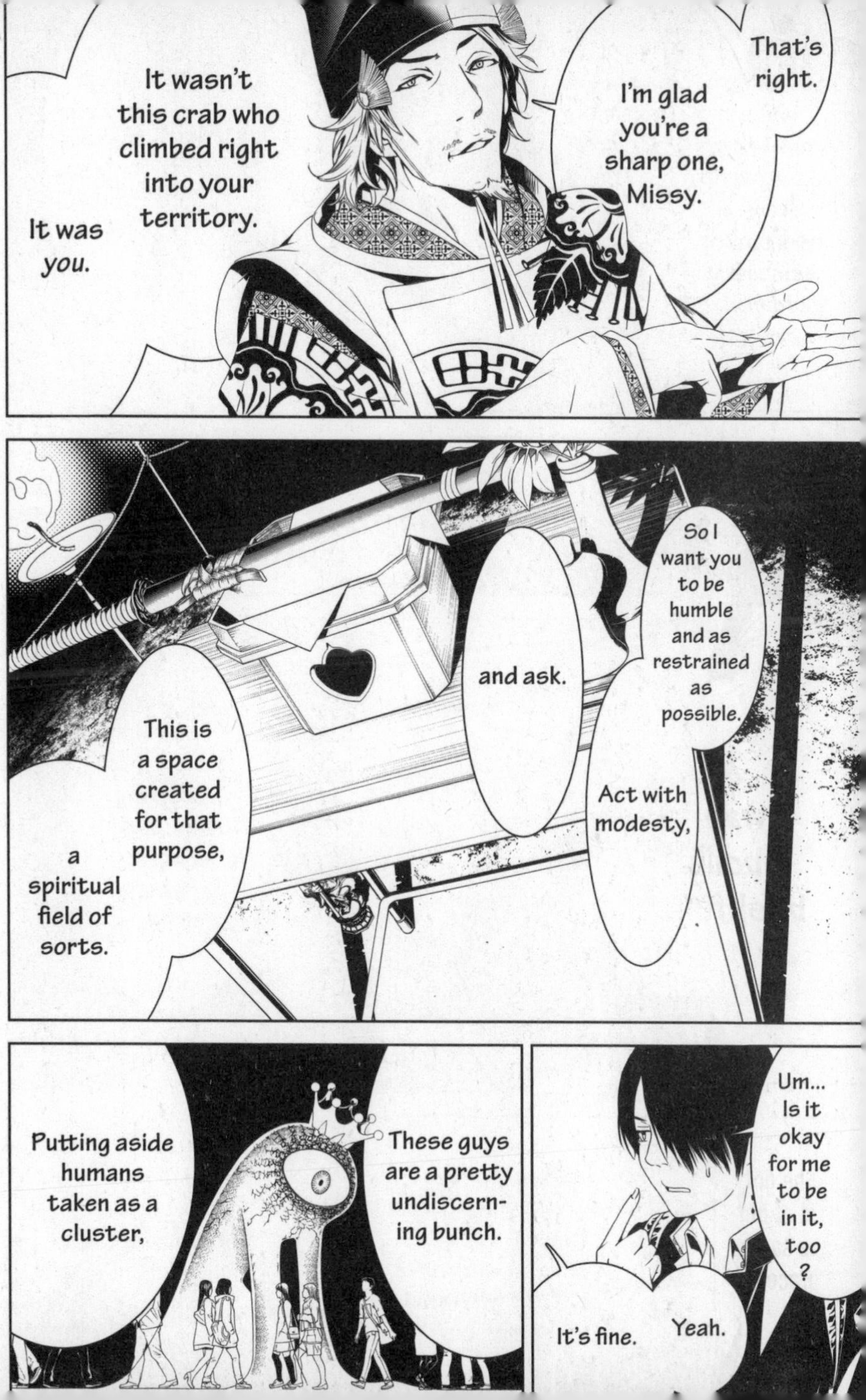
That's right.
I'm glad you're a sharp one, Missy.
It wasn't this crab who climbed right into your territory.
It was you.
So I want you to be humble and as restrained as possible.
Act with modesty,
and ask.
This is a space created for that purpose,
a spiritual field of sorts.
Um... Is it okay for me to be in it, too?
Yeah.
It's fine.
These guys are a pretty undiscern-ing bunch.
Putting aside humans taken as a cluster,

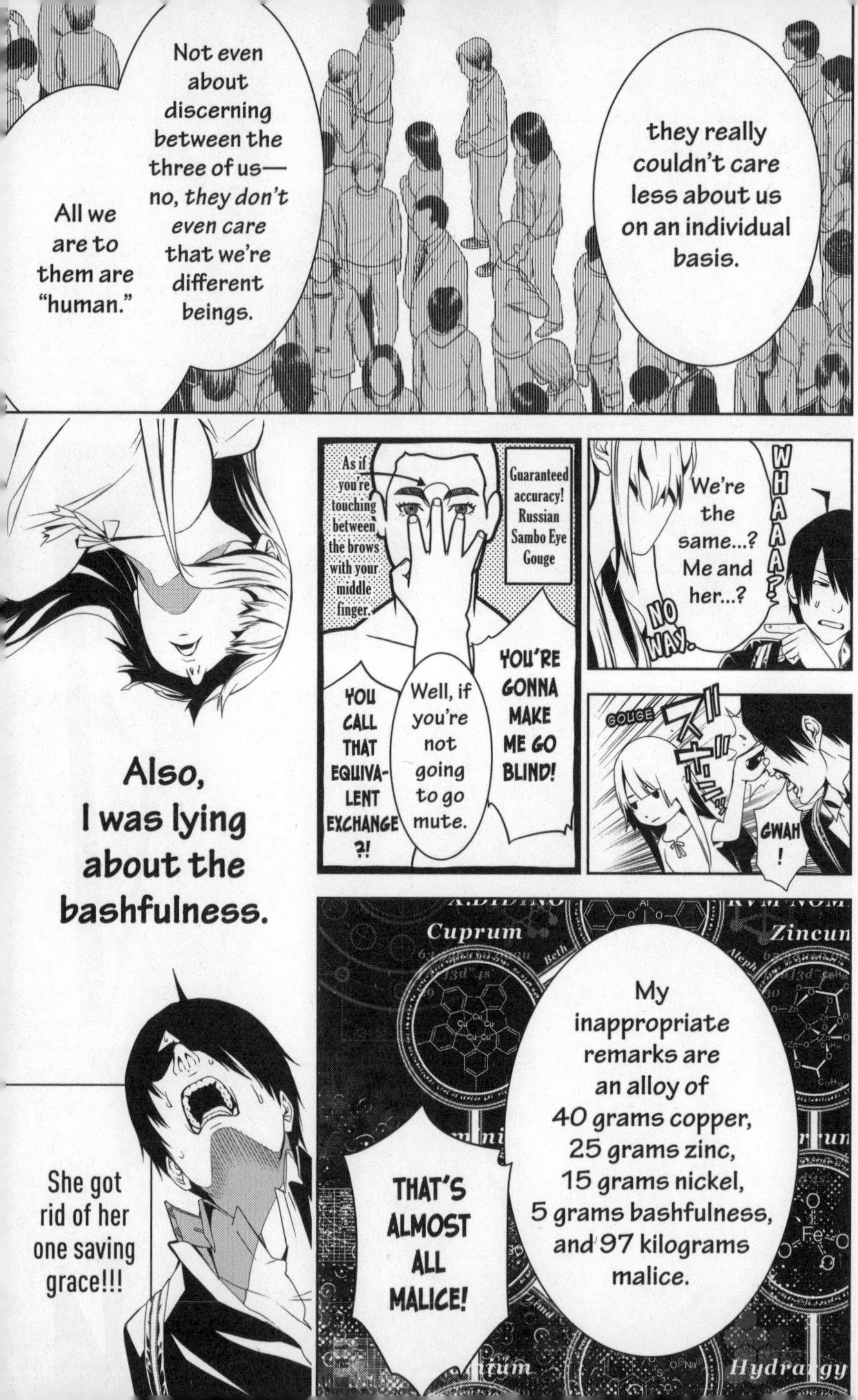
they really couldn't care less about us on an individual basis.
Not even about discerning between the three of us— no, *they don't even care* that we're different beings.
All we are to them are "human."
WHAAAA?!
We're the same...? Me and her...?
NO WAY.
GOUGE
GWAH!
Guaranteed accuracy! Russian Sambo Eye Gouge
As if you're touching between the brows with your middle finger.
YOU'RE GONNA MAKE ME GO BLIND!
Well, if you're not going to go mute.
YOU CALL THAT EQUIVALENT EXCHANGE?!
Also, I was lying about the bashfulness.
Cuprum
My inappropriate remarks are an alloy of 40 grams copper, 25 grams zinc, 15 grams nickel, 5 grams bashfulness, and 97 kilograms malice.
THAT'S ALMOST ALL MALICE!
She got rid of her one saving grace!!!

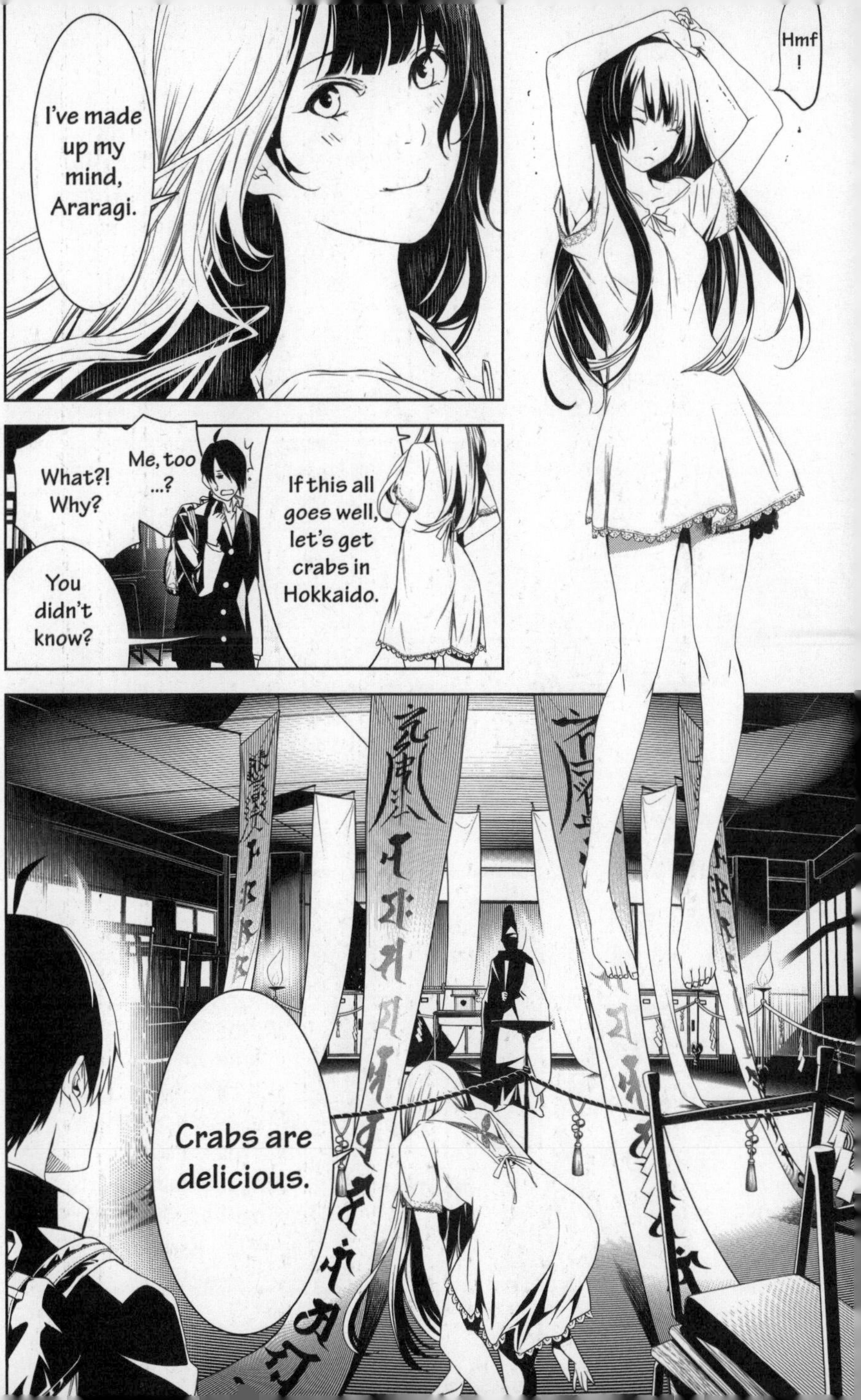
Hmf
!
I've made up my mind, Araragi.
If this all goes well, let's get crabs in Hokkaido.
Me, too ...?
What?! Why?
You didn't know?
Crabs are delicious.

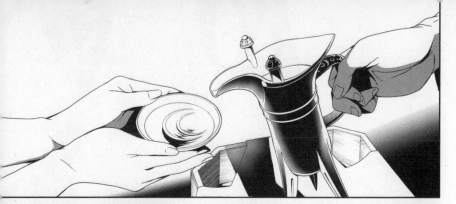

HOO

Start by
letting your
guard down.

Relax.

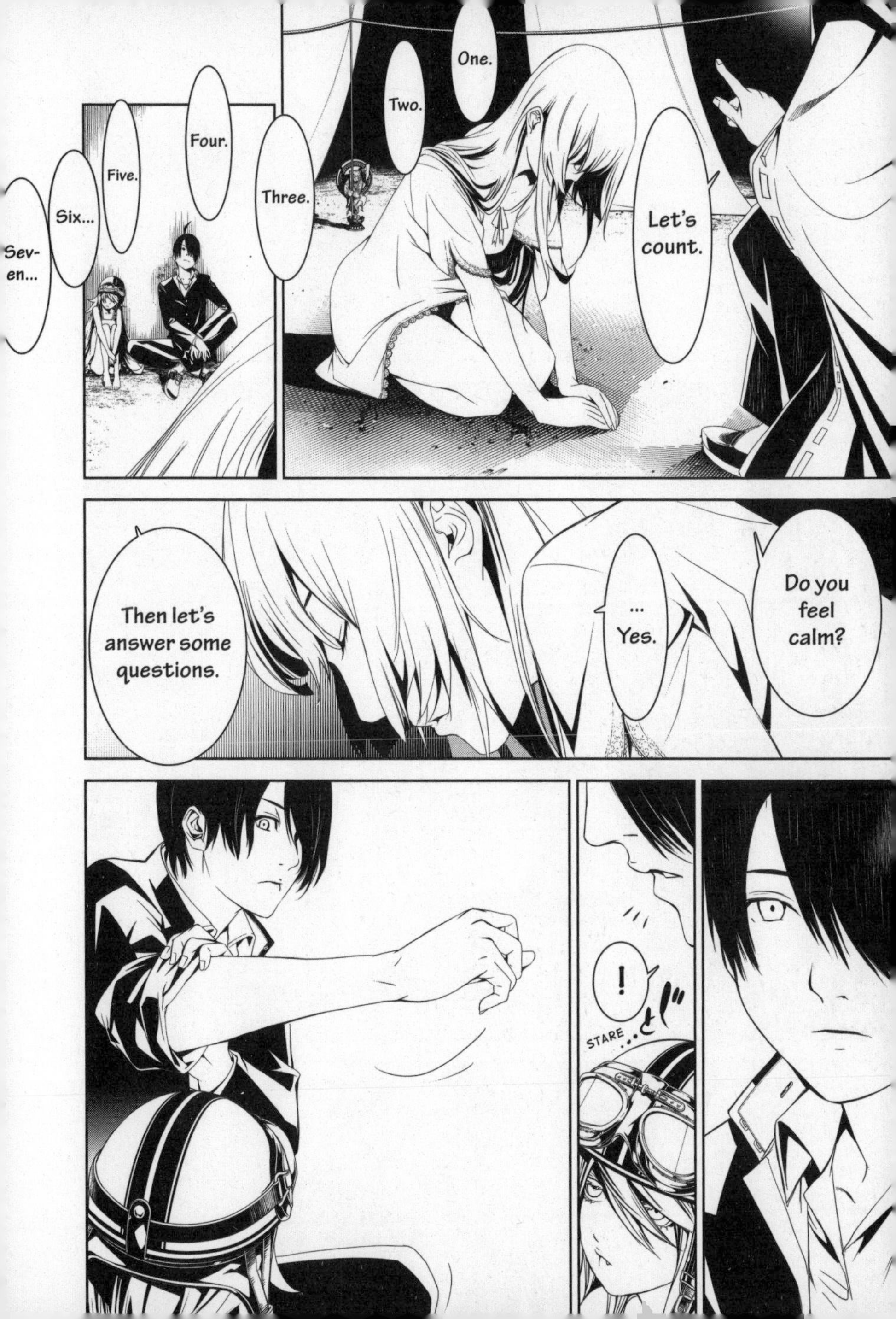
Let's count.
One.
Two.
Three.
Four.
Five.
Six...
Sev-en...
Do you feel calm?
... Yes.
Then let's answer some questions.
!
STARE

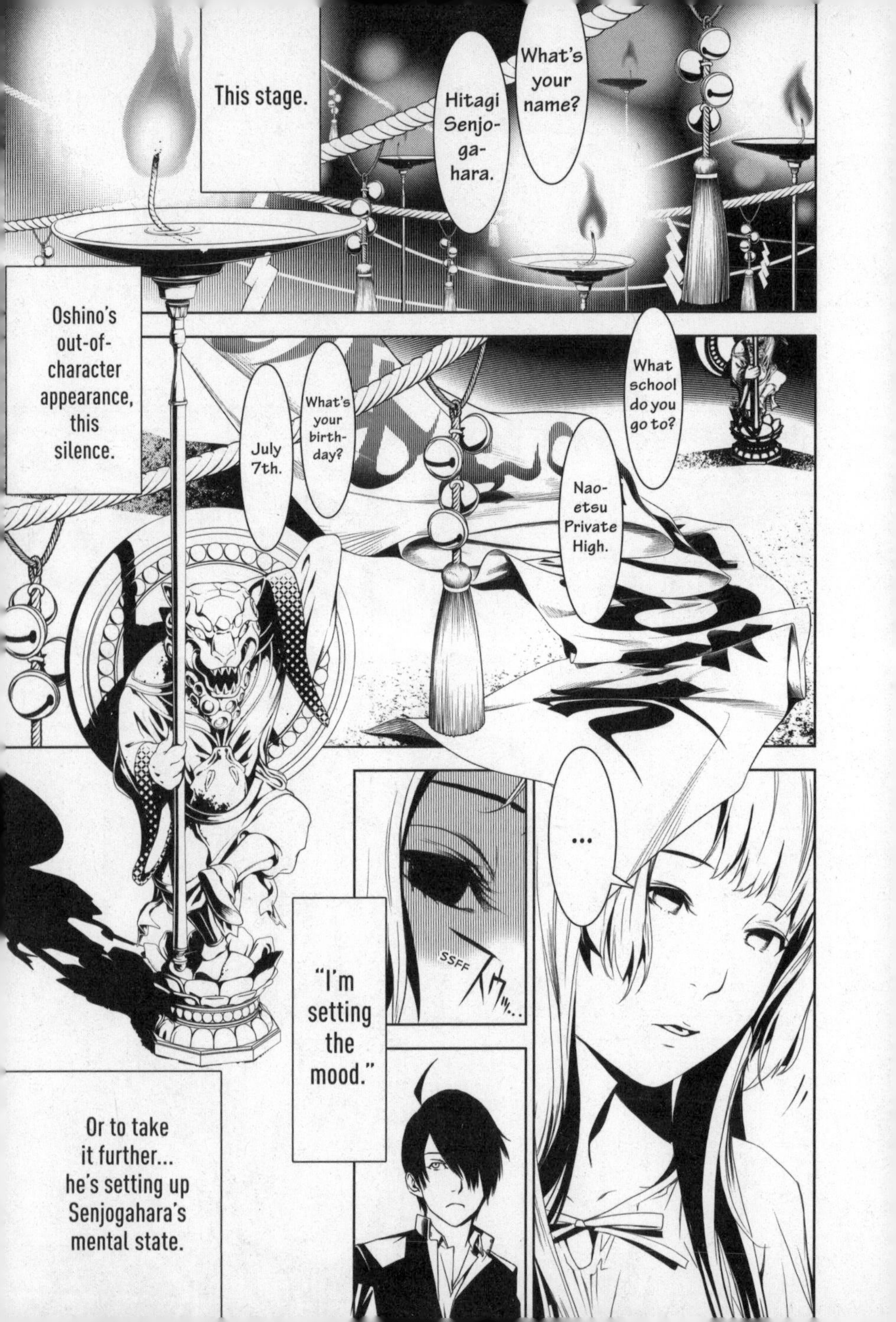
What's your name?
Hitagi Senjo-ga-hara.
This stage.
What school do you go to?
Nao-etsu Private High.
What's your birth-day?
July 7th.
Oshino's out-of-character appearance, this silence.
...
SSFF
"I'm setting the mood."
Or to take it further... he's setting up Senjogahara's mental state.

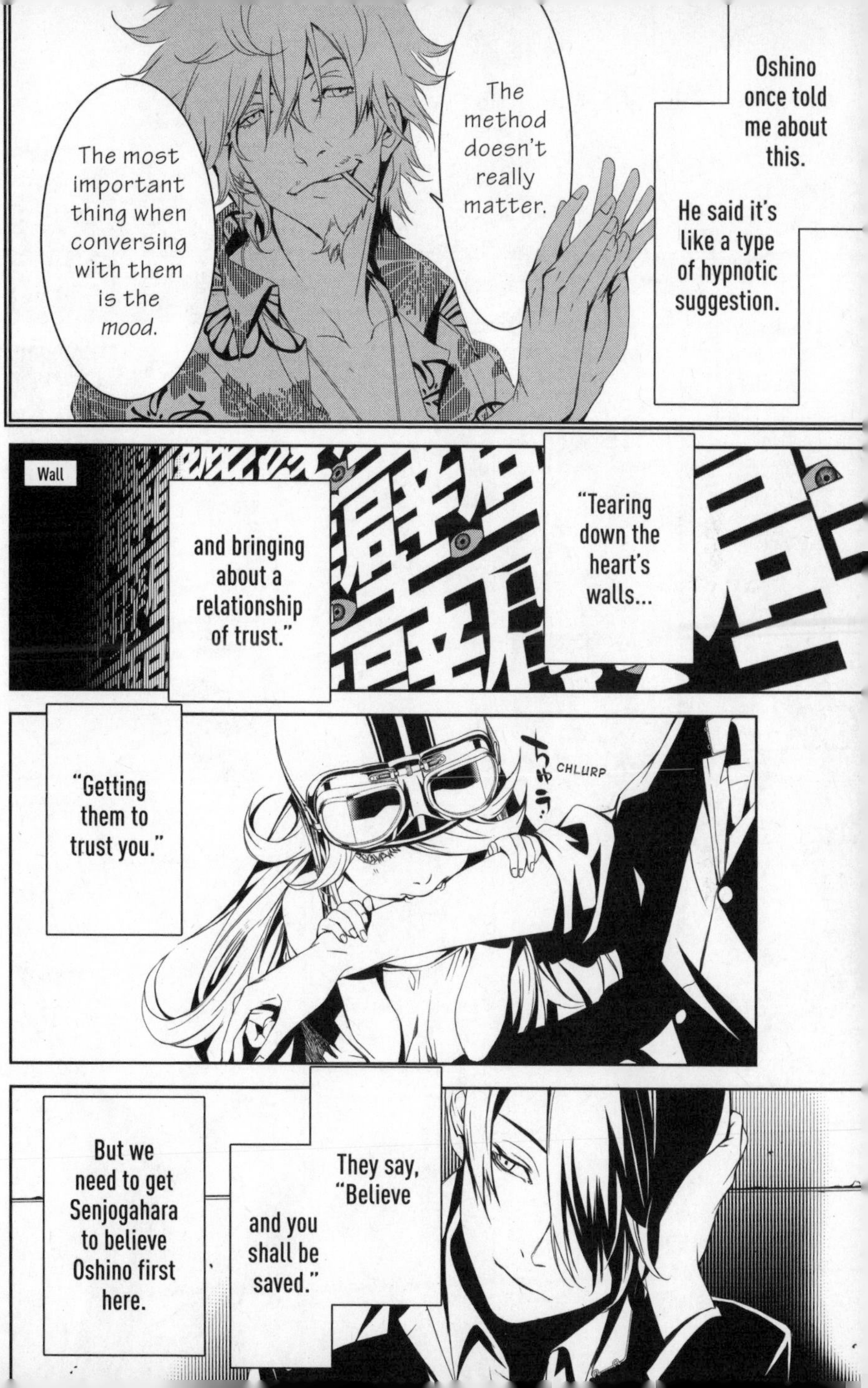

Oshino once told me about this.
He said it's like a type of hypnotic suggestion.
The method doesn't really matter.
The most important thing when conversing with them is the *mood*.
"Tearing down the heart's walls...
and bringing about a relationship of trust."
Wall
CHLURP
"Getting them to trust you."
They say, "Believe
and you shall be saved."
But we need to get Senjogahara to believe Oshino first here.

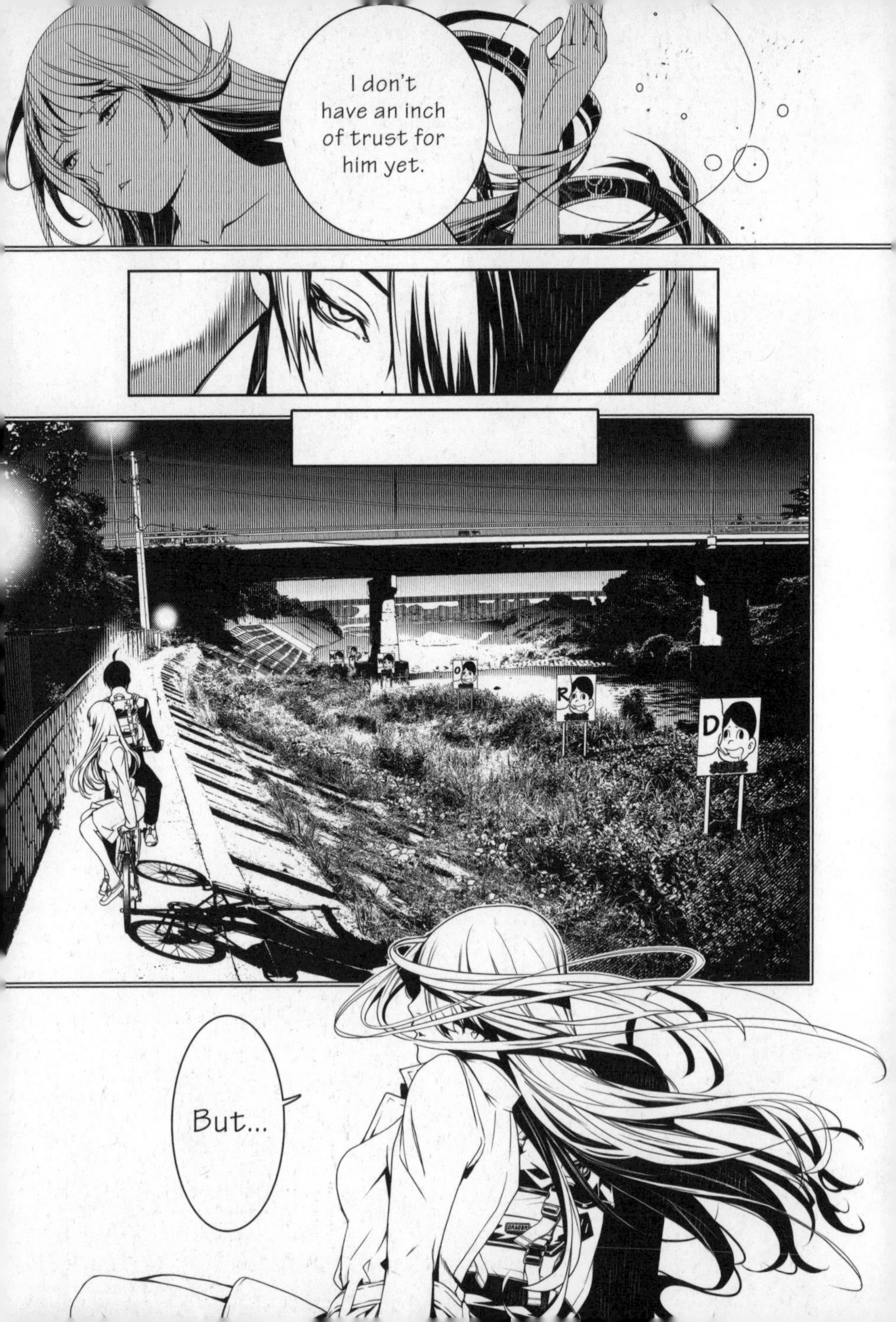
I don't have an inch of trust for him yet.
But...

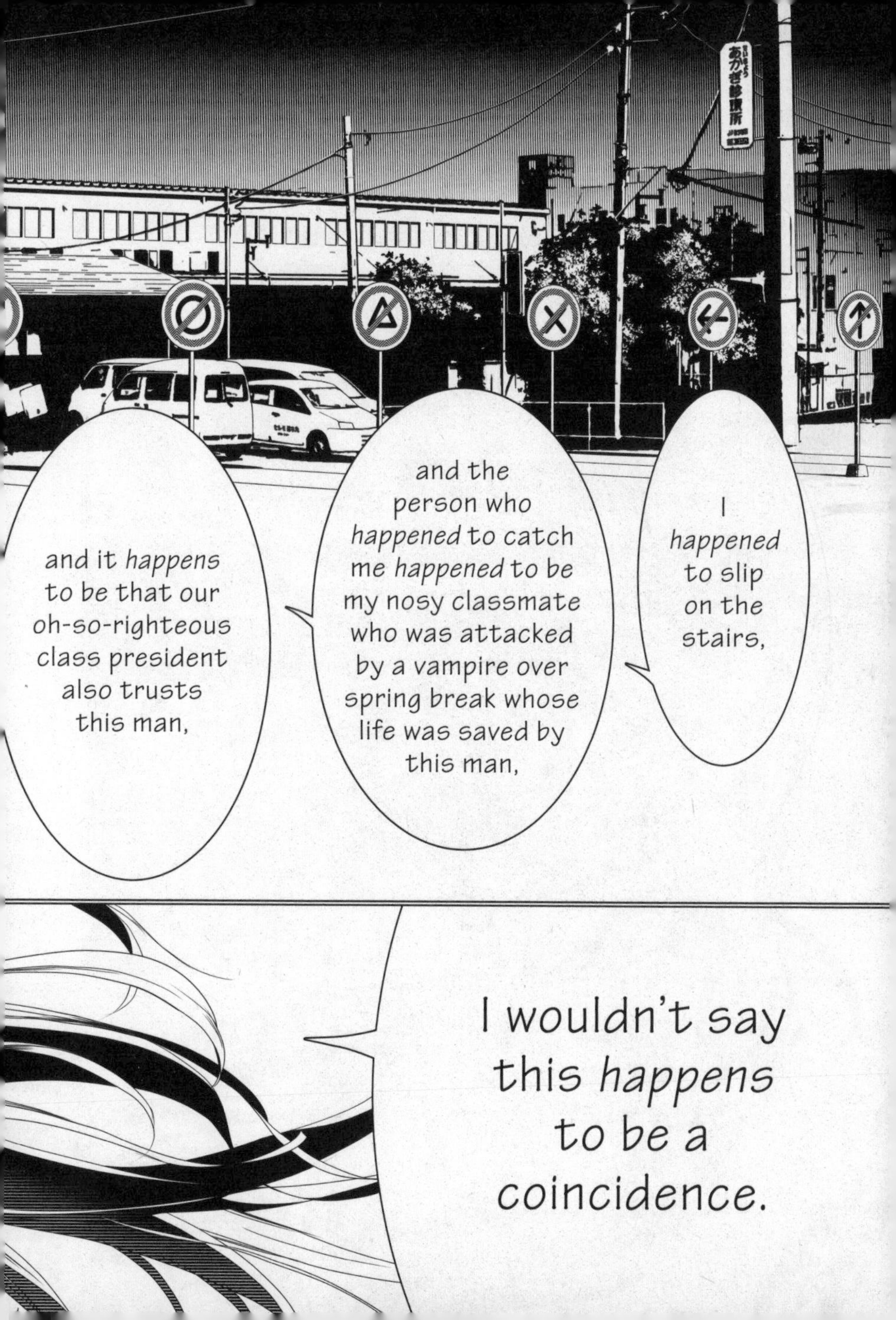
I *happened* to slip on the stairs,
and the person who *happened* to catch me *happened* to be my nosy classmate who was attacked by a vampire over spring break whose life was saved by this man,
and it *happens* to be that our oh-so-righteous class president also trusts this man,
I wouldn't say this *happens* to be a coincidence.

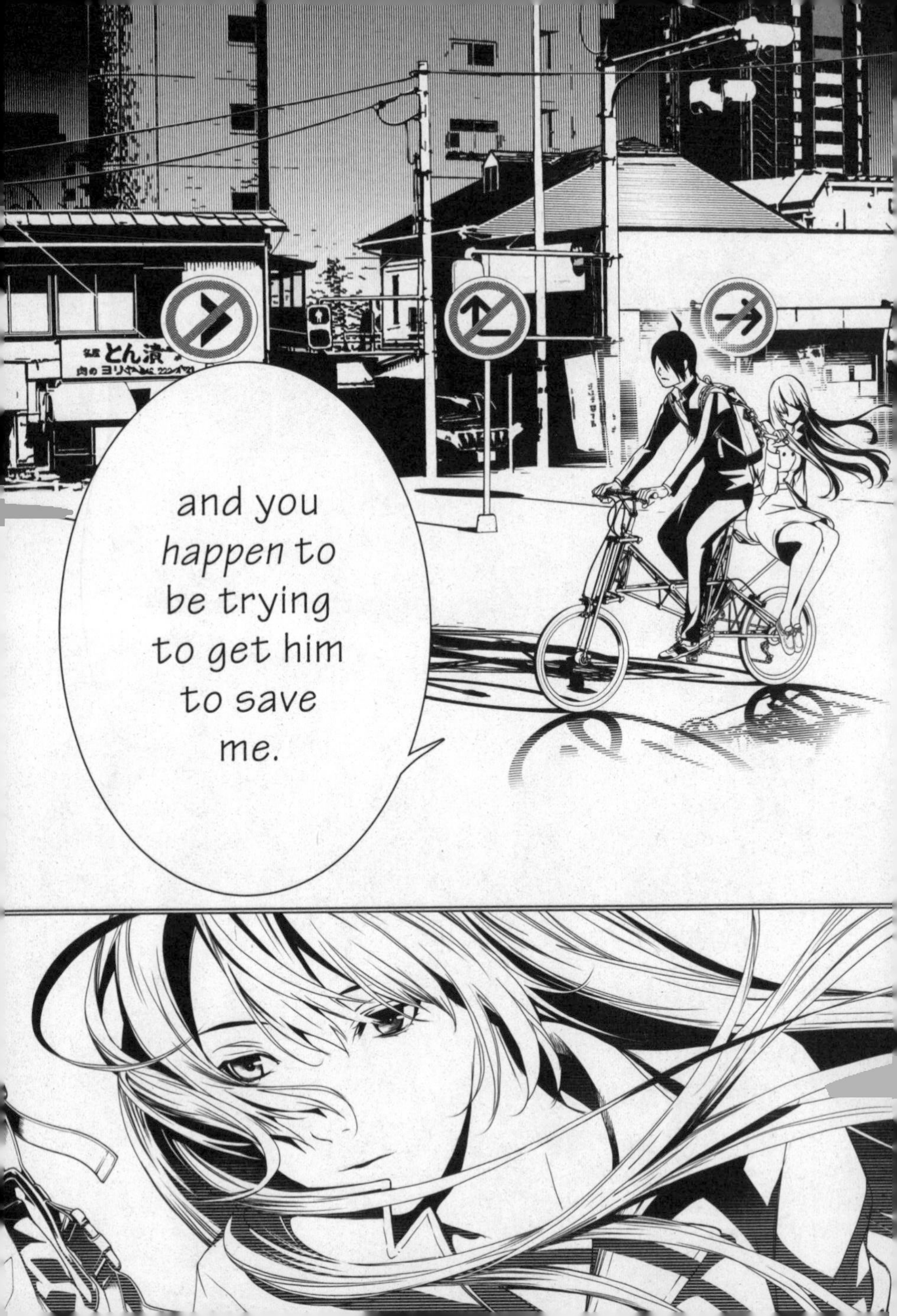
とん漬
and you *happen* to be trying to get him to save me.

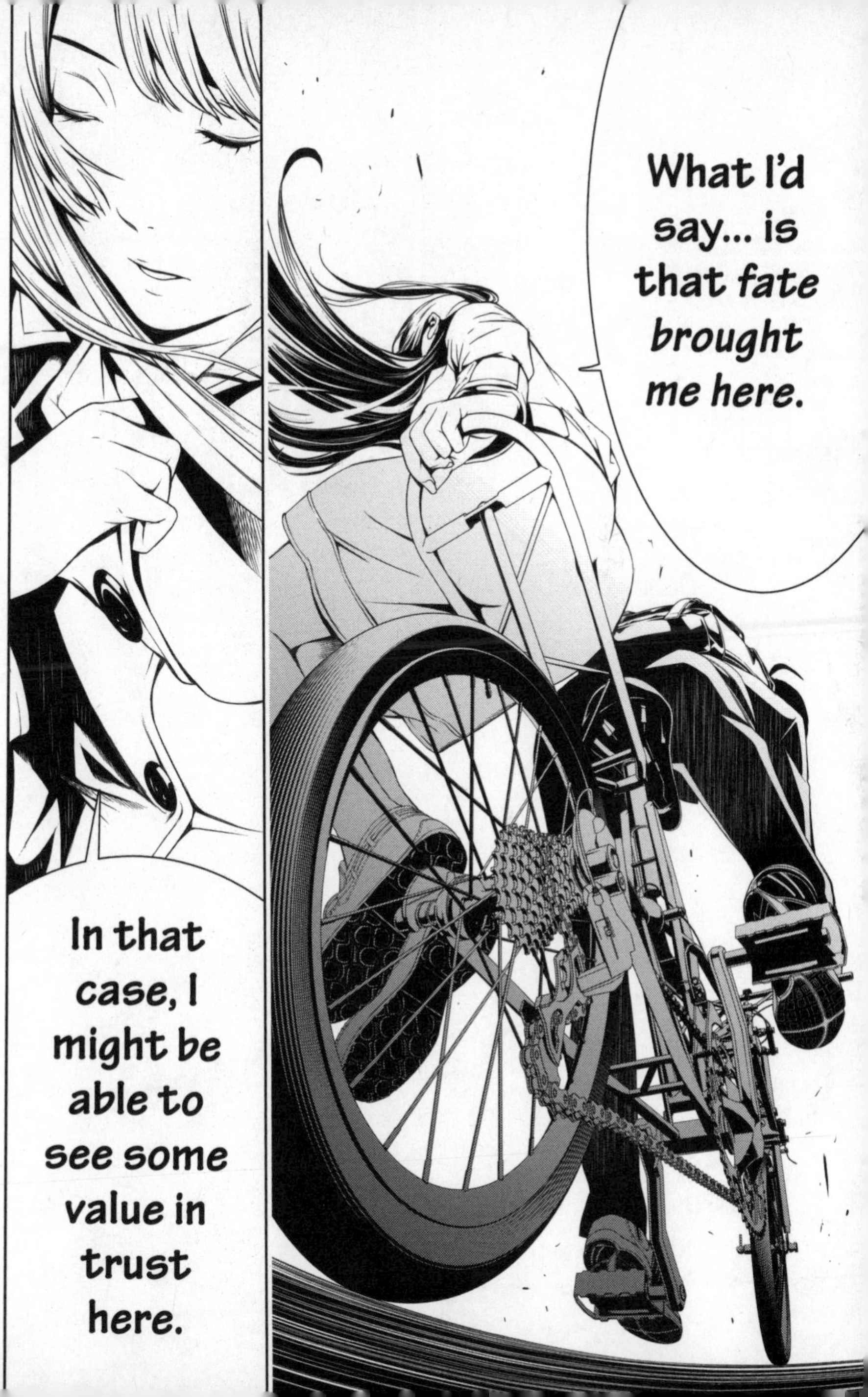
What I'd say... is that fate brought me here.
In that case, I might be able to see some value in trust here.

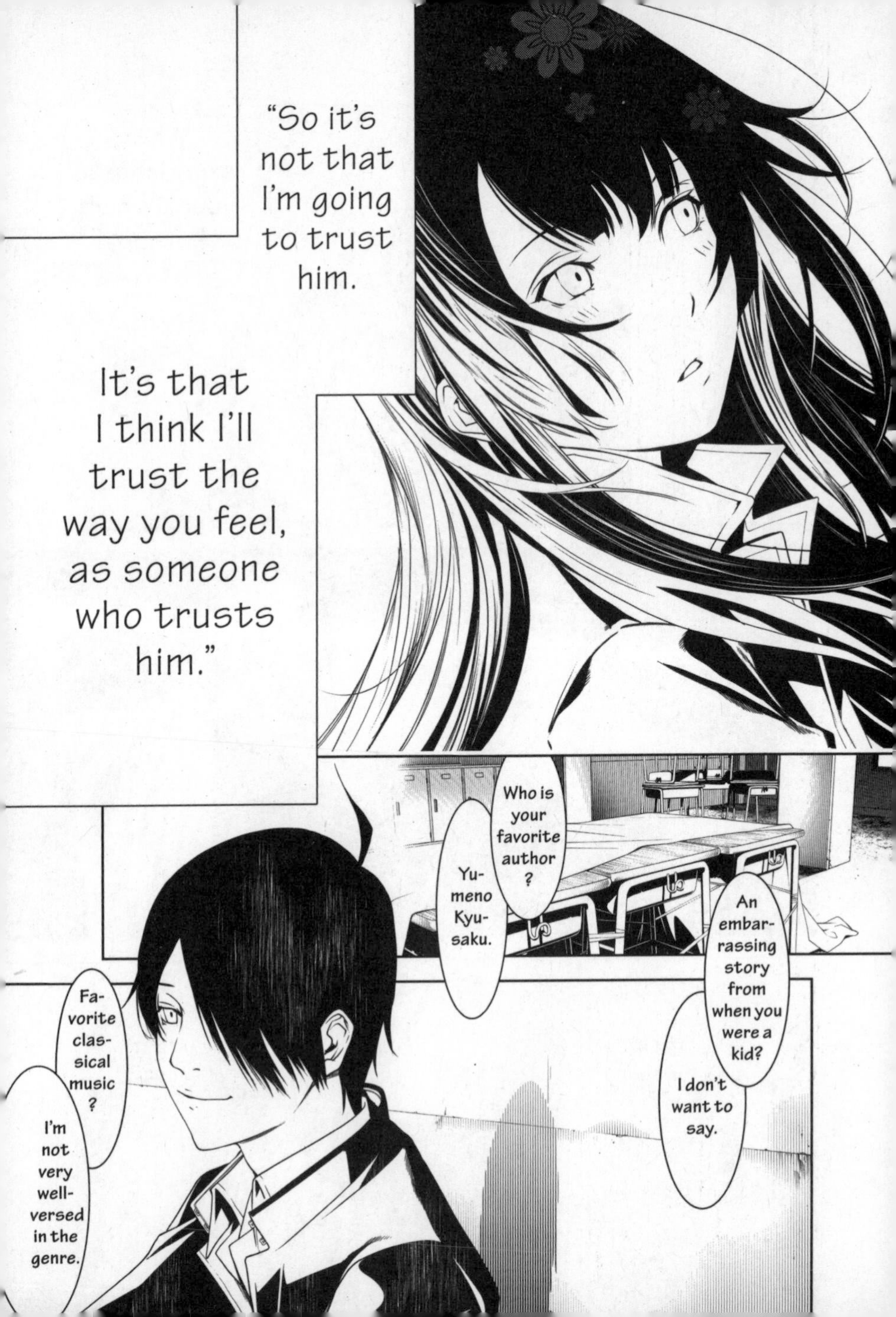
"So it's not that I'm going to trust him.
It's that I think I'll trust the way you feel, as someone who trusts him."
Who is your favorite author?
Yumeno Kyusaku.
An embarrassing story from when you were a kid?
I don't want to say.
Favorite classical music?
I'm not very well-versed in the genre.

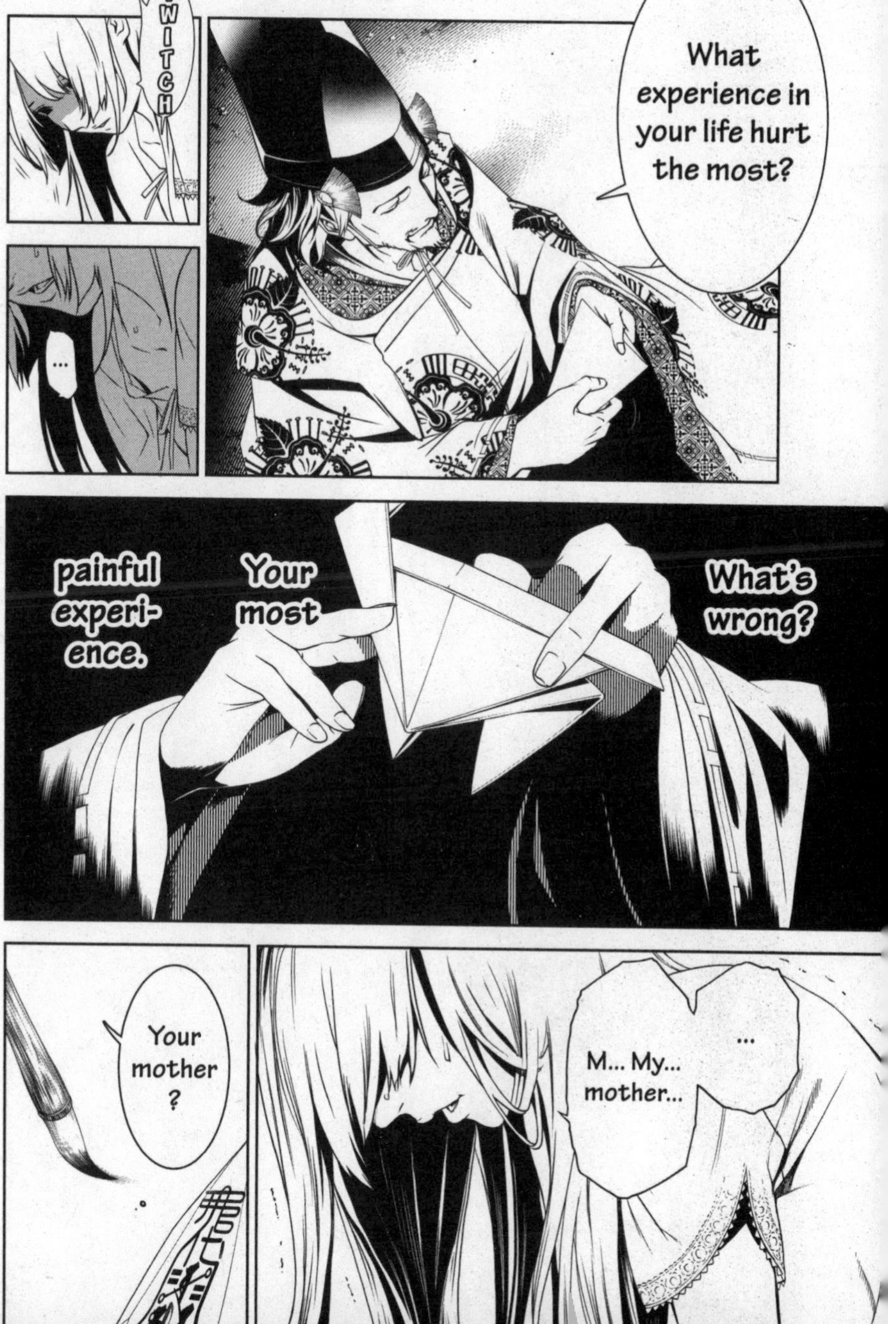
What experience in your life hurt the most?
TWITCH
...
What's wrong?
Your most
painful experi-ence.
...
M... My... mother...
Your mother?

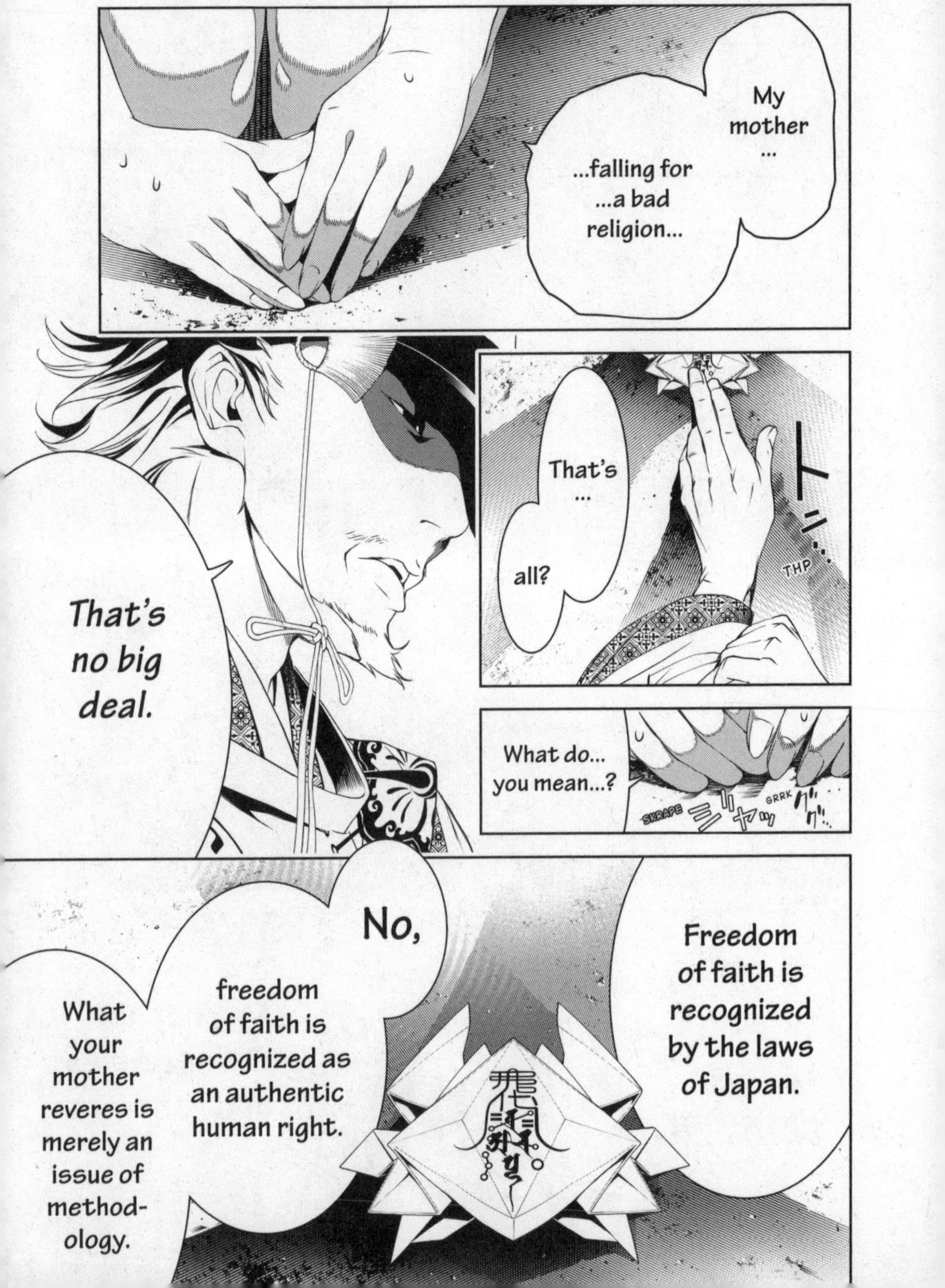
My mother...
...falling for ...a bad religion...
That's... all?
THP
What do... you mean...?
GRRK
SKRAPE
That's no big deal.
Freedom of faith is recognized by the laws of Japan.
No,
freedom of faith is recognized as an authentic human right.
What your mother reveres is merely an issue of methodology.

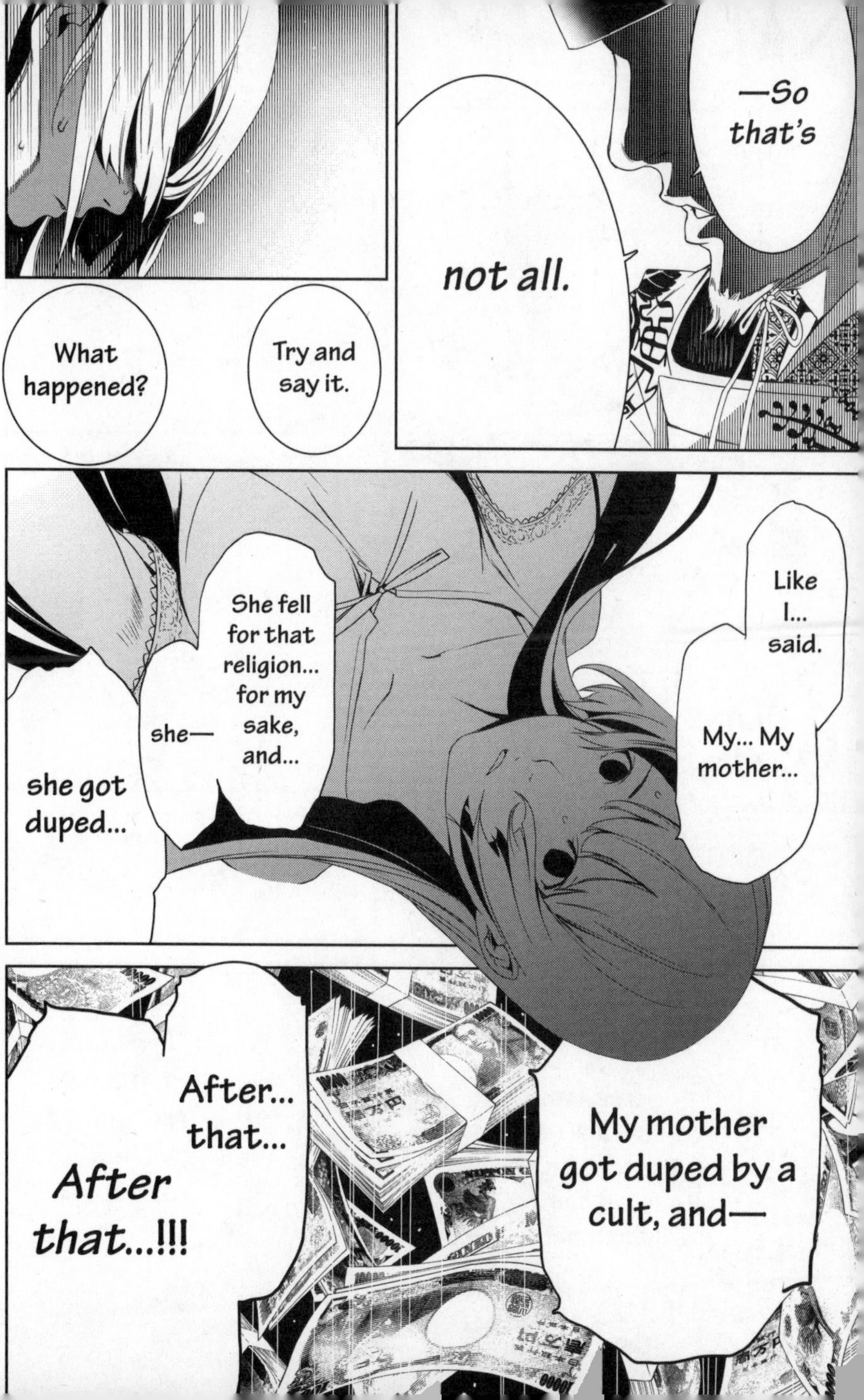
—So that's not all.
Try and say it.
What happened?
Like I... said.
My... My mother...
She fell for that religion... for my sake, and...
she—
she got duped...
My mother got duped by a cult, and—
After... that...
After that...!!!

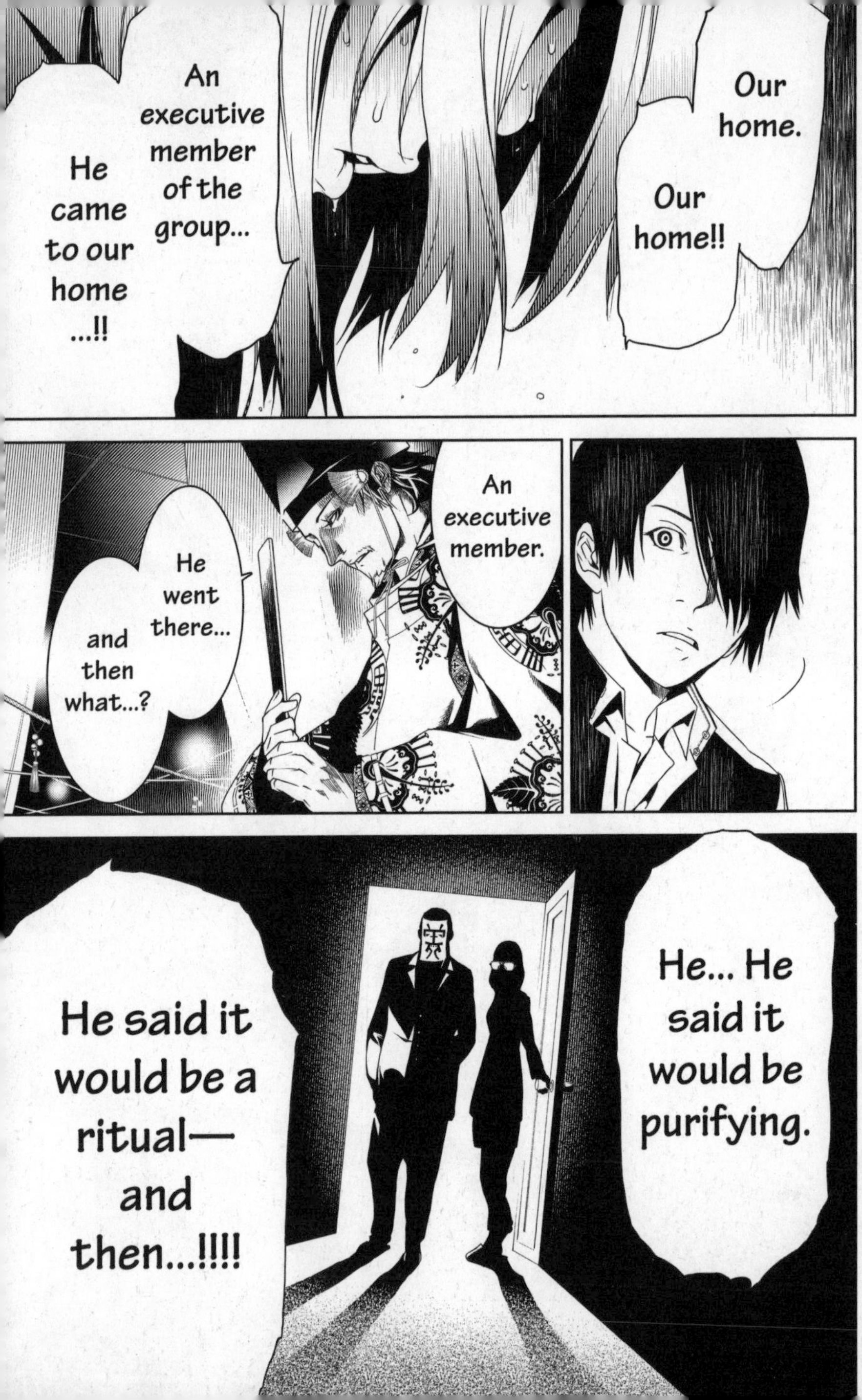
Our home.
Our home!!
An executive member of the group...
He came to our home ...!!
An executive member.
He went there...
and then what...?
He... He said it would be purifying.
He said it would be a ritual— and then...!!!!

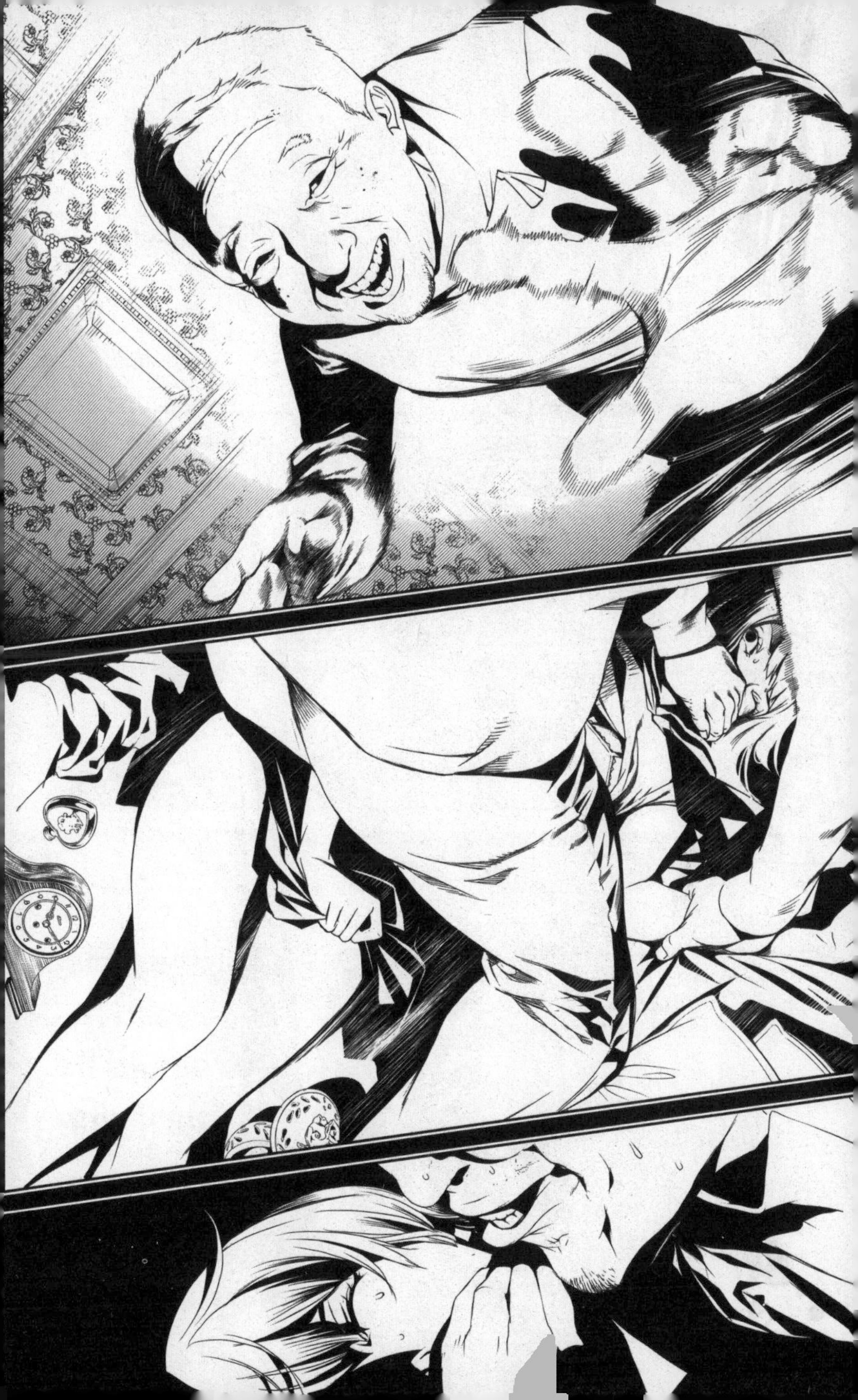

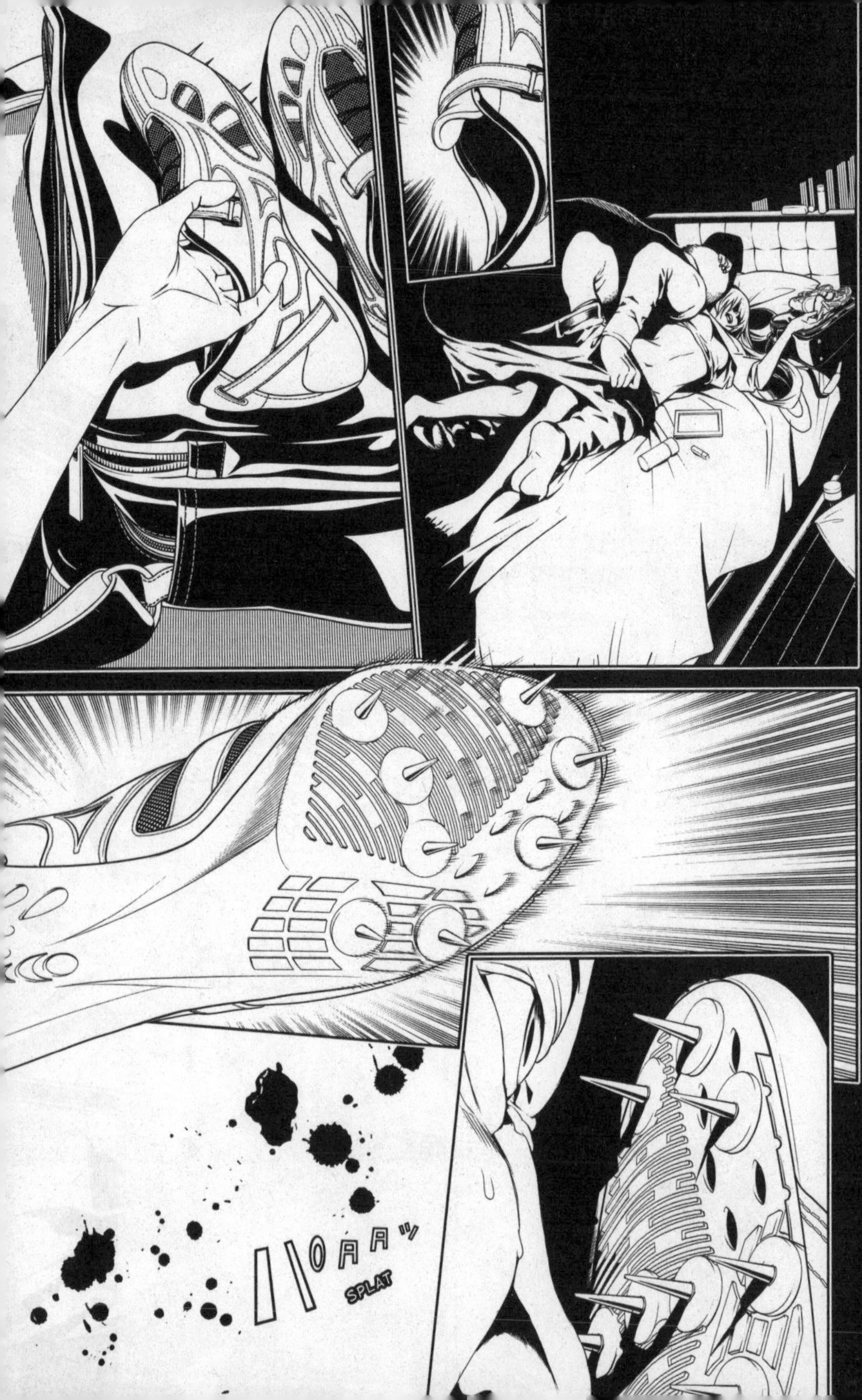
SPLAT

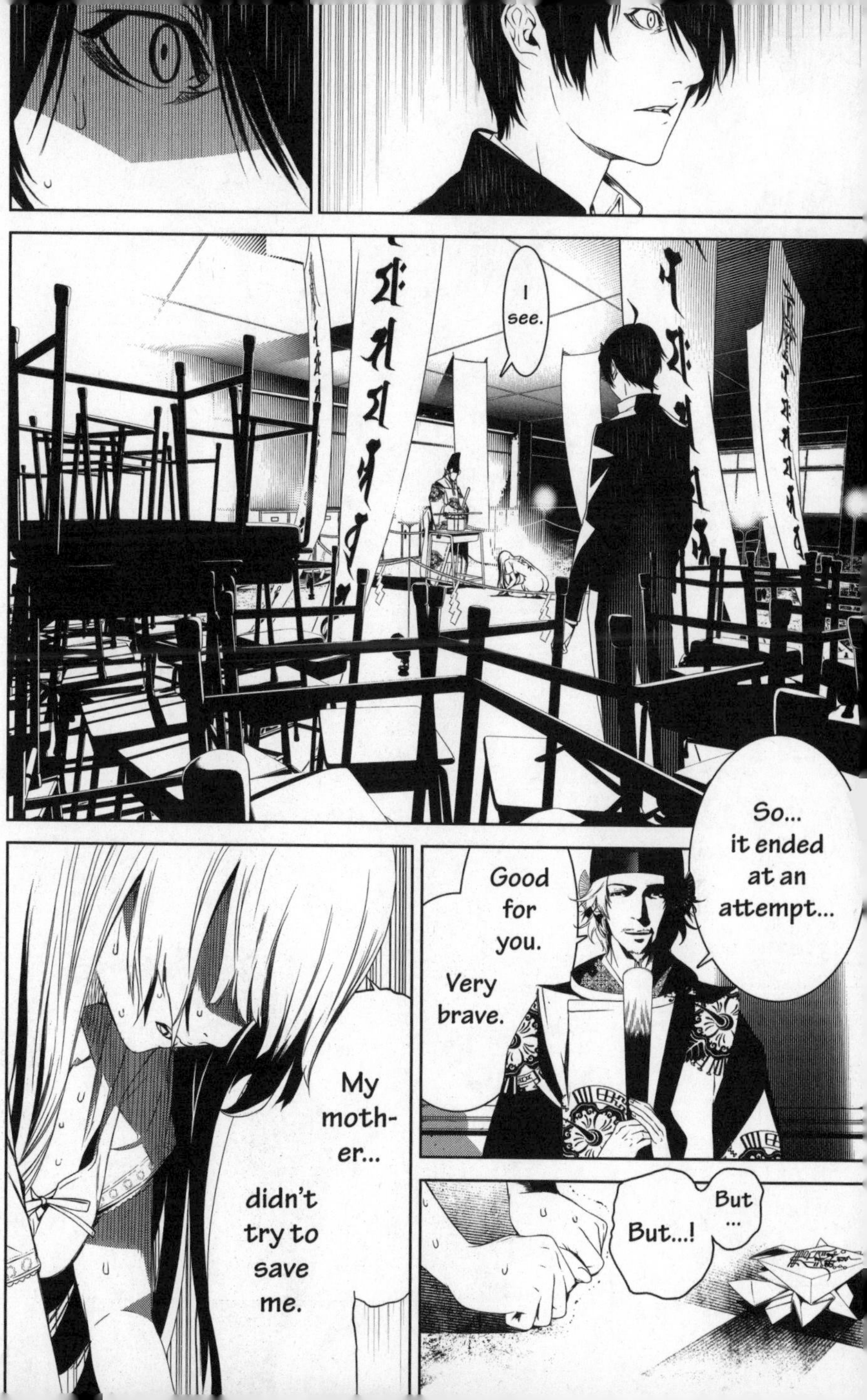
I see.
So... it ended at an attempt...
Good for you.
Very brave.
But ...
But...!
My moth- er...
didn't try to save me.

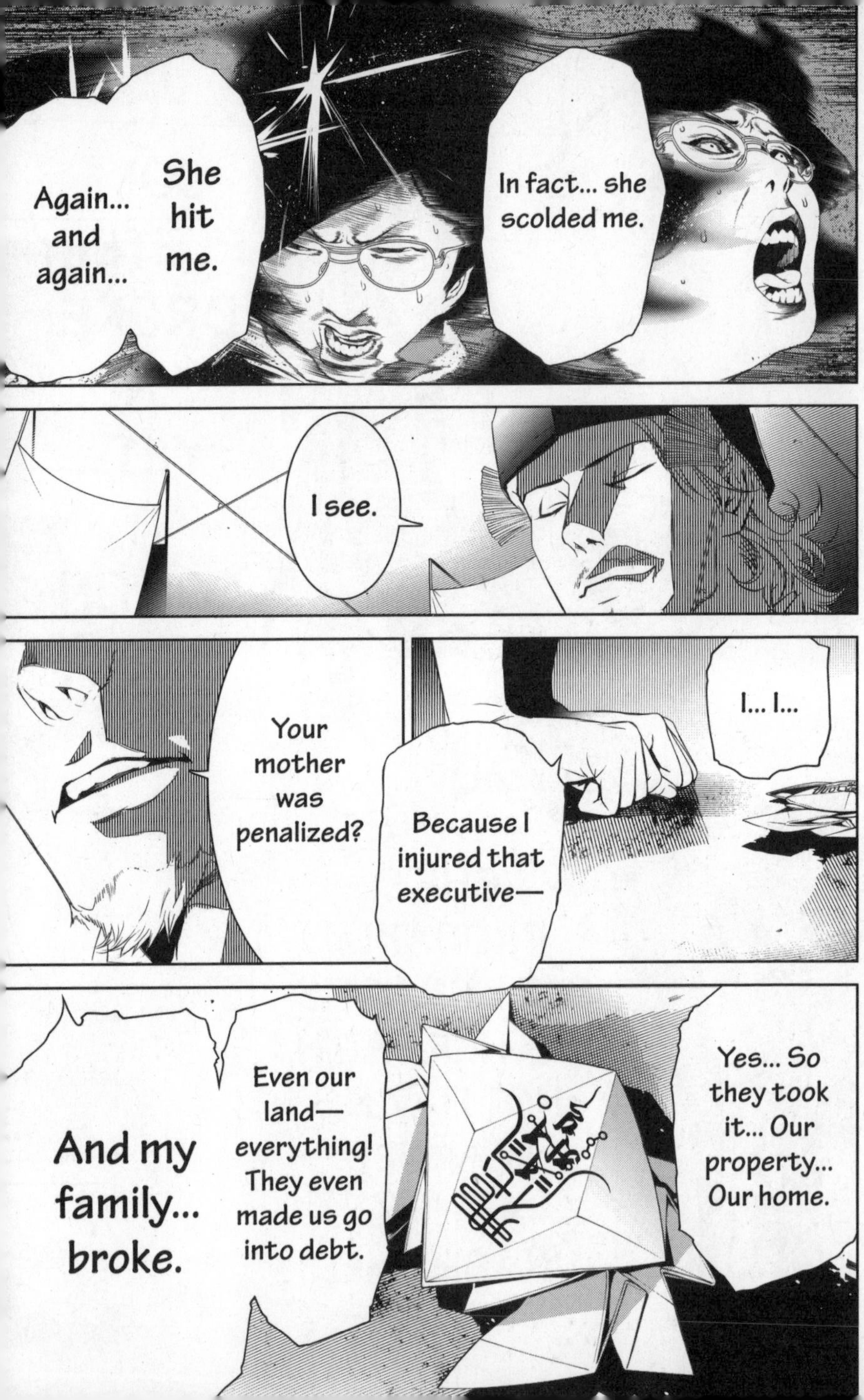
In fact... she scolded me.
She hit me.
Again... and again...
I see.
I... I...
Because I injured that executive—
Your mother was penalized?
Yes... So they took it... Our property... Our home.
Even our land— everything! They even made us go into debt.
And my family... broke.

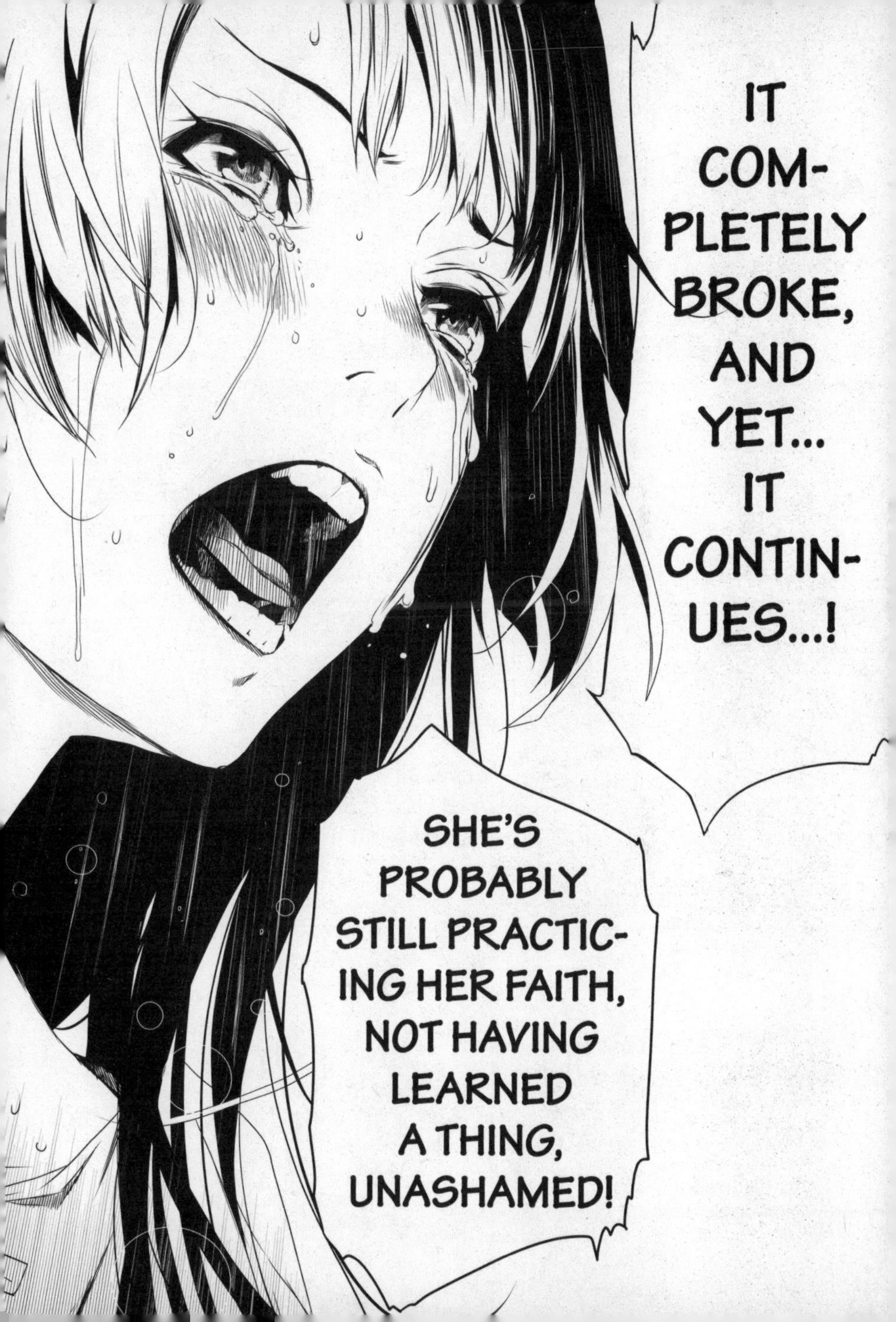
IT COM-PLETELY BROKE, AND YET... IT CONTIN-UES...!
SHE'S PROBABLY STILL PRACTIC-ING HER FAITH, NOT HAVING LEARNED A THING, UNASHAMED!

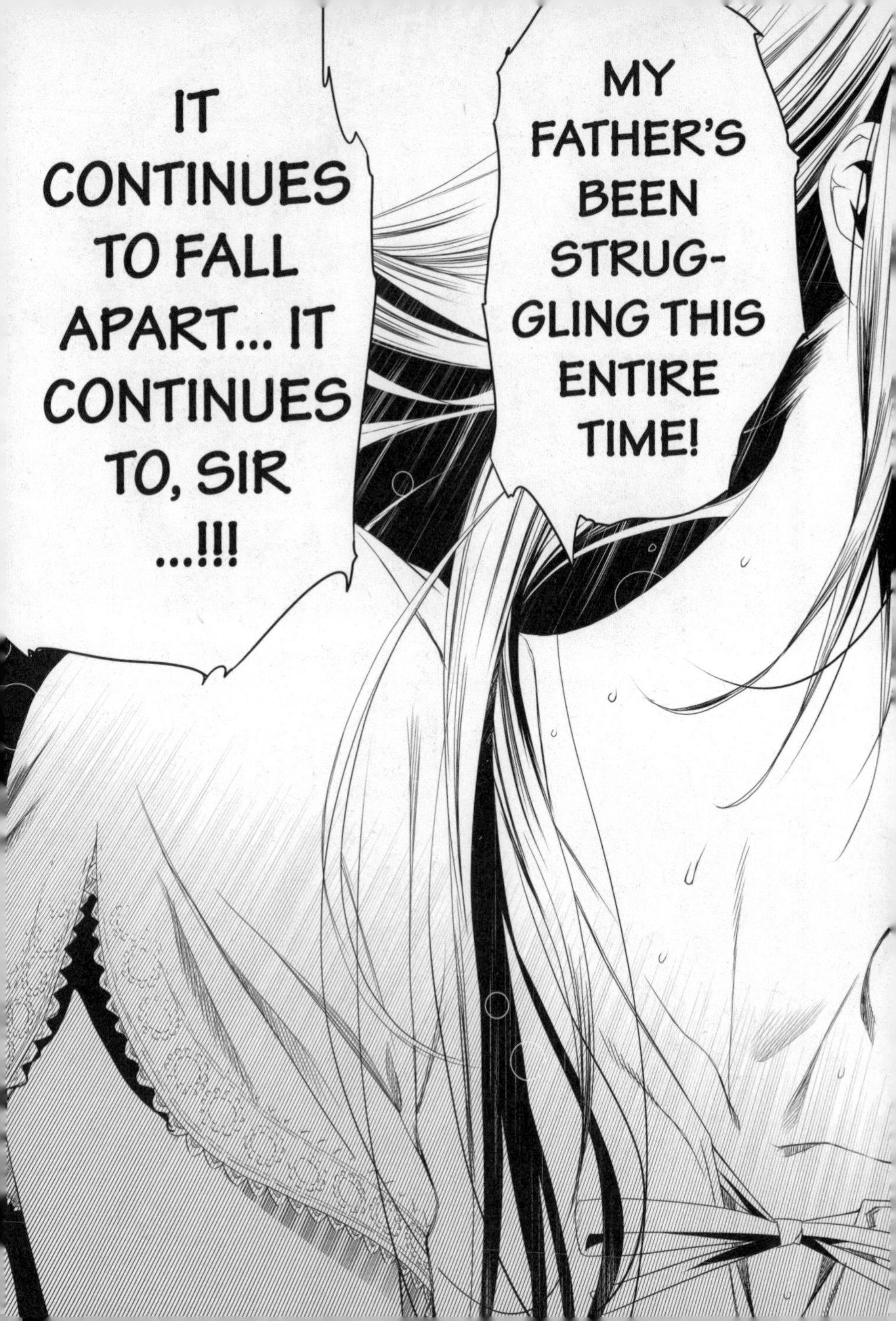
MY FATHER'S BEEN STRUG-GLING THIS ENTIRE TIME!
IT CONTINUES TO FALL APART... IT CONTINUES TO, SIR ...!!!

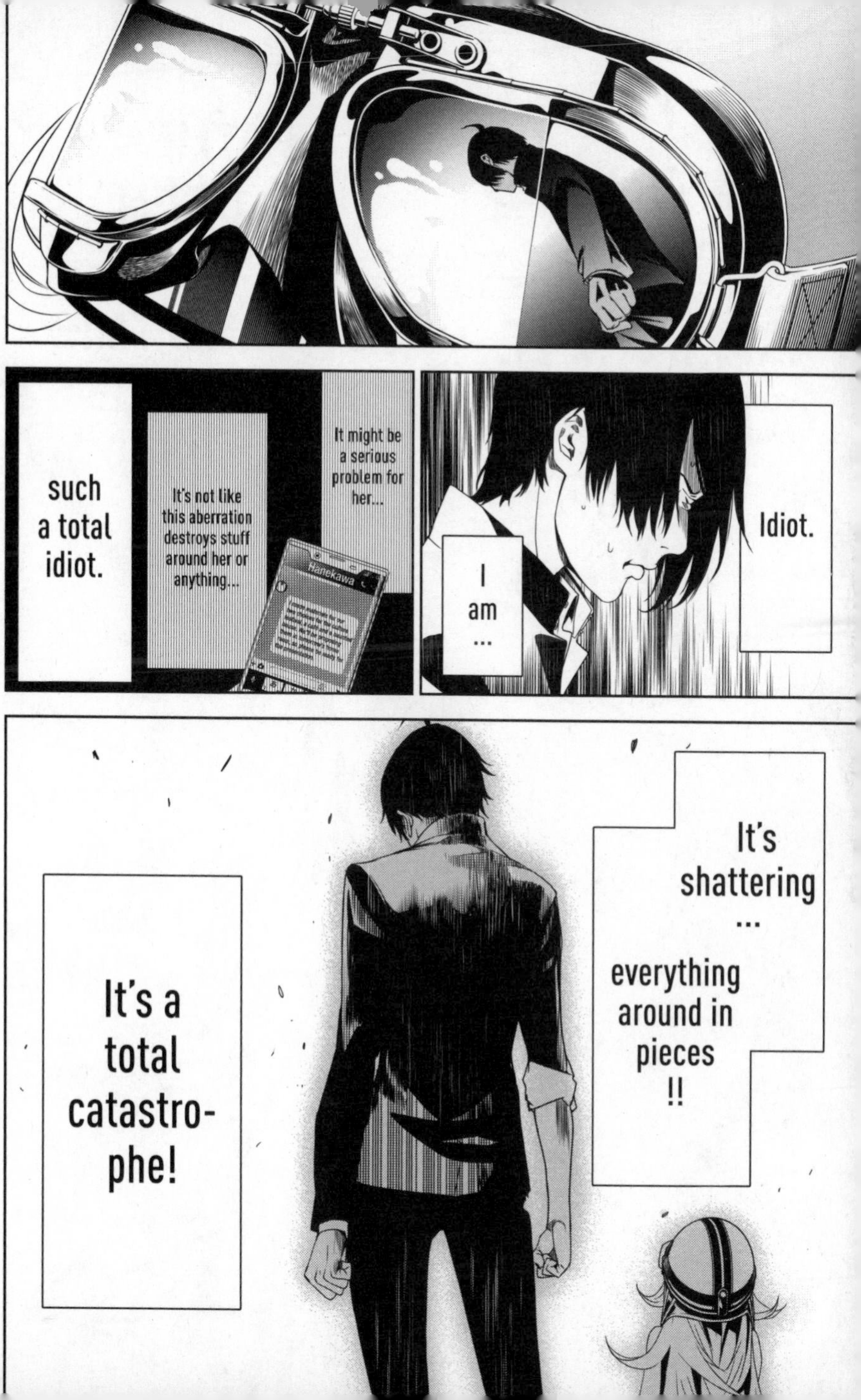
Idiot.
I am ...
It might be a serious problem for her...
Hanekawa
It's not like this aberration destroys stuff around her or anything...
such a total idiot.
It's shattering ... everything around in pieces !!
It's a total catastrophe!

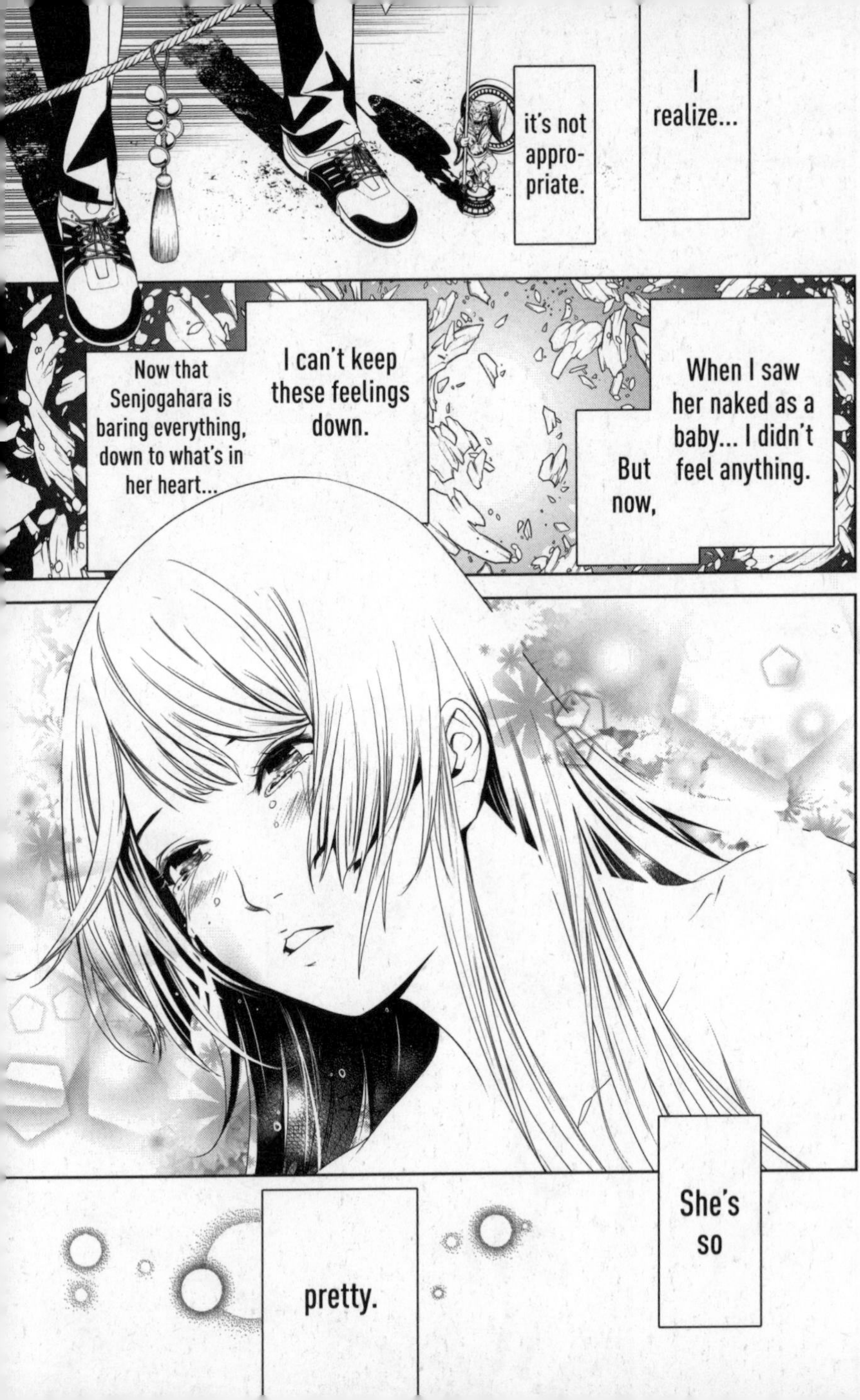
I realize...
it's not appro-priate.
When I saw her naked as a baby... I didn't feel anything.
But now,
I can't keep these feelings down.
Now that Senjogahara is baring everything, down to what's in her heart...
She's so
pretty.

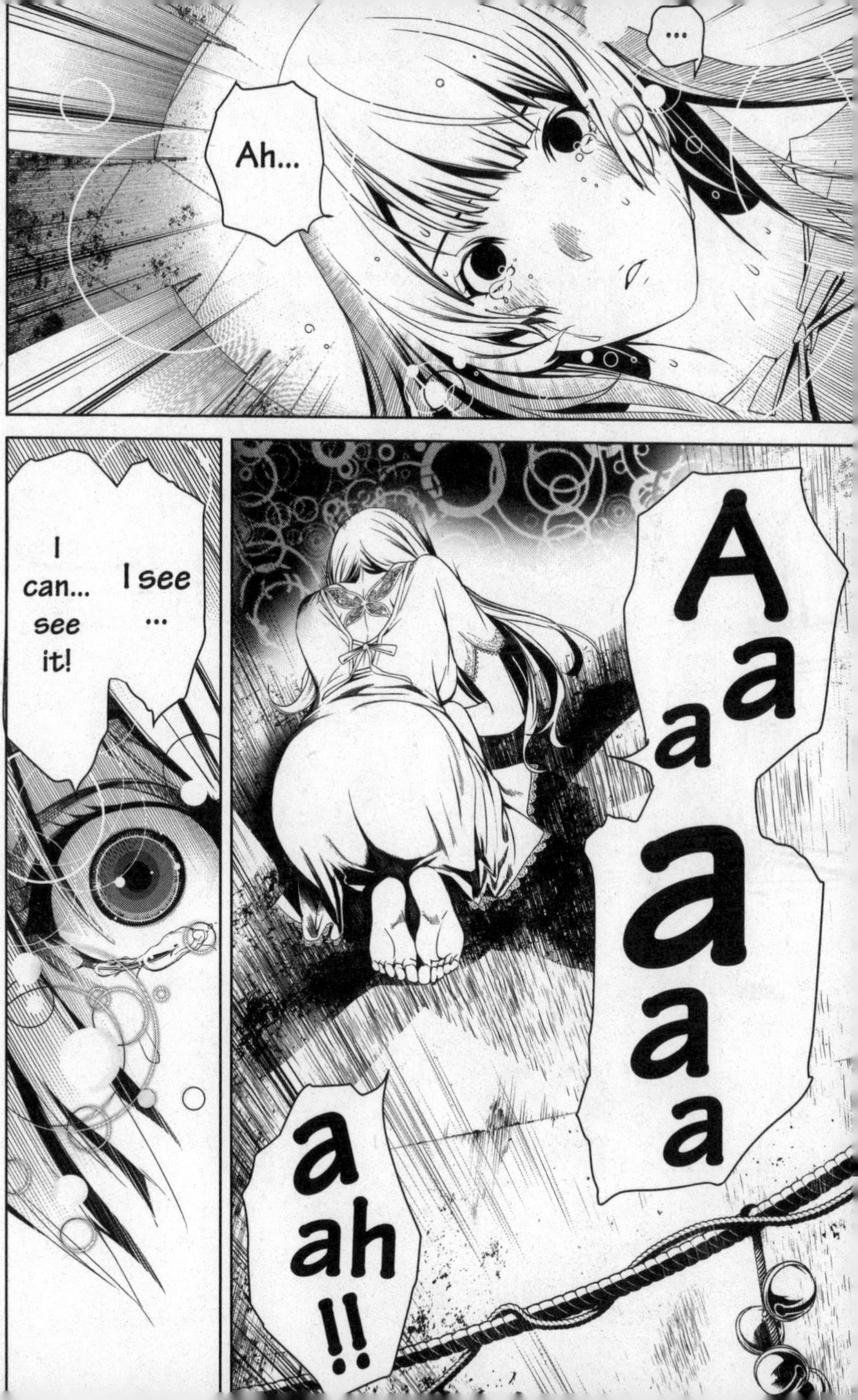
...
Ah...
Aaaaaaa
aah!!
I see ...
I can... see it!

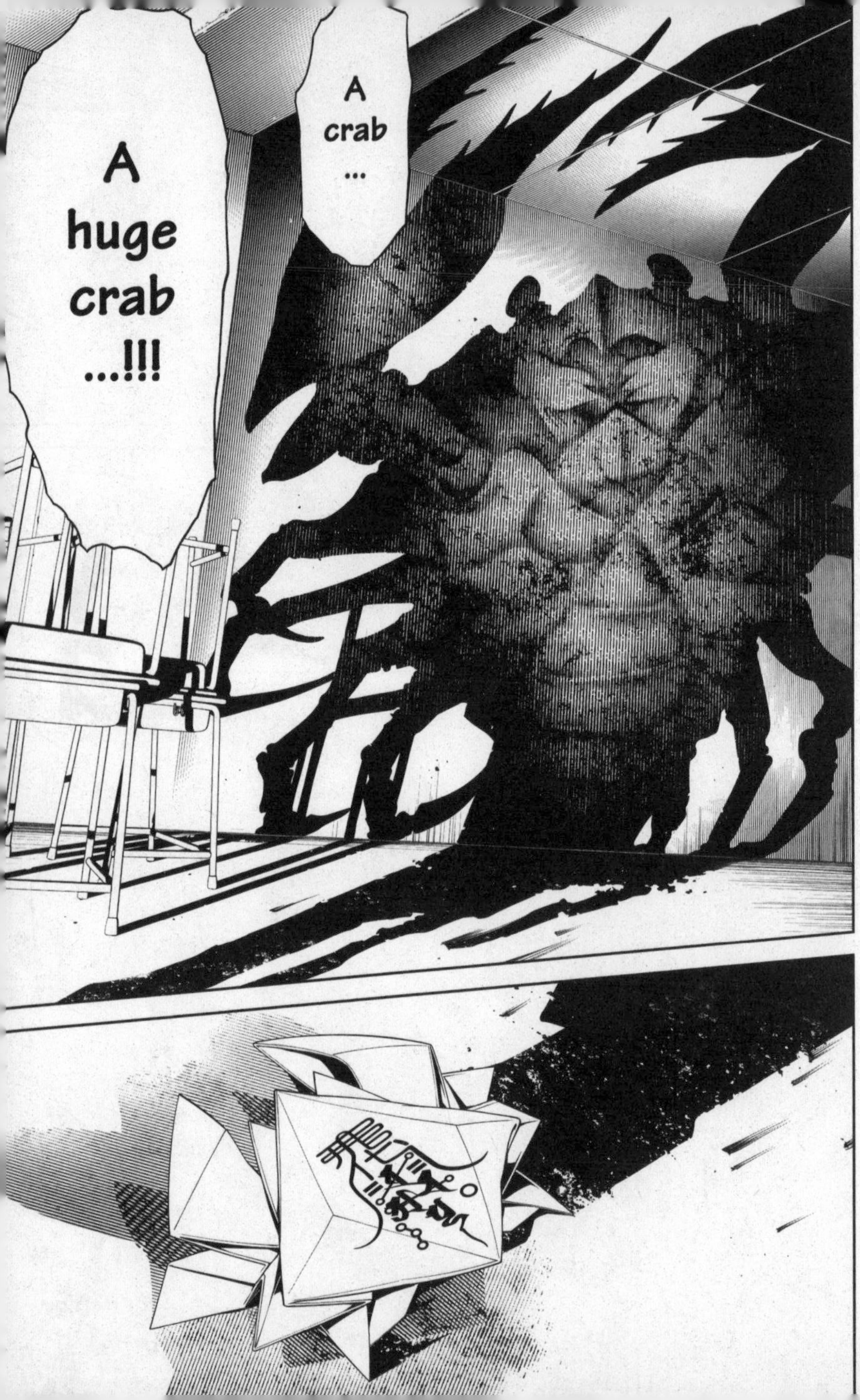
A crab ...
A huge crab ...!!!

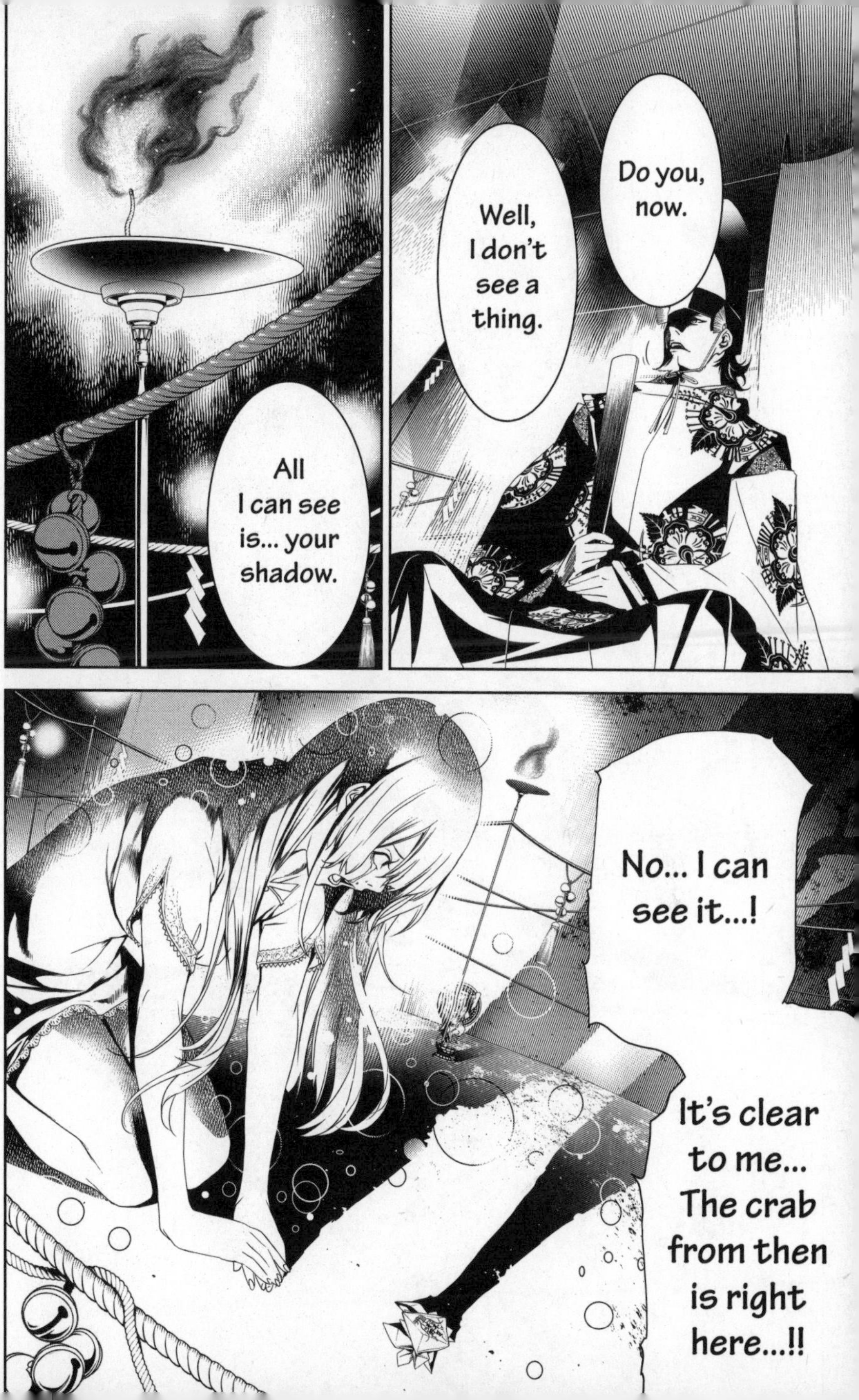
Do you, now.
Well, I don't see a thing.
All I can see is... your shadow.
No... I can see it...!
It's clear to me... The crab from then is right here...!!

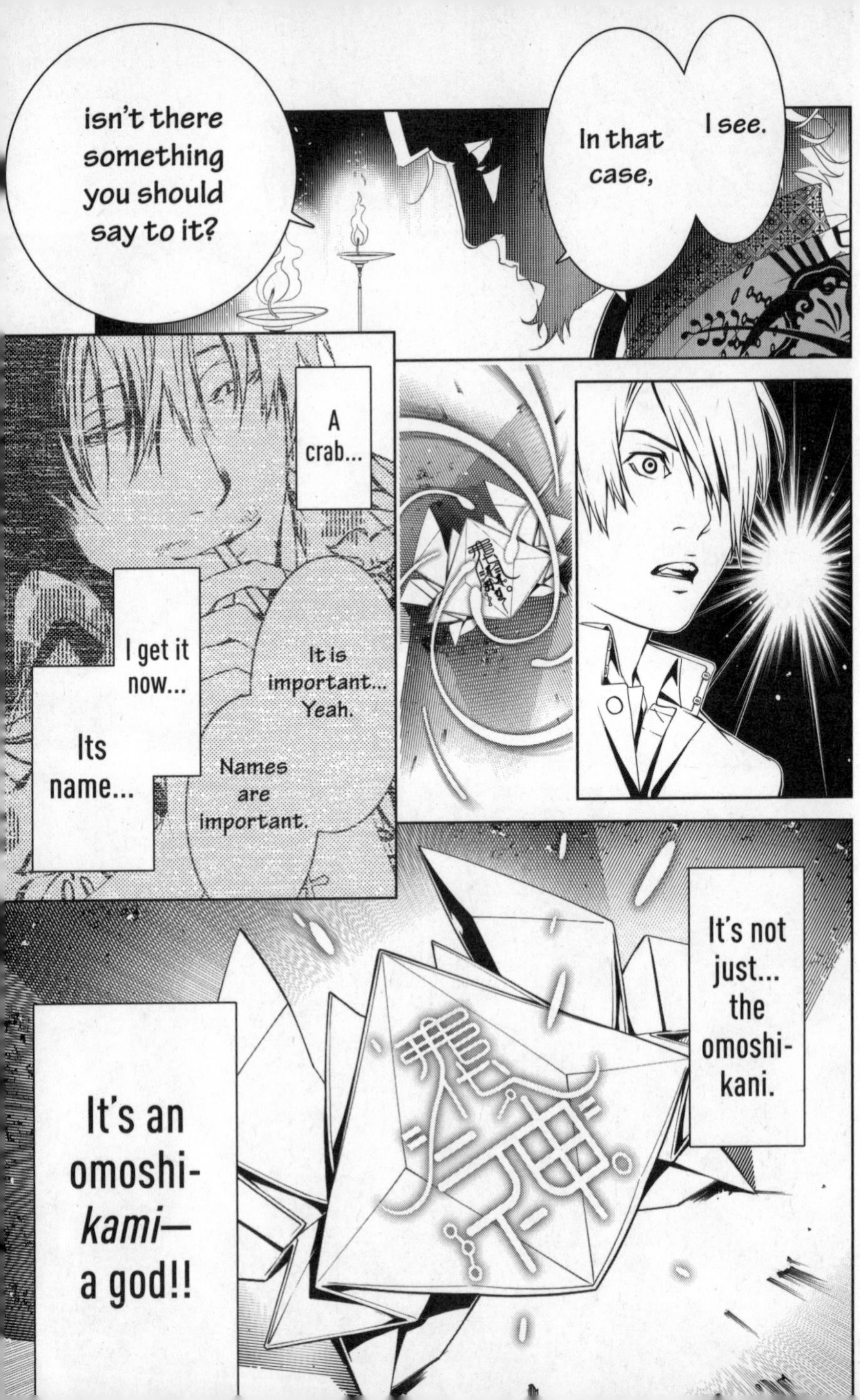
I see.
In that case,
isn't there something you should say to it?
A crab...
It is important... Yeah.
Names are important.
I get it now...
Its name...
It's not just... the omoshi-kani.
It's an omoshi-*kami*—a god!!

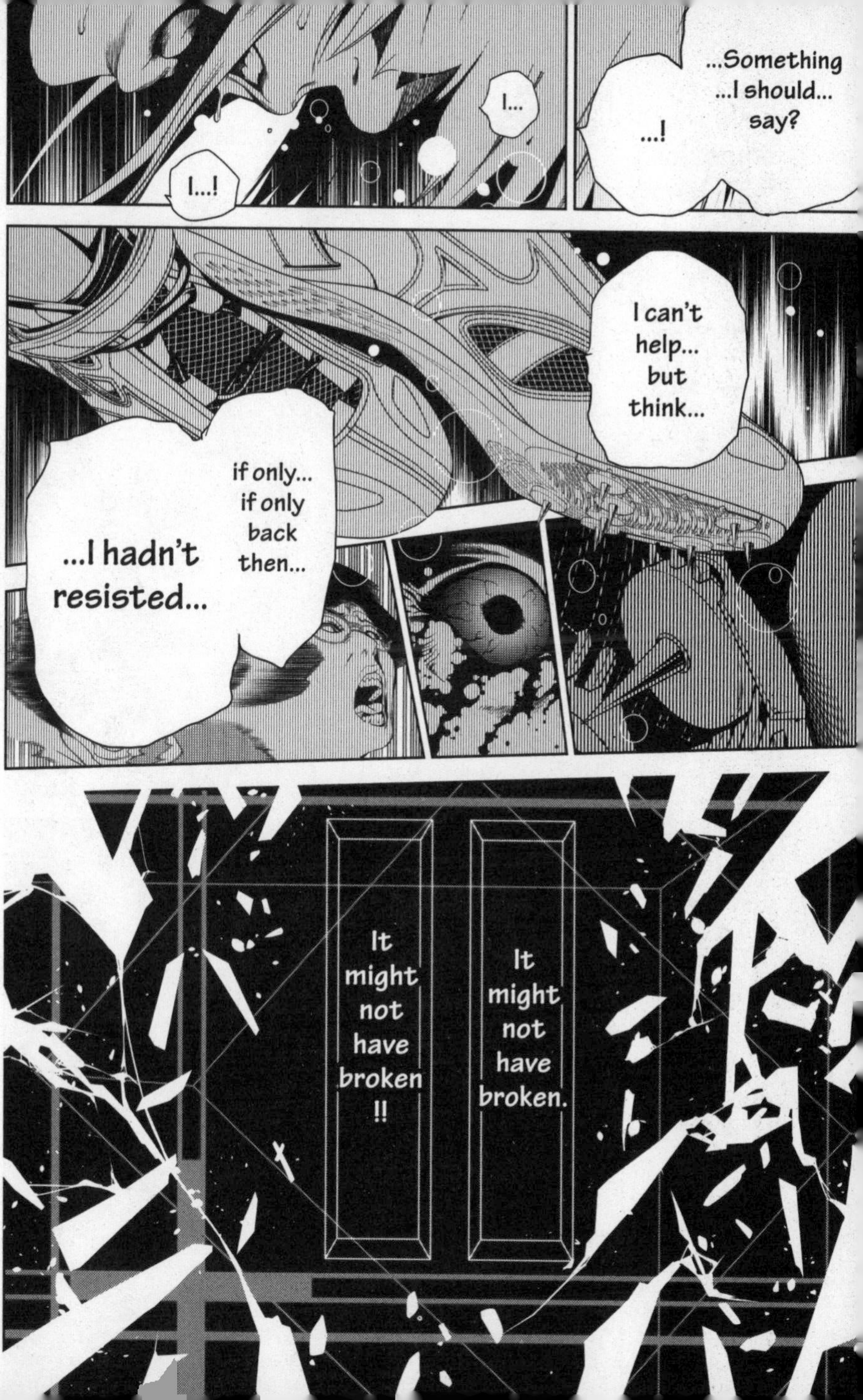
...Something ...I should... say?
...!
I...
I...!
I can't help... but think...
if only... if only back then...
...I hadn't resisted...
It might not have broken.
It might not have broken !!

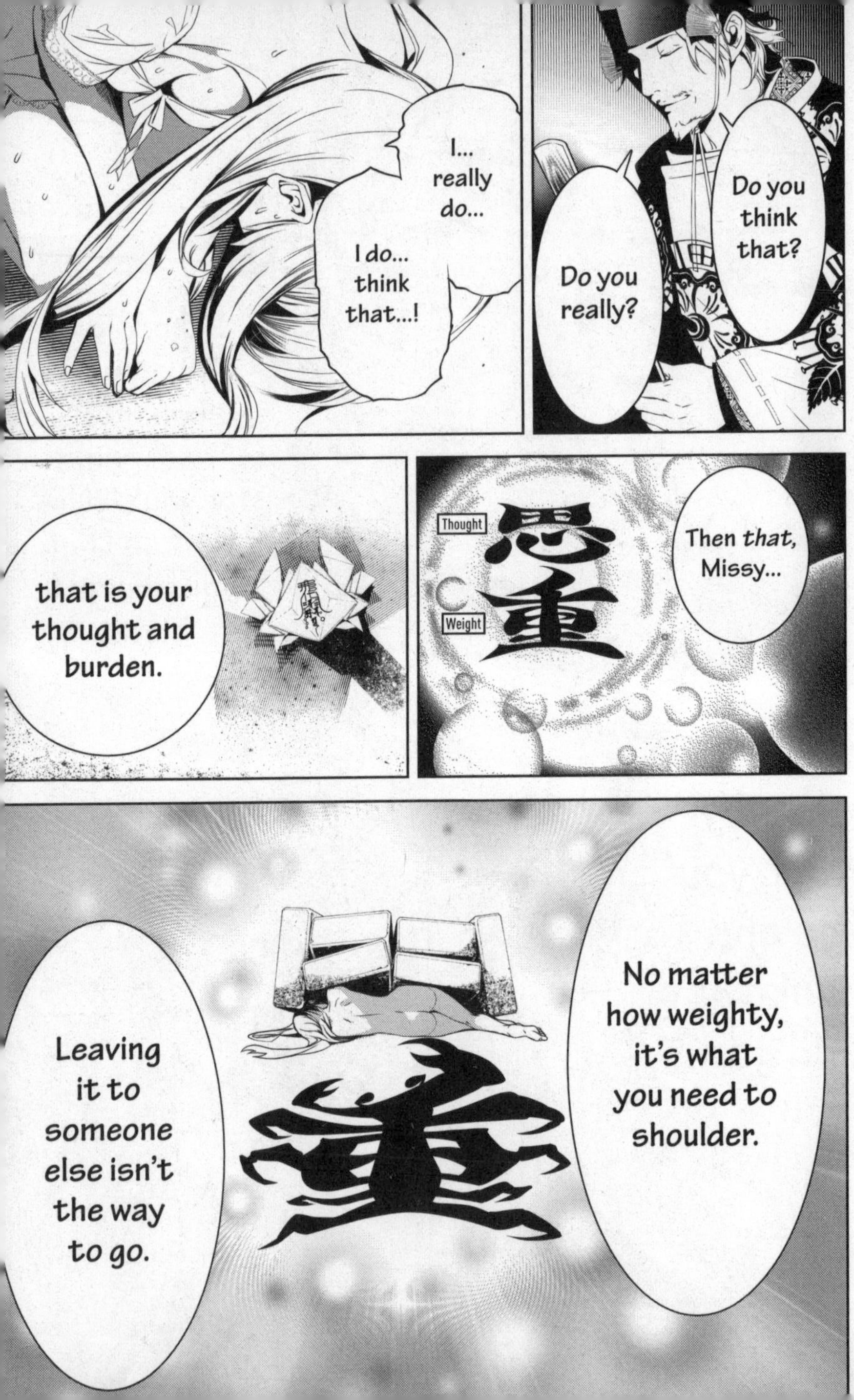
Do you think that?
Do you really?
I... really do...
I do... think that...!
Then *that*, Missy...
Thought
Weight
that is your thought and burden.
No matter how weighty, it's what you need to shoulder.
Leaving it to someone else isn't the way to go.

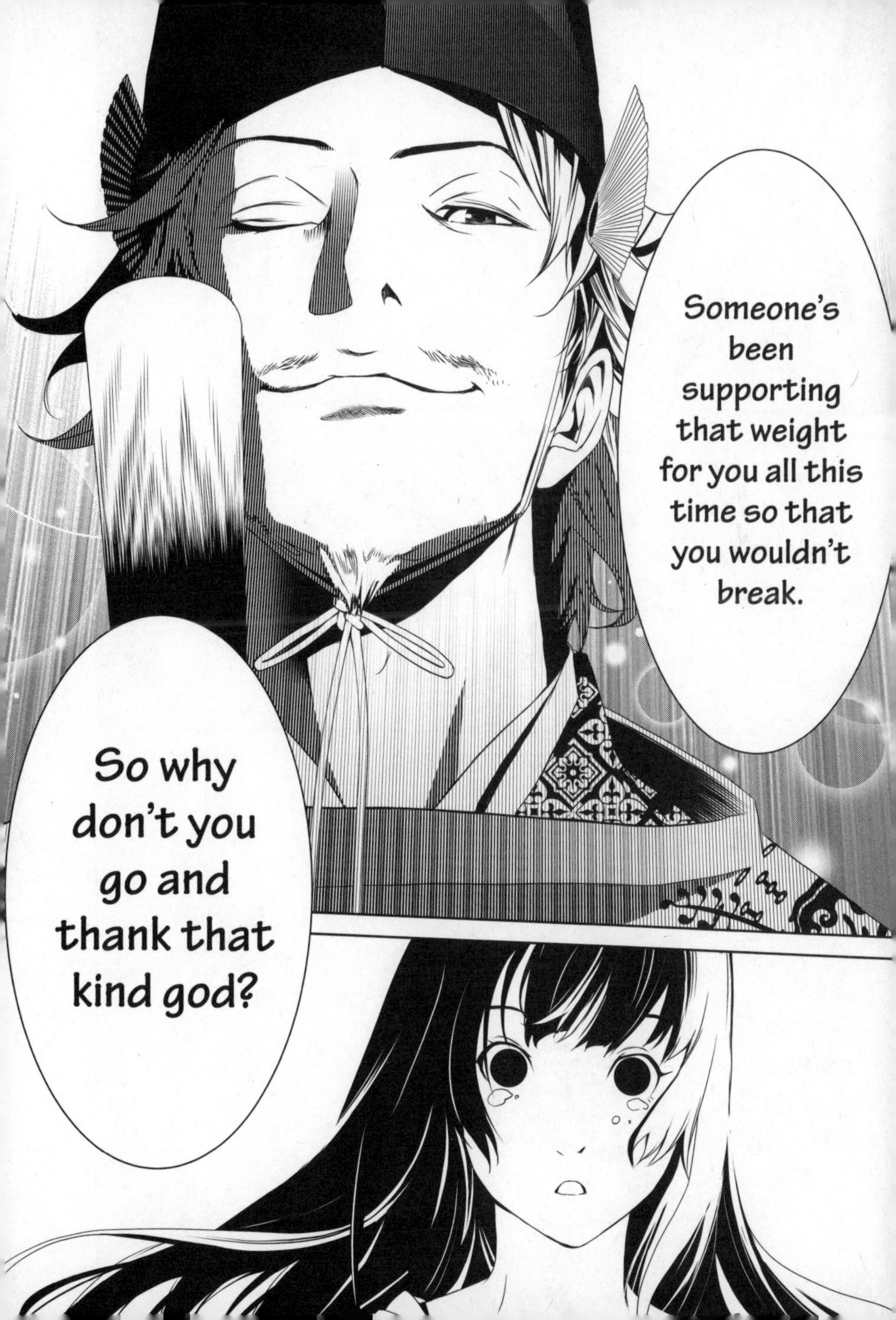
Someone's been supporting that weight for you all this time so that you wouldn't break.
So why don't you go and thank that kind god?

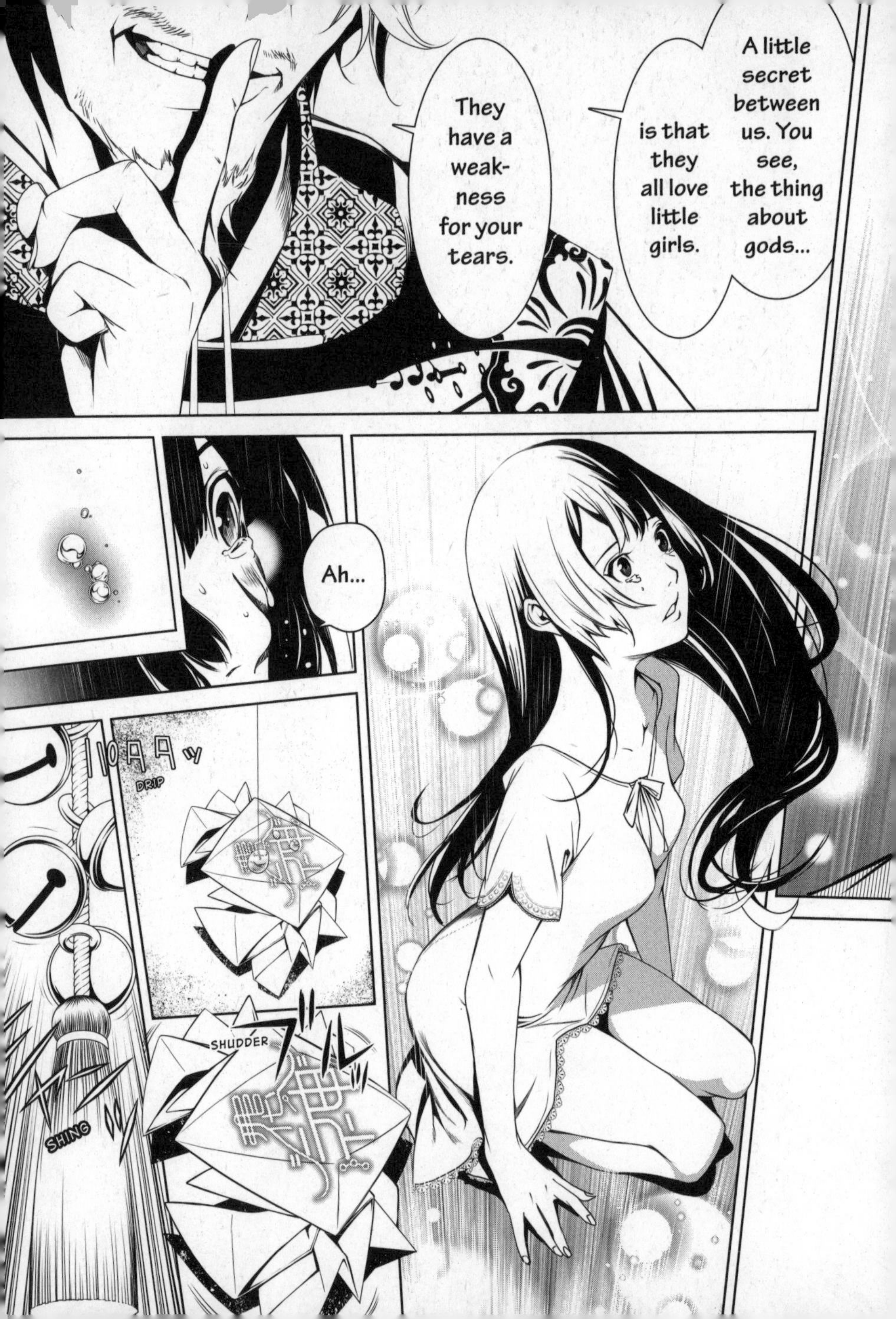
A little secret between us. You see, the thing about gods...
is that they all love little girls.
They have a weakness for your tears.
Ah...
DRIP
SHUDDER
SHING

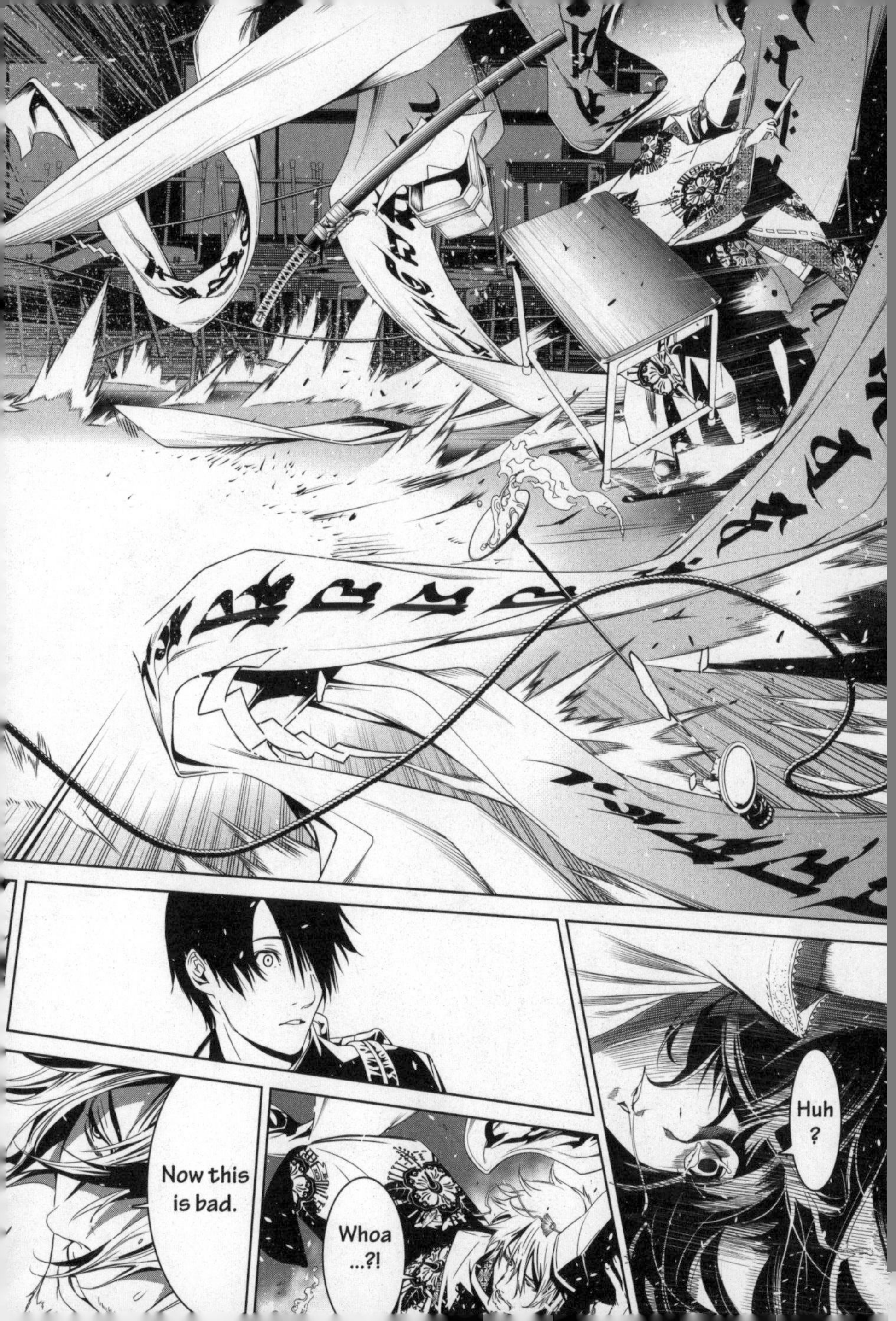
Huh?
Whoa...?!
Now this is bad.

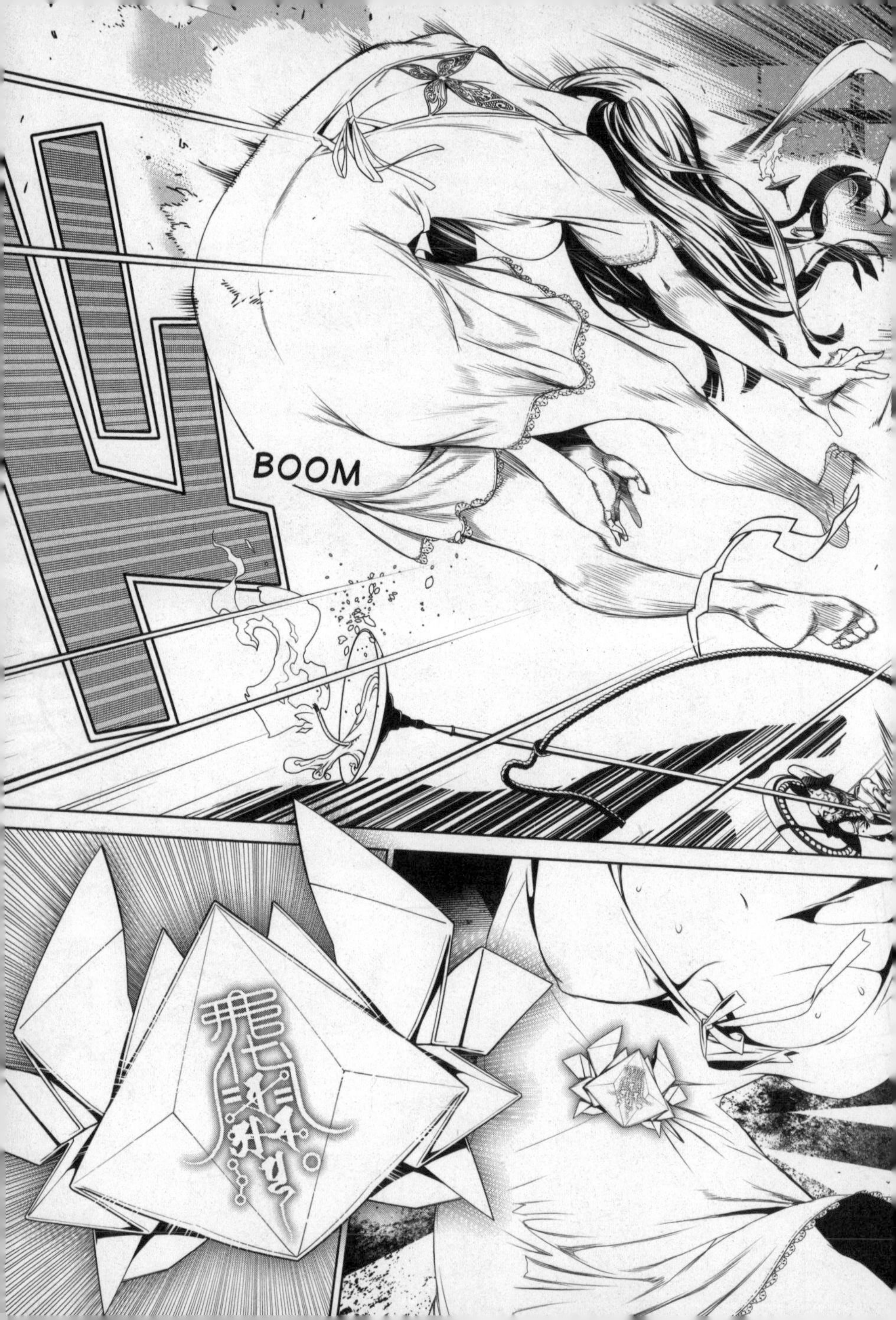
BOOM

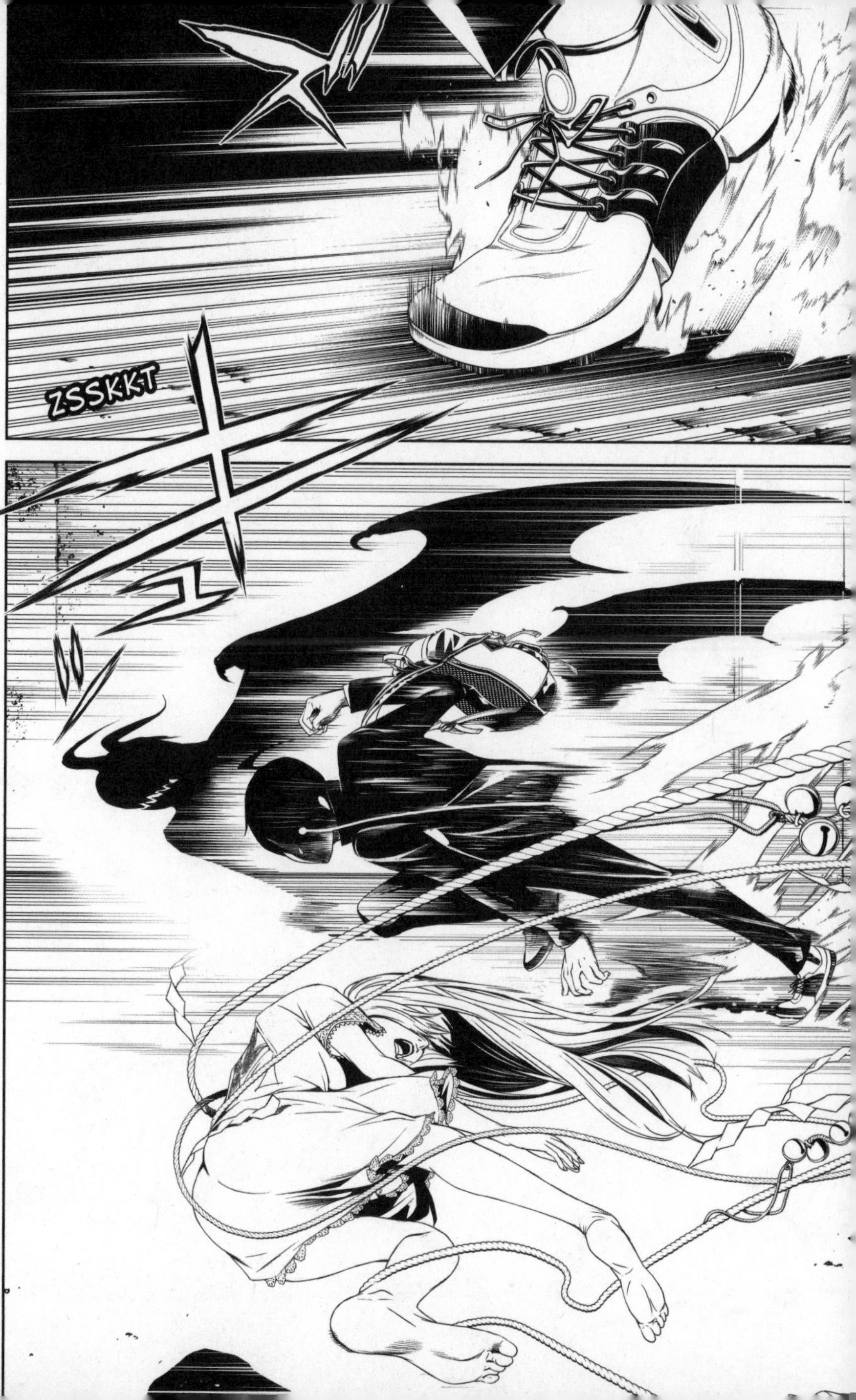
ZSSKKT

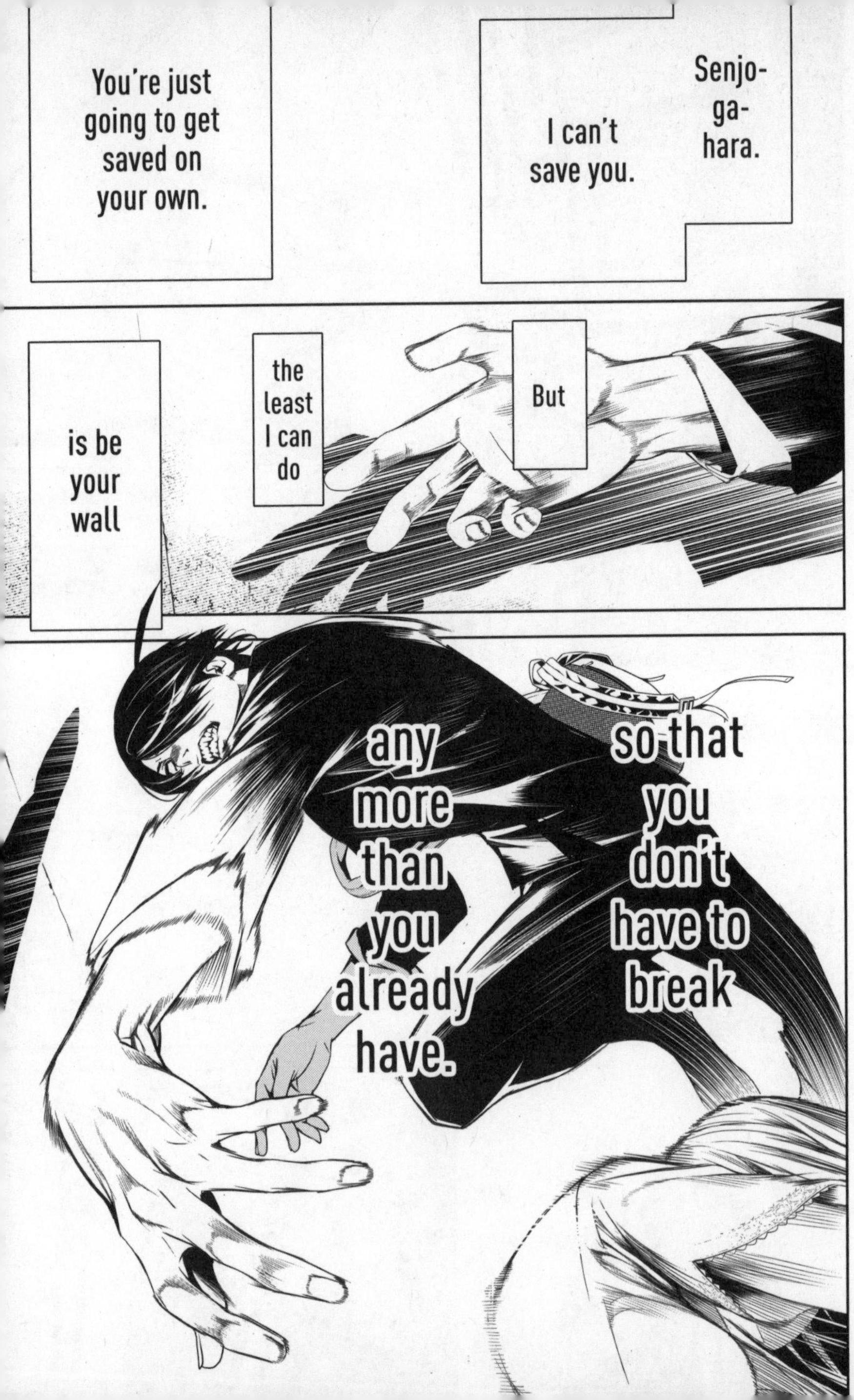
Senjo-ga-hara.
I can't save you.
You're just going to get saved on your own.
But
the least I can do
is be your wall
so that you don't have to break
any more than you already have.

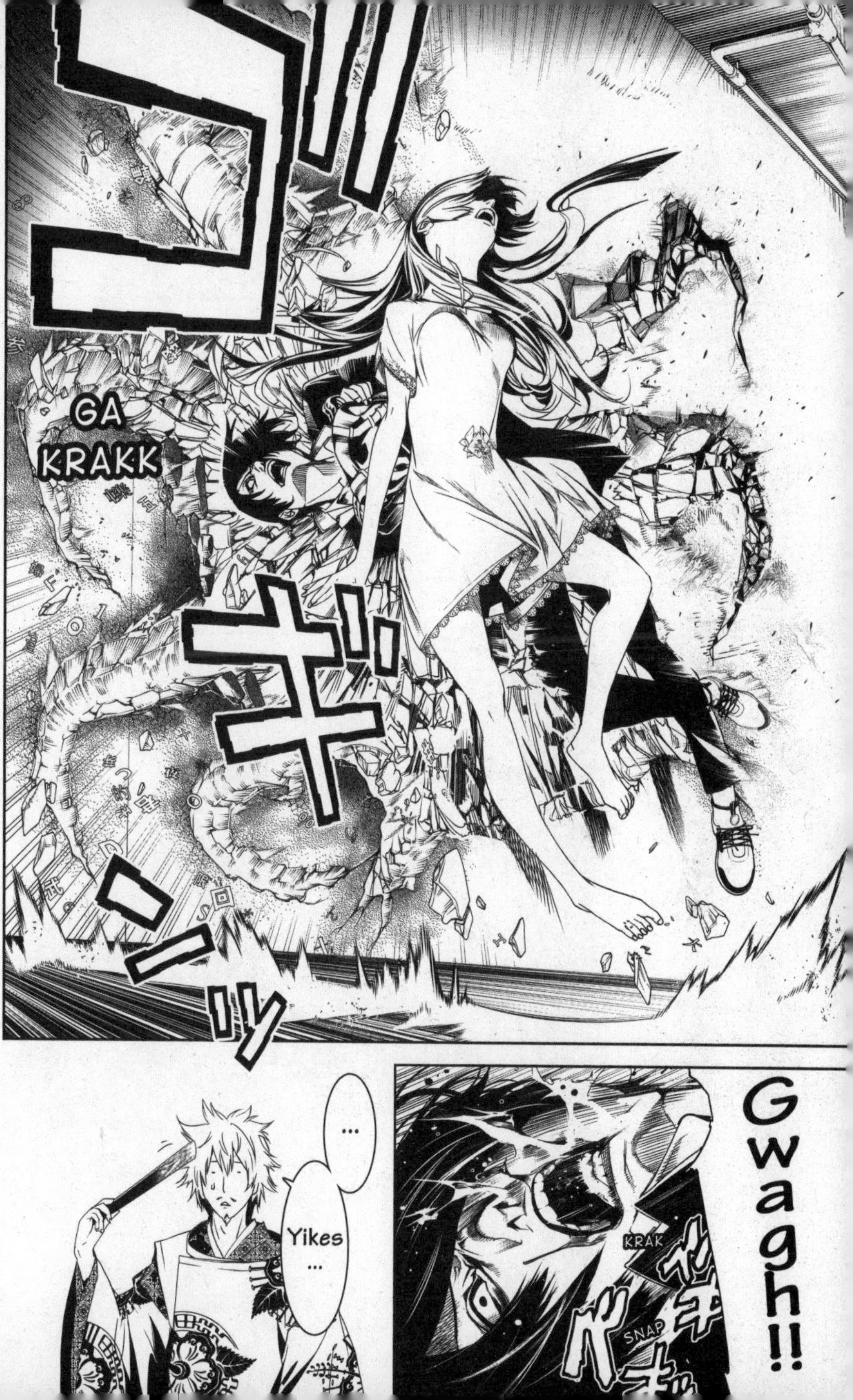
GA KRAKK
Gwagh!!
KRAK
SNAP
...
Yikes ...

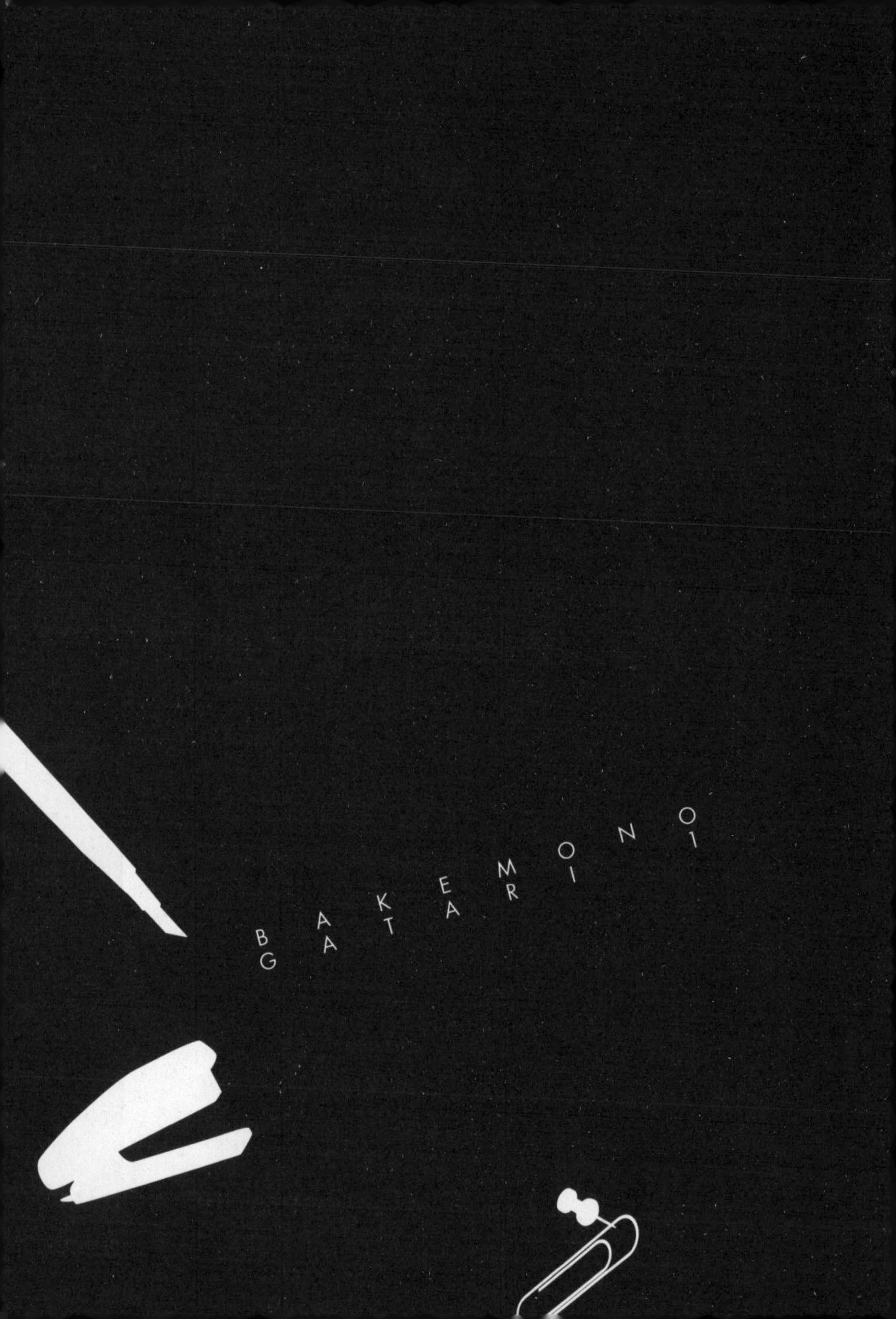
BAKEMONO
GATARI 1

BAKEMONO
GATARI 1

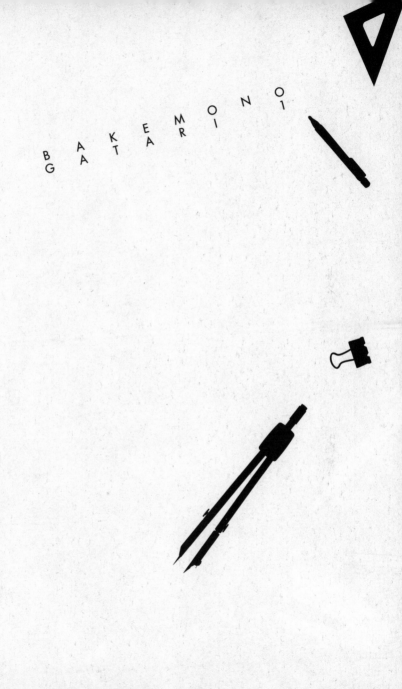

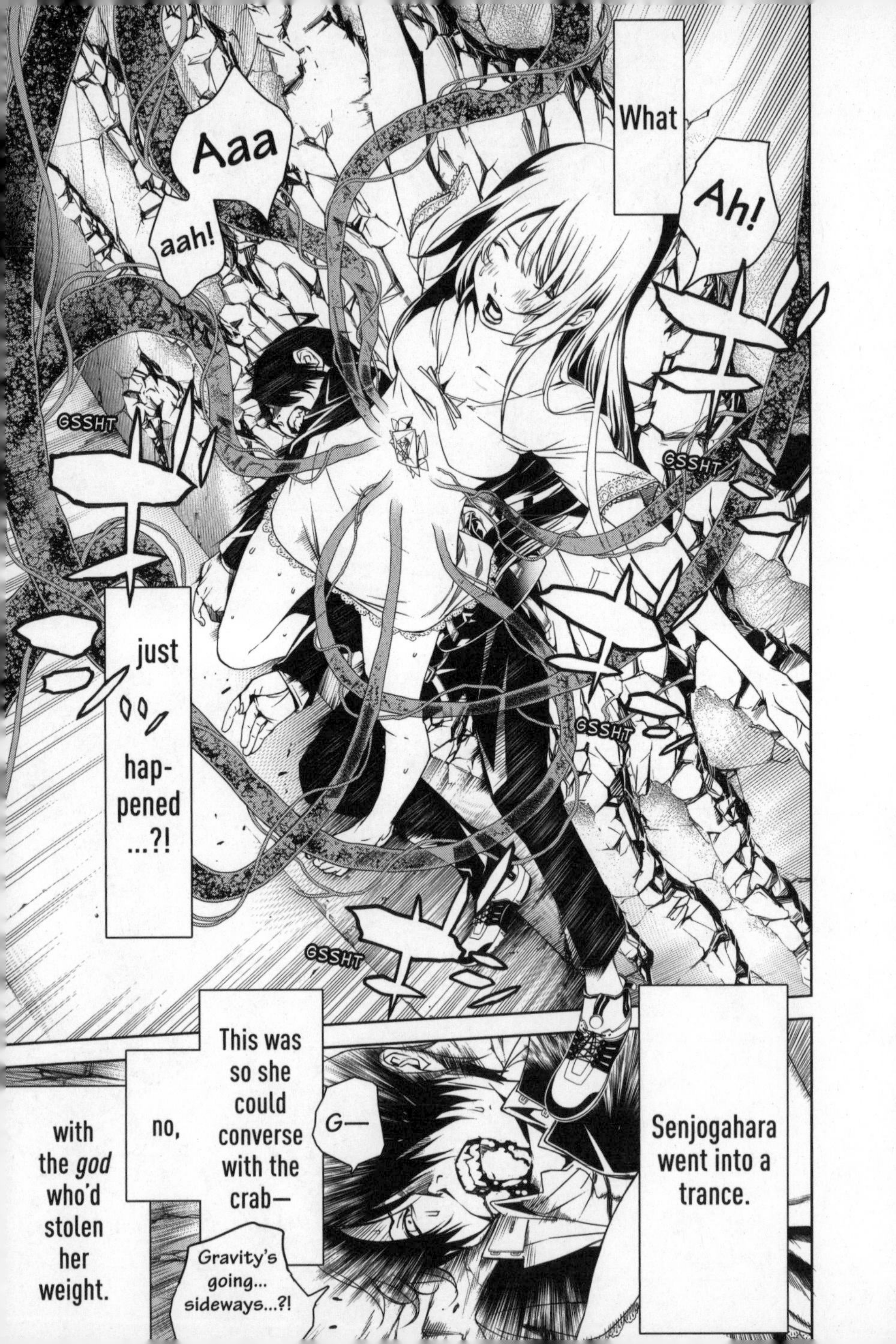
What
Ah!
Aaa
aah!
GSSHT
GSSHT
just hap-pened...?!
GSSHT
GSSHT
Senjogahara went into a trance.
This was so she could converse with the crab—
G—
no,
with the *god* who'd stolen her weight.
Gravity's going... sideways...?!

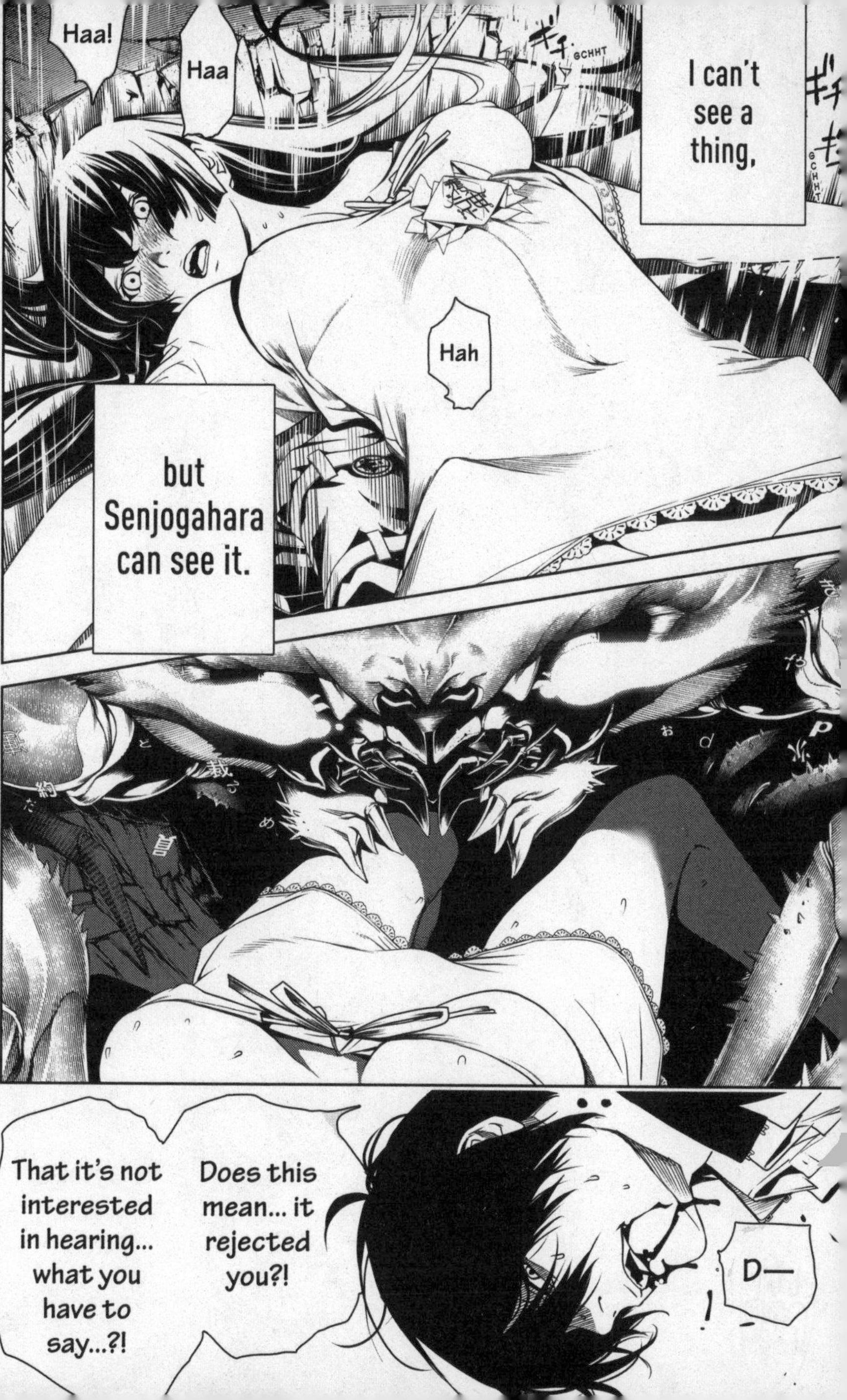
GCHHT
I can't see a thing,
GCHHT
Haa
Haa!
Hah
but Senjogahara can see it.
D—
Does this mean... it rejected you?!
That it's not interested in hearing... what you have to say...?!

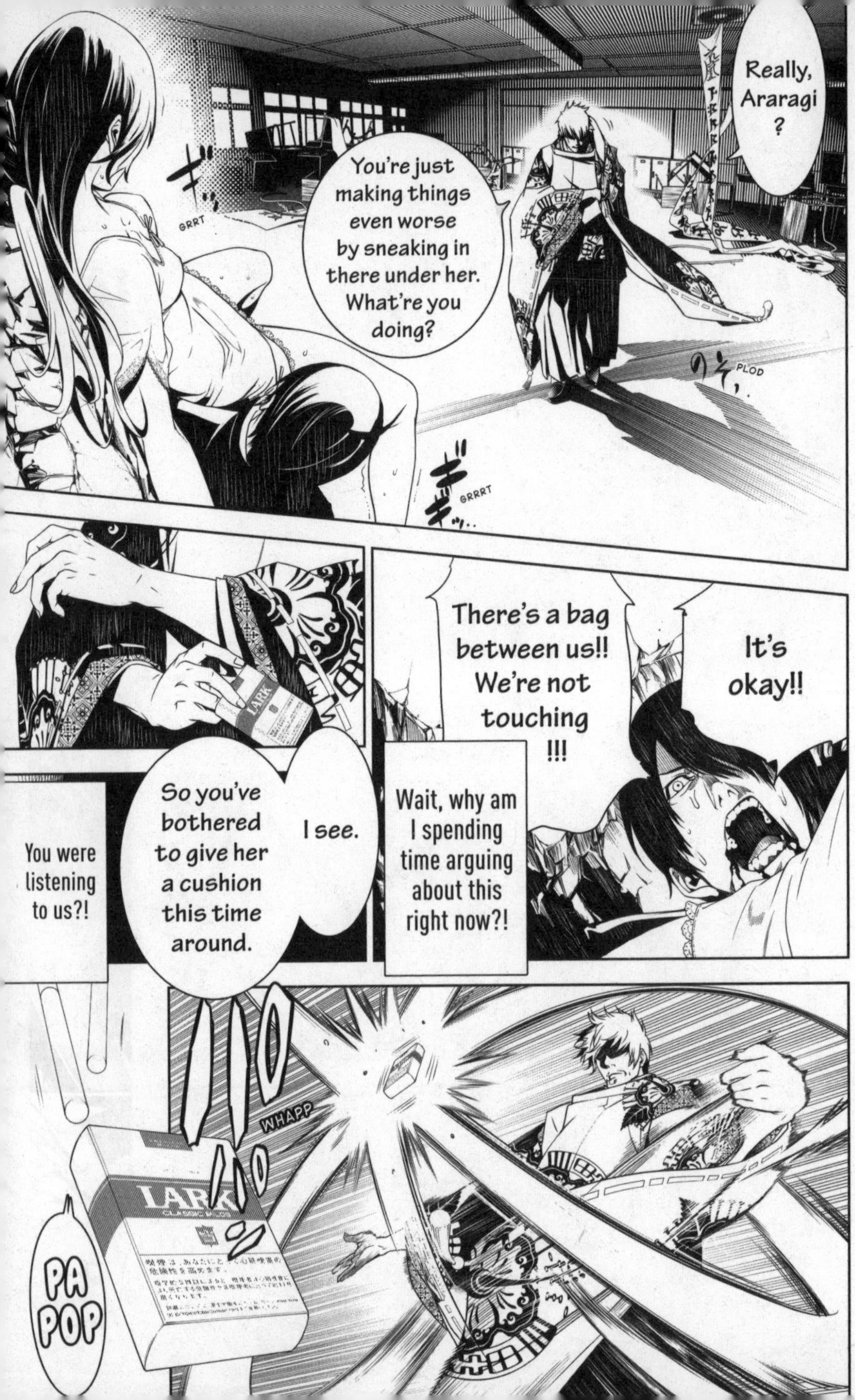
Really, Araragi?
You're just making things even worse by sneaking in there under her. What're you doing?
GRRT
PLOD
GRRRT
It's okay!!
There's a bag between us!! We're not touching!!!
Wait, why am I spending time arguing about this right now?!
I see.
So you've bothered to give her a cushion this time around.
You were listening to us?!
WHAPP
PA POP

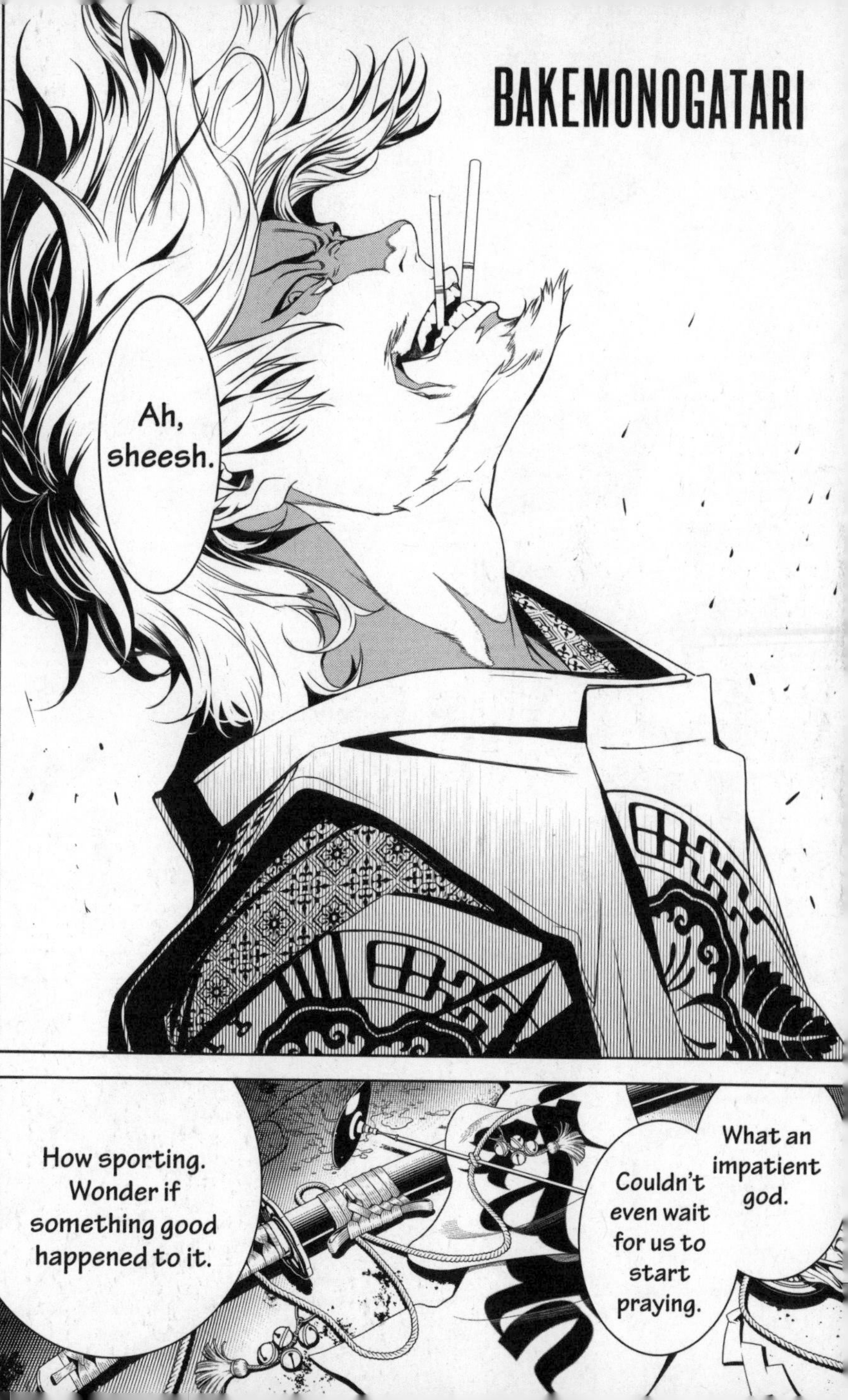
BAKEMONOGATARI
Ah, sheesh.
What an impatient god.
Couldn't even wait for us to start praying.
How sporting. Wonder if something good happened to it.

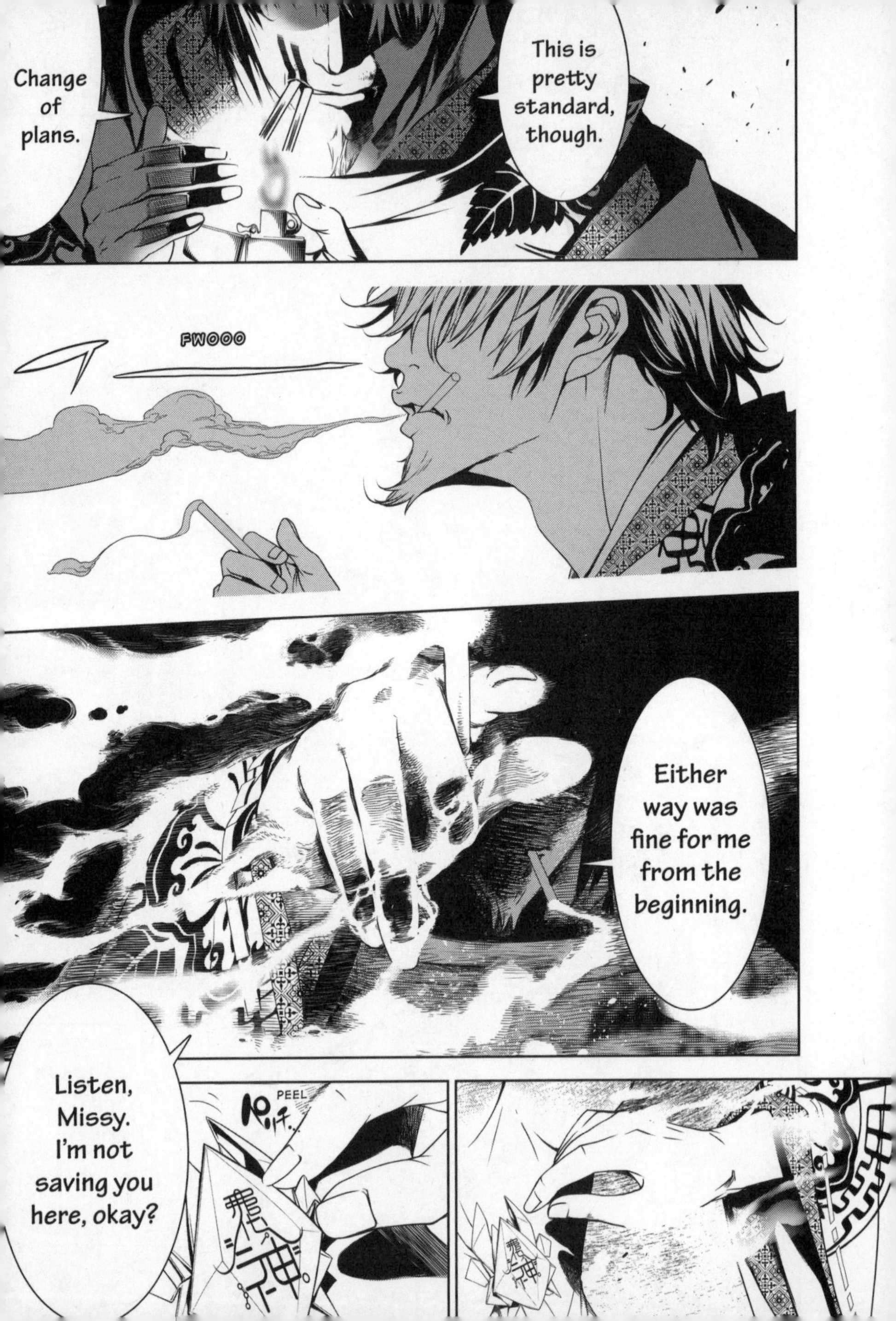
This is pretty standard, though.
Change of plans.
FWOOO
Either way was fine for me from the beginning.
Listen, Missy. I'm not saving you here, okay?
PEEL

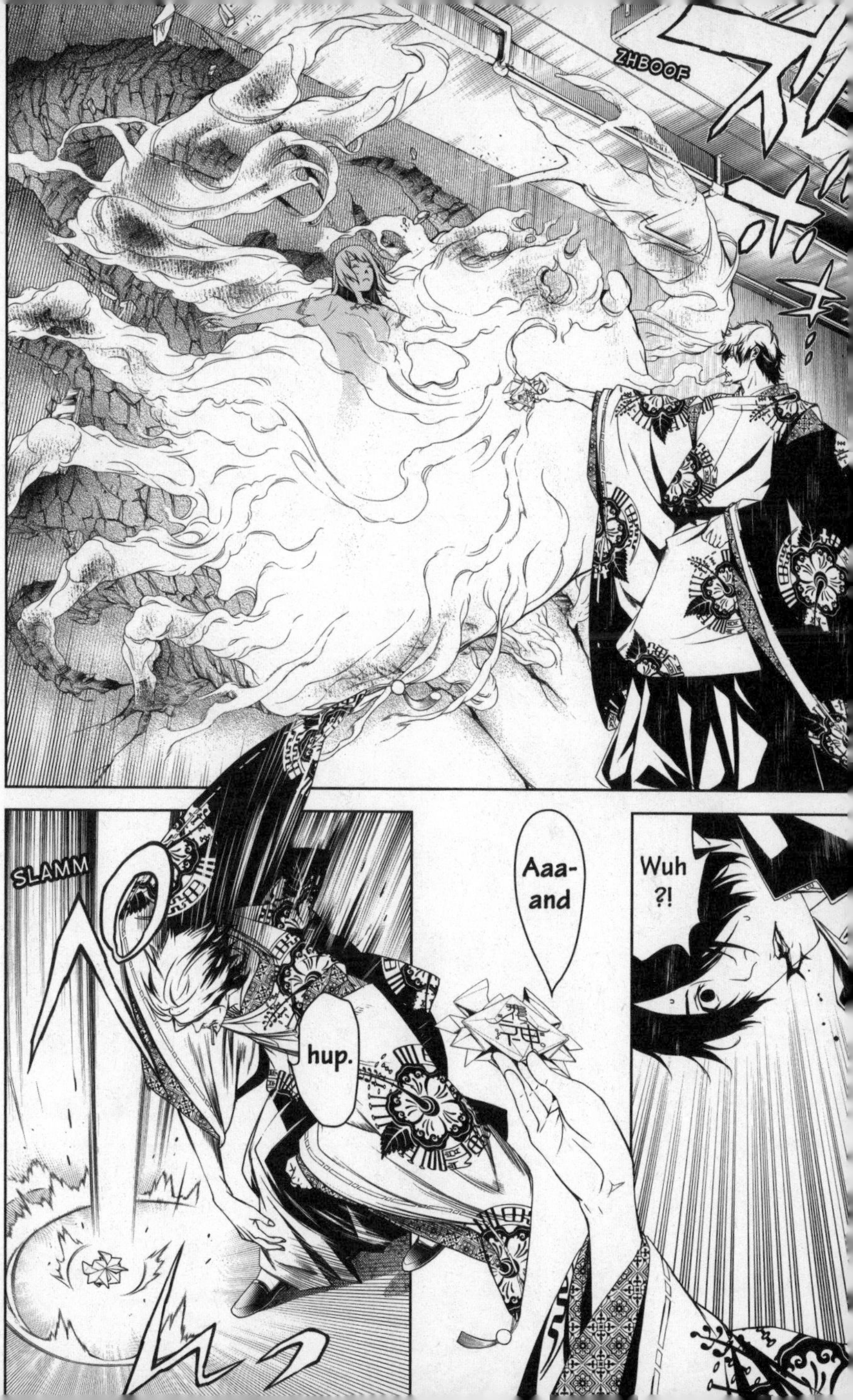
ZHBOOF
Wuh ?!
Aaa-and
hup.
SLAMM

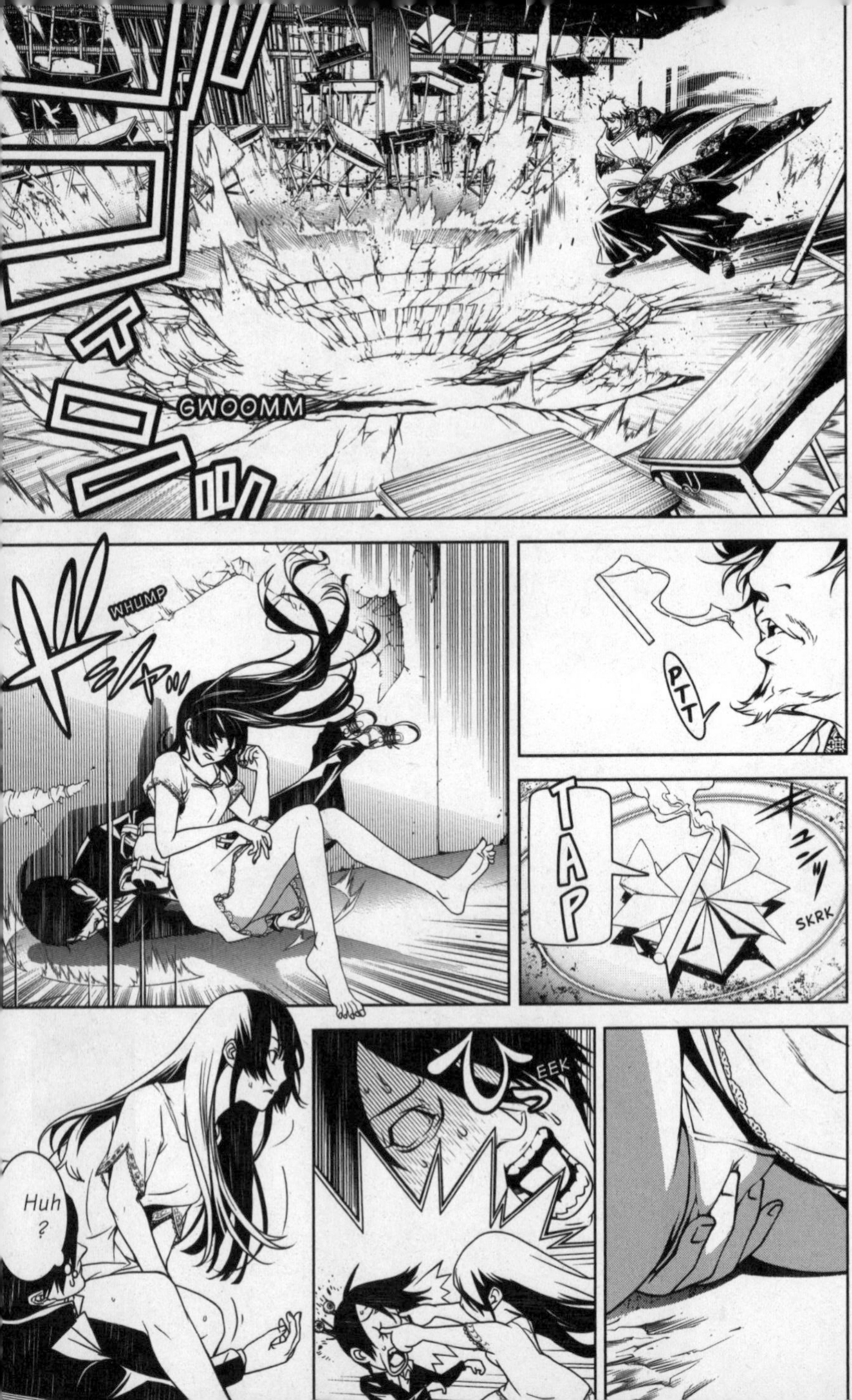
GWOOMM
PTT
TAP
SKRK
WHUMP
EEK
Huh
?

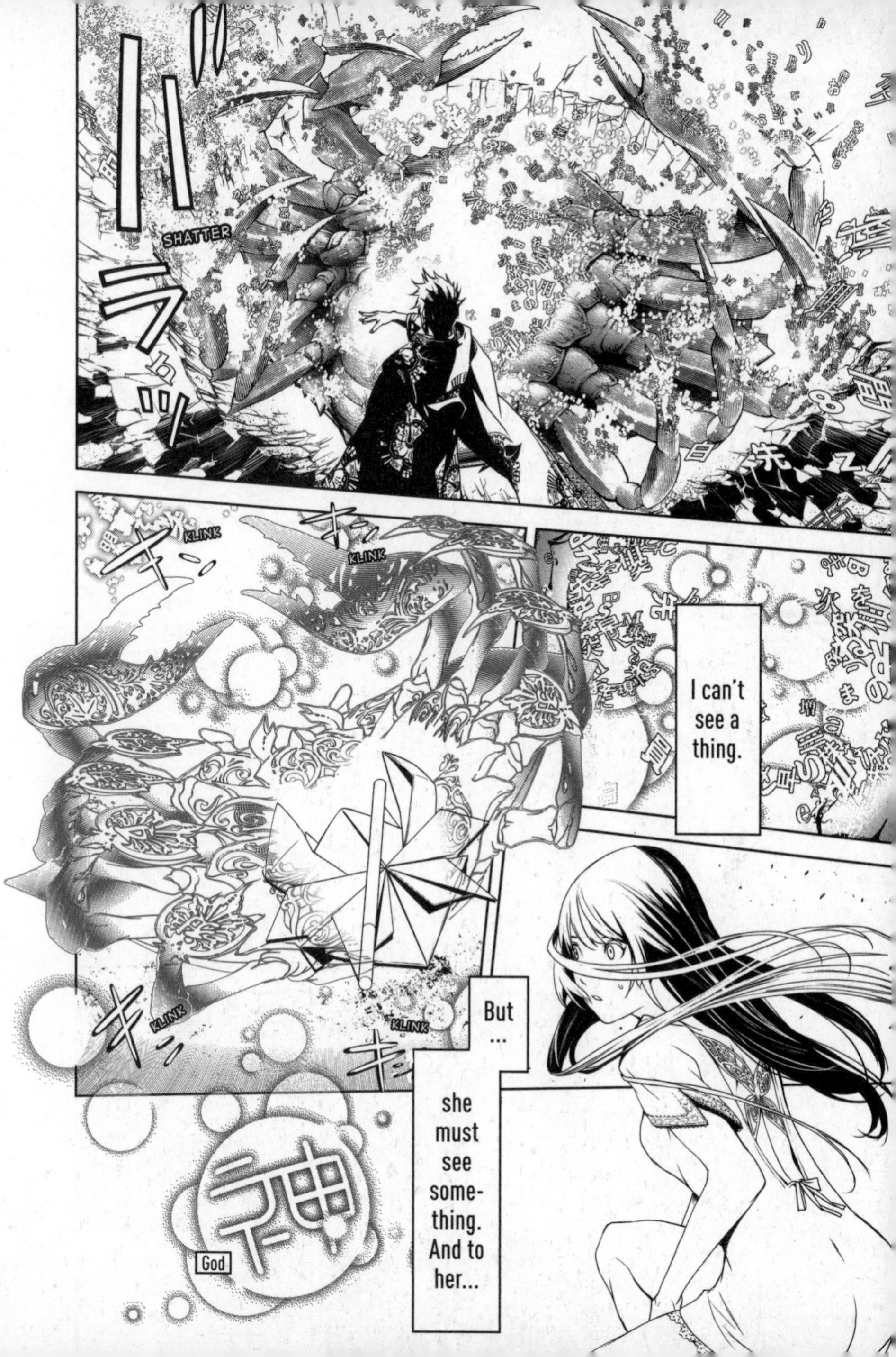
SHATTER
I can't see a thing.
KLINK
KLINK
KLINK
KLINK
But ...
she must see something. And to her...
God

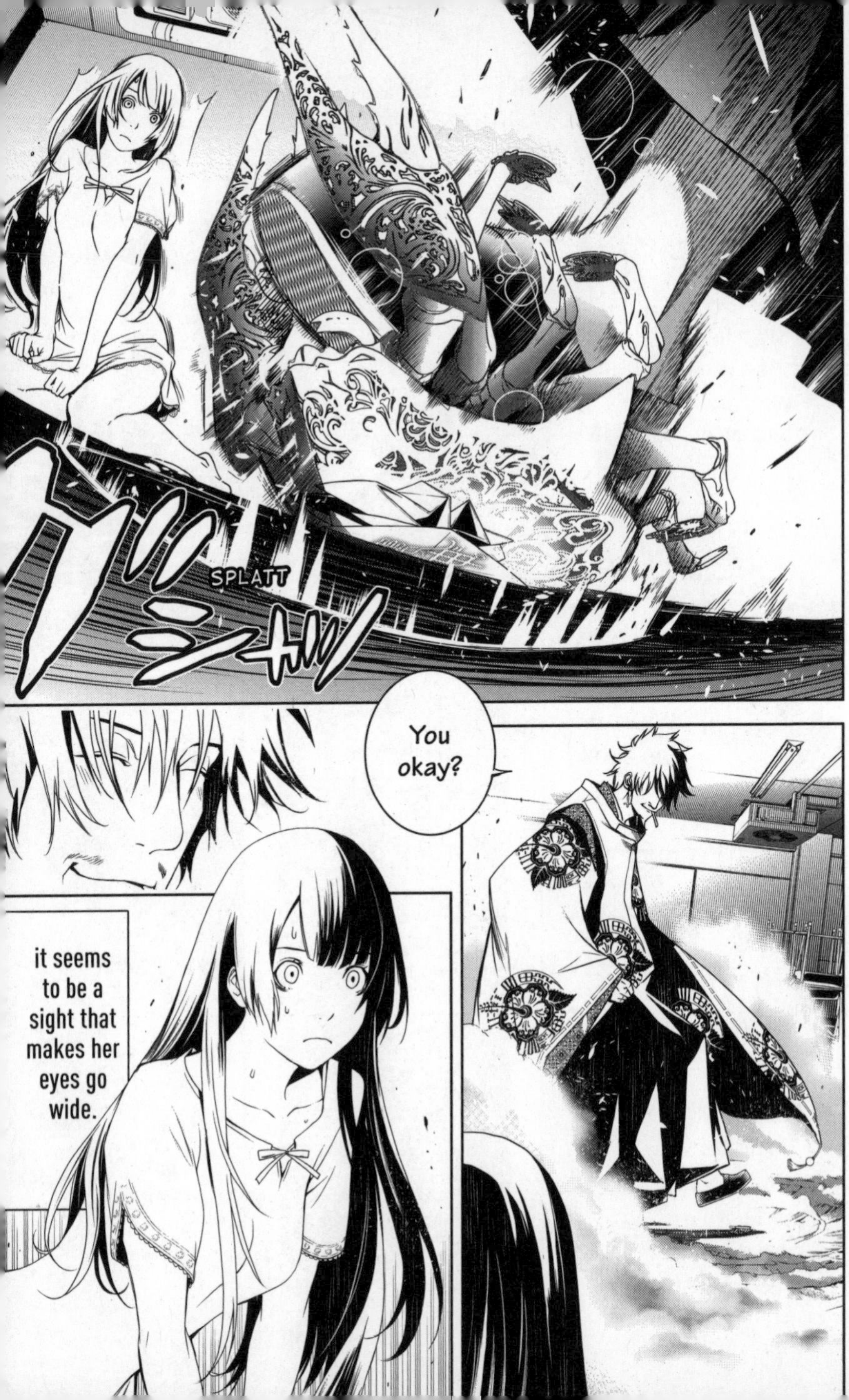
SPLATT
You okay?
it seems to be a sight that makes her eyes go wide.

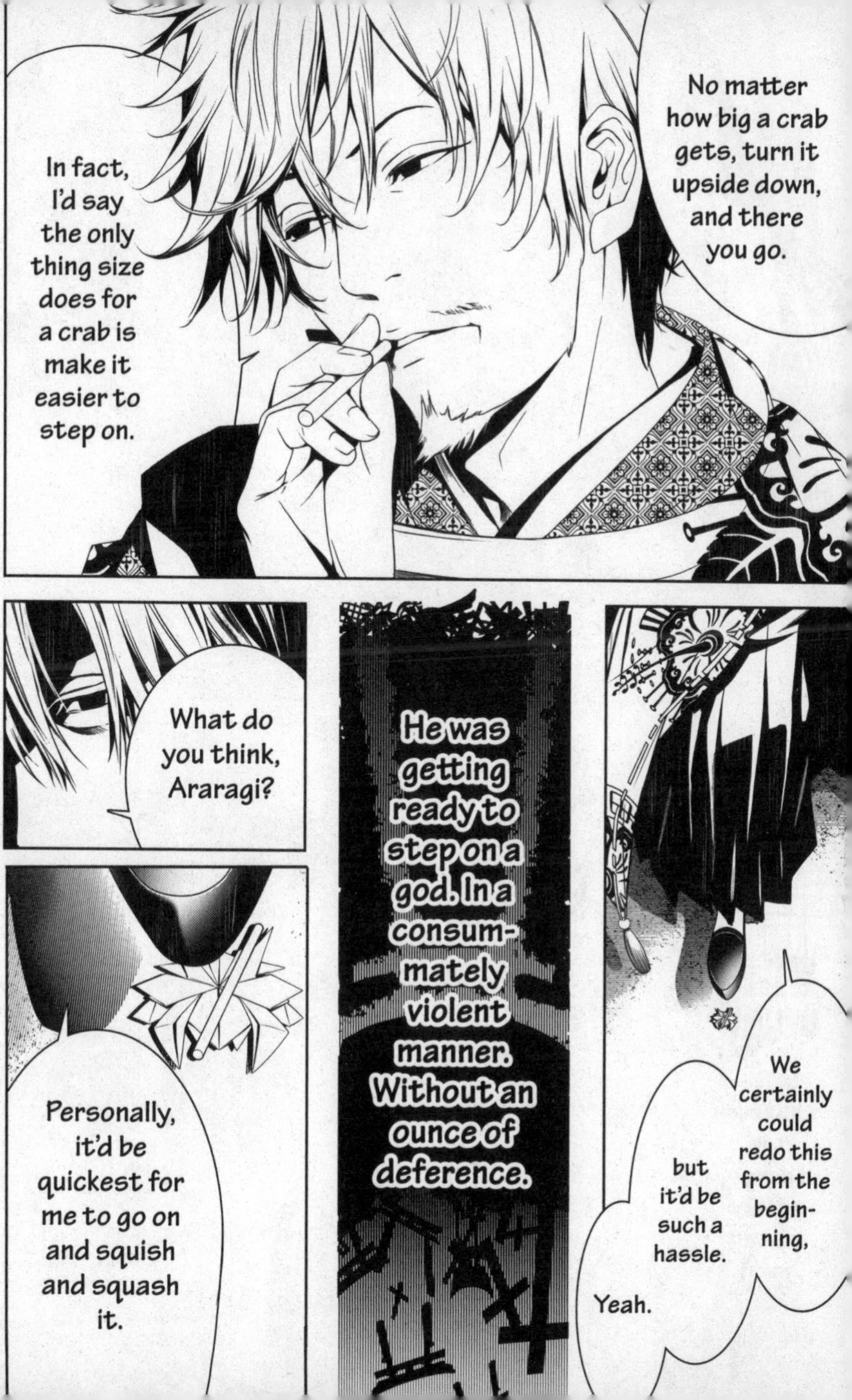
No matter how big a crab gets, turn it upside down, and there you go.
In fact, I'd say the only thing size does for a crab is make it easier to step on.
We certainly could redo this from the beginning,
but it'd be such a hassle.
Yeah.
He was getting ready to step on a god. In a consummately violent manner. Without an ounce of deference.
What do you think, Araragi?
Personally, it'd be quickest for me to go on and squish and squash it.

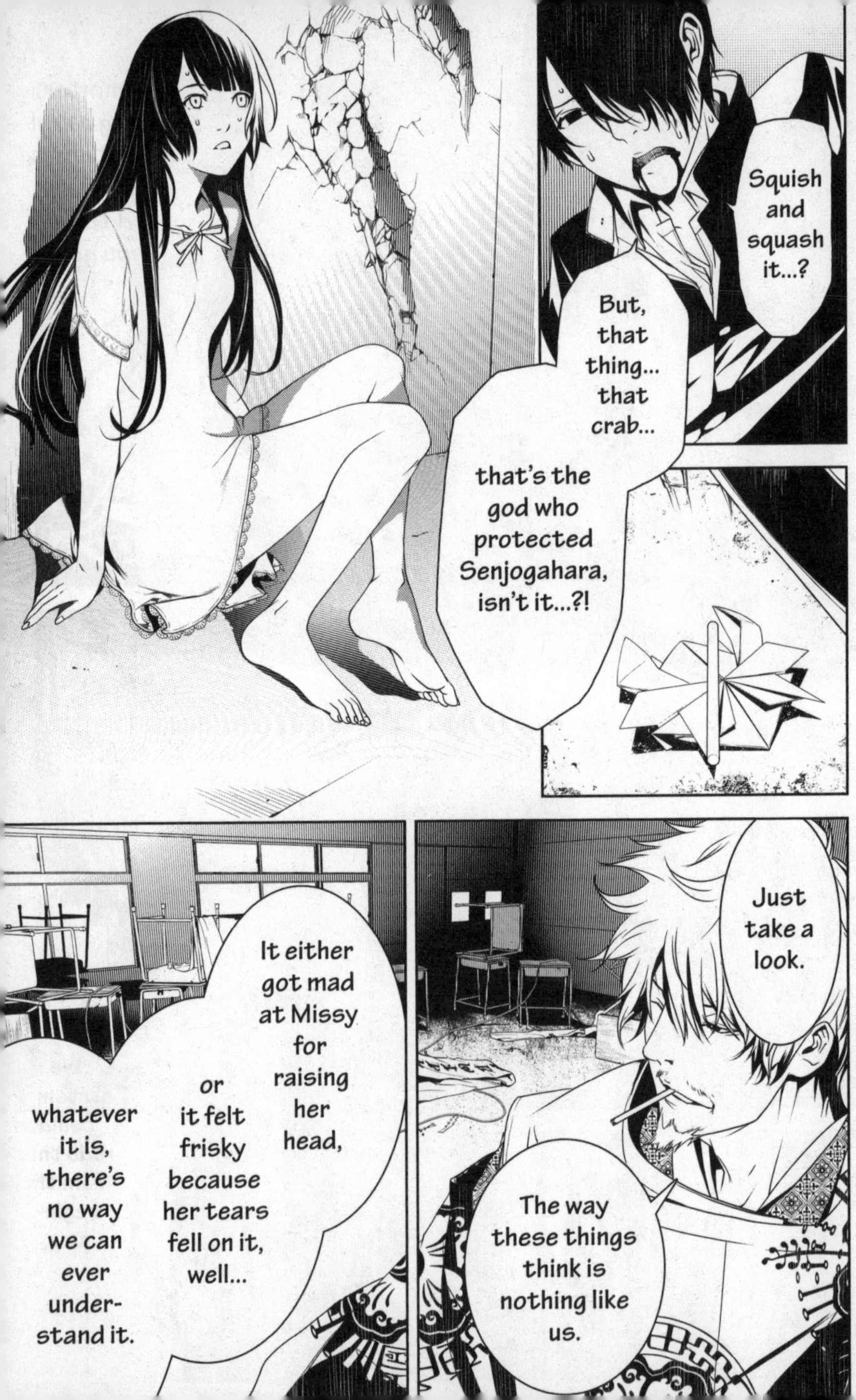
Squish and squash it...?
But, that thing... that crab...
that's the god who protected Senjogahara, isn't it...?!
Just take a look.
The way these things think is nothing like us.
It either got mad at Missy for raising her head,
or it felt frisky because her tears fell on it, well...
whatever it is, there's no way we can ever under-stand it.

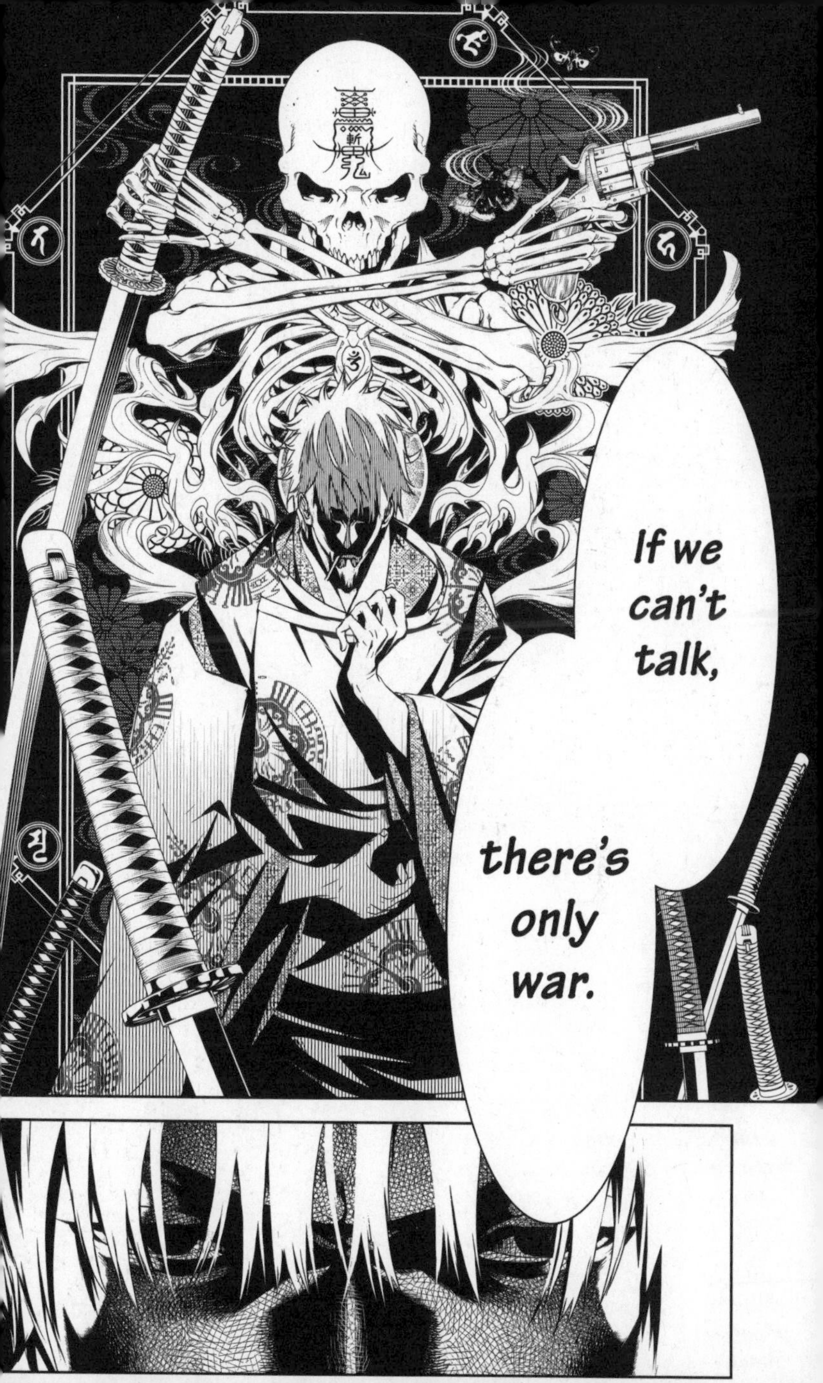
If we can't talk, there's only war.

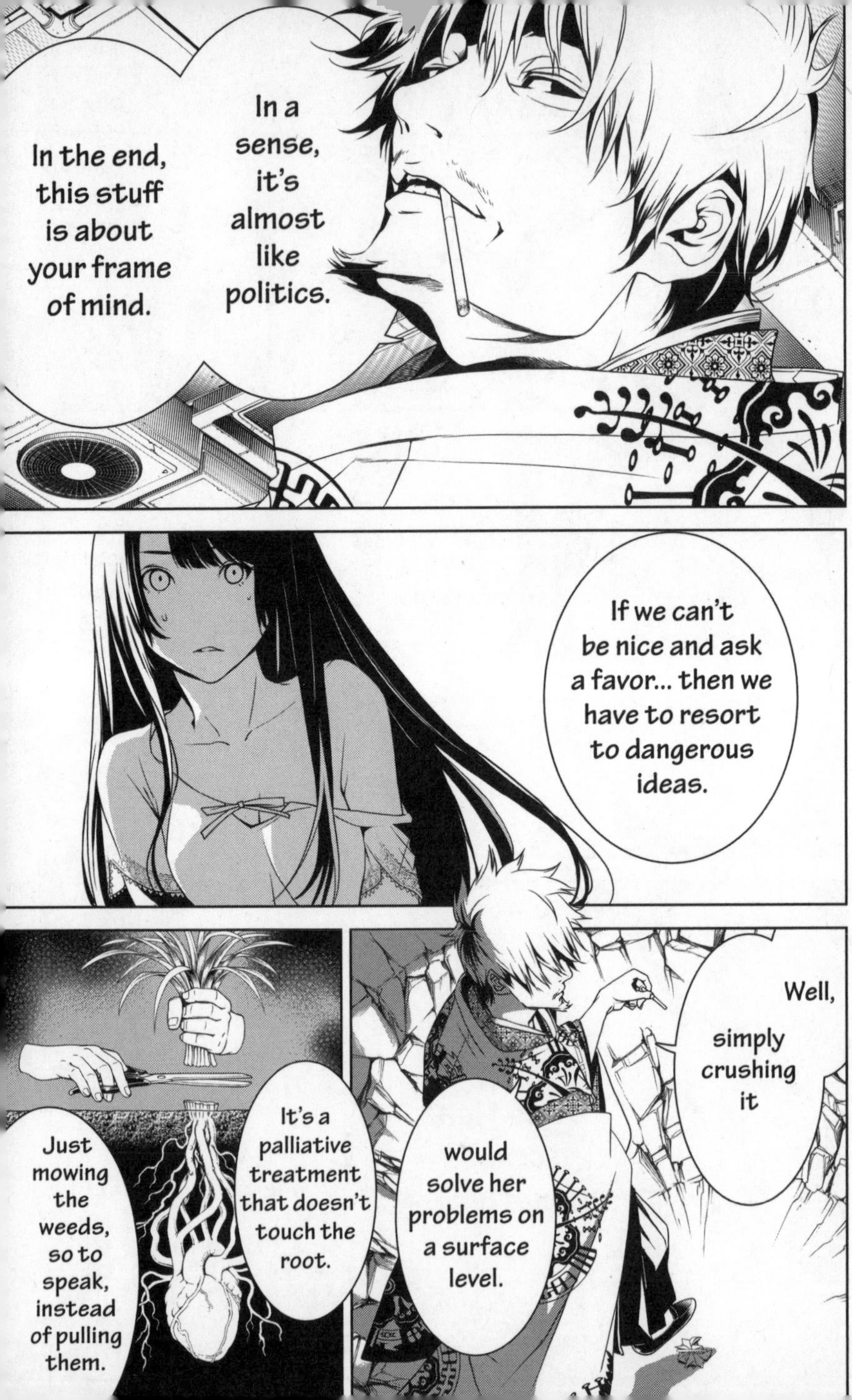
In a sense, it's almost like politics.
In the end, this stuff is about your frame of mind.
If we can't be nice and ask a favor... then we have to resort to dangerous ideas.
Well,
simply crushing it
would solve her problems on a surface level.
It's a palliative treatment that doesn't touch the root.
Just mowing the weeds, so to speak, instead of pulling them.

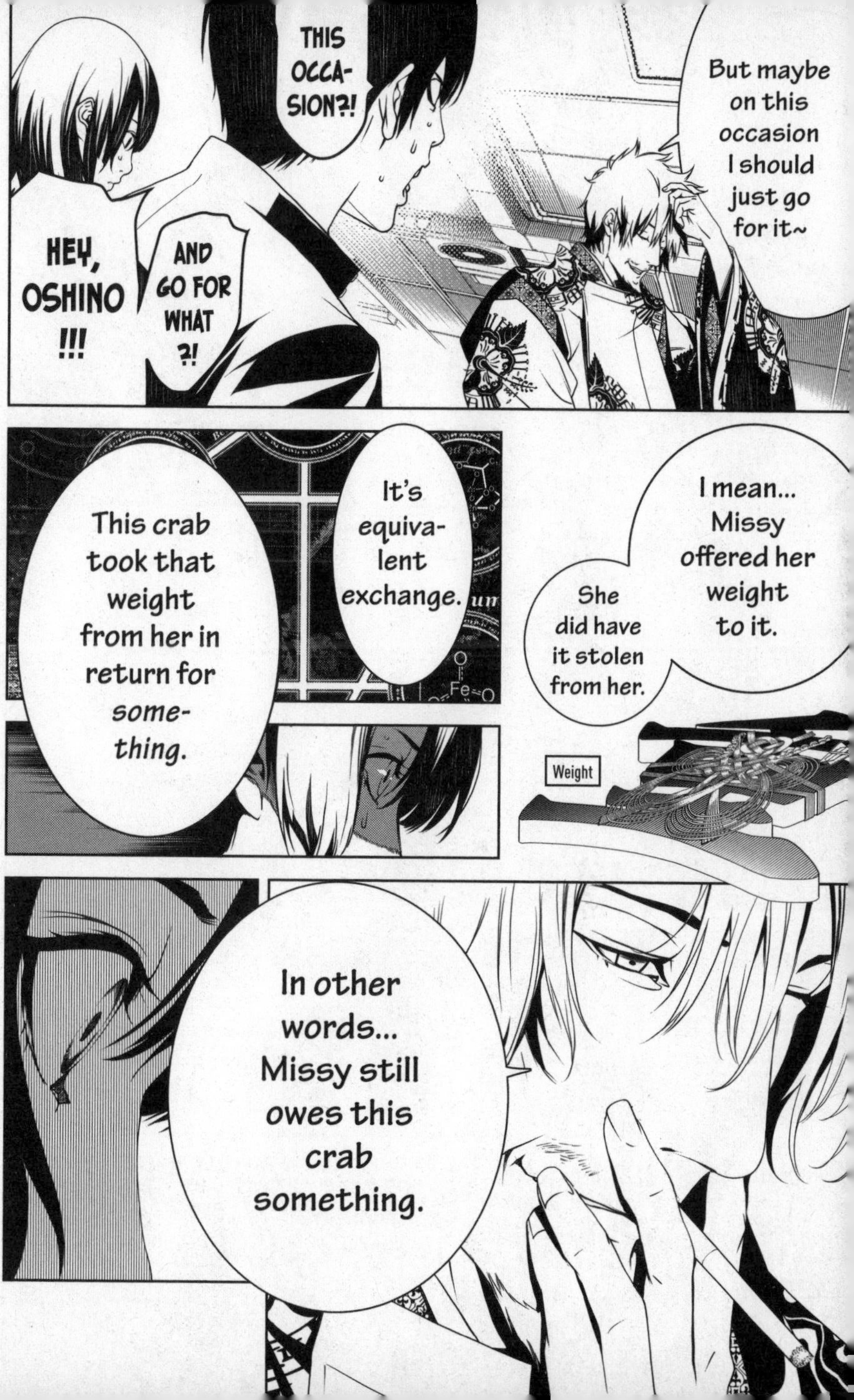
But maybe on this occasion I should just go for it~
THIS OCCASION?!
AND GO FOR WHAT?!
HEY, OSHINO!!!
I mean... Missy offered her weight to it.
She did have it stolen from her.
Weight
It's equivalent exchange.
This crab took that weight from her in return for something.
In other words... Missy still owes this crab something.

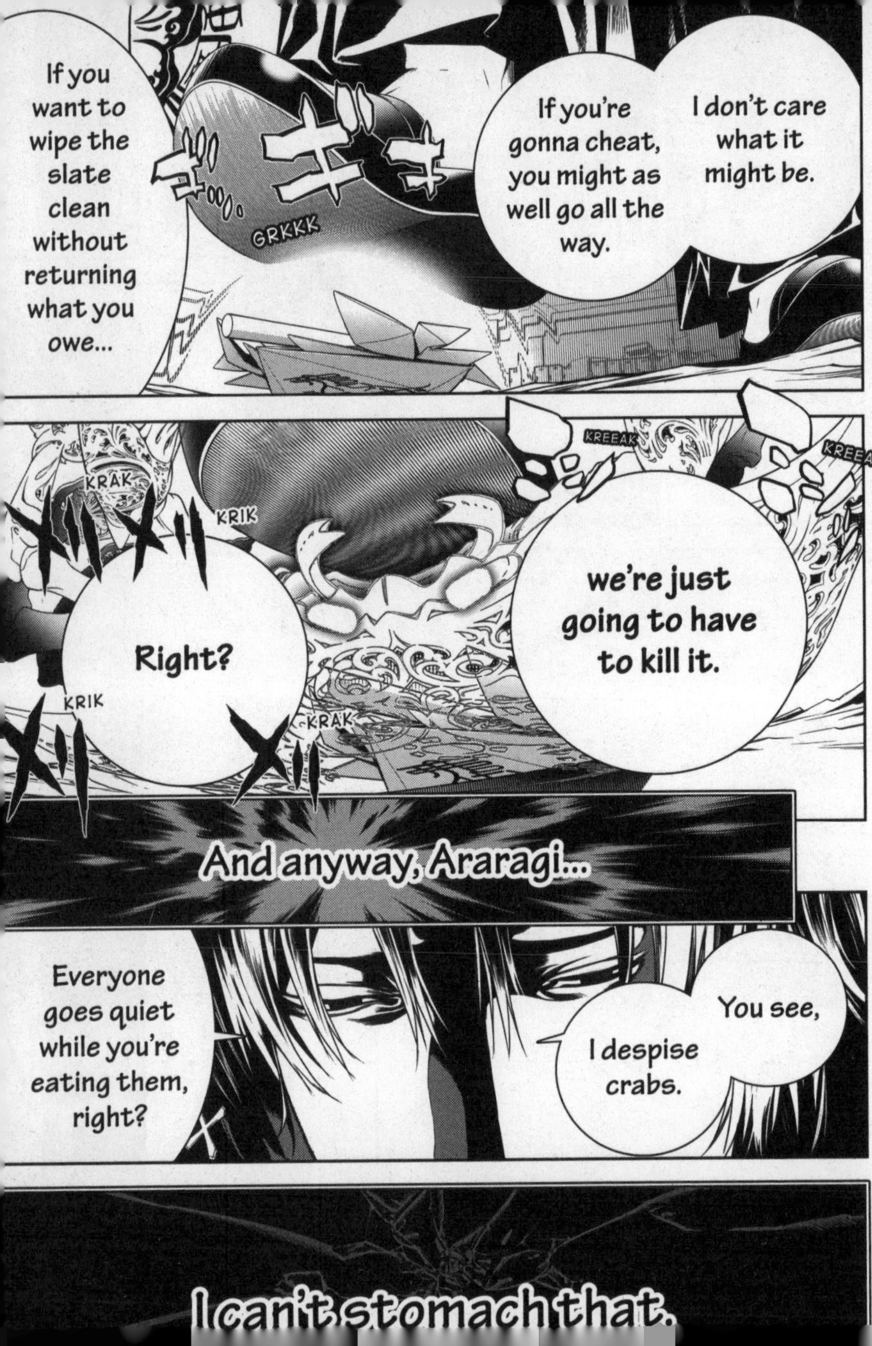
I don't care what it might be.
If you're gonna cheat, you might as well go all the way.
GRKKK
If you want to wipe the slate clean without returning what you owe...
KREEAK
KREEAK
we're just going to have to kill it.
KRAK
KRIK
Right?
KRIK
KRAK
And anyway, Araragi...
You see, I despise crabs.
Everyone goes quiet while you're eating them, right?
I can't stomach that.

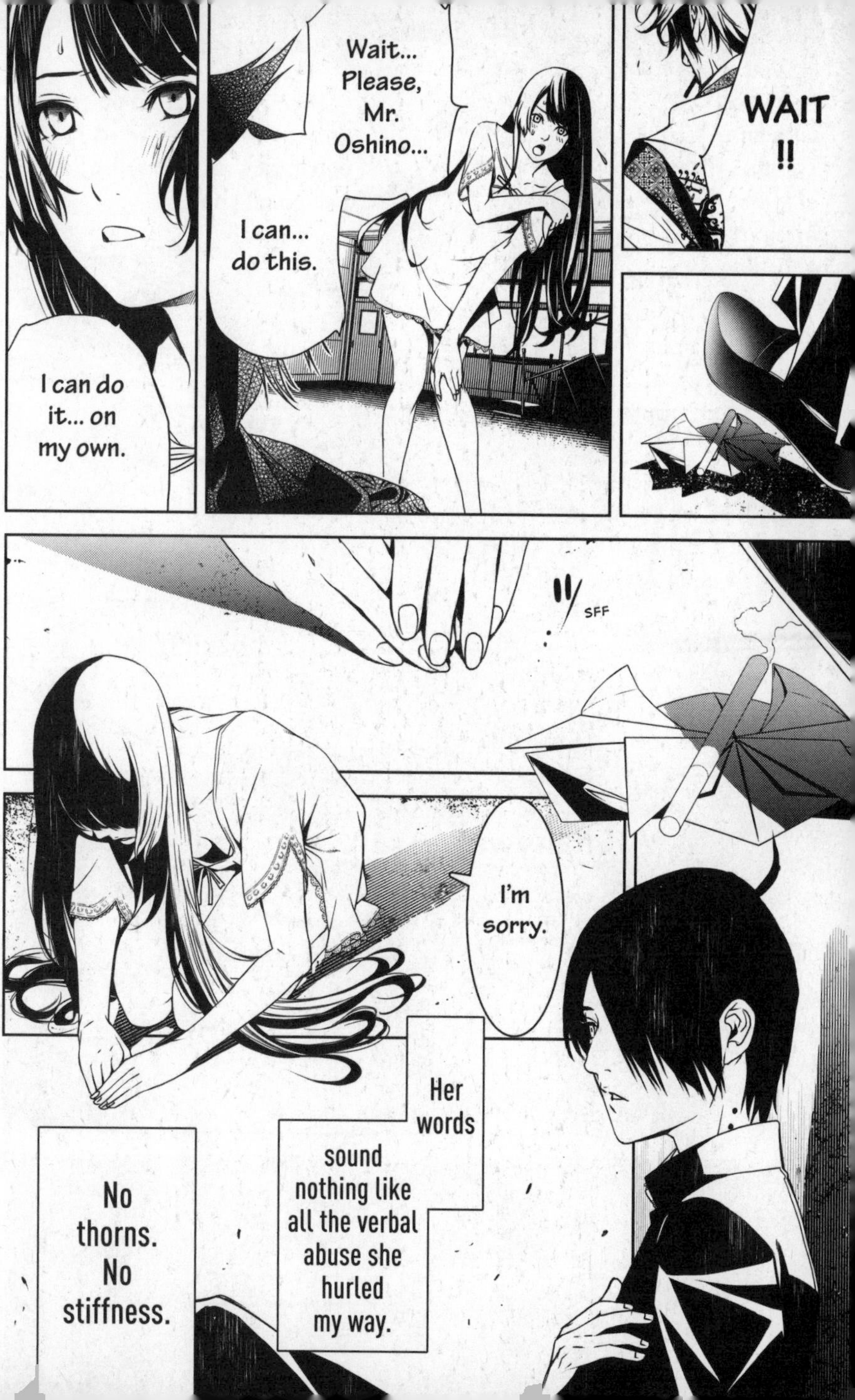
WAIT !!
Wait... Please, Mr. Oshino...
I can... do this.
I can do it... on my own.
SFF
I'm sorry.
Her words sound nothing like all the verbal abuse she hurled my way.
No thorns. No stiffness.

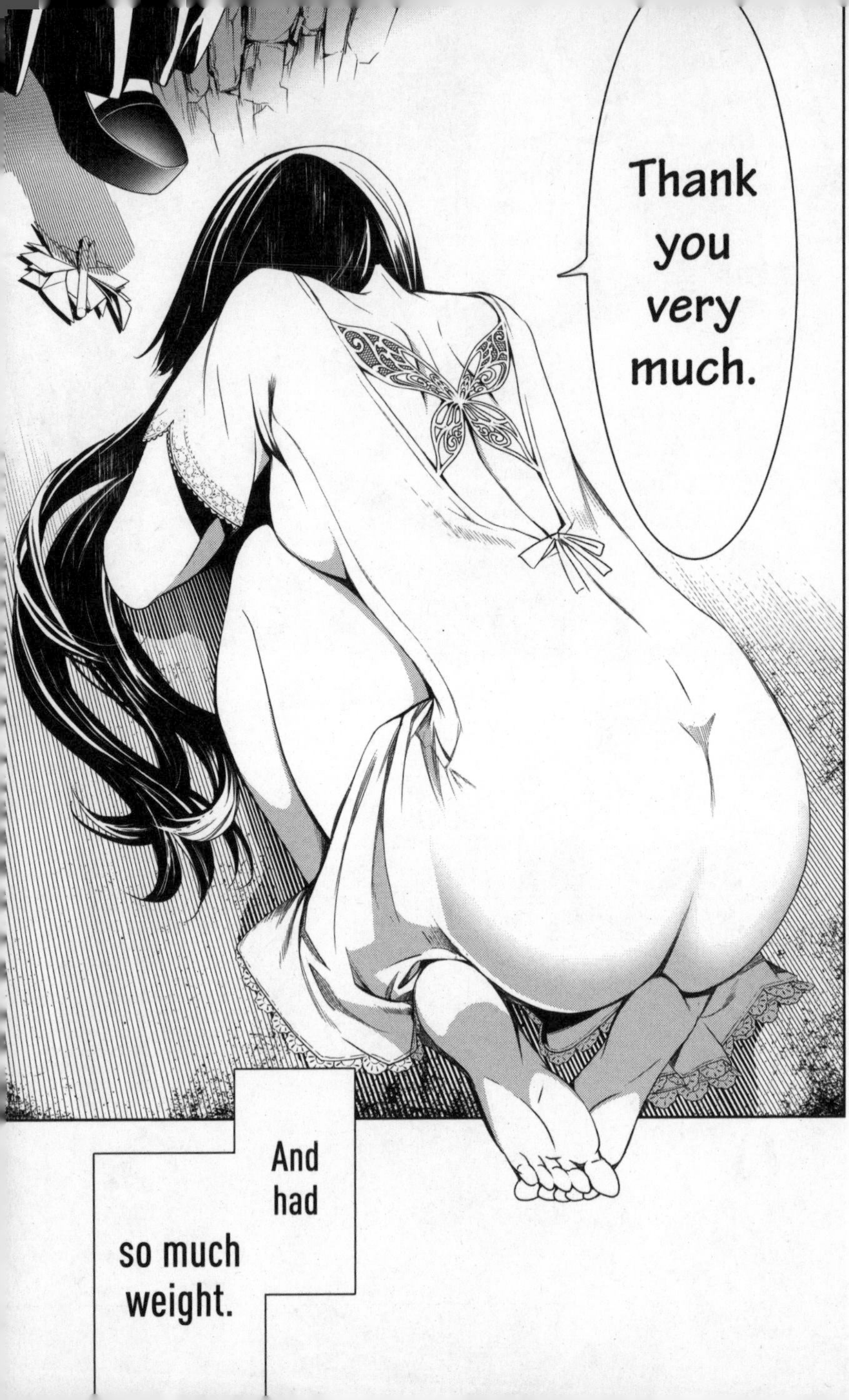
Thank you very much.
And had so much weight.

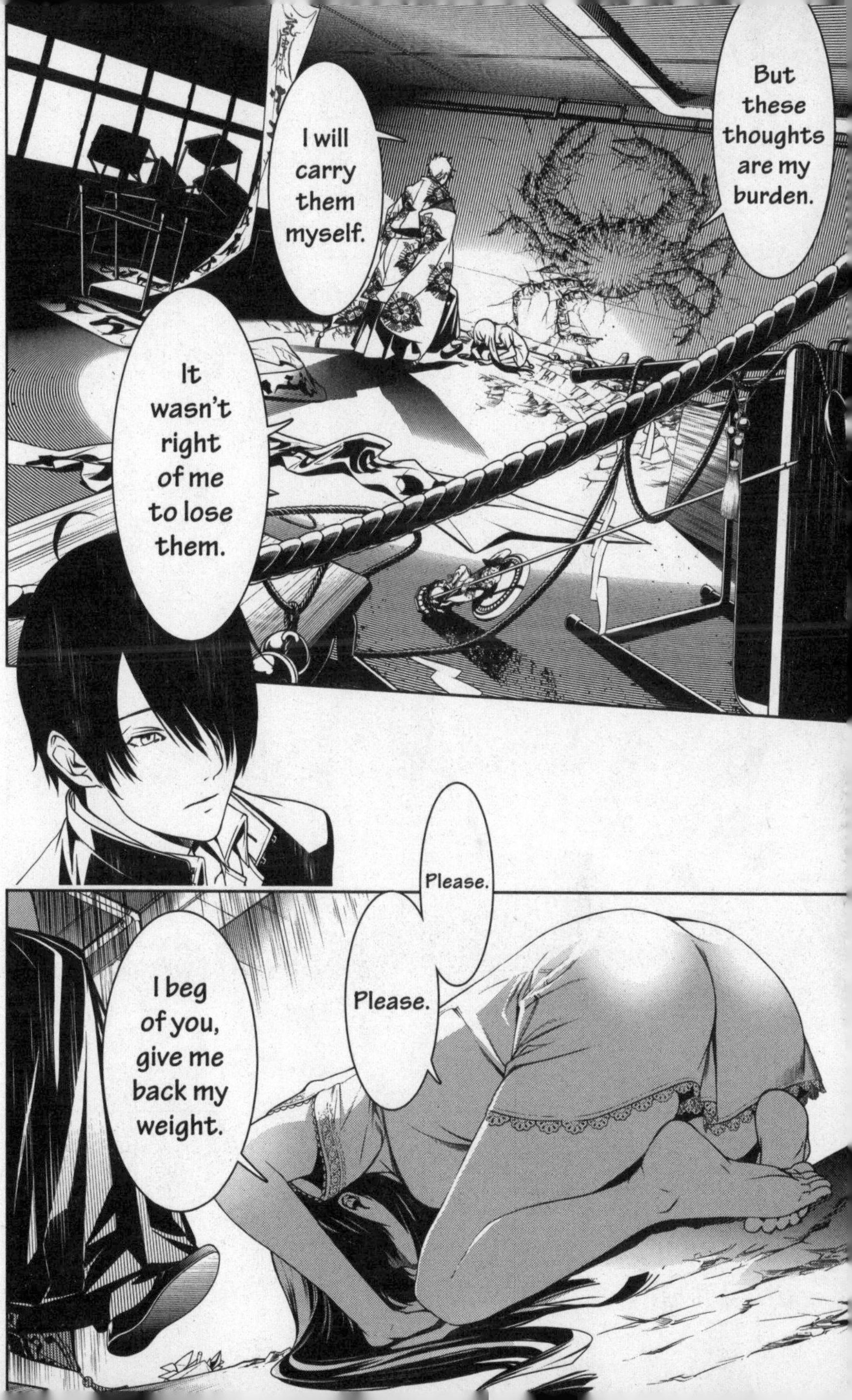
But these thoughts are my burden.
I will carry them myself.
It wasn't right of me to lose them.
Please.
Please.
I beg of you, give me back my weight.

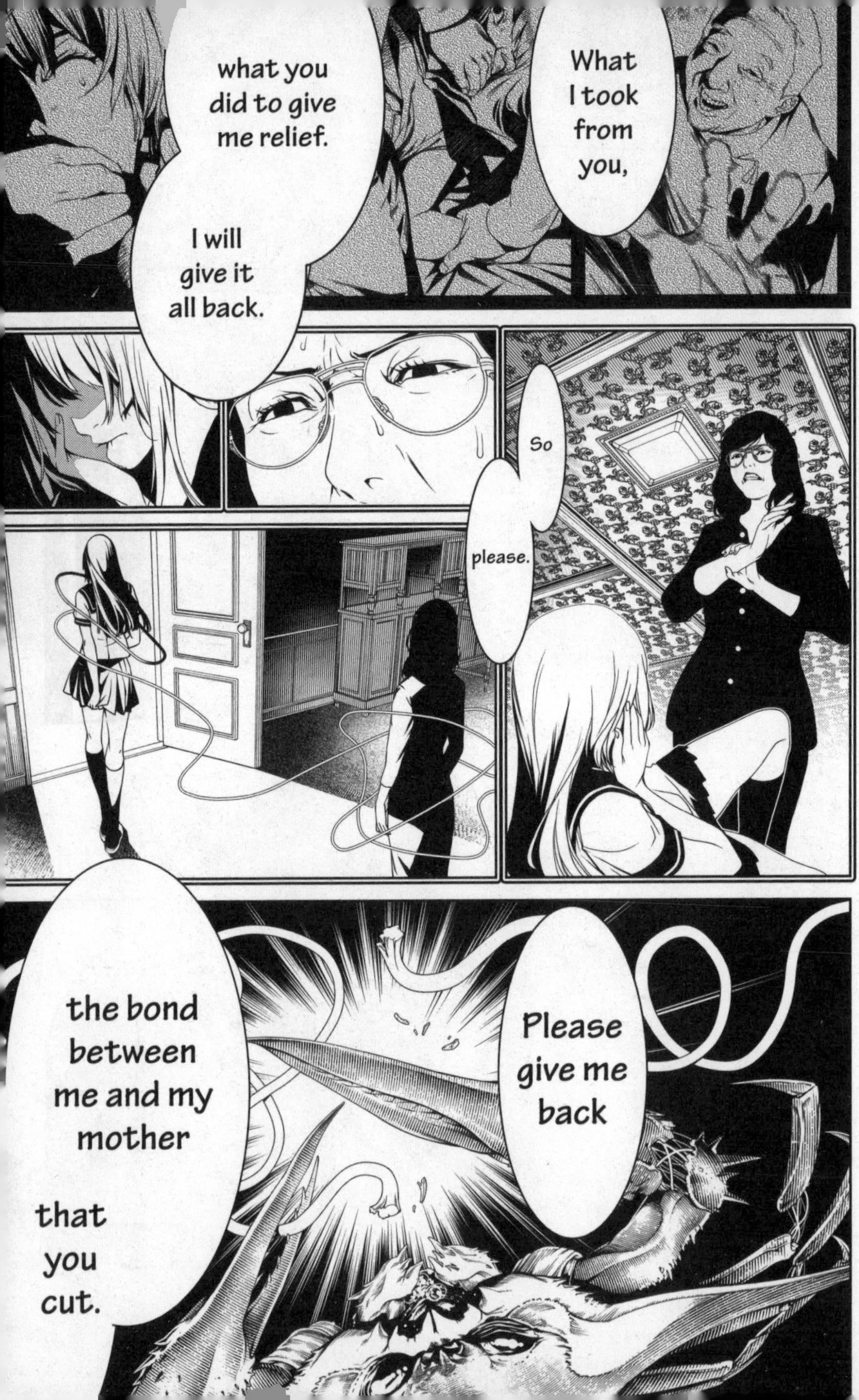
What I took from you,
what you did to give me relief.
I will give it all back.
So
please.
Please give me back
the bond between me and my mother
that you cut.

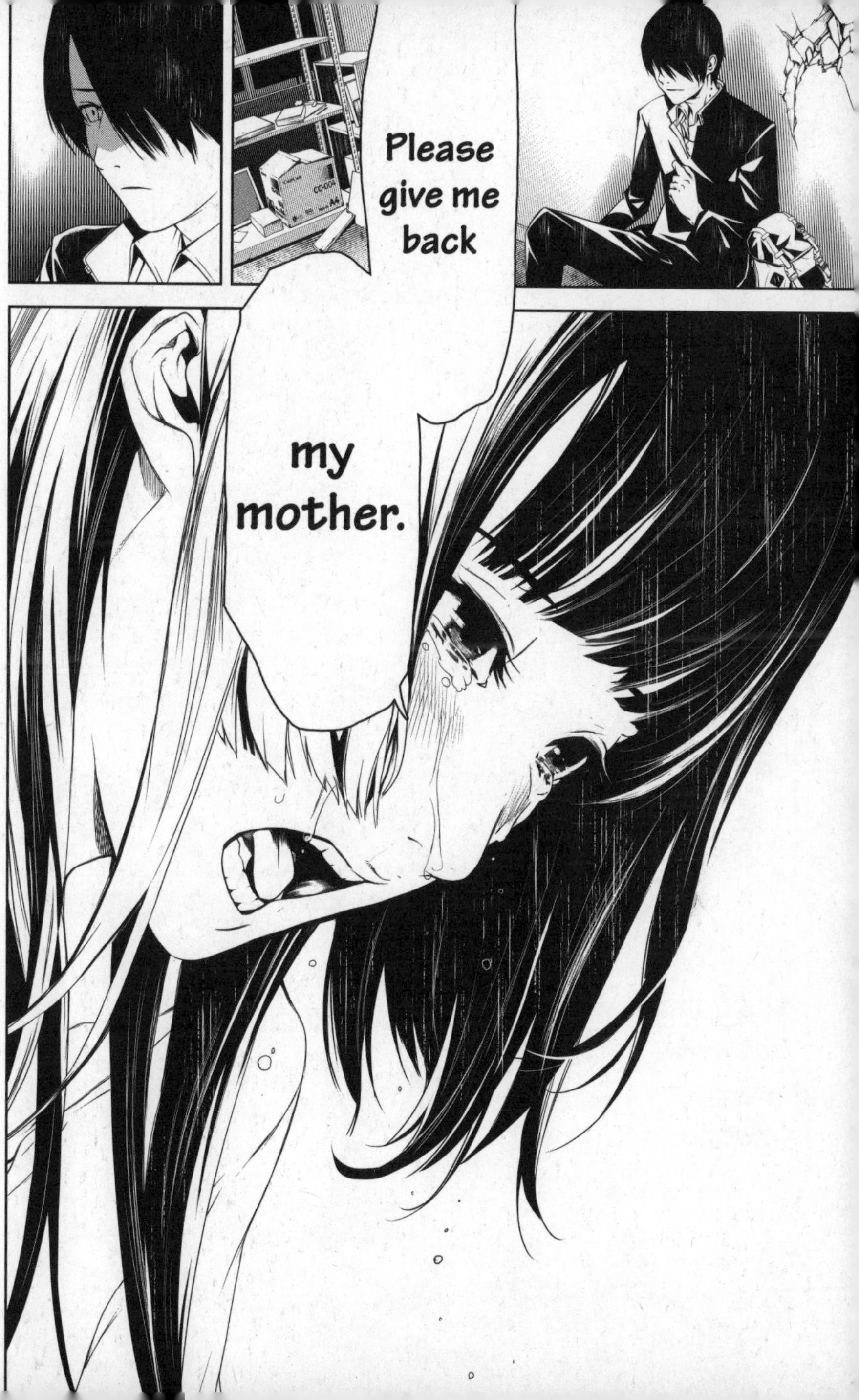
Please give me back
my mother.

Continued in Volume 2

BAKEMONOGATARI in Detail

The Path of the Series

2005
- "Hitagi Crab" runs in the September 2005 issue of *Shousetsu Gendai Zoukan Mephisto*

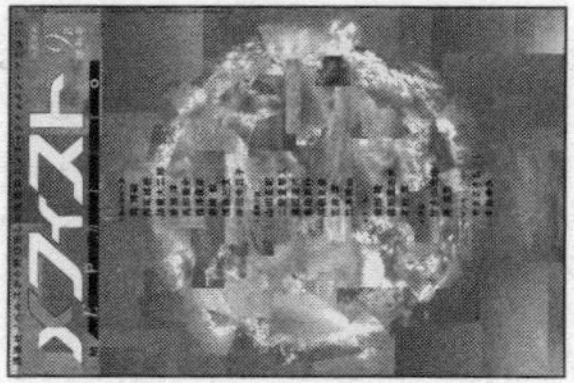

2006
- Bakemonogatari (Part 1), Bakemonogatari (Part 2) released

2008
- Kizumonogatari, Nisemonogatari (Part 1) released

2009
- Nisemonogatari (Part 2) released
- Bakemonogatari TV anime broadcast

2010
- Nekomonogatari (Black), Nekomonogatari (White), Kabukimonogatari released

2011
- Hanamonogatari, Otorimonogatari, Onimonogatari, Koimonogatari released

2012
- Tsukimonogatari released

What is BAKEMONOGATARI?

A novel written "entirely as a hobby" by NISIOISIN published by the Kodansha BOX label. The series, which started with *Bakemonogatari*, is known as the *Monogatari* series. Taiwanese illustrator VOFAN is responsible for the cover art and insert illustrations. It has now been adapted into various forms of media, including a TV anime series.

The Path of the Manga Until Now

Before entering high school:

Hitagi encounters a crab and has her weight taken from her.

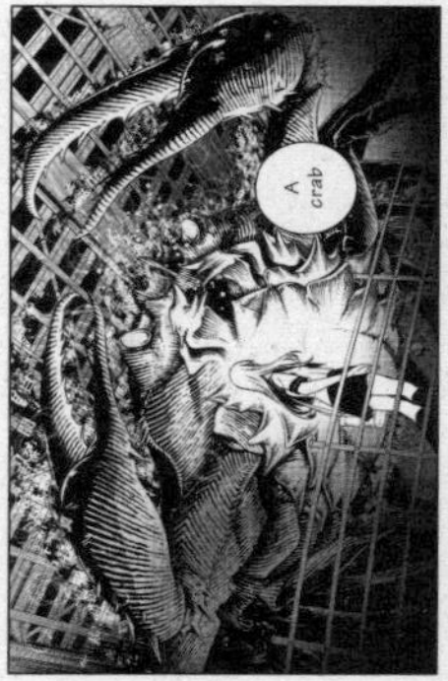
A crab

Second year of high school:

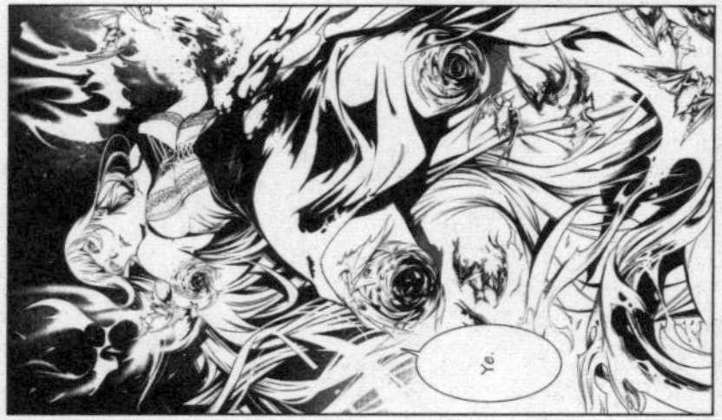
Ye.

3/25 (spring break)

Koyomi encounters a vampire on the verge of death.

2013 • Koyomimonogatari, Owarimonogatari (Part 1) released

2014 • Owarimonogatari (Part 2), Owarimonogatari (Part 3), Zoku Owarimonogatari released

2015 • Orokamonogatari released

2016 • Kizumonogatari 1: Tekketsu-hen anime released in theaters
Wazamonogatari, Nademonogatari released

2017 • Musubimonogatari, Shinobumonogatari released

2018 • Bakemonogatari manga version begins serialization in issue 15 of *Weekly Shonen Magazine*

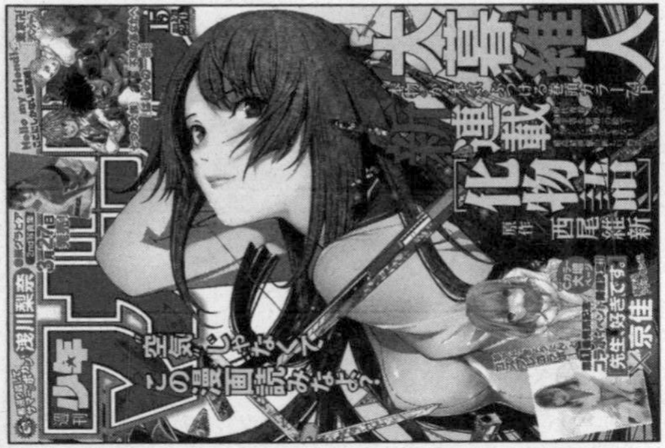
週刊少年マガジン
浅川梨奈
3月27日
Hello my friend!
空気じゃなくてこの漫画読みなよ?
大暮維人
新連載
化物語
原作 西尾維新
先生、好きです。
×京佳

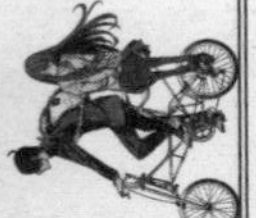

PRESENT DAY

• Yoimonogatari released

Currently in the manga: Senior year of high school:

April 29 (Golden Week)	May 8
Hanekawa comes to owe Oshino a debt of gratitude	Morning: Koyomi catches Hitagi Night: Koyomi and Hitagi visit Mème

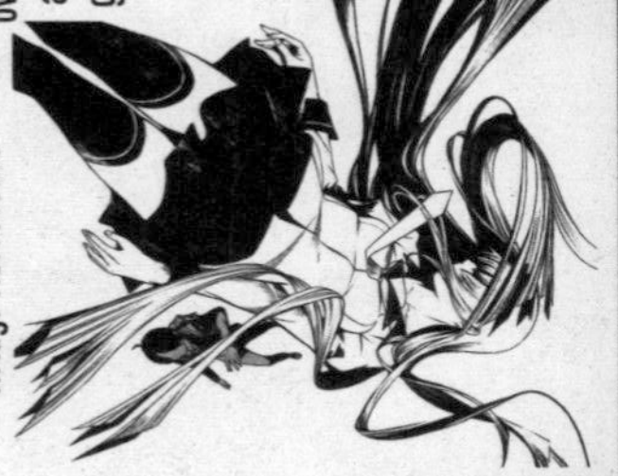

Mayoi Snail

Suruga Monkey

Nadeko Snake

Tsubasa Cat

A List of Works in the Monogatari Series

First Season: Bakemonogatari (Part 1), Bakemonogatari (Part 2), Kizumonogatari, Nisemonogatari (Part 1), Nisemonogatari (Part 2), Nekomonogatari (Black)

Second Season: Nekomonogatari (White), Kabukimonogatari, Hanamonogatari, Otorimonogatari, Onimonogatari, Koimonogatari

Final Season: Tsukimonogatari, Koyomimonogatari, Owarimonogatari (Part 1), Owarimonogatari (Part 2), Owarimonogatari (Part 3), Zoku Owarimonogatari

Off-Season: Orokamonogatari, Wazamonogatari, Nademonogatari, Musubimonogatari

Monster Season: Shinobumonogatari, Yoimonogatari

...and more?!

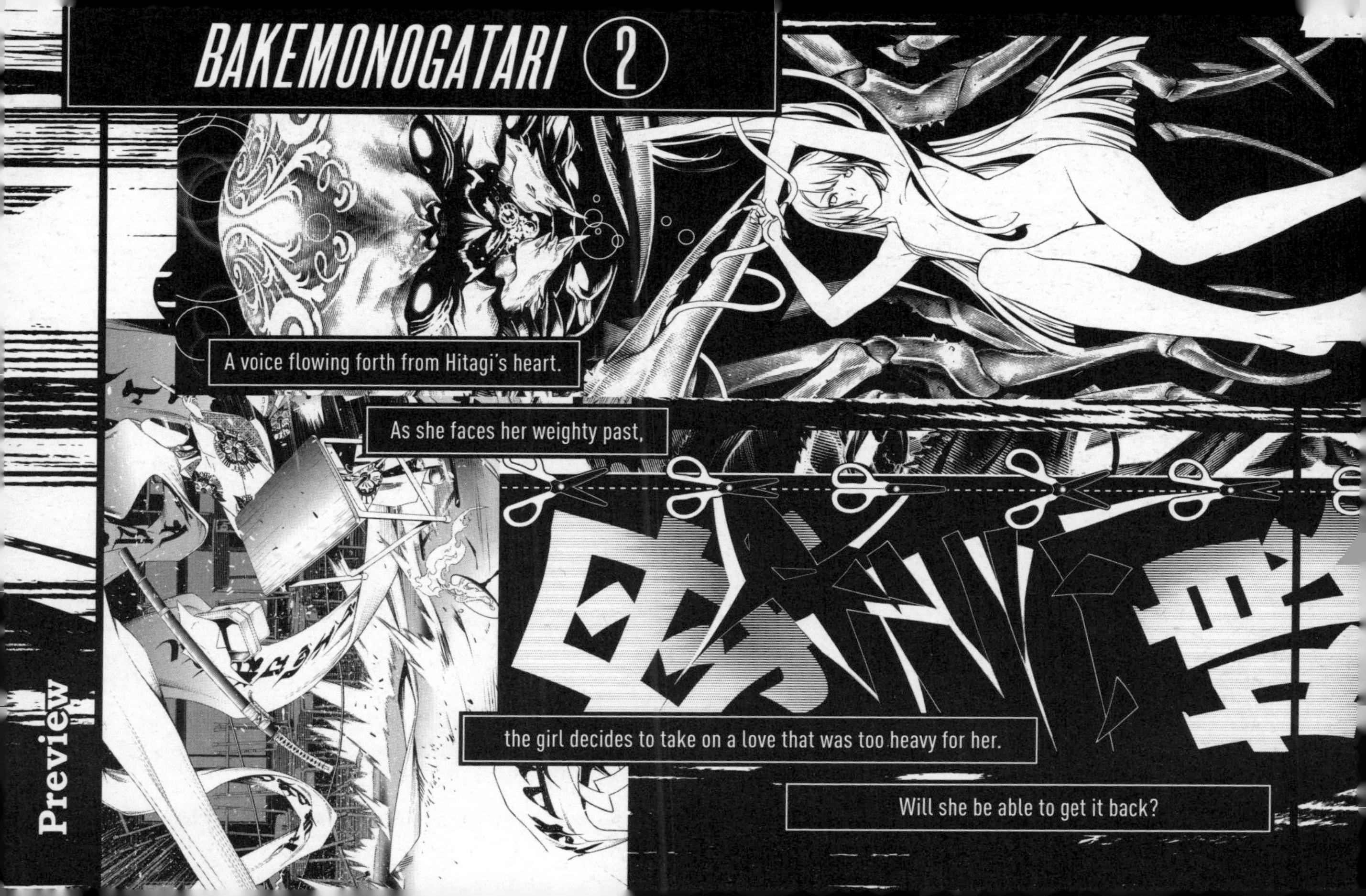
Preview
BAKEMONOGATARI 2
A voice flowing forth from Hitagi's heart.
As she faces her weighty past,
the girl decides to take on a love that was too heavy for her.
Will she be able to get it back?

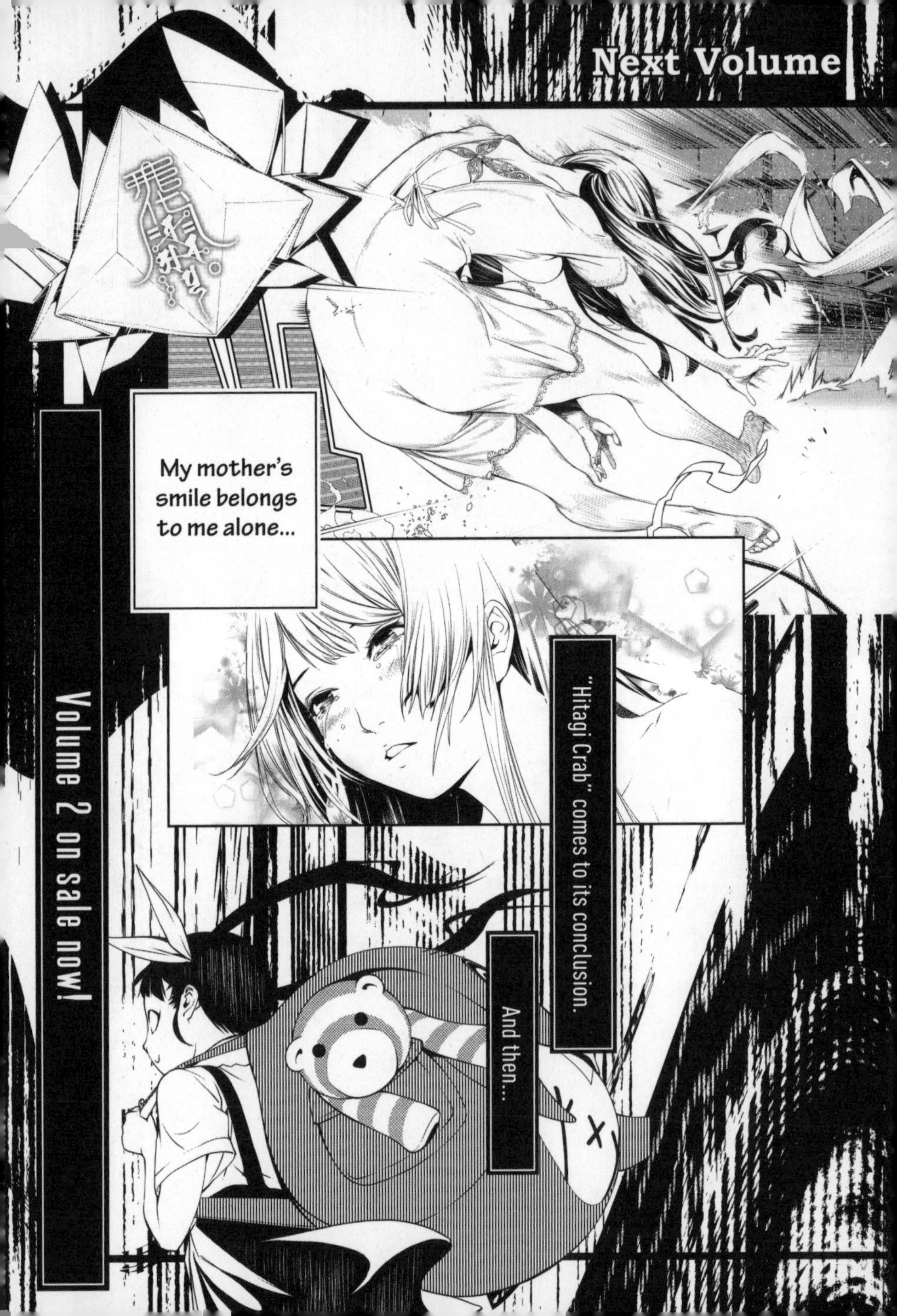
Next Volume
My mother's smile belongs to me alone...
"Hitagi Crab" comes to its conclusion.
And then...
Volume 2 on sale now!

JOIN THE CLUB

Ten years ago, Mayumi Dojima saw a star...and she's been searching for it ever since. The mysterious organization that solves (and causes?) all the problems at Yubiwa Academy—the *Pretty Boy Detective Club* is on the case! Five beautiful youths, each more eccentric than the last, united only by their devotion to the aesthetics of mystery-solving. Together they find much, much more than they bargained for.

A new series from the inimitable NISIOISIN!

The Dark Star that Shines for You Alone

The Swindler, the Vanishing Man, and the Pretty Boys

The Pretty Boy in the Attic

AVAILABLE NOW!

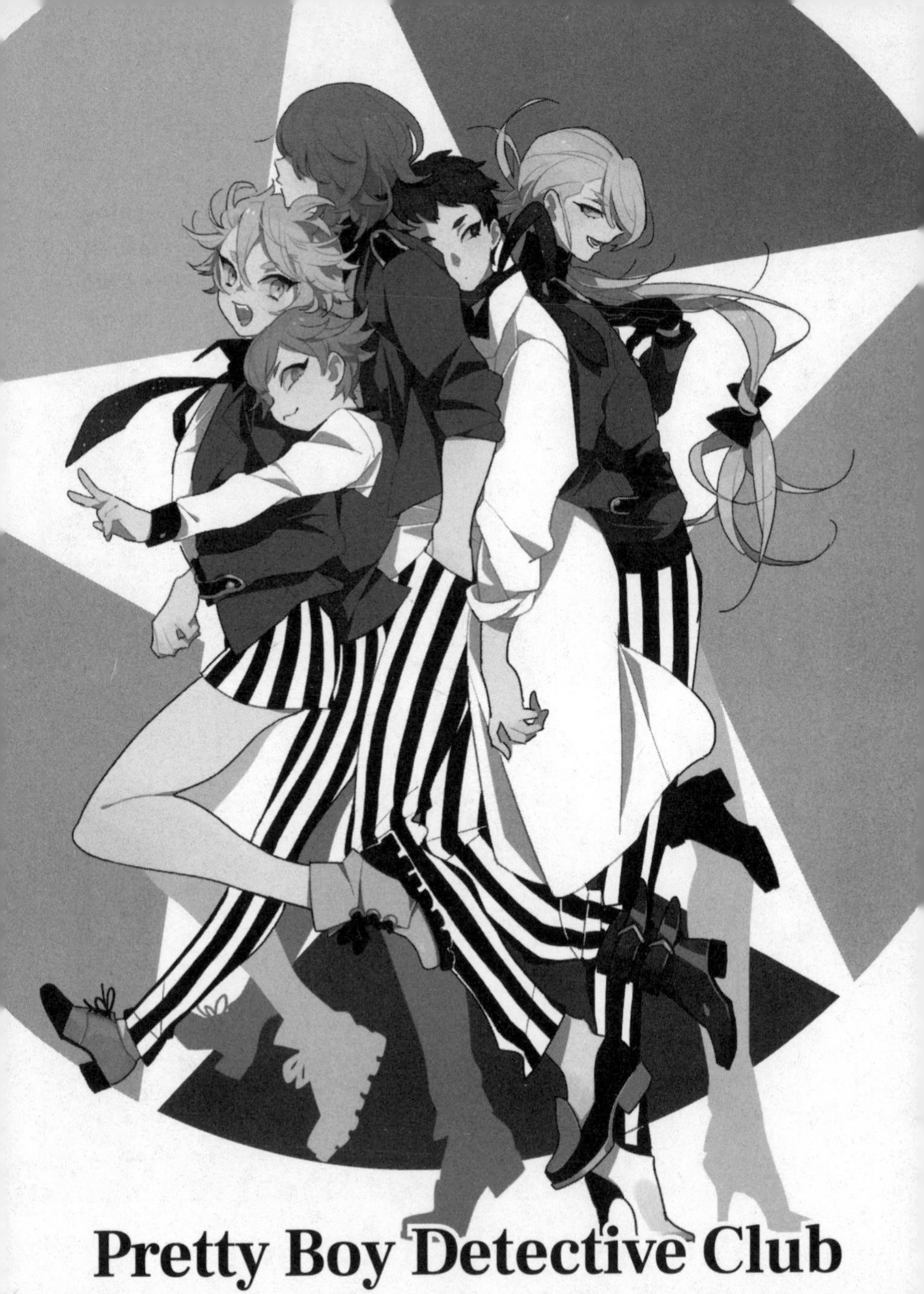

Pretty Boy Detective Club

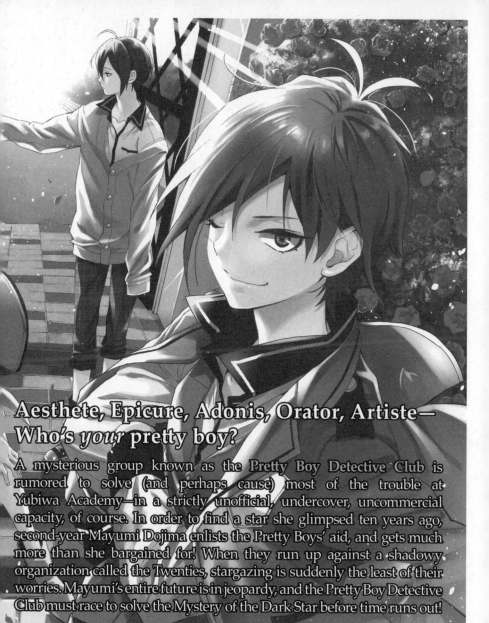

Aesthete, Epicure, Adonis, Orator, Artiste— Who's *your* pretty boy?

A mysterious group known as the Pretty Boy Detective Club is rumored to solve (and perhaps cause) most of the trouble at Yubiwa Academy—in a strictly unofficial, undercover, uncommercial capacity, of course. In order to find a star she glimpsed ten years ago, second-year Mayumi Dojima enlists the Pretty Boys' aid, and gets much more than she bargained for! When they run up against a shadowy organization called the Twenties, stargazing is suddenly the least of their worries. Mayumi's entire future is in jeopardy, and the Pretty Boy Detective Club must race to solve the Mystery of the Dark Star before time runs out!

Volume 1 Available Now!

PRETTY BOY DETECTIVE CLUB

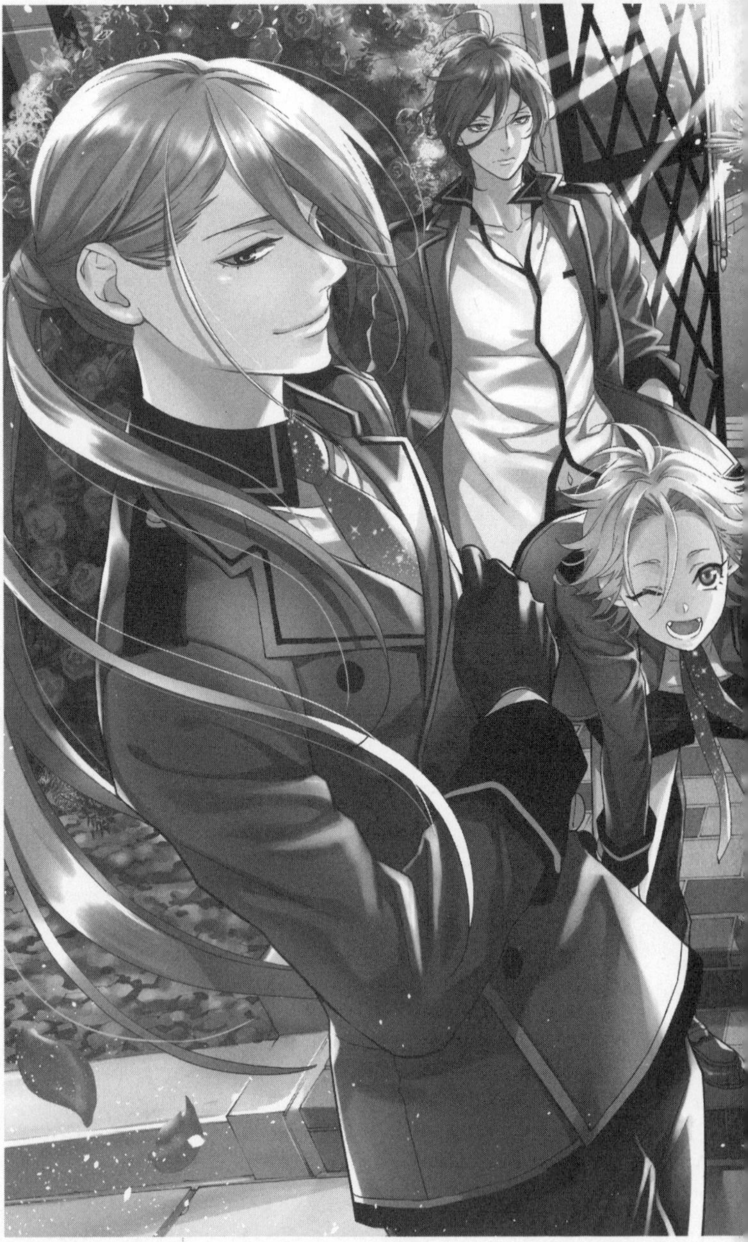

Original Story NISIOISIN
Manga Suzuka Oda
Original Character Design Kinako

BAKEMONOGATARI

volume 1

A Vertical Comics Edition

Translation: Ko Ransom
Production: Grace Lu
            Hiroko Mizuno

First published in Japan in 2018 by Kodansha, Ltd., Tokyo
Publication for this English edition arranged through Kodansha, Ltd., Tokyo
English language version produced by Vertical Comics,
an imprint of Kodansha USA Publishing, LLC

Translation provided by Vertical Comics, 2019
Published by Kodansha USA Publishing, LLC, New York

Originally published in Japanese as *BAKEMONOGATARI 1* by Kodansha, Ltd.
BAKEMONOGATARI first serialized in *Weekly Shonen Magazine*,
Kodansha, Ltd., 2017-

This is a work of fiction.

ISBN: 978-1-947194-97-7

Manufactured in the United States of America

First Edition

Third Printing

Kodansha USA Publishing, LLC
451 Park Avenue South
7th Floor
New York, NY 10016
www.kodansha.us

Vertical books are distributed through Penguin-Random House Publisher Services.